The purpose of this series is to provide comprehensive expository and critical surveys of the work of major philosophers. Each volume, which contains commissioned essays by an international group of scholars, as well as a substantial bibliography, will serve as a reference work for students and nonspecialists. One aim of the series is to dispel the intimidation such readers often feel when faced with the work of a difficult and challenging thinker.

Martin Heidegger is now widely recognized alongside Wittgenstein as one of the greatest philosophers of the twentieth century. He transformed mainstream philosophy by defining its central task as asking the "question of being," and he has had a profound impact on such fields as literary theory, theology, psychotherapy, political theory, aesthetics, and environmental studies. His thought has contributed to the recent turn to hermeneutics in philosophy and the social sciences and to current postmodern and poststructuralist developments. Moreover, the disclosure of his deep involvement in the ideology of Nazism has provoked much debate about the relation of philosophy to politics. This volume contains both overviews of Heidegger's life and works and analyses of his most important work, *Being and Time.* In addition there are discussions of Heidegger's thought in relation to politics, theology, ecology, psychotherapy, Eastern thought, and the philosophy of language. The volume also contains an in-depth study of what has been called Heidegger's second greatest work, the *Beiträge zur Philosophie.*

New readers and nonspecialists will find this the most convenient, accessible guide to Heidegger currently available. Advanced students and specialists will find a conspectus of recent developments in the interpretation of Heidegger.

THE CAMBRIDGE COMPANION TO

HEIDEGGER

OTHER VOLUMES IN THIS SERIES OF CAMBRIDGE COMPANIONS:

AQUINAS *Edited by* NORMAN KRETZMANN *and* ELEONORE STUMP
ARISTOTLE *Edited by* JONATHAN BARNES
BACON *Edited by* MARKKU PELTONEN
DESCARTES *Edited by* JOHN COTTINGHAM *(published)*
FOUCAULT *Edited by* GARY CUTTING
FREUD *Edited by* JEROME NEU *(published)*
HABERMAS *Edited by* STEPHEN WHITE
HEGEL *Edited by* FREDERICK BEISER
HOBBES *Edited by* TOM SORRELL
HUME *Edited by* DAVID FATE NORTON
HUSSERL *Edited by* BARRY SMITH *and* DAVID WOODRUFF SMITH
KANT *Edited by* PAUL GUYER *(published)*
LEIBNIZ *Edited by* NICHOLAS JOLLEY
LOCKE *Edited by* VERE CHAPPELL
MARX *Edited by* TERRELL CARVER *(published)*
MILL *Edited by* JOHN SKORUPSKI
NIETZSCHE *Edited by* BERND MAGNUS
PLATO *Edited by* RICHARD KRAUT *(published)*
SARTRE *Edited by* CHRISTINA HOWELLS *(published)*
SPINOZA *Edited by* DON GARRETT
WITTGENSTEIN *Edited by* HANS SLUGA *and* DAVID STERN

The Cambridge Companion to

HEIDEGGER

Edited by Charles B. Guignon

CAMBRIDGE
UNIVERSITY PRESS

PUBLISHED BY THE PRESS SYNDICATE OF THE UNIVERSITY OF CAMBRIDGE
The Pitt Building, Trumpington Street, Cambridge, United Kingdom

CAMBRIDGE UNIVERSITY PRESS
The Edinburgh Building, Cambridge CB2 2RU, UK http: //www.cup.cam.ac.uk
40 West 20th Street, New York, NY 10011-4211, USA http: //www.cup.org
10 Stamford Road, Oakleigh, Melbourne 3166, Australia

First published 1993
Reprinted 1993, 1994, 1995, 1996, 1997, 1998, 1999

Printed in the United States of America

Typeset in Trump Mediaeval

A catalogue record for this book is available from the British Library

Library of Congress Cataloguing-in-Publication Data is available

ISBN 0-521-38597-0 paperback

The Cambridge Companion to

HEIDEGGER

Edited by Charles B. Guignon

PUBLISHED BY THE PRESS SYNDICATE OF THE UNIVERSITY OF CAMBRIDGE
The Pitt Building, Trumpington Street, Cambridge, United Kingdom

CAMBRIDGE UNIVERSITY PRESS
The Edinburgh Building, Cambridge CB2 2RU, UK http: //www.cup.cam.ac.uk
40 West 20th Street, New York, NY 10011-4211, USA http: //www.cup.org
10 Stamford Road, Oakleigh, Melbourne 3166, Australia

First published 1993
Reprinted 1993, 1994, 1995, 1996, 1997, 1998, 1999

Printed in the United States of America

Typeset in Trump Mediaeval

A catalogue record for this book is available from the British Library

Library of Congress Cataloguing-in-Publication Data is available

ISBN 0-521-38597-0 paperback

For Michele and Christopher

CONTENTS

CONTRIBUTORS

JOHN D. CAPUTO, David R. Cook Professor of Philosophy at Villanova University, is the author of *Radical Hermeneutics* (1987), *Heidegger and Aquinas* (1982), and *The Mystical Element in Heidegger's Thought* (1978). He is currently preparing a book on ethics and deconstruction.

ROBERT J. DOSTAL, Rufus M. Jones Professor of Philosophy at Bryn Mawr College, is the author of numerous articles on Kant, Heidegger, and hermeneutics. He has been a Humboldt Fellow at the universities of Cologne and Freiburg and is currently working on a book on the phenomenological ontology of time.

HUBERT L. DREYFUS is Professor of Philosophy at the University of California, Berkeley. He is the author of *Being-in-the-World: A Commentary on Heidegger's "Being and Time," Division I* (1991) and has recently edited a collection of papers with Harrison Hall entitled *Heidegger: A Critical Reader* (1992).

DOROTHEA FREDE is Professor of Philosophy at the University of Hamburg in Germany. Her main field is ancient philosophy, and she has published widely in classical and Hellenistic philosophy. She has also published essays on Heidegger emphasizing his criticism of, and dependence on, the history of Western philosophy.

CHARLES B. GUIGNON, Associate Professor of Philosophy at the University of Vermont, is the author of *Heidegger and the Problem of Knowledge* (1983) as well as articles on Wittgenstein, Rorty, and hermeneutics. He is currently coauthoring a book on hermeneutics and psychotherapy theory.

HARRISON HALL is Professor of Philosophy at the University of Delaware. He has written on Husserl, Heidegger, and Merleau-Ponty, and is coeditor of *Husserl, Intentionality and Cognitive Science* (1982) and *Heidegger: A Critical Reader* (1992).

PIOTR HOFFMAN is Professor of Philosophy at the University of Nevada, Reno. His most recent writings include *Violence in Modern Philosophy* (1989) and *Doubt, Time, Violence* (1987).

DAVID COUZENS HOY, Professor of Philosophy at the University of California, Santa Cruz, has also taught at Yale, Princeton, Barnard, Columbia, and the University of California, Los Angeles. In addition to many articles on modern and postmodern European philosophers, his publications include *The Critical Circle: Literature, History, and Philosophical Hermeneutics* (1978) and *Foucault: A Critical Reader* (1986). He is coauthoring a book with Thomas McCarthy, *Critical Theory, For and Against.*

FREDERICK A. OLAFSON has taught at Harvard, Vassar, Johns Hopkins, and the University of California, San Diego. He is the author of *Principles and Persons: An Ethical Interpretation of Existentialism* (1967), *The Dialectic of Action: A Philosophical Interpretation of History and the Humanities* (1979), and *Heidegger and the Philosophy of Mind* (1987).

RICHARD RORTY is University Professor of the Humanities at the University of Virginia. He recently published *Objectivity, Relativism and Truth* (1991) and *Essays on Heidegger and Others* (1991).

THOMAS SHEEHAN is Professor of Philosophy at Loyola University of Chicago. He is the editor of *Heidegger, the Man and the Thinker* (1981) and the author of *Karl Rahner: The Philosophical Foundations* (1987), *The First Coming: How the Kingdom of God Became Christianity* (1986), and numerous articles on Heidegger.

CHARLES TAYLOR has been Chichele Professor of Social and Political Theory at Oxford and is currently Professor of Political Science and Philosophy at McGill University. His writings include *Hegel* (1975), the two-volume *Philosophical Papers* (1985), and, most recently, *Sources of the Self: The Making of the Modern Identity* (1989).

MICHAEL E. ZIMMERMAN is Professor and Chair of Philosophy at Tulane University. He has published many scholarly articles, as well as two books, *Eclipse of the Self* (rev. ed., 1986) and *Heidegger's Confrontation with Modernity* (1990). Currently he is writing a book on radical ecology and postmodernism and is editing a textbook on environmental philosophy.

ACKNOWLEDGMENTS

A number of people were especially helpful in the preparation of this volume. I want to thank H. L. Dreyfus, Richard Polt, and Frank Richardson for offering valuable comments on my introduction. Special thanks are due to Thomas Sheehan for making an accurate chronology of Heidegger's life possible. Dennis Mahoney and Wolfgang Mieder generously helped with information on German culture and history in the 1930s. I am grateful to Robert Hall for suggestions for the bibliography and to Bill Dunlop and Bea Harvey at the University of Vermont library for their efforts in updating information on publications and obtaining books. Sally-Marie Angier patiently talked me through some difficult times in the final preparation of the manuscript. At Cambridge University Press, Terence Moore and Christine Murray remained supportive and helpful through some trying delays. The deepest debt of gratitude I owe to Leslie Weiger, who not only typed most of the manuscript and all of the bibliography, but also revised (and, in some cases, rewrote) some troublesome essays by myself and others. Without her steady help and sharp eye, this volume would not have been possible.

ABBREVIATIONS

BP — *The Basic Problems of Phenomenology.* Translated by Albert Hofstadter. Bloomington: Indiana University Press, 1982.

BT — *Being and Time.* Translated by John Macquarrie and Edward Robinson. New York: Harper & Row, 1962.

BW — *Basic Writings.* Edited by David F. Krell. New York: Harper & Row, 1977.

DT — *Discourse on Thinking.* Translated by John M. Anderson and E. Hans Freund. New York: Harper & Row, 1966.

EGT — *Early Greek Thinking.* Translated by David F. Krell and Frank Capuzzi. New York: Harper & Row, 1975.

EP — *The End of Philosophy.* Translated by Joan Stambaugh. New York: Harper & Row, 1973.

ER — *The Essence of Reasons.* Translated by Terence Malick. Evanston, Ill.: Northwestern University Press, 1969.

FS — *Frühe Schriften.* Frankfurt am Main: Klostermann, 1972.

G — *Gelassenheit.* Pfullingen: Neske, 1959.

GA 1 — *Gesamtausgabe,* Vol. 1: *Frühe Schriften.* Edited by Friedrich-Wilhelm von Hermann. Frankfurt am Main: Klostermann, 1978.

GA 5 — *Gesamtausgabe,* Vol. 5: *Holzwege.* Edited by Friedrich-Wilhelm von Hermann. Frankfurt am Main: Klostermann, 1977.

GA 9 *Gesamtausgabe,* Vol. 9: *Wegmarken.* Edited by Friedrich-Wilhelm von Hermann. Frankfurt am Main: Klostermann, 1976.

GA 12 *Gesamtausgabe,* Vol. 12: *Unterwegs zur Sprache.* Edited by Friedrich-Wilhelm von Hermann. Frankfurt am Main: Klostermann, 1985.

GA 13 *Gesamtausgabe,* Vol. 13: *Aus der Erfahrung des Denkens.* Edited by Hermann Heidegger. Frankfurt am Main: Klostermann, 1983.

GA 24 *Gesamtausgabe,* Vol. 24: *Die Grundprobleme der Phänomenologie* (1927 lectures). Edited by Friedrich-Wilhelm von Hermann. Frankfurt am Main: Klostermann, 1989.

GA 29/30 *Gesamtausgabe,* Vol. 29/30: *Die Grundbegriffe der Metaphysik. Welt, Endlichkeit, Einsamkeit* (1929–30 lectures). Edited by Friedrich-Wilhelm von Hermann. Frankfurt am Main: Klostermann, 1983.

GA 40 *Gesamtausgabe,* Vol. 40: *Einführung in die Metaphysik* (1935 lectures). Edited by Petra Jaeger. Frankfurt am Main: Klostermann, 1983.

GA 42 *Gesamtausgabe,* Vol. 42: *Schelling: Vom Wesen der menschlichen Freiheit.* Edited by Ingrid Schüssler. Frankfurt am Main: Klostermann, 1988.

GA 56/57 *Gesamtausgabe,* Vol. 56/57: *Zur Bestimmung der Philosophie* (1919 Freiburg lectures). Edited by Bernd Heimbüchel. Frankfurt am Main: Klostermann, 1987.

GA 59/60 *Gesamtausgabe,* Vol. 59/60: *Vorlesungen Sommersemester 1920 und 1921. 1. Phänomenologie der Anschauung und des Ausdrucks. Theorie der philosophischen Begriffsbildung. 2. Augustinus und der Neuplatonismus.* Edited by Claudius Strube and Bernd Heimbüchel. Frankfurt am Main: Klostermann, forthcoming.

GA 61 *Gesamtausgabe,* Vol. 61: *Phänomenologische Interpretationen zu Aristoteles. Einführung in die phänomenologische Forschung* (1921–22 lectures). Edited by Walter Bröcker and Käte Bröcker-Oltmanns. Frankfurt am Main: Klostermann, 1985.

GA 65 *Gesamtausgabe,* Vol. 65: *Beiträge zur Philosophie.* Edited by Friedrich-Wilhelm von Hermann. Frankfurt am Main: Klostermann, 1989.

HCT *History of the Concept of Time: Prolegomena.* Translated by Theodore Kisiel. Bloomington: Indiana University Press, 1985.

ID *Identity and Difference.* Translated by Joan Stambaugh. New York: Harper & Row, 1969.

IM *An Introduction to Metaphysics.* Translated by Ralph Manheim. New Haven, Conn.: Yale University Press, 1959.

KPM *Kant and the Problem of Metaphysics.* Translated by James Churchill. Bloomington: Indiana University Press, 1962.

MFL *The Metaphysical Foundations of Logic.* Translated by Michael Heim. Bloomington: Indiana University Press, 1984.

N 1 *Nietzsche I: The Will to Power as Art.* Edited and translated by David E. Krell. New York: Harper & Row, 1979.

N 2 *Nietzsche II: The Eternal Recurrence of the Same.* Edited and translated by David F. Krell. New York: Harper & Row, 1984.

N 3 *Nietzsche III: The Will to Power as Knowledge and as Metaphysics.* Translated by Joan Stambaugh, David F. Krell, and Frank A. Capuzzi. New York: Harper & Row, 1987.

N 4 *Nietzsche IV: Nihilism.* Edited by David F. Krell; translated by Frank A. Capuzzi. New York: Harper & Row, 1982.

OGSU "Only a God Can Save Us: *Der Spiegel*'s Interview with Martin Heidegger." Translated by Maria P. Alter and John D. Caputo. *Philosophy Today,* 20 (Winter 1976): 267–84.

OWL *On the Way to Language.* Translated by Peter D. Hertz. New York: Harper & Row, 1971.

PLT *Poetry, Language, Thought.* Translated by Albert Hofstadter. New York: Harper & Row, 1971.

PT	*The Piety of Thinking.* Translated by James Hart and John Maraldo. Bloomington: Indiana University Press, 1976.
QCT	*The Question Concerning Technology and Other Essays.* Translated by William Lovitt. New York: Harper & Row, 1977.
SD	*Zur Sache des Denkens.* Tübingen: Niemeyer, 1969.
SG	*Der Satz vom Grund.* Pfullingen: Neske, 1971.
Sp	"Nur Noch ein Gott kann uns retten." *Spiegel*-Gespräch mit Martin Heidegger am 23 September, 1966. *Der Spiegel,* No. 26 (May 31, 1976): 193–219.
SZ	*Sein und Zeit.* Tübingen: Niemeyer, 1957.
TB	*On Time and Being.* Translated by Joan Stambaugh. New York: Harper & Row, 1972.
TK	*Die Technik und die Kehre.* Pfullingen: Neske, 1962.
US	*Unterwegs zur Sprache.* Pfullingen: Neske, 1965.
VA	*Vorträge und Aufsätze.* Pfullingen: Neske, 1959.
WM	*Wegmarken.* Frankfurt am Main: Klostermann, 1967.

CHRONOLOGY

Sept. 26, 1889	Born in Messkirch, Baden-Württemburg
1903–11	Studies for the priesthood at the Seminary of the Archdiocese of Freiburg
1903–9	Concurrent high school studies: State Gymnasium, Constance (1903–6); Berthold Gymnasium, Freiburg (1906–9)
1907	Receives a copy of Franz Brentano's *On the Manifold Meaning of Being in Aristotle* (1862), the book that led him to formulate the "question of being"
1909	Spends two weeks in the Jesuit novitiate, Feldkirch, Austria; leaves due to poor health
1909–13	Studies at the University of Freiburg: theology until 1911, then mathematics and philosophy
1912	First philosophical publications: "The Problem of Reality in Modern Philosophy" and "New Research on Logic"
1913	Awarded Ph.D. under Arthur Schneider (chair); dissertation, "The Doctrine of Judgment in Psychologism"
1915	Habilitation (teaching qualification dissertation) under Heinrich Rickert, "The Doctrine of Categories and Signification in Duns Scotus"
1915–23	*Privatdozent* (lecturer) at the University of Freiburg
1915–18	Military service
1917	Married to Elfriede Petri
1919–23	Assistant to Husserl at Freiburg

1919, 1920	Birth of sons Jörg and Hermann
1923–8	Associate professor, University of Marburg
1927	*Sein und Zeit* (Being and time) published
1928	Appointed Husserl's successor, professor of philosophy, at the University of Freiburg
1929	Break with Husserl
1929	Publishes *Kant und das Problem der Metaphysik* (Kant and the problem of metaphysics), "Was ist Metaphysik?" (What is metaphysics?), and "Vom Wesen des Grundes" (The essence of reasons)
Apr. 22, 1933	Becomes rector of the University of Freiburg
May 1, 1933	Joins the National Socialist Party
Nov. 11, 1933	Radio address supporting Hitler's withdrawal of Germany from the League of Nations
Apr. 27, 1934	Resigns as rector
1934–42	Lectures on Hölderlin and Nietzsche
1935	Lectures: "Der Ursprung des Kunstwerkes" (The origin of the work of art) and *Einführung in die Metaphysik* (Introduction to metaphysics)
1936–8	Composes *Beiträge zur Philosophie* (Contributions to philosophy)
Nov. 1944	Drafted into the People's Militia (Volkssturm)
1945	Denazification hearings; banned from teaching
1946	Nervous breakdown
1947	"Brief über den Humanismus" (Letter on humanism) published
1950	Reinstated to teaching position
1951	Granted emeritus status
1953	*Einführung in die Metaphysik* (Introduction to metaphysics) published
1957	*Der Satz vom Grund* (The principle of reason) published
1959	*Unterwegs zur Sprache* (On the way to language) published
1961	Two-volume *Nietzsche* published
May 26, 1976	Dies in Freiburg

Introduction

As the twentieth century draws to a close, it is increasingly clear that Heidegger will stand out as one of the greatest philosophers of our times. His writings have had an immense impact not only in Europe and the English-speaking world, but in Asia as well.[1] And his influence has been felt in areas as diverse as literary theory, psychoanalysis, rhetoric, ecology, and theology. The recent explosion of interest in Heidegger has come as a surprise to even his most ardent admirers. In the fifties and sixties it was still possible to consign Heidegger to the "Phenomenology and Existentialism" bin of the philosophy curriculum, treating him as the student of Husserl and precursor of Sartre. His talk about angst, guilt, death, and the need to be authentic seemed to place his work well outside the range of topics making up the mainstream Anglo-American curriculum. Though he was read in France, he was largely ignored in the English-speaking world.

In the past few decades, however, a number of events have brought about a wider appreciation of the achievement of this fertile and complex thinker. First, in North America, the writings of such influential figures as Richard Rorty, Charles Taylor, and H. L. Dreyfus have helped us to see Heidegger as the seminal figure in what David Hoy calls a "hermeneutic turn," a new orientation with profound repercussions for such issues as the nature of the human sciences, the possibility of artificial intelligence, and the prospects for a postfoundationalist culture. As such respected theorists as Clifford Geertz, Thomas Kuhn, Michael Walzer, and Roy Schafer come to describe their approaches as "hermeneutic," there is a greater tendency to go back to the seminal texts that shaped contemporary hermeneutics. Second, the growing interest in Continental philosophers who start out from Heidegger – including Gadamer in his debates with Habermas, and "postmodern" thinkers like Derrida, Foucault, and Bourdieu – has provoked curiosity about the figure who is a constant presence in all their work.[2] Third, and most recently, the latest revelations concerning the extent of Heidegger's involvement with the Nazis has led to a flurry of reflections on the relation of his thought – and of philosophy in general – to politics and culture.[3]

Heidegger's lofty ambition was to rejuvenate philosophy (and, at the same time, Western culture) by clearing away the conceptual rubbish that has collected over our history in order to recover a clearer, richer understanding of what things are all about. Since this calls for appropriating the underlying ideas that have formed our culture, his thought weaves together many different historical strands. The essays written for this volume reveal the complex range of sources of Heidegger's thought. He draws on St. Paul, the pre-Socratics, Aristotle, Aquinas, Duns Scotus, Meister Eckhart, Kant, Hegel, Schelling, Schleiermacher, Kierkegaard, Nietzsche, Dilthey, Bergson, Husserl, and Scheler, and he does so in order to formulate an alternative to the assumptions that make up the tradition extending from Plato to Descartes to contemporary scientific naturalism. What is most striking about Heidegger's appropriation of historical sources is the way he blends together points of view generally regarded as irreconcilably opposed. Thus, we find Kierkegaardian passion combined with a commitment to systematic rigor, a Romantic concern with individual fulfillment together with a Hegelian communitarianism, a deep respect for German Idealism along with a hard-headed realism, and an awareness of the historicity and finitude of life together with the search for a stable "ground."

These overlapping themes steadily evolve during a philosophical career spanning nearly seventy years. Considering the diversity and scope of Heidegger's writings, it is hardly surprising that his influence has been so extensive. His thought has contributed to phenomenology (Merleau-Ponty), existentialism (Sartre, Ortega y Gasset), hermeneutics (Gadamer, Ricoeur), political theory (Hannah Arendt, the early Marcuse), psychotherapy theory (Medard Boss, Ludwig Binswanger, Rollo May), theology (Rudolph Bultmann, Paul Tillich), as well as current postmodern and "new pragmatist" trends.

Heidegger explicitly rejected epigonism and pedantic scholarship, calling on thinkers to travel along the paths he traversed instead of pondering his words. As a result, the finest scholarly work done on his writings tends to reflect widely divergent readings of what he has to offer. In addition, his claim that what is most important in any thinker is what remains "unsaid," together with his belief that authentic interpretation always requires doing "violence" to the texts, further fans the flames of the conflict of interpretations surrounding his works today. The contributions to this volume, written by philosophers whose primary goal is enriching our understanding of ourselves and our world, show the very different ways of understanding what Heidegger has to say.

The essays can be roughly divided into four groups. The first three essays, those by Frede, Sheehan, and Olafson, provide an overview of Heidegger's lifework. The next four essays, those by Hall, Dostal, Hoy, and Hoffman, focus primarily on themes developed in *Being and Time.* The essays by Guignon, Zimmerman, Caputo, and Dreyfus deal with Heidegger's contributions to such areas of inquiry as psychotherapy theory, ecology, aesthetics, politics, and theology. The final essays by Taylor and Rorty present two different assessments of Heidegger's philosophical contribution. These divisions could have been made differently, however. For instance, the subject of language is central to Rorty's contribution, as well as to the essays by Frede, Olafson, and Hoy. The crucial question of Heidegger's involvement with the Nazis is dealt with not just by Sheehan, but by Zimmerman, Caputo, and Dreyfus. And though all the authors engage in critical reflection, Rorty launches an especially powerful critique of the later Heidegger in defending a view of philosophy he finds in the early Heidegger and later Wittgenstein.

My aim in this introduction is to sketch out a broad picture of Heidegger's lifework in order to provide a background for the essays that follow. The first section deals with the account of "Dasein" (human existence) and of the worldhood of the world in *Being and Time.* The following two sections deal with the "turn" to the so-called later Heidegger and with his involvement in National Socialism in the thirties. I should say here that my account of Heidegger's complicity with the Nazis represents my own personal perspective concerning this issue and that its meliorative tone is at odds with the brilliant and insightful work of Sheehan and Caputo, as well as with the majority of other commentators on this topic.[4] My goal, however, is not to justify Heidegger's actions (I find them disgraceful and contemptible), but to try to understand how a bookish academic from the backwoods of Germany – a person admired throughout his life by decent people who regarded him as a friend – could have become involved in such horrors. In presenting one more take on this hotly debated affair, of course, I do not pretend to have said the last word on it.

FUNDAMENTAL ONTOLOGY IN *BEING AND TIME*

Being and Time (1927) remains Heidegger's best-known and most influential work. Despite its heavy Teutonic tone and tortuous style (especially in the English translation), it can seem to bring a breath of fresh air to traditional philosophical puzzles. Heidegger's insight there is that many of the knots in thinking that characterize philosophy are due to a particular way of understanding the nature of reality, an outlook that arose at the dawn of Western history and dominates our thought to this day. This outlook is what Dorothea Frede in her essay calls the "substance ontology": the view that what is ultimately real is that which underlies properties – what "stands under" (*sub-stantia*) and remains continuously present throughout all change. Because of its emphasis on enduring presence, this traditional ontology is also called the "metaphysics of presence." It is found, for example, in Plato's notion of the Forms, Aristotle's primary substances, the Creator of Christian belief, Descartes's *res extensa* and *res cogitans,* Kant's noumena, and the physical stuff presupposed by scientific naturalism. Ever since Descartes, this substance ontology has bred a covey of either/ors that generate the so-called problems of philosophy: either there is mind or everything is just matter; either our ideas do represent objects or nothing exists outside the mind; either something in me remains constant through change or there is no personal identity; either values have objective existence or everything is permitted. These either/ors lay out a grid of possible moves and countermoves in a philosophical game that eventually can begin to feel as predictable and tiresome as tic-tac-toe.

Heidegger's goal is to undercut the entire game by challenging the idea that reality must be thought of in terms of the idea of substance at all. His claim is not that mind and matter do not exist, but that they are derivative, regional ways of being for things, the detritus of some fairly high-level theorizing that is remote from concrete, lived existence. As Thomas Sheehan notes, Heidegger in 1919 already regarded the objectifying outlook as originating not so much from natural science as from the theoretical attitude itself: "It is not just naturalism, as [Husserl] thought, . . . but the general domination of the *theoretical* that is messing up the real problematic" (GA 56/57 87). It is therefore possible to see the history of philosophy from Plato to contemporary naturalism – and including Husserlian phenomenology itself – as one extended misinterpretation of the nature of reality. This misinterpretation is inevitable once one adopts the detached standpoint of theoretical reflection, for when we step back and try to get an impartial, objective view of things, the world, so to speak, goes dead for us – things lose the meaningfulness definitive of their being in the everyday life-world. Following the lead of the influential turn-of-the-century movement called "life philosophy" (then seen as including Nietzsche, Bergson, and Dilthey), Heidegger hoped to recover a more original sense of things by setting aside the view of reality we get from theorizing and focusing instead on the way things show up in the flux of our everyday, prereflective activities.

To pave the way to a new understanding of ourselves and the world, *Being and Time* begins by asking the question posed by traditional ontology: What is the being of entities? But Heidegger quickly notes that ontology as such, the question of being, "remains itself naive and opaque" if it fails to inquire first into the *meaning* of being (BT 31). In other words, since what things *are* (their being) is accessible only insofar as they become intelligible to us (insofar as they show up for us as relevant or as counting in some determinate way), we need a "fundamental ontology" that clarifies the meaning (i.e., conditions of intelligibility) of things in general. And since *our* existence or "being-there" (Dasein) is "the horizon in which something like being in general becomes intelligible," fundamental ontology must begin by "clarifying the possibility of having any understanding of being at all – an understanding which itself belongs to the constitution of the entity called Dasein" (BT 274). This inquiry into the conditions for the possibility of having any understanding whatsoever, the analytic of Dasein, makes up the published portion of *Being and Time.* The investigation starts, then, with an inquiry into our own being, insofar as we are the entities who have some understanding of being, and it does so in order to lay a basis for inquiring into the being of entities in general (rocks, hammers, squirrels, numbers, constellations, symphonies).[5]

The question of being is therefore reformulated as a question about the conditions for the accessibility or intelligibility of things. The constant references to Kant in the essays that follow (especially in those by Hoy, Dostal, and Frede) show how this project can be seen as a continuation of Kant's "Copernican revolution," the shift from seeing the mind as trying to hook up with an antecedently given world to seeing the world as being made over in order to fit the demands of the mind. But Heidegger's analytic of Dasein also marks an important break from Kant and from German Idealism generally. For Heidegger brackets the assumption that there is such a thing as a mind or consciousness, something immediately presented to itself in introspection, which must be taken as the self-evident starting point for any account of reality. Instead, though it is true that the first-person standpoint is basic (as Hoffman clearly shows), it is not the mental that is basic but rather what Taylor calls "engaged agency." We start out from a description of ourselves as we are in the midst of our day-to-day practical affairs, prior to any split between mind and matter. Our inquiry must begin from the "existentiell" (concrete, specific, local) sense we have of ourselves as caught up in the midst of a practical world (in the "life-world" sense of this term found in such expressions as "the world of academia" or the "business world").

In Heidegger's view, there is no pure, external vantage point to which we can retreat in order to get a disinterested, presuppositionless angle on things. So fundamental ontology begins with a description of the "phenomena" where this means what "shows itself," what "becomes manifest" or "shows forth" *for us,* in relation to our purposes as they are shaped by our forms of life.[6] But this need to start from an insider's perspective is not a restriction in any sense. On the contrary, as Taylor shows, it is only because we are "always already" in on a way of life, engaged in everyday dealings with things in a familiar life-world, that we have some "pre-understanding" of what things are all about. It is our being as participants in a shared practical world that first gives us a window onto ourselves and reality.

The existential analytic therefore starts out from a description of our average everydayness as agents in practical contexts. Heidegger's early writings are filled with descriptions of such mundane activities as hammering in a workshop, turning a doorknob, hearing motorcycles, and operating the turn signal on a car. But the goal of the inquiry is to identify the "essential structures" that make up the "formal scaffolding (*Gerüst*)" of any Dasein whatsoever. For this reason the phenomenology of everydayness is coupled with a hermeneutic or interpretation designed to bring to light the hidden basis for the unity and intelligibility of the practical life-world. Because interpretation reveals that in virtue of which (*woraufhin*) everything hangs together, Heidegger says that it formulates "transcendental generalizations" concerning the conditions for any interpretations or worldviews whatsoever (BT 244). It is, as Hoy points out, *Interpretierung* aimed at revealing the "primary understanding of world" that underlies and makes possible our day-to-day existentiell interpretations (*Auslegungen*). Since the goal of the inquiry is not to give an account of entities but rather to grasp the being of entities (what lets things be what they are, what "determines entities as entities" in their various ways of being), phenomenology seeks what generally "does not show itself at all," the hidden "meaning and ground" of what does show up (BT 25, 59). In the course of this investigation, it becomes clear that the entities taken as basic by certain regional sciences – for example, the material objects in causal interactions of classical mechanics – are theoretical constructs with no privileged status in helping us grasp the nature of reality.

Insofar as our commonsense outlook is pervaded by past theorizing, and especially by the Cartesian ontology of modernity, fundamental ontology will involve "*doing violence*" to the complacent assumptions of common sense. Nowhere is this challenge to common sense more evident than in Heidegger's description of being human, or Dasein.[7] This description is sharply opposed to the picture of humans we have inherited from Descartes. According to the Cartesian view, we are at the most basic level minds located in bodies. And this is indeed the way we tend to think of ourselves when we step back and reflect on our being. The binary opposition between mind and matter colors all our thinking in the modern world, and it leads to a kind of Cartesian extortion which tells us that if we ever question the existence of mental substance, we will sink to the level of being crude materialists who can never account for human experience and agency.

Heidegger's way of dealing with this extortion is to subvert the binary opposition that sets up the narrow range of options in the first place. In my own essay (Chapter 8), I try to show that instead of defining Dasein as a thing or object of any sort, Heidegger describes human existence as a "happening," a life story unfolding "between birth and death" (BT 427). This conception of existence as the "historicity" or "temporalizing" of a life course arises quite naturally when we reflect on the nature of human agency. For what a person is *doing* at any moment can be regarded as action (and not just as inadvertent movement) only because of the way it is nested in the wider context of a life story. For instance, what I am doing now can be seen as writing a philosophy essay only because of the relation of my current activity to my background (my training, my academic career) and to my future-directedness (the outcome of this activity in relation to my undertakings in general). In fact, it seems that what is most important to an event being an action is not just the beliefs and desires going on in a mental substance, since all sorts of things might be going through my mind as I type away here. Rather, what is crucial to this movement being *action* is its rootedness in meaningful contexts of the past and its directedness toward some future end state (despite the fact that this is all probably far from my "mind" when I am busily engaged in everyday activities).

When we think of a human being as the temporal unfolding of a life course, we can identify three structural elements that make up human existence. First, Dasein always finds itself "thrown" into a concrete situation and attuned to a cultural and historical context where things already count in determinate ways in relation to a community's practices. This prior thrownness into the medium of shared intelligibility, disclosed in our moods, makes up Dasein's "facticity." Second, agency is "discursive" in the sense that in our activities we are articulating the world and interacting with situations along the guidelines of interpretations embodied in our public language. Third, Dasein is "understanding" in Heidegger's special use of this term: it has always taken some stand on its life insofar as it has undertaken (or drifted into) the vocations, roles, life-styles, personal relationships, and so on that give content to its life. Because our familiar skilled activities embody a generally tacit "know-how," a sense of what things are all about in relation to our practical concerns, taking a stand is said to be a "projection" of possibilities of meaningfulness for things and ourselves.

As having taken a stand, Dasein's existence is "futural" in the sense that it is under way toward realizing some outcome (though this goal-directedness might never expressly come into one's mind). Thus, agency is characterized as "coming-toward" (*zu-kommend*) the realization of one's undertakings, that is, as being-toward the future (*Zu-kunft*). I attend a parent–teacher conference, for example, as part of my "project" of being a concerned parent, and I do so even though this way of doing things is so deeply ingrained in me, so "automatic," that I never think about *why* I am doing it. According to Heidegger, the future has priority over both the past and the present in defining the being of the self. This is so, first of all, because what a person is shooting for in life determines both how the past can be encountered as providing assets for the present and how the present can show up as a situation demanding action. But the future also has priority because, insofar as my actions commit me to a range of possible ways of being in the future, their future-directedness defines what my life – that is, my "being" – is adding up to as a totality, "right up to the end."

According to this description, Dasein's "being" or personal identity is defined by the stands it takes in acting in day-to-day situations over the course of its lifetime. Heidegger expresses this by saying that Dasein is an "ability-to-be," which comes to realization only through the ways it is channeled into concrete "possibilities," that is, into specific roles, relationships, personality traits, lifestyles, and so on, as these have been made accessible in its cultural context.[8] Thus, when I hold a door open for a friend or get on line at the theater, I am constituting myself as a fairly well behaved person as this is understood in my culture. Here I just *am* what I make of myself by slipping into familiar patterns of action and reaction throughout my life.

The conception of human existence as an emergence-into-presence provides an insight into the understanding of being that Heidegger is trying to work out, a conception Zimmerman calls "ontological phenomenalism." My being – who I am – is nothing other than what unfolds in the course of my interactions with the world over the course of my life. In saying that "the 'essence' of Dasein lies in its existence" (BT 67), Heidegger suggests that there is no role to be played by the notion of an underlying substance or a hidden essence allegedly needed to explain the outward phenomena. What makes agency possible is not some underlying substrate, not some mental substance, but is rather the way our life stories unfold against the backdrop of practices of a shared, meaningful world. From Heidegger's standpoint, then, the ability to think of ourselves as minds located in physical bodies is a highly specialized self-interpretation rooted in detached theorizing, an interpretation lacking any broader implications for understanding human existence.

The power of the Cartesian extortion lies in its ability to keep us in line by telling us that doubts about the mind lead inevitably to crude materialism. Heidegger sidesteps this move by suggesting that not only mind but matter as well is a theoretical construct with no indispensable role to play in making sense of the everyday life-world. To get this point across, he undertakes a description of how things show up for us most "primordially" in the course of our everyday dealings with the world. In his now-well-known example of hammering in a workshop, he suggests that what we encounter when we are absorbed in such an activity is not a "hammer-thing" with properties to which we then assign a use value. On the contrary, what shows up for us initially is the hammering, which is "in order to" nail boards together, which is "for" building a bookcase, which is ultimately "for the sake of" being, say, a person with a neat study. As Hall's essay shows, the ordinary work-world as a whole – the light in the room, the workbench, the saw, the glue – all of these show up in their interconnected functionality in relation to our projects.

It follows, then, that what is "given" in average everyday dealings with the world is a holistic "equipmental totality," a web of functional relationships in which things are encountered in their interdependent functions and in terms of their relevance to what we are doing. The hammer is what it is by virtue of its reference to these nails and boards in hammering on this workbench under this lighting for this purpose. In Heidegger's vocabulary, the world of average everydayness is not an aggregate of "present-at-hand" objects, things that just occur, but is a holistic contexture of relations, the "ready-to-hand," where what something *is* – its "ontological definition" – is determined by its role within the projects under way within the workshop.[9] The totality of these functional relations – the general structure of "in order tos," "by doing whichs," "for whichs," and "for the sakes of" as laid out in our culture's practices – Heidegger calls the "worldhood" of the world. His claim, as I understand it, is that the present-at-hand items taken as basic by traditional theorizing (for instance, physical objects and their causal relations) are derivative from and parasitic on the world understood as a context of involvements directed toward accomplishing things. To think that there are "at first" mere present-at-hand things "in a space in general," which then get concatenated into equipmental relations, is an "illusion" (BT 421), according to Heidegger (though it may be useful to assume that such things exist for the purposes of certain regional inquiries).[10]

The description of average everydayness leads us to see that what is most basic is a world of "significance" in which things show up as *counting* or *mattering* in relation to our practical affairs. This meaningful life-world is inseparable from Dasein's future-directedness, its being "for the sake of itself" in the various self-interpretations and roles it picks up from the public "we-world" into which it is thrown. Dasein is said to be a "clearing" or a "lighting" through which entities can stand forth *as* such and such. In other words, it is because we take a stand on our being in the world – because we are "understanding," in Heidegger's special use of this word – that we engage in familiar, skillful practices in everday contexts, and we thereby open a leeway or field of free play (*Spielraum*) where things can stand out as counting or mattering in some determinate ways. Given my self-understanding as a cook in the kitchen, for example, I handle things there in such a way that the spatula and pan stand out as significant while the linoleum and wainscotting recede into insignificance.

This projection of possibilities opened by understanding is realized and made concrete in "interpretation" (*Auslegung,* literally "laying out"). Interpretation is our way of "explicitly appropriating" the world "in preparing, putting to rights, repairing, improving [and] rounding out," that is, in our familiar activities within ordinary contexts. Interpretation seizes on the range of possibilities laid out in advance by the "fore-structure" of understanding and works it over into a concrete "*as*-structure" of uses – using the pan to boil an egg, for instance, rather than to simmer a white sauce (BT §§31–2). Given this description of everydayness, we can see why Heidegger claims that the *being* of everyday equipment in use – its readiness-to-hand – is defined by our ways of using things in the course of our prereflective activities.

It should now be clear why Heidegger tells us that being-in-the-world is a "unitary phenomenon." On the one hand, the being of everyday functional contexts is inseparable from the specific uses we put things to in the course of our shared practical involvements in the world. On the other hand, who *I am* as an agent is determined by the equipmental contexts and familiar forms of life that make up the worldly "dwelling" in which I find myself. Since there is no ultimate ground or foundation for the holistic web of meaning that makes up being-in-the-world, Heidegger suggests that the meaning of being (i.e., the basis of all intelligibility) is an "absence of ground" or "abyss" (*Abgrund*) (BT 194).[11]

What must be explained given such a picture of being-in-the-world, as Hoy points out, is not how an initially worldless subject can get hooked up with a pregiven collection of objects "out there" in a neutral space–time coordinate system. Rather, what we need to show is why the tradition has overlooked this unified phenomenon, and how the disjunction of self and things ever arises in the first place. To explain the appeal of the substance ontology, Heidegger describes how the spectator attitude and the objectifying ontology result from a "breakdown" in average everydayness. When everything is running smoothly in the workplace, he suggests, the ready-to-hand and the surrounding work-world remain unobtrusive and unnoticed. The ready-to-hand must "withdraw" into its usability, Heidegger says, "in order to *be* ready-to-hand quite authentically" (BT 99). As Hall points out, we see through it, so to speak, in zeroing in on what we are out to accomplish.

When something goes wrong in the workshop, however, there is a "changeover" in the way things show up for us. If the handle breaks off the pot or the spatula is missing, the whole project grinds to a standstill and we are put in the position of just looking around to see what to do next. It is when things are temporarily unready-to-hand in this way that we can catch a glimpse of the web of functional relations in which they played a part. Thus, a breakdown makes it possible to catch sight of the worldhood of the world. If the breakdown persists, however, items can begin to obtrude in their unusability, and we can look at things as brute present-at-hand objects to be investigated from a theoretical perspective. As we adopt a stance in which things are explicitly noticed, we can be led to believe that what have been there "all along" are value-free, meaningless objects whose usefulness was merely a product of our own subjective interests and needs. Heidegger's point, however, is that this conception of reality as consisting of essentially contextless objects can arise only derivatively from a more "primordial" way of being absorbed in a meaningful life-world.[12] Such contextless objects are by-products of the "disworlding of the world," and so cannot be thought of as the basic components from which the world is built up.

According to Heidegger's phenomenology of being-in-the-world, what is most primordial is neither humans nor objects, but rather the "clearing" in which specific forms of human existence along with particular sorts of equipmental context emerge-into-presence in their reciprocal interdependence. Entities in general – the tools in a workshop, the unknown chemical in the chemist's beaker, even the precise kinds of sensation and emotion we can have – these can show up *as* what they *are* (i.e., in their *being* such and such) only against the background of the interpretive practices of a particular historical culture. Yet it is also true that *we* can be the kinds of people we are in our everyday affairs only by virtue of the practical contexts of worldly involvement in which we find ourselves. In the kitchen I can be a culinary artist or a klutz, but not a world leader signing a treaty. Thus, "Self and world belong together in the single entity Dasein. Self and world are not two beings, like subject and object; . . . [instead,] self and world are the basic determination of Dasein in the unity of the structure of being-in-the-world" (BP 297).

With its emphasis on our facticity, thrownness, and embeddedness in a concrete world, we might think of Heidegger's fundamental ontology as moving toward something like a "Ptolemaic reaction" to Kant's Copernican revolution. Humans do not construct the world. Rather, humans *and* things are constituted by the totality of what Heidegger in his earliest writings called the "worlding of the world." And *being* is understood neither as an essential property of things, nor as the mere fact that they occur, nor as something cast onto things by humans. Instead, being comes to be thought of as a temporal event, a "movement into presence" inseparable from the understanding of being embodied in Dasein's forms of life. It is the event (*Ereignis*) of disclosedness in which entities come to be appropriated into intelligibility.[13]

It follows from Heidegger's account of average everydayness that there can be no presuppositionless knowledge, no access of the sort philosophers sought when they dreamed of getting in touch with "reality as it is in itself." We are always caught up in a "hermeneutic circle": though our general sense of things depends on what we encounter in the world, we can first discover something as significant in some determinate way only because we have soaked up a "preontological understanding" of how things in general can count through being initiated into the practices and language of our culture.

Of course, to say that we always encounter entities *as* counting in such and such ways does not entail that, in some sense, a veil has been pulled over things so that we can never make contact with the things themselves. On the contrary, since the ways things show up – the appearances – just are what those things really *are,* access to what appears just is access to those things. Heidegger tries to clarify this point by considering what is involved when a city "presents a magnificent view" from the vantage point of a particular scenic overlook. Here it is the city itself that offers itself "from this or that point of view" (IM 104). It remains true, needless to say, that the city can present *this* panorama only because *we* are viewing it from a particular position. But this relativity to a standpoint does not entail that we are cut off from the city, having access to, say, only a mental picture of the city. It is not, after all, a representation of the city we encounter, but a *presentation* of the city as it shows itself from this particular point of view.

This example shows how Heidegger tries to undercut traditional skepticism about the external world by undermining the representationalist model that gets it going in the first place. The perspectival modes of access to the city, far from being barriers between us and reality, are in fact the conditions making possible any access to things at all. They *place* the city before us, and they place *us* in the setting, letting us be the observers we are. Thus, we can make no sense of the idea of getting a "view of the city as it *really* is," independent of all points of view and perspectives. For even aerial photographs and street maps are just more points of view; they are not privileged, "purely objective" indicators of what the city is "really" like. The idea of a pure, colorless, objective geographic or geological locale, distinct from all possible modes of presentation, is an illusion bred by the dominance of representationalism in our thinking. As a result, Heidegger's recognition of the Dasein-relativity of the being of entities is consistent with a full-blooded realism that affirms the reality of what shows up for us. *The* world just is the human world in its various manifestations.[14]

THE TURN TO THE HISTORY OF BEING

In his writings after *Being and Time,* Heidegger's thought began to shift in important ways, moving toward the often baffling writings of the later period. Heidegger himself speaks of a "turn" (*Kehre*) in his thought, which begins with the 1930 essay "On the Essence of Truth." In order to try to get a handle on this turn, we might distinguish two tightly interwoven strands of the shift that took place in his outlook through the thirties. First, there are his attempts to answer charges that *Being and Time* is merely a new move in the tradition of transcendental philosophy stemming from Kant – that it is "anthropocentric" and treats Dasein as a detached, "standpoint-free" source from which "the entirety of non-Daseinal . . . being" can be derived (ER 99). Second, there are Heidegger's responses to the "conservative revolution" in Germany that swept the Nazis into power in 1933. As we shall see, these strands are interdependent and ultimately arrive at the same point.

The first source of change consists in the shift away from fundamental ontology, with its focus on Dasein as the source of the intelligibility of things, to the project of thinking the "history of being," where humans and their modes of understanding are themselves treated as offshoots of a wider historical unfolding. In the new *seynsgeschichtlich* approach that took shape in the mid-thirties, being is seen as a complex "happening" that, although it "needs" and "uses" humans, is not to be thought of as something humans create. As Caputo puts it in Chapter 10, being has to be thought of as "the event of manifestness, the happening of the truth of being, the coming to pass of the history of the epochal manifestations of being." And because being just *is* the history of unfolding epochs of self-manifestation, Heidegger says that "the history of being is being itself" (EP 82). Humans are then seen more as respondents who are "called" to the task of the "safekeeping" of being than they are creators who constitute being. In this respect, as Olafson points out, being is very similar to language. When we talk to one another we say things that are often quite original and inventive. But we can do this only by drawing on the linguistic resources of our language. What we can say, then, is always preshaped by the articulations and schematizations built into our historical language. In the same way, our actions and thoughts contribute to the transmission of history, but even our most original articulations and creations are always guided and regulated by the generally tacit understanding embodied in the practices of our historical culture. This formative understanding of being "happens behind our backs," as it were, leading us at times to recapitulate the very patterns we might hope to overcome.

To understand Heidegger's turn to the history of being, we need to sketch out the rough contours of his historical story. It starts with the assumption, based on a reading of pre-Socratic texts, that at the dawn of Western civilization there was a "first beginning," in which the Greeks brought to light the ontological difference – the difference between being and entities – by asking the question, What are entities? or What is the *being* of entities? This has been the "guiding question" (*Leitfrage*) of Western thought to this day. The first answer to the question was *physis*, or presence understood as "emerging and abiding," as "self-blossoming emergence . . . , unfolding, that which manifests itself in such unfolding and perseveres and endures in it" (IM 14). Being, according to this earliest Greek experience, is "*appearance* as a definite mode of emerging self-manifestation" in which things emerge from concealment into "*truth* in the sense of unconcealment" (IM 109).

An analysis of Sophocles' "Ode to Man" suggests that the Greeks were aware, if only in a dim and confused way, of the role of human practices and language in articulating how things can count within a world. For the earliest Greeks, the more-than-human, the "overpowering surge," is "made manifest and made to stand" through the "gathering" and "collecting collectedness" brought about by the comportment of a historical people (IM 171). By means of the "capturing and subjugating that opens entities *as* sea, *as* earth, *as* animal," humans "undertake to govern and succeed in governing the power of the overpowering" (IM 157, 172). Heidegger regards this insight into the connection between the coming-into-presence of entities and the role of human practices in articulating what shows up as fundamental to understanding being. In its "historical, history-disclosing essence," he writes, "human-being is *logos*, the gathering and apprehending of the being of entities" (IM 171). The event of being – *that* things stand forth, for example, as holy or as natural resources – is made possible by the understanding of being embodied in the practices of a historical culture, for example, *that* there are people who worship or people who challenge forth the energies of nature.

The first beginning makes up what the unpublished "de-structuring of the history of ontology" in *Being and Time* proposed to find when it spoke of retrieving the "wellsprings" of our understanding of being, "those primordial experiences in which we achieved our first ways of determining the nature of being – the ways which have guided us ever since" (BT 44).[15] It is because those initial experiences have shaped how Western people understand being to this day that Heidegger can say that "the beginning, conceived in an originary way, is being itself" (*Der Anfang – anfänglich begriffen – ist das Seyn selbst*) (58).[16] Since the first beginning has predefined all subsequent ways of experiencing things, it follows that the historically shifting interpretations of being in our culture have all been permutations on the understanding that took shape at the dawn of our civilization. Thus, the early Greek understanding of being as *physis* is not one outlook among others. Rather, it is definitive of who we are as participants in Western history. As a result, any new beginning will involve recapturing the insights flowing from those initial "wellsprings" of understanding that set our civilization on its course: the new beginning is "realizable only in a dialogue (*Auseinandersetzung*) with the *first*" (58).

Nevertheless, the unfolding of different "epochs" in the understanding of being over the past millennia – the "history of metaphysics" – has involved a progressive masking or concealing of what was revealed in that primordial experience. In asking about entities and experiencing entities as what comes to presence, the Greeks overlooked what makes this presence possible – that is, the "presencing" of what is present. Thus, according to Heidegger's story, *being* itself "remains forgotten" in the first beginning (IM 18). Instead of thinking of being (*Sein,* or as Heidegger begins to write it, *Seyn*), the Greeks focused on "beingness" (*Seiendheit*) understood as the essential property of actually existent entities.

The history of metaphysics is therefore a history of forgetfulness or "withdrawal," in which entities obtrude as actually existing and as having essential properties while being – that which first makes it possible for anything to show up in its *existentia* and *essentia* – remains concealed. This withdrawal is evident in Plato's interpretation of the beingness of entities as the aspect (*idea*) or perfect prototype, knowable through pure rational contemplation, that produces those diverse material things that come to be in our visible world. Later developments lead to a conception of entities as "what has been produced" and of being as "being produced" (by nature or by God). In the modern age, this production is seen as what "stands before" (*vor-stellend*) a subject or a Will. To be, then, is to be the stably persisting outcome of a productive act – that which "lies before" the producer as his or her product.[17]

As a result of the first moves at the dawn of history, being comes to be thought of as what endures, what is permanent, what is always there. It is the continuous presence of a substance (*ousia*) – that which "remains" through all changes (as Descartes later puts it when reflecting on the essence of a piece of wax in the second *Meditation*). To the extent that metaphysics focuses on "beingness" and is blind to the conditions that let anything whatsoever show up, metaphysics has been dominated by "error" or "going astray." Because Plato inaugurated this interpretation of beingness, the entire history of metaphysics can be called "Platonism." And since Nietzsche still operates within the range of oppositions opened by Plato, Heidegger can say that Nietzsche is "the most unbridled Platonist."[18] It follows, then, that the entire history of Western thought consists of variations on the initial answer to the question, What are entities?: "The first beginning and its end comprise the entire history of the guiding question from Anaximander up to Nietzsche" (232).

Nevertheless, it is important to keep in mind that the history of metaphysics, far from being something people have *done* over the centuries, is something that happens from out of being itself *to* humans, though their practices play a role in its realization. Epochs in the history of being are brought about through what Heidegger calls an *Ereignis*, a word meaning "event" but tied to the idea of "ownness" or "appropriation" (*eigen*), and so suggesting "an event of coming-into-its-own." If unconcealment results from an event within being and so is not something humans do, it follows that the concealment running through the history of metaphysics is *also* something that happens within being itself. Concealment inevitably accompanies every emerging-into-presence in this sense: just as the items in a room can become visible only if the lighting that illuminates them itself remains invisible, so things can become manifest only if this manifesting itself "stays away" or "withdraws." This first-order concealment is unavoidable and innocuous. But it becomes aggravated by a second-order concealment that occurs when the original concealment itself is concealed. That is, insofar as humans are oblivious to the fact that every disclosedness involves concealment, they fall into the illusion of thinking that nothing is hidden and that everything is totally out front. Thus, to take a familiar example, the emergence of modern individualism concealed the role of shared social practices in making possible such a mode of self-understanding as individualism. This initial concealment in turn leads to the complacent assurance that individualism is the final, incontrovertible truth about human reality, and that collectives and social practices of any sort must be explainable in terms of artificial aggregates of initially isolated individuals. This second-order forgetfulness then reinforces and sustains the initial concealment that opened up the individualist understanding of life in the first place.

Because concealment occurs when a particular form of presenting comes to be taken as the ultimate truth about things, Heidegger says that being (as appearing) "cloaks itself *as* appearance insofar as it shows itself *as* being" (IM 109, my emphasis). In other words, what shows up at a particular time presents itself as the last word about reality, as the "only game in town," with the result that the current epoch's interpretation of reality comes to be taken as self-evident and beyond discussion. When a totalizing, homogenized understanding of things comes to seem so obvious that there is no longer any room for reflection about the being of entities, nothing is any longer genuinely *at stake* or *at issue* for a people. All the significance of what shows up in the world is bleached out. As the world becomes more constricted and inflexible, all that presents itself is a collection of fixed items on hand for us to use or discard as we like. This nearsighted preoccupation with entities understood as fixed and antecedently given, just there on hand for our use, conceals both the "world" (defined as the open arena of possibilities in which a historical people dwells) and that which resists all human mastery, the "earth." Where everything is leveled down to the familiar and the commonplace – the "actual" – things are no longer "possible" and challenging for us.

The characteristic of our age is that being's inevitable withdrawal has been aggravated into complete "abandonment" in the form of modern technology. Heidegger's later diagnosis of technology, discussed in detail by Dreyfus (Chapter 11), first began to take shape in the *Beiträge zur Philosophie.* According to that work, our age is characterized by the fact that "nothing is any longer essentially impossible or inaccessible. Everything 'can be done' and 'lets itself be done' ['*wird gemacht' und 'lässt sich machen*'] if one only has the will for it" (108). The stance toward things in the modern age is that of "machination" (*Machenschaft*), which interprets all entities as representable (*Vor-stellbar*) and capable of being brought forth in production (108–9). Technology, then, is "the *priority* of machination, of discipline, and of method over *what* it is that goes into them and is affected by them"; it is "the priority of ordering over what it is supposed to accomplish" (336, 397).

The domination of ordering takes the form of "enframing" or "configuring" (*Ge-stell*), which reduces all entities, including humans, to the homogenized level of resources on hand to be ordered and used with maximum efficiency. This fascination with ordering for its own sake colors all our ways of understanding things. As Heidegger says, "*Immediate* graspability and usefulness and serviceability . . . self-evidently constitute *what is in being* and what is not" (30). Entities "are presupposed as what can be arranged, produced, and fixed (*idea*)" (493). The understanding of entities as whatever is at our disposal reinforces the self-certainty of the "greatness of the subject" in modern subjectivism (441). We experience reality as a "world-picture" set before (*vor-gestellt*) us, and ourselves as subjects who can challenge and control whatever there is. The result of this abandonment of being is that "entities appear as objects merely on hand, as if being were not [*als ob Seyn nicht wese*]" (115). Being – that which imparts focus, coherence, belongingness, and a richness of possibilities to things – is blotted out of view. This withdrawal of being is evident in the objectifying procedure of modern natural science that conceals the "essential fullness [*Wesensfülle*] of nature" (QCT 174), that is, the rich possibilities for cohering and belonging together harbored within things. When entities are treated as interchangeable bits cut off from any proper place or "region" to which they belong, they are "un-beings," devoid of the kind of connectedness to contexts of meaning that could let them become manifest in their being.

Only by coming to experience fully the distress of this abandonment of being can we begin to move beyond the mode of understanding dominated by technology and metaphysics. Heidegger speaks of a "new" or an "other" beginning that stands as a possibility before us if we can hear the "echo" (*Anklang*) of being. This "other beginning" will bring about a transformed relationship of humans and being. By bringing us face to face with the concealment itself, the transition to a new beginning will lead us to experience exactly what was forgotten in metaphysics: the *truth* of being. In Heidegger's words, "The *first beginning* experience[d] and posit[ed] the *truth of entities* without asking about truth as such. . . . The *other beginning* experiences the truth of being and asks about the being of *truth* in order to thereby ground the essencing of being" (179). Instead of the "guiding question" concerning the beingness of entities (What are entities?) there will be the "basic question" (*Grundfrage*) that asks "about being in respect to its ground" (IM 32) – What is the truth of being? What is being itself?" Or, as Sheehan puts it, "How come truth?"

As was the case for the first beginning, this new beginning will be not something humans do, but something that happens within being itself. In Heidegger's writings of the thirties, humans are always participants in a wider event. Projection, for example, is no longer described as a structure of human agency, but instead is something that *happens to* humans in the "thrownness of a . . . clearing" (448). And *truth,* understood in the sense of the Greek word for truth, which means unhiddenness or unconcealment,[19] is what lets humans show up in the midst of things: "Truth contains and grants that which *is,* grants beings in the midst of which man himself is a being, in such a way that he relates to beings" (N 3 24). The new beginning, because it recognizes this embeddedness and indebtedness, will carry with it an intensified sense of humans as "thrown" into an open space (Da-sein, or "there-being"), where their task is to preserve and protect the being in entities. In reply to the critics of *Being and Time* who saw that work as a continuation of traditional transcendental philosophy, Heidegger insists that human understanding is not to be thought of as a transcendental condition in any sense. It is necessary to "leap beyond *transcendence,*" he says, "and ask in an original way about being and truth" (250–1). The "experience of thrownness and the belongingness to being" marks the "essential difference" of this form of thinking from "all *transcendental* ways of knowing" (239).

As Dreyfus shows, we can get a clue to what the new beginning will look like from Heidegger's essay "The Origin of the Work of Art." According to this essay, a great work of art is a world-transforming event that crystallizes an understanding of being for a people, giving them a coherent focus and direction for their lives. Heidegger's description of a Greek temple shows how a focal work, what Dreyfus calls a "cultural paradigm," defines how things can *count* for a community:

> Standing there, the building holds its ground against the storm raging above it and so makes the storm itself manifest in its violence. The luster and gleam of the stone . . . first brings to light the light of the day. . . . Tree and grass, eagle and bull, snake and cricket first enter into their distinctive shapes and thus come to appear as what they are. (PLT 42)

What Heidegger wants us to see in this description is the way a world-defining work first opens a clearing in which things become accessible and intelligible, and thereby brings to realization the *being* of entities in a world. What was initially only inchoate and partial is given a shape and allowed to stand forth *as* something or other. "But men and animals, plants and things, are never [just] present and familiar as unchangeable objects, only to represent incidentally also a fitting environment for the temple, which one fine day is added to what is already there." On the contrary, the appearance of the temple lets things show up as having a definite articulation, and so as *belonging* in some determinate way within the totality of a world: "The temple, in its standing there, first gives to things their look and to men their outlook on themselves" (PLT 42–3).

The account of the working of the temple in the ancient Greek world shows how an "event of being" can bring to realization a world of a particular sort. Here it makes no sense to think of a world as something humans create, since it is this newly emergent world that first *lets humans be the kinds of beings they are* in this world. It is only in the light of the world opened by the temple that humans can understand themselves as – and so *be* – the builders and creators that they are. The world is described as "the self-disclosing openness of the broad paths of the simple and essential decisions in the destiny of an historical people" (PLT 48). In opening a world, the temple defines the "measure" (*Mass*) or standards that disclose how things are *at stake* for a people. At the same time, it brings into focus what is "measureless for that people," what is yet "not mastered, something concealed, confusing" and so in need of a decision (PLT 55).

Heidegger says that because truth always happens through being articulated or composed (*gedichtet*, literally "condensed" or "bound together"), all art is essentially "poetry" (*Dichtung*) in the broadest sense of this term (PLT 70). But poetry in the narrow sense as a linguistic art has a special position among the arts. Poetry draws on the background "saying" (*Sagen*) of a people – that is, their proverbs, anecdotes, and oral traditions, but also the tacit interpretations embodied in their customs, rituals, and festivals – and transforms that "saying" into a configuration that articulates for a people their understanding of reality. Poetry "transforms the people's saying so that now every living word fights the battle and puts up for decision what is holy and what unholy, what great and what small, what brave and what cowardly" (PLT 43). Thus, the epics of Homer, the psalms of David, or the Sermon on the Mount are not merely aesthetically pleasing embellishments tacked on to a previously existing prosaic form of life. Instead, they formulate and bring to realization what is definitive of a people's form of life.

A great work of art therefore can inaugurate a new beginning for a community. What before had been humdrum and self-evident suddenly stands forth as strange and challenging as a result of this reconfiguration of the world: the work contains "the undisclosed abundance of the unfamiliar and the extraordinary, which means that it also contains strife with the familiar and the ordinary" (PLT 76). Through the work, the "dawning world brings out what is as yet undecided and measureless, and thus discloses the hidden necessity of measure and decisiveness" (PLT 63).

In this way the great poetic works of a historical community play the role of "founding" the existence of that community. The artwork is founding first of all in the sense that it is an "endowment" defining the tasks for the future "preservers" whose world has been opened by the work. In the poetic work, "truth is thrown toward the coming preservers, that is, toward a historical human community." The work sketches out in advance "the concepts of a historial people's essence, i.e., of its belonging to world history," and it thereby transports "a people into [their] appointed task" (PLT 75, 77). We can see this in the way the Gospels, by opening up a new understanding of the point of life in the ancient world, thereby laid out in advance what is demanded of future Christians. But second, world-defining works are also founding in the sense that they establish a "beginning" (*Anfang*) understood not just as the first event in a sequence, but as an origin that, filled with promise, "already contains the end latent in itself." A "genuine beginning," Heidegger says, "is always a leap forward, in which everything to come is already leaped over, even if as something disguised" (PLT 76). In this way, the possibilities of being a Christian are already anticipated in its beginning, though it is up to future Christians to realize and define what was implicit and "disguised" in that origin.

By sketching out the endowment and tasks of a community, the work of art provides a people with a narrative schema that lets them weave their own lives into a wider, future-directed, and so life-orienting historical unfolding. For Heidegger, the founding beginning for the West occurred "for the first time in Greece. What was in the future to be called 'being' was set into work in a way which set the measure" for what was to come (PLT 76–7). Heidegger points out that insofar as the power of a beginning can never sustain itself, "decline" is inevitable,[20] so that the beginning needs to be "repeated" or "retrieved" (*wiederholt*) if its promise is to be brought to realization. It is "only by thoughtful repetition [*denkende Wiederholung*] that we can deal appropriately with the beginning" (IM 191), recovering what is always there though in a concealed form. This requires that we act as "preservers" who, carrying forward what was undertaken at the dawn of our civilization, work to realize its latent possibilities. And that in turn means overcoming the forgetfulness pervading modern existence. Since the technological understanding of being is rigid and calcified, more a source of concealment than of genuine disclosedness, what is needed now is a new poet who can poetize the background in the way the earliest Greek poets and thinkers did in the first beginning.

Such a repoetizing Heidegger finds in Hölderlin, and especially in the late hymns, which, he says, hit him and others "like an earthquake" when they were first published in an edition by Norbert von Hellingrath in 1914 (OWL 78). Frank H. W. Edler sees Heidegger's reading of Hölderlin as rooted in Hellingrath's interpretation of Hölderlin's later poetry as the attempt to bring to language a "hidden or secret Germany [*das geheime Deutschland*]" that, though it does not yet exist, defines the essence of the Germany yet to come.[21] Hölderlin's poetry provides a language that can find new names to invoke the gods of antiquity: "The old gods are dead [and] live on only in mythical language [*Sage*] but their shadows crowd around for a new birth."[22] Heidegger's own conception of language as a Saying (*Sage*) whose "soundless voice" has the power to summon forth what is forgotten or concealed (OWL 124) seems to be quite in tune with this reading of Hölderlin.

What is most striking about Heidegger's vision of the "history of being" in the thirties is the soteriological and apocalyptic "metanarrative" that seems to underlie it. History is seen as a monolithic "happening" that, springing from primordial origins, passes through a "dark night of the soul" of forgetfulness, yet embodies the prospects for a redemption in the final recovery of its concealed origins. Just as "futurity" is basic to human temporality, so the future is definitive of history. As Heidegger says, "History as a happening is an acting and being acted upon which, passing through the present, *is determined from out of the future* and takes over the past" (IM 44, my emphasis).

This conception of history was already articulated in *Being and Time*. There Heidegger claimed that historiography must begin by projecting "monumental" possibilities for the future to serve as a basis for formulating our sense of where history is headed as a totality. This futural moment is unavoidable, for it is only in terms of some anticipated vision of the end state of historical development that we have a basis for *selecting* the events that can be taken as historically relevant in formulating our account of what history is adding up to. That is, we can narrativize the confusing array of events of the past in order to find some significance in them only on the basis of some conception of the future outcome of history. The projected sense of the possible achievement of history lets us see what should be "reverently preserved" from the past as the historical record of our culture's achievements (BT 447–8). This is why Dasein must "choose its hero" if it is to identify what is worthy of being retrieved from the past (BT 437). And only on the basis of such a monumentalized understanding of the past can we then have a standpoint for criticizing the "today." Authentic historiography is necessarily a "critique of the present," "a way of painfully detaching oneself from the falling publicness of the 'today'" (BT 449). Heidegger's point, it seems, is that a critique of the present can be carried out only on the basis of a vision of alternative ways of living that are possible for us, a "utopian" vision that itself could be *drawn only from our understanding of the past.* In other words, we can criticize what we *are now* only in the name of a monumentalized picture of what, given our history, we *could be.*

The aim of philosophy is "to restore humanity's historical Dasein – and that always includes our own *future* Dasein in the totality of the history allotted to us – to the domain of being, which it was originally incumbent on humans to open up for themselves" (IM 41–2, my emphasis). Understanding the task set for us by the future throws us back onto the need to "win back our roots in history," to take "a creative view of [our] tradition," and to "repeat the beginning . . . in order to transform it into a new beginning" (IM 38–9). To ask the question of being, then, is not just to dabble in an abstract academic pursuit. On the contrary, the question opens the "happening" of human existence to "yet unquestioned possibilities, futures, and at the same time binds it back to its past beginning, so sharpening it and giving it weight in the present" (IM 44). Behind this thinking there seems to be a belief that the unfolding event of being is itself eschatological: it is because "being itself is inherently eschatological," Heidegger wrote in 1950, that "we must someday anticipate the former dawn in the dawn to come" (EGT 18). Yet it is also clear from these writings that there can never be anything like a final, conclusive account of being: "the essence of being is never conclusively sayable" (460). The most we can do is try to think along with the poet who, hearing what is said in the silent Saying (*Sage*) of language, can "compose" it into a poetry that awakens a renewed experience of the truth of being.

HEIDEGGER AND THE NAZIS

One strand of the "turn" in Heidegger's thought in the thirties, then, is found in his shift away from a Dasein-centered account of being to one that starts from the history of being. This first strand is closely bound up with a second aspect of the turn, the shift connected with his involvement with the Nazis. In the great outpouring of heated debate that followed the publication of Victor Farías's *Heidegger and Nazism* in 1987, what has often been missing is a reflection on Heidegger's place within the wider arena of events of the time.[23] Certainly it does not *excuse* his behavior to observe that he was in most ways a fairly minor, almost laughable actor in a much wider wave of support for Hitler. Within the context of the so-called conservative revolution that swept the Nazis into power, the backlash against modernization and liberalism that was building steadily in Germany from the 1870s to 1933, Heidegger's own contributions seem relatively paltry.[24]

It is perhaps hard for us to imagine the shock and bewilderment that accompanied the unification of Germany and the sudden rush of industrialization and urbanization at the end of the nineteenth century. The time of Heidegger's youth was a period of sudden, wrenching change, a time when "Germany was transformed from a relatively backward and predominantly agricultural nation into one of the greatest industrial powers in the world."[25] Especially among disaffected intellectuals and those living in rural areas, the result was a mood of despair over the collapse of traditional culture. We can see this response in the correspondence between Wilhelm Dilthey and Count Yorck, which made such a strong impression on the young Heidegger.[26] Dilthey and Yorck both bemoan the secularization of everyday life, the loss of all sense of hierarchy, the ascendancy of the *Naturwissenschaften,* and the encroaching dangers of what they call "Nietzscheanism," a term referring primarily, it seems, to Nietzsche's skeptical reflections on history in his early work *The Use and Abuse of History.* The reaction against modernization is also evident in that spontaneous uprising, the Youth Movement at the turn of the century. The quest for *Bunderlebnis,* or a "feeling of belonging," the emphasis on youth, nature, health, and the simple life, and above all the search for firm values and the "longing for a Caesar, for an ultimate authority"[27] – these were the ideals that the young *Wandervögel* (wandering birds) set against what they regarded as the decadence of their bourgeois parents. Running through these conservative movements was the theme of recovering the essence of the *Volk* (people or folk) – the unique "blood and soil" and ancient bonds of the German people – from the forces of Westernization.[28]

In the first decades of the twentieth century this undercurrent of distrust of modernity continued to spread through intellectual circles. Heidegger speaks of those "exciting years between 1910 and 1914" that brought the first complete edition of Nietzsche's *The Will to Power* and the translation of the works of Kierkegaard and Dostoyevski (FS x). It would be hard to overestimate the impact of Dostoyevski on German intellectuals generally and, I suspect, on Heidegger in particular.[29] As Stern observes, "No other modern writer save Nietzsche had as great an impact on German thought as Dostoevski." Part of this impact was due to the influence of the editor of Dostoyevski's complete works, Arthur Moeller van den Bruck. In his introductions to the translations, Moeller quoted Dostoyevski as saying, "We are revolutionaries out of conservatism," and he portrayed the Russian as offering an escape from the West "via the theology of Kierkegaard."[30] Dostoyevski's critique of both liberal individualism and secularized collectivism paved the way for Moeller's own vision of a "third way" between capitalism and Marxism (what he called *das dritte Reich* in his 1922 book of the same name), a truly national, German socialism.

The defeat in the Great War and the seemingly endless economic crises under the Weimar Republic intensified the smoldering resentment of the conservatives. Through the spiraling inflation of the twenties and the collapse of the early thirties, the Republic appeared divided, defenseless, shabby, and hopelessly unstable. In contrast, the conservative Cult of the Young – the "rebellion of the young *for* authority, not *against* authority" – seemed to promise community, rejuvenation, purity, vigor, and *Bodenständigkeit* (rootedness in the earth).[31] By the thirties, parliamentary democracy appeared to be a failure, and extremists from both the Left and Right squeezed out the defenders of the Republic. In what most at the time saw as a face-off between the Bolsheviks and the conservatives, it was the conservatives who seemed to offer the more truly German option. The conservatives "sought a breakthrough to the past, and they longed for a new community in which old ideas and institutions would once again command universal allegiance." Their aim of "destroy[ing] the despised present in order to recapture an idealized past in an imaginary future"[32] parallels Heidegger's own nostalgic and apocalyptic vision of history. In the words of a recent book title, their appeal was in "the new politics of old values."

Raised in a lower-middle-class household in an agrarian, primarily Catholic part of the Black Forest region, Heidegger was, not surprisingly, conservative and often quite provincial in his outlook. Like many other inhabitants of the rural backwaters of Germany, which had suffered the greatest economic losses from sudden industrialization, Heidegger voted for a conservative regional party, the party of Württemberg winegrowers, as late as the Reichstag election of 1932.[33] In the first decades of the twentieth century his views were generally in step with the prevailing currents of cultural despair. His attacks on the theoretical attitude and his adoption of the vocabulary of life philosophy were motivated by a sense of the "loss of meaning" associated with the ascendancy of the natural sciences and modernization in general.

In 1919 Heidegger spoke to his students about the "de-vitalizing" (*Ent-lebnis*) of life in contemporary scientific pursuits and the "extinguishing of the situation" (*Situation*) in the current context of life (*Lebenszusammenhang*). A "situation" is what imparts unity and meaning to the natural flow of life experience. Heidegger speaks of three fundamental characteristics of a situation: (1) a situation is "an 'event' ['*Ereignis*'], not a 'process' ['*Vorgang*']"; (2) a situation is relatively closed (*Geschlossenheit*); and (3) in a situation the "I" is never "detached" or "disengaged" (*Unabgehobenheit*) – "The 'I' never needs to come into view, [for] it swims within the situation" (GA 56/57 205–6).

It is our being-in-a-situation, where things are clearly *at stake*, that gives our lives focus and direction. At the current time, however, the character of there being a situation is disappearing: "The unity of the situation explodes. Experiences possess no unity of meaning, no unity of content [*Sacheinheit*]; they lose the unity the situation gave them" (GA 56/57 206). Only where life is marked by genuine possibilities of motivation does it produce an "intensification of life." Such an intensification is found in the "Youth Movement for a Free Germany," though not in those (presumably internationalist) forms of "activism" (*Activismus*) that are nothing but "machination" (*Machenschaft*). When the situation collapses, however, the contents of experience present themselves as mere states of affairs detached from any clear relevance to our lives. Everything is leveled down to the indifferent, the familiar, the commonplace (GA 56/57 208–9).

It was during this period that Heidegger broke with the Catholic church and threw himself into the religious radicalism he found in Pauline eschatology, in Kierkegaard and Dostoyevski, and above all in Luther.[34] His writings of this period suggest that we can recover a sense of the weightiness of our "factical" existence in the secularized world only by recapturing something like the world-defining "venture of faith" of authentic, primitive Christianity. As Heidegger sees it, our "worldly" existence as "average everydayness" is characterized by "falling," the tendency to be engrossed in day-to-day preoccupations and to drift along with the fads and trends of the crowd – the anonymous "they" or "anyone" (*das Man*). In this humdrum everydayness, life is leveled down to the lowest common denominator of doing what "one" does in typical, familiar circumstances. We are, as Piotr Hoffman puts it, "replaceable," mere points of intersection of social roles and functions we share with others. As placeholders in the public world, we become caught up in the turbulence of mindless busy-ness, yet we are at the same time "tranquilized," complacently assured that everything has already been worked out and that nothing really calls for a decision.

In my essay (Chapter 8) I run through Heidegger's description of inauthentic existence. Heidegger tells us that the totalizing commonsense interpretation reduces all undertakings to the level of what is "fitting and proper" (BT 239). In contexts calling for action, the "they" knows only "rules and public norms," and it therefore "deprives the particular Dasein of its responsibility [*Verantwortlichkeit*]" for what it does (BT 165, 334). "This leveling off of Dasein's possibilities to what is proximally at its everyday disposal also results in a *dimming down of the possible as such*" (BT 239, my emphasis). In other words, in the complacency of worldly existence we become so absorbed in the things that show up on the current scene – taking them as the "last word" about what is real – that we lose sight of our own contribution to opening the clearing of possibilities in which things can stand forth *as* such and such in the first place. Preoccupied with the entities that show up in the lighting, we are blind to what makes it possible for there to be any lighting at all. In average everydayness, Heidegger says, Dasein "becomes blind to its possibilities, and tranquilizes itself with that which is merely 'actual' " (BT 239).

What is needed, then, is a way of recovering a sense of the openness of the possible and of our own responsibility as individuals in articulating and bringing to realization the worldly contexts in which we find ourselves. And that means being able to experience our predicament not as a mere set of "circumstances" (*Lage*) subsumable under universally valid (and hence anonymous) principles, but as a "situation" where the choice demanded of us is defined by the concrete characteristics of the context itself. To become an authentic individual is to achieve the kind of clear-sighted, committed resoluteness that first "*gives* itself the situation, and *brings* itself into that situation" by defining how things are to count in relation to one's stance. In contrast to the "they," which "knows only the '*general circumstances*,' [and] loses itself in those '*opportunities*' which are closest to it," the resolute individual finds him- or herself already in a *situation* of "taking-action," and so directly sees what the situation demands (BT 347, 355).

What kind of stand is one to take in the situation? Heidegger answers, "*Only* the resolution itself can give the answer. . . . *The resolution is precisely the disclosive projection and determination of what is factically possible at the time*" (BT 345). Resoluteness lets us achieve clear-sightedness about what is possible and what is demanded in the current situation because it totally immerses us in that setting. No longer "losing *itself* in the object of its concern," authentic Dasein in a *moment of vision* "makes the situation authentically present." This authentic presence holds on to both the future and the past, and it thereby provides the kind of coherence, continuity, and "*constancy* of the self" that gives one "time *for* what the situation demands" (BT 463). Only such an intense and unified stance gives one's life story the "steadiness" it needs to let one grasp what is genuinely *at stake* in the situation, and so to take a stand "*for* what is world-historical in [one's] current situation" (BT 442).

What is demanded of us as individuals, according to Heidegger's early view, is the courage to "simplify" ourselves and to seize on our lives as our "fate." Authenticity "snatches one back from the endless multiplicity of possibilities which offer themselves as closest to one . . . and brings Dasein into the simplicity of its *fate*" (BT 435). Fate in turn is always tied into a wider "struggle" (*Kampf*) that makes up one's *destiny* "in and with [one's] 'generation' " (BT 436). This struggle will most likely require "*doing violence* . . . to the claims of the everyday interpretation, or to its complacency and its tranquilized obviousness" (BT 399). And as "The Origin of the Work of Art" makes clear, it runs the risk of "going astray" into "the indefeasible severity of error" (PLT 55). But it is only by overthrowing what is calcified and stale – the familiar, the commonplace, the ordinary – that a new "measure" (*Mass*) can be found, a new world order brought to pass.

For Heidegger in the early thirties, the Nazi movement seemed to promise the sort of rejuvenation through retrieval envisioned by his apocalyptic view of history. Like many other conservative Germans, Heidegger must have "shudderingly admired the terroristic idealism of Hitler's movement,"[35] convinced that conditions had reached such a desperate state that only an act of violence could lead to a breakthrough to a purer, more stable form of life. At least this seems to be what is implied by Heidegger's Rectoral Address, delivered in May 1933, when he speaks of "the German fate in its most extreme distress" and of the need to recover "the *beginning* of our spiritual-historical being," that "first beginning" inaugurated by the Greeks.[36] This beginning "still *is*," Heidegger says. "It does not lie *behind us*, as something that was long ago, but stands *before* us. As what is greatest, the beginning has passed in advance beyond all that is to come. . . . The beginning had invaded our future. There it awaits us, as a distant command bidding us catch up with its greatness." It is part of the "spiritual mission of the German *Volk*," then, to "resolutely submit to this distant command to recapture the greatness of the beginning."[37] What previously was treated as solely the task of the individual is now seen as the task of an entire nation. Heidegger's constant references in his speeches and popular writings to the *Volk*, the ideal of a *völkische Wissenschaft* (people's science), and the protection of the *Volkstum* (character of the cultural group) reveal his commitment to the *völkische* ideology of Nazism and his belief in the unique destiny and essence of the German people.[38]

By 1936, however, Heidegger was pulling back from his involvement in the political arena. There are still apocalyptic tirades about the darkening of the world and the need for rejuvenation. Our task, according to the *Beiträge*, is "the renewal of the world through the salvation of the earth," and for this we need to prepare ourselves "for the appearance of the last god" (411–12).[39] Humans still have a central role in this recovery. The truth of being can happen, Heidegger claims, only if we make a decision to achieve *Inständigkeit*, that is, "insistence," a steadfast "standing-in-a-site" which lets that site be a situation where things can show up in the fullest way. The "*truth* of being . . . comes-to-pass [*west*] only in the steady standing-in-a-site [*Inständigkeit*] of Da-sein, in the experience of thrownness into the There out of the calling-forth [*Zuruf*] of the *Ereignis*" (233). Insistence establishes a "grounded relation" to being, a relation that makes possible the "safeguarding of being in that which . . . shows itself as an entity in the clearing of the There" (467). The idea here seems to be that a necessary condition of entities fully manifesting their being is that we do not treat things as bits in the mosaic of a world picture laid out before our detached representation (*Vorstellen*), but instead experience our thrownness into a setting where we are "called" to the task of letting things show up in their full significance and belongingness together. This mode of "insistent caring [*Besorgung*]" (71) Heidegger later calls "dwelling," a way of abiding on the earth that opens a clearing where things can "gather" the surrounding environment into a coherent whole (a "region" or "play of time-space" [*Zeit-Spiel-Raum*]). The essay "Building Dwelling Thinking," for example, speaks of how the dwelling of peasants, embodied in a farmhouse built centuries ago, contributed to "the power [that] let earth and heaven, divinities and mortals enter *in simple oneness* into things," and so ordered the house in the world of the Black Forest (PLT 160).

From this new point of view, however, the *Volk* (and humans generally) come to be treated more as facilitators and participants in the wider event of a "Fourfold" in which mortals, gods, earth, and heaven are gathered into the "belonging-together" of a world. The term "Da-sein" now refers not to humans but to "the self-opening medium of the interplay of calling-forth and belongingness; . . . the *between* between humans . . . and gods . . ." (311). Increasingly, it is *things* that play the central role in letting a world happen, while we humans "are *called by* the thing as thing" precisely because "we are bethinged [*be-dingt*], the conditioned ones" (PLT 181, my emphasis).

The *Beiträge* still speaks of the need for us to make a "decision." This need, however, is revealed not by reflecting on the current political situation, but by coming to terms with the history of being. "Certainly this basic 'fact' of our history [i.e., the need for a decision] becomes apparent not through an 'analysis' of the 'spiritual' or 'political' 'situation' of the time." Indeed, an absorption in intellectual and political currents conceals the need to experience "authentic history – the struggle [*Kampf*] of the appropriation [*Ereignung*] of humanity through being" (309). Political involvement – including National Socialism – now comes to be regarded as a symptom of abandonment and nihilism rather than as their potential cure.

By 1936 the concern with the *Volk* is treated as merely a continuation of the domination of subjectivism and humanism of Western metaphysics. The *Volk* can "never be the goal and purpose," Heidegger says. On the contrary, belief in the priority of the people is "only a '*völkische*' expansion of 'liberal,' 'me-centered' thinking and of the economic representation of the maintenance of 'life' " (319). The Nazi slogan "Everything must be at the service of the people" trivializes entities to the level of what is useful and at our disposal (30). But this shows that the Nazi movement itself is nothing more than one more stage in the ongoing story of the abandonment of being in metaphysics. As being withdraws, there is an "*idolizing* of the *conditions* for historical being – the *Völkisch*, for example, with all its ambiguity – to the [level of the] *unconditional*" (117). Heidegger's anti-Humanism now comes to be formulated in sharp opposition to the core beliefs of the Nazis. In response to what is perceived as nihilism – the loss of life-defining goals – the Nazis have made the people into the highest goal. But in doing so, Heidegger says, they take what is in fact merely a *means* to achieving goals – the *Volk* – and treat that as if it were the *goal itself* (139). The futility of Nazism becomes evident, however, once we recognize that it is precisely this humanistic tendency to treat humans as the ultimate goal, rather than as a means to achieving the authentic goal, that has created the sense of the aimlessness and nihilism of modern existence. The concern with recovering goals by, for example, making culture available to all the people, or by providing rich, meaningful "experiences," actually engenders greater nihilism: the "noisy drunkenness with 'experiences' " – seen in the "*gigantic* meetings" organized to overcome the people's fears – "is the greatest nihilism, the organized blindness to the aimlessness of humanity" (139).

Heidegger is contemptuous of the idea of a "people's philosophy," the idea that philosophy is one cultural accomplishment among others like a style of dress or a local cuisine. With his characteristic air of paradox he asserts that a people does not create a philosophy, but rather a philosophy creates a people (42–3). In the same way, the ideal of a "*völkische* science" is just another symptom of nihilism, as is the idea that "blood and race" are the agents and bearers of history – as if it were "*pre*history that gives history its validity" (493). Thus Heidegger's verdict: the Nazi "revolution" is rootless, unable to face its own lack of ground to stand on, its own *Bodenlosigkeit* (122).

The task set before us, as Heidegger sees it, is to "open up the simplicity and greatness" of entities and to secure "the truth of being in entities, in order thereby to give a *goal* to historical humanity: *to become the grounder and preserver of the truth of being,* to *be* the There as the ground that is used by the essence of being itself" (16). The point of this obscure passage seems to be that, since humans are at the deepest level participants in a wider scheme of things (what later will be called the "play" of the Fourfold of earth, sky, humans, and gods), their proper function is to articulate and preserve a clearing in which things can become manifest in their "simplicity" and "greatness." Humans have a genuine goal, then, to the extent that they abandon their quest for self-aggrandizement and instead realize their function by doing what they are called on to do by the "destining" (*Geschick*) of being. Genuine *care* (*Sorge*) is needed, then, in order "to be simply '*for the sake of being,*' not for the sake of man but for the sake of the being of entities in totality" (16, cf. 99).

To achieve this sense of purpose, according to Heidegger, we need to experience ourselves as recipients of the "gift" of being. What is suggested here is the idea of treasuring things for what they are rather than for what they can do for us. Perhaps the only examples of what Heidegger envisions as this impending "new beginning" are such non-Western experiences as the Hopi sense of the land as a gift to be cared for and returned at the end of our dwelling on earth or the Japanese experience of "national treasures" that people are charged with preserving. It is such experiences of receiving a gift that Heidegger tries to capture when he speaks of a kind of thinking that is thankfulness. Because Western metaphysics has been anthropocentric from the earliest misreading of *physis,* however, it is hard for us to conjure up comparable experiences from our own heritage. Heidegger's reminders of temples from the past or anticipations of new ways of encountering a jug in the future give us only intimations of what the new beginning might bring. The later writings, as the essays by Caputo and Zimmerman show, move toward an ideal mode of comportment called *Gelassenheit,* a nonmanipulative, nonimposing way of "letting things be" what they are.

In treating Heidegger as a product of his times, we run the risk of either trivializing his thought by reducing it to its sociohistorical causes or "explaining away" his actions as "what everyone did" at the time. It is certainly not true, of course, that "everyone did" what he did in the thirties. Heidegger's friends at the time felt his attempts to "work within the system" and to provide leadership to the chaotic political upheavals were at best naive and were quite possibly opportunistic and self-serving. The fact that he was largely ignored by the Nazis makes his dream of a life-transforming "national religion" almost pathetic. Yet at least one friend, Hans-Georg Gadamer, wonders whether his own way of dealing with the events – keeping a low profile and waiting for it all to blow over – was really any better.[40]

Given Heidegger's actions, and given his own firm belief that those actions followed quite naturally from his philosophy, there is no way to buy into his philosophy without reflecting deeply on its moral and political implications. We must keep in mind that, as is true with Nietzsche, there is no way to make Heidegger's thought consonant with our own deepest democratic sentiments without distorting it. His nonegalitarian outlook is evident, for example, even as late as his 1950 essay "The Thing," in which he says that from among "the measureless mass of men as living beings" there may be some "living beings [who can] first *become* mortals" and so can be in the right relation to being (PLT 179, 182). And his lifelong belief in the possibility of a new dispensation of being leaves innumerable questions about why we should think, once being is detached from Christian providence or Stoic rationality, that such an event will be *good* in any sense. Nevertheless, while there is no way to play down the moral worries raised by Heidegger's thought, there is also no way to deny that this at times mystifying man from the backwoods of Germany more than once redrew the philosophical map of the twentieth century, laying out lines of questioning for generations to come.

NOTES

1 Zimmerman's essay (Chapter 9) details some of this influence. See especially Graham Parkes, ed., *Heidegger and Asian Thought* (Honolulu: University of Hawaii Press, 1987).

2 Hoy sums up some of this discussion in Chapter 6. For insight into how Heidegger can be treated as the wellspring of current movements, see John D. Caputo, *Radical Hermeneutics: Repetition, Deconstruction, and the Hermeneutic Project* (Bloomington: Indiana University Press, 1987).

3 The new wave of interest in Heidegger's involvement with the Nazis was sparked by the appearance in 1987 of Victor Farías's *Heidegger et le nazisme,* translated as *Heidegger and Nazism,* ed. J. Margolis and T. Rockmore (Philadelphia: Temple University Press, 1989). Thomas Sheehan provides an excellent review of Farías's book in *New York Review of Books,* June 16, 1988, pp. 38–47. For an overview of key texts on Heidegger and politics, see Michael Zimmerman, "The Thorn in Heidegger's Side: The Question of National Socialism," *Philosophical Forum,* 20 (Summer 1989): 326–65, and, more recently, *Heidegger and the Political,* ed. Marcus Brainard with David Jacobs and Rick Lee, special issue of the *Graduate Faculty of Philosophy Journal,* 14, No. 2, and 15, No. 1 (1991).

4 In addition to Sheehan's review mentioned in note 3, see John D. Caputo, "Thinking, Poetry and Pain," in *Heidegger and Praxis,* ed. Thomas J. Nenon, 1989 Spindel Conference, supplement to *Southern Journal of Philosophy,* 28 (1990): 155–81.

5 The contributions by Frede, Zimmerman, and Caputo (Chapters 1, 9, and 10) are especially helpful in showing how Heidegger's view of the connection between being and human understanding builds on medieval thought, and especially on the Scotist account of the connection between the *modus intelligendi* of things (how they are comprehended) and their *modus essendi* (type of objectivity).

6 It seems that Heidegger drew this conception of phenomena not so much from Husserl as from Aristotle. As Martha Nussbaum points out, Aristotle held that philosophy starts from phenomena defined as "the world *as it appears to,* as it is experienced by, observers of our kind." Phenomena are found in "interpretations, often revealed in linguistic usage." Philosophy's aim, in Aristotle's view, is not to get at something *beneath* the appearances, but to grasp that in virtue of which appearances are unified and intelligible. In this sense, "the appearances go all the way down." See Nussbaum, *The Fragility of Goodness: Luck and Ethics in Greek Tragedy and Philosophy* (New York: Cambridge University Press, 1986), pp. 24–45, 251. Heidegger more than once expressed his debt to Aristotle's phenomenological method (cf. BP 232; TB 79).

7 I fully agree with Dreyfus's definition of "Dasein" as the basic structure of humans: *that* each human's own way of being is an issue for it. Thus, when Heidegger says, "*More primordial than man is the finitude of the Dasein in him*" (KPM 237), I take that to mean that Dasein *qua* finitude, though instantiated in each (normal) human, is conceptually distinct

from the anthropological entity, *Homo sapiens.* This is where I differ from Olafson. On my view, to say that Dasein makes possible the world where entities can show up is not to suggest that *each* Dasein has its own monadic world, but rather that it is *because* an "understanding of being as essentially existent finitude" (KPM 238) has emerged, and is now deposited and preserved in communal practices, monuments, libraries, and so forth, that there is a field of intelligibility in which various sorts of things show up (for all of us) in familiar ways.

8 Dasein's understanding is a "self-projective being toward its ownmost ability-to-be. This ability is that for the sake of which any Dasein is as it is. In each case Dasein has already put itself together, in its being, with a possibility of itself" (BT 236).

9 For detailed examinations of Heidegger's conception of worldhood, see Hubert L. Dreyfus, *Being-in-the-World: A Commentary on Heidegger's "Being and Time," Division I* (Cambridge, Mass.: MIT Press, 1991), and Mark Okrent, *Heidegger's Pragmatism: Understanding, Being, and the Critique of Metaphysics* (Ithaca, N.Y.: Cornell University Press, 1988).

10 When I say that Heidegger is a "realist," then, I mean something different from what Dreyfus means in his *Being-in-the-World* (pp. 251–65) when he speaks of Heidegger's "minimal hermeneutic realism about nature." According to my interpretation, Heidegger's claim is that it is the ready-to-hand world of familiar things that is real (or is "as real as anything can get"), whereas the entities held to exist by the natural sciences are products of working over or redescribing those familiar equipmental entities for particular purposes. On my interpretation, Heidegger seems quite close to what John Dewey is saying in his distinction between water and H_2O in the opening chapters of *The Quest for Certainty* (New York: Putnam's, 1960).

11 Hoffman's essay (Chapter 7) shows how we become aware of this ultimate lack of foundations in the experience of anxiety.

12 Taylor (Chapter 12) shows how this kind of "primordiality" claim is similar to the Kantian argument that experiencing particular sensations as sensations is derivative from and parasitic on a background in which we experience a world of real, concrete things.

13 Thomas Sheehan points out that, in his 1928 seminar on Aristotle's *Physics,* Heidegger already was thinking of being (or *physis*) as a "movement" or "event" (*Ereignis*), the "disclosive event" of "appropriatedness into intelligibility" from out of concealment. See Sheehan, "On Movement and the Destruction of Ontology," *Monist,* 64 (October 1981): 534–42.

14 Nevertheless, I am not convinced that Heidegger's attempt to pull the rug out from under the skeptic is the last word on skepticism. One

might still ask, for instance, how we are to deal with cases of *conflicting* presentations or appearances – that is, with disputes involving incompatible perspectives – once we abjure the traditional notion of a final "truth of the matter." Moreover, Heidegger's repeated claims that there are entities independent of Dasein's understanding, together with the plausible assumption that they can enter into our intelligibility only because they have what Dorothea Frede in Chapter 1 calls a "fittingness" to our modes of understanding, seems to pave the way to questions about the nature of these entities. Once again the Kantian *Ding an sich* threatens to rear its ugly head.

15 As a matter of fact, it appears that in *Being and Time* the primordial sources were to be found in primal Christian experience, especially the Pauline experience of the *kairos*, and that Paramenides already represented an initial stage of forgetfulness (cf. BT 133). As Caputo shows, however, by the thirties this priority given to Christian experience had dropped away in favor of a notion of "primal experience," which is, in fact, a Christianized reading of pre-Socratic thought. The possibility that at the core of Western civilization there is essentially dissension, a *conflict* of cultures and traditions (Greek, Judeo-Christian, African, etc.), is something Heidegger never considered, perhaps because he assumed that history, which he said is always "mythology" (IM 155), requires a unified beginning in order to have a coherent narrative structure.

16 All plain page citations in parentheses are from the *Beiträge zur Philosophie* (Contributions to philosophy), Vol. 65 of the *Gesamtausgabe*, first published in 1989. For my interpretation of this work I am deeply indebted to Richard Polt's excellent study, "Heidegger and the Place of Logic" (Ph.D. dissertation, University of Chicago, 1991). I have also made use of F. W. von Hermann's "Technology, Politics and Art in Heidegger's *Beiträge zur Philosophie*," delivered at the Yale Colloquium "Art, Politics, Technology," October 1989, and forthcoming in a volume edited by Karsten Harries and Otto Pöggeler.

17 Zimmerman succinctly traces these developments in Chapter 9. For an illuminating account of Heidegger's thought as a sustained reflection on "productionist metaphysics," see his book, *Heidegger's Confrontation with Modernity: Technology, Politics, and Art* (Bloomington: Indiana University Press, 1990).

18 "Platons Lehre von der Wahrheit," *Wegmarken*, p. 133. Quoted in Robert J. Dostal, "Beyond Being: Heidegger's Plato," *Journal of the History of Philosophy*, 23 (January 1985): 71–98, p. 79.

19 In *The Fragility of Goodness*, Martha Nussbaum points out that the Greek word for truth, *a-letheia*, means etymologically "what is brought out from concealment" (p. 241).

20 This seems to be the point of the statement in *Being and Time* that "in the field of ontology, any 'springing from' is degeneration" (BT 383).

21 Norbert von Hellingrath, *Hölderlin: Zwei Vorträge,* 2d ed. (Munich: Hugo Bruckmann, 1922), pp. 41, 47. Quoted in Frank H. W. Edler, "Philosophy, Language, and Politics: Heidegger's Attempt to Steal the Language of the Revolution in 1933–34," *Social Research,* 57 (Spring 1990): 197–238, p. 208.

22 Hellingrath, *Hölderlin,* p. 44, quoted in Edler, "Philosophy, Language, and Politics," p. 214.

23 The essay by Sheehan (Chapter 2) is one exception. Other notable exceptions are Pierre Bourdieu's *The Political Ontology of Martin Heidegger,* trans. P. Collier (Stanford, Calif.: Stanford University Press, 1991), which first appeared in French in 1975, and Zimmerman's *Heidegger's Confrontation with Modernity.* Hans Sluga is preparing an extended study of this topic for Harvard University Press.

24 According to Hans Sluga, "The historical record shows . . . that [Heidegger] was of no central importance within the world of Nazi philosophy, and that he was, if anything, an outsider to the philosophical establishment of the time." "Metadiscourse: German Philosophy and National Socialism," *Social Research,* 56 (Winter 1989): 795–818, p. 817.

25 Fritz K. Ringer, *The Decline of the German Mandarins: The German Academic Community, 1890–1933* (Cambridge, Mass.: Harvard University Press, 1969), p. 43.

26 Heidegger devotes an entire section of *Being and Time* (§77) to a discussion of Count Yorck's thoughts on history as formulated in the *Briefwechsel zwischen Wilhelm Dilthey und dem Grafen Paul Yorck von Wartenburg, 1877–1897* (Halle: Niemeyer, 1923).

27 Fritz Stern, *The Politics of Cultural Despair: A Study in the Rise of the Germanic Ideology* (Berkeley and Los Angeles: University of California Press, 1961), p. xxviii.

28 See George L. Mosse, *The Crisis of German Ideology: Intellectual Origins of the Third Reich* (New York: Schocken Books, 1981), for a study of how *völkische* ideology contributed to Nazi anti-Semitism.

29 According to Otto Pöggeler, Heidegger held that among all early critics of the European tradition, "the greatest importance then surely belonged to Dostoyevski." See Pöggeler, *Martin Heidegger's Path of Thinking,* trans. D. Magurshak and S. Barber (Atlantic Highlands, N.J.: Humanities Press, 1987), p. 265. Karl Löwith recalls that of the two portraits Heidegger kept on the desk in his office, one was of Dostoyevski. "The Political Implications of Heidegger's Existentialism," *New German Critique,* 45 (Fall 1988): 117–134, p. 121.

30 Stern, *Politics of Cultural Despair,* pp. 209–10.

31 Ibid., pp. 224–25.

32 Ibid., p. xvi.

33 According to a letter from Heidegger's son, Dr. Hermann Heidegger, as reported by Edler in "Philosophy, Language, and Politics" (pp. 237–8). The record suggests that the Nazis drew most of their support from the small local parties. V. R. Berghahn shows that, in the 1930 Reichstag election, smaller regional and conservative parties accounted for about 21% of the electorate, whereas only 15% voted for the Nazis. By November 1932, support had shifted to 10% for local and right-wing parties as opposed to 27% for the Nazis. See V. R. Berghahn, *Modern Germany: Society, Economy and Politics in the Twentieth Century* (Cambridge: Cambridge University Press, 1982), p. 113.

34 In Chapter 10, Caputo describes this shift toward Protestantism as Heidegger's "first turn." It is interesting that, according to Hans-Georg Gadamer, Heidegger once said his life's goal was "to be a new Luther" (personal communication). The theologian Rudolf Bultmann, whose seminar on St. Paul Heidegger attended in 1923, described Heidegger as "*the* Luther expert" and said of him, "He comes out of Catholicism, but he is totally Protestant." See Hugo Ott, *Martin Heidegger: Unterwegs zu einer Biographie* (Frankfurt: Campus, 1988), pp. 11, 123. Karl Löwith reports that Heidegger "knew Luther's works better than many a professional theologian" ("The Political Implications of Heidegger's Existentialism," p. 122). That Heidegger saw himself as in protest against mainstream Christendom is evident in such remarks as his 1928 reference to "the enormously phoney religiosity" of the times (MFL 165n).

35 Stern, *Politics of Cultural Despair,* p. xxx.

36 "The Self-Assertion of the German University," trans. K. Harries, *Review of Metaphysics,* 38 (March 1985): 467–502, p. 471.

37 Ibid., pp. 473, 476.

38 See, e.g., the "Declaration of Support for Adolph Hitler and the National Socialist State" of November 11, 1933, "A Word from the University" of January 6, 1934, or "National Socialist Education" of January 22, 1934, in Guido Schneeberger, *Nachlese zu Heidegger: Dokumente zu seinem Leben und Denken* (Bern: Suhr, 1962), translated by W. S. Lewis in Richard Wolin, "Martin Heidegger and Politics: A Dossier," *New German Critique,* 45 (Fall 1988): 91–114.

39 In Chapter 11 Dreyfus tries to clarify this important notion of the coming of a new "god."

40 The comment was made as, with characteristic candor, Gadamer reminisced about the past with his former students at a conference in Heidelberg in 1989.

DOROTHEA FREDE

1 The question of being: Heidegger's project

An on-the-way in the field of paths for the changing questioning of the manifold question of Being.[1]

It may remain forever a matter of debate how much truth there is in the old claim that every important thinker has essentially one fundamental idea. In the case of famous philosophers, its vindication may oblige us to summarize the "one great idea" in such broad terms as to make it almost meaningless. What can probably be claimed with more justification is that for most great minds there has been *one question* that guided their thinking or research. This certainly applies to Martin Heidegger, and the question that fascinated him throughout his long philosophic life can be stated simply: what is the meaning of being? Ontology, in the widest possible sense, was his main concern throughout his life. This does not mean, of course, that he was forever looking for an answer to the same old question. As his thinking evolved, the meaning of the question changed; but Heidegger to the end of his life remained convinced that the "questionability" of the *Seinsfrage* was the main thrust of his life's work (cf. GA 1 438).

Impressive as such single-mindedness may seem, the phrase "meaning of being" on careful examination seems so vague that philosophers and nonphilosophers alike may wonder what kind of question this is. The meaning of being? Does this refer to all beings, to whatever we may say that it *is* – rocks, trees, clouds, colors, sounds, dreams, or irrational numbers alike? Or does the question presuppose some high-flying metaphysical concept like Being as such, as seems to be indicated by the fact that English translations usually capitalize the letter "B"? Heidegger made it his task to show that there is a meaningful concept of the being of all beings, a conception that underlies all our understanding of reality. As he saw it, this conception has been the aim of all metaphysical thinking, even if it was not always properly understood. The search for an answer remained a search for a clarification of the question, as Heidegger's reference to "the changing questioning" in the epigraph to this chapter shows.

It is not possible in one short essay to trace the meaning of this question throughout Heidegger's lifetime – why he continued to think it worth asking, and why it seemed so elusive. The discussion here will have to be confined to a clarification of the sense in which the "question of being" came to vex the young Heidegger, and why he treated its "neglect" after a promising start in early Greek philosophy as the most serious omission in the history of Western philosophy. Basing the origins of the problems he is dealing with in ancient Greek philosophy is more than the conventional homage paid to the Greeks by educated Germans of Heidegger's generation. Understanding Heidegger's reference to that tradition is indispensable for a proper understanding of the question of the meaning of being itself.[2] As he never tired of repeating, the problem of the meaning of being, the guiding star of his philosophical thought, started to concern him while he was still a high school student. It began when one of his teachers presented him with Franz Brentano's book *On the Several Senses of Being in Aristotle.*[3] A brief summary will provide a rough picture of the history of Aristotelian ontology, for in its traditional ramifications, this is the conception that Heidegger pits himself against with his claim that the meaning of the question of being must be revived. This chapter will therefore try to point out in a kind of dialectical discussion how Heidegger relates himself to the tradition.

THE QUESTION OF BEING IN HEIDEGGER'S EARLY WRITINGS

Certain peculiarities of the Greek language favored the development of ontology, the "science of being," as Aristotle called metaphysics. Even in prephilosophical Greek it was quite common to refer to "beings," to "what there is," both in the sense of "things" and in the sense of what we would call "states of affairs." The fact that there is a clear linguistic distinction between "beings," *ta onta,* referred to by the participle with the definite article, the verb "to be," *einai,* and the abstract noun "being," *ousia* (the nature of beings), makes the development of such a philosophical discipline much more natural than our contrived renderings in English (or in German for that matter) would suggest.[4] Once a certain level of abstraction and conceptual reflection was reached, it became only natural to raise the question whether there is a unified meaning of *being* that accrues to all beings (in contradistinction to "what is not") or whether *being* has irreducibly many different meanings that fall into different categories, depending on the kind of entity that is under investigation. It became natural to ask whether there is a unitary meaningful concept that demarcates the realm of being as such.

Plato was the first to raise this question explicitly in the *Sophist;* he calls the problem of being a *gigantomachia,* a "battle among giants," that has to be settled if there is to be any chance of solving problems about the meaning of not-being. Whether the conception of being as "what has the power to act or be acted on," offered as a compromise in the *Sophist* (242c ff.), is in effect Plato's own answer cannot be examined here.[5] Heidegger was well aware of Plato's struggle with this problem, since he used the passage in the *Sophist* as his point of departure in *Being and Time* (BT 19). Nevertheless, whatever Plato may have thought about the "unity of being," it was the *Aristotelian* doctrine of a *manifold* of meanings of being that came to dominate the history of Western metaphysics. It is Aristotle's doctrine of the *categories* of beings that Heidegger refers to when he presents his view of the historical development of Western thought that ended in complete "forgetfulness of the question of being." To understand Heidegger's reaction to this tradition that made the conception of "substance" its main focus, we have to take a closer look at Aristotle's theory.

Aristotle distinguished as many meanings of "being" as there are categories of entities. There is the primary category of *substance,* designating natural "things" that exist in their own right,[6] while all other entities are *attributes of substances* either inhering in them or standing in some other relation to them (quality, quantity, relation, place, time, action, affection, possession, position). Although it is not entirely clear how Aristotle arrived at his list of categories of all the things there are, it is fairly obvious that he used linguistic criteria as one of his guides. Thus, when we take a naturally existing independent object (e.g., a stone) and try to determine what predicates we assign to it, what characteristics it has, we get different types of answers about its nature in all its respects (its quantity, qualities, place, time, etc.). That the way we speak about entities provides the guideline for their classification does not imply, however, that Aristotle regarded his system of categories as a man-made conceptual scheme. He regarded the categories as distinctions contained in the nature of things; they are read off nature and are not schemas read into or imposed on nature by us.

Aristotle therefore remained a metaphysical realist with respect to his "discovery" of the natural structure of reality. This structure is based on the *primacy of substances,* naturally existing *independent* entities that form the building blocks of Aristotle's universe. Substances are the only entities that can exist in their own right, while all other entities are attributes that need substances as the substrate for their existence. "To be" then means either to be a substance or to be (one of the nine other kinds of) attributes of a substance. And since the being of a substance, a quality, a quantity, or other attributes are *irreducibly different,* there is no unified sense of "being" that could be predicated of items in all categories. There is only an "analogy of being" that has in recent years been dubbed "focal meaning" to indicate the centrality of the substance, without permitting a univocal definition of the term "being."

Since this focus of the conception of being on *substantiality* determined the future development of metaphysics, not only in later antiquity but through the Middle Ages into the modern age, "substance" remained the central term in traditional ontology, and substances or "things," natural entities with attributes and the capacities to interact causally with one another, remained the building blocks – and became Heidegger's main challenge.[7]

The young Heidegger's apparent unease at the "untidiness" of this allegedly natural order of things, with its resulting emptiness of the concept of being itself, increased when he immersed himself in medieval philosophy. He could see how heavily Christian doctrine was leaning on Aristotelian metaphysics, as neo-Thomism does to this day. In spite of all changes in the adaptation of Greek philosophy to Christian theology, the handmaiden exerted a decisive influence over her mistress: the substance-oriented ontology of the Aristotelians dominated the medieval discussion and determined what solutions were even considered viable.

It took Heidegger some time to find his own way and to overcome this tradition, founded by Aristotle and carried on by the Aristotelians, a tradition that continued to exert its influence even over Kantian and post-Kantian philosophy. We will have to follow some further steps in Heidegger's development to see what he found so pernicious in the "substance ontology" and how he arrived at the solution to the difficulties. His self-attested continued perplexity concerning the question of being helps to explain an otherwise rather surprising feature of his philosophical biography. A contemporary of the young Heidegger who had to evaluate his early published work (before *Being and Time*) could not have had an inkling that Heidegger would become one of the most important and influential philosophers of the twentieth century. His early work, if not actually dull, is at least rather conventional and must look at first blush as of historical interest at best. Neither his thesis, "The Doctrine of Judgment in Psychologism" (1913), nor his monograph, *The Theory of Categories and Meaning of Duns Scotus* (1915), would seem to promise great originality, let alone revolutionary thinking. Had Heidegger done no more, he would rightly have vanished without a trace in the archives.

A closer look at these early writings (which we can only touch on here) would show, however, that Heidegger had not been wasting his time. As early as his thesis, his critique of psychologism – at that time still a fashionable trend in the philosophy of mind in Germany – shows that he was firmly convinced that the key to *meaning* cannot lie in the empirical observation of the actual psychological processes that constitute our thoughts. This conviction formed the basis of his later allegiance to Husserlian phenomenology. The act of judging must not be confused with the meaning of what is judged (GA 1 110). If we want to know what our thoughts are *about* (what philosophers after Brentano call the "intentionality" of acts of consciousness), we must analyze the *content of thought* itself, as distinct from the psychic events that are at work.

Nevertheless, Heidegger gained valuable insights concerning the *Seinsfrage* from this discussion of a philosophy that he regarded as fundamentally mistaken. His reflections on the psychologistic philosophers' explanations of how psychological processes constitute the objects of our thoughts forced Heidegger to reflect more on the connection between the act of thinking in contradistinction to the *meaning* of the thought and on its relationship with the *language* in which it is expressed. Tentative results of these reflections are found in side remarks which indicate that Heidegger was moving toward a characterization of "being" that is rather different from the one generated in the Aristotelian naturalist ontology.

He envisages the future task of the theory of knowledge to be to "divide the whole realm of 'being' into its different *modes of reality* [*Wirklichkeitsweisen*]" and regards epistemology as crucial for such a division: "The characteristics of the different forms of reality must be sharply demarcated and determined, including the appropriate method of knowing [*Art ihrer Erkenntnis*] and its limitations" (GA 1 186). The "division of being" into the realms of the physical, psychic, metaphysical, and logical (GA 1 160)[8] makes no claims to being comprehensive, however; it is rather tentative, and it follows conventional lines. Heidegger is clearly still far from seeing any way to provide for the possibility of a unified meaning of being. But although he advocates a strict separation of the realm of the psychic and that of logical validity, what is important for him is the question of how *meaning* as a whole is embedded in the actual life of the person who entertains a thought; the distinction between the different "realms" is not as rigid as his adherence to the terminology might suggest.

A major step forward in the search for a clearer conception of the different meanings of being can be found in Heidegger's second monograph, the discussion of the theory of categories and meaning found in Duns Scotus. What intrigued him in particular was why Duns Scotus came to see the Aristotelian system of categories as only one of several such systems, a subclass that fits one special part or *specific realm* of being but does not exhaust reality as such. The need for a widening of the ontological categories seems to have occurred to Scotus first for theological reasons. If the most fundamental concepts apply to God at all, then they can do so only in an analogous sense. For God is not a substance like other substances, nor can the concepts of unity, truth, and goodness apply to him in the same sense that they do to other entities (GA 1 260, 263). But it was not just a widening and a diversification that separated Scotus's treatment of the problem of the categories of being from the traditional treatment by the Aristotelians. As Heidegger saw it, Scotus did not just assign different realms of reality to the different subject matters of different disciplines; rather he saw the need for a new conception of *reality* as such. Behind this revision stands the insight that if different disciplines import different (senses of the) categories, then the categories of reality cannot simply be *read off* nature, as they were for Aristotle, but they are obviously also read *into* nature by us, or rather into reality as a whole. The "question of being" becomes then the question of the givenness of the object to the subject. For Scotus, therefore, the conditions of *subjectivity* (how does the subject grasp or interpret its objects?) attain central importance. If all "objects" depend on the meaning that is bestowed on them by the subject, and if they are always part of a wider network of a referential totality, then it must be the philosopher's task to work out in what sense there is a *structure of meaning* that stands in relation to or conditions what one might call the *structure of reality.*

Scotus realized at the same time that all meanings find their expression in linguistic signs, and this explains the importance that he attributed to the reflection on language as the tool to work out the structure of meanings. The question whether language, particularly its grammatical structure, imposes a definite analyzable *form* on our thinking acquired special importance, since Scotus was aware of the fact that it provides the basic concepts that hold together the different realms of reality, of all that "can be experienced and thought."[9] The question is then how the meaning of linguistic terms (the *ratio significandi*) reflects and conditions the concepts of the mind (the *ratio intelligendi*), and how both of them are based on and constitute at the same time the mode of being of the actually existing object that is understood (the *ratio essendi*). To express it in less abstract and scholastic terms: the meaning of the name "Socrates" and the aspect under which Socrates is referred to by the speaker are interdependent (e.g., whether Socrates is being regarded as a living individual, a figure of history, or merely a stand-in exemplifying any man, as was common usage in medieval philosophy). The example makes clear why the "being" of the subject matter is in each case determined by the *mode* in which it is referred to in a judgment: only the whole statement determines in what sense and whether we are in fact referring to the individual Socrates at all. "Being" then means "object-givenness," the aspect under which the entity is understood ("It is the function of the form in the complex of meaning to give the object its *being*" [GA I 325; cf. 215, 266]). The meaning of the concepts employed, the formal structure of judgments as a functional whole, reveals the givenness of objects.

The discovery of this structure of meaning also brought it home to Scotus, according to Heidegger, that this "logical reality" that is intended by the subject cannot be identical to or isomorphic with the *empirical* reality of what lies outside the realm of meaning. Scotus therefore distinguishes between the "*ens rationis*" and the "*ens naturae,*" the being of reason and the being of nature, and he comes to realize that there cannot be any simple correspondence theory of truth in the sense that our thoughts could be a mirror of reality. The signs "stand for" but do not bear any similarity to what they signify, just as the sign that advertises wine outside a tavern need not resemble the wine itself (GA I 265 ff., 271). Following Scotus, Heidegger came to dismiss "mirror theories" of language and truth early on. The categories of "all that is" become the categories of our *understanding of being:* the categories become the "elements and means of the interpretation of the meaning of what is experienced" (GA I 400). Aristotle's metaphysical realism has been challenged.

The subtlety of the scholastic philosopher Duns Soctus is not our topic here. If we follow Heidegger's reception of Scotus's theory of categories and meaning, it is because Scotus clearly realized that *objective* reality is determined by the thinking *subject's* understanding (cf. GA I 318–19, 337). That there can be "objective subjectivity" and that there is an overall order and structure underlying all "object-givenness" is the most important principle in Scotus's structural analysis of what the different parts of language signify. The importance of the interdependence between language, interpretation, and "outside reality" that is to become so crucial in *Being and Time* may have impressed Heidegger here for the first time. The interconnection between meaning and the intended object also drew Heidegger's attention to the question of what constitutes the "fitting" between the realm of meaning and the real object in the world. So we find here several indications of seminal ideas that will gain major importance in *Being and Time,* namely that it is *our* comprehension that assigns a "significance" to the object and that the object in turn must be able to bear such a significance, a significance that is determined by the context of our understanding and our activities, whether they are of a practical or a theoretical nature.[10]

Of particular importance is Scotus's doctrine of the *intentionality* of the nature of all objects – that all things have to be regarded as the intentional objects of acts of comprehension, and so depend on the general structure of our understanding (GA 1 281). Heidegger came to realize, however, that such an attempt to "fix" the different kinds of meanings once and for all in a purely formal way must remain sterile as long as it does not include the "living experience" of the speaker in whose understanding all intentionality must be grounded.[11] As he emphasizes, all understanding is at the same time historically conditioned understanding of the living spirit (GA 1 405, 407). Heidegger's most important critical qualification in his admiration of Duns Scotus's effort to overcome the "poverty of categorical systems" as such is the recognition that medieval thought, with its transcendent orientation toward the being of God, and its rigid division of being into the two fundamental categories of "created being" and "uncreated being," was not flexible enough to accommodate historical and individual conditioning.

If his work on Duns Scotus represents a decisive advance toward the realization that the meaning of being must be sought in human understanding (i.e., that to be means "to be understood as something"), Heidegger still had a long way to go in the development of his own fundamental ontology. While he realized the sterility of an abstract search for categories of being that did not take into account the individual "living experience," in his book on Scotus Heidegger willingly follows the division of being into different "realms of being and reality" (*Seinsbereiche, Wirklichkeitsbereiche* [GA 1 211]) that exist more or less comfortably but *unconnected* side by side. Each of the realms of mathematical, natural, metaphysical, logical, and psychic reality has its own structure and order, which depend on a particular point of view (cf. *Scotus,* Chaps. 1 and 2). Even though Heidegger realized that there can be no isolated significance of any object because it is always part of a referential totality (GA 1 212, 202), he does not go beyond Scotus's compartmentalization of being into different realms with their separate meanings and systems of order.

There is as yet no sign of Heidegger's own holistic conception of human existence as "Dasein," that is, as being-in-a-world, or of "care" as the meaning of our existence, which comprises and unifies in its understanding all the different conceptions of what there is, let alone of temporality as the transcendental horizon of the overall meaning of being as such. What is clear, however, is that the research on Duns Scotus had not put to rest Heidegger's old concern with the manifold meanings of being, but that it had rather sharpened his perception of its difficulties. The very fact that he found the Scotist schematization and formal structuring inadequate to capture living experience as a whole or to overcome what he calls the "impression of a deadly emptiness of all previous systems of categories" (GA 1 399, 408) shows that he was searching for a way of getting beyond abstract schemes of classification. His conclusion indicates that he was already aware of one major shortcoming underlying all such purely formal categorizations of beings: that they regard the *theoretical* attitude as the only one that gives shape to reality. He calls it a fateful error (GA 1 406). To remove that error will become one of the main tasks of Heidegger's mature philosophy.

THE QUESTION OF BEING IN *BEING AND TIME*

What made the difference? What led to the "breakthrough" that provided Heidegger with the clue for attacking the question of the meaning of being in a new way, so new that he found it necessary to invent an original philosophical language in order to prevent any confusion of his new approach with traditional lines of thought? It is often maintained that the "new Heidegger," who had not published anything for twelve years before he produced the monumental work *Being and Time,* owes the incentive for his own philosophy to the influence of Edmund Husserl, whom he met personally only after the completion of his early writings. But this is true only in a very limited sense. First of all, Husserl's phenomenology clearly (and with Heidegger's acknowledgment) already formed the background of Heidegger's critique of psychologism and had supplied him with the necessary conceptual framework for the discussion of Scotus's theory of language and meaning. Heidegger in fact reports that he had already been intrigued by Husserl's *Logical Investigations* when he was a student, but at that time he could not see how it would help him to solve his problem of *being.* Only when he came into personal contact with Husserl and the practice of the phenomenological method did he see more clearly what phenomenology could do – and, increasingly over the years, its shortcomings. As we shall see, it was these shortcomings that guided him on the way to the ideas he developed in *Being and Time.*

A short characterization of Husserl's phenomenology will be necessary to clarify the issue. Husserl had adopted Brentano's conception of the intentionality ("directedness toward") of all mental acts in order to give a comprehensive depiction of all phenomena as *objects of* – or, more precisely, the contents of – different types of acts of consciousness. Every object is to be interpreted as it is grasped by an act of comprehension in consciousness; it is something thought of, wished for, doubted, imagined, seen, heard, or known. If we want to understand the nature of all phenomena, we therefore have to work out the precise way in which consciousness intends its objects.

As Husserl saw it, such a precise description of the working of consciousness must furnish us with a proper understanding of all the *types* or ways of intending the objects of consciousness.[12] This claim is based on the notion, familiar since Descartes, that the content of consciousness is transparent and indubitable to the pure *I,* or *ego,* which forms the basis of consciousness, while facts about the world are at best probable. For Husserl the precise examination of the intended objects leads to a comprehension of their being or *essence;* if we want to know what phenomena really are, we have to look at consciousness itself rather than at the results of the empirical sciences. He therefore tried to establish philosophy as a strict *ego-centered* science that furnishes all other disciplines with the *a priori* conditions of their specific modes of cognition. Husserl can therefore be characterized as a "transcendental subjectivist"; that is, he held the view that it is the *subject* that provides the conditions of all determinations of the *objects* of experience and thought. Reflections on the acts of consciousness were supposed to render the essence not only of the acts of consciousness themselves, but also of the objects, while questions of actual external facts of experience were to be kept aside. The importance of the actual world that transcends consciousness was not denied by Husserl, but it was "bracketed," or kept out of consideration, for phenomenological purposes; only the experience of the subject and the *content* of the intentional acts of consciousness were to be studied.

Heidegger acknowledged with Husserl that the "being" of all entities lies in the sense we gain of them in our understanding. This much he shared with both Husserl's *transcendental subjectivism* and modern *anthropocentrism.* What Heidegger saw as crucial difficulties in Husserl's approach (apart from the fact that Husserl's phenomenology leaves him still with an unanalyzed multiplicity of meanings of being) can be summed up as three interrelated points. (1) He objected to treating the subject in whose understanding all ontology must center as an impersonal and *transparent ego* that is infallible in its intuitions about the activity and the content of its consciousness. That the "I" is in a sense closest to me does not mean that I comprehend it; we may be very far from possessing any such self-transparency. As Heidegger takes great pains to show, our self-understanding in fact is usually not at all authentic. (2) Heidegger questioned the feasibility or advisability of "bracketing" the *world.* He regarded Husserl's "immanentism" as mistaken, since it came dangerously close to turning the objects *of* consciousness exclusively into objects *in* consciousness, and it made Husserl dispense with the question of the ties there are to the actual world that transcends consciousness. (3) In spite of Husserl's attempt to capture all modes of consciousness including emotional attitudes, for Heidegger the very fact that the objects of consciousness are assumed as simply given in the stream of consciousness and to be studied in a detached "viewing" or "intuition" showed that Husserl's ontology remained tied to the traditional theoretical stance and ontology of the "occurent." Since all three of these points are crucial issues to Heidegger, they can be used as a key to understanding what is characteristic of Heideggerian ontology in *Being and Time.*

(1) Heidegger's realization that the picture we form of ourselves may be influenced (and even distorted) by our personal interests and propensities, and that it is conditioned by the general historical situation, made it seem questionable whether there is such a neutral transcendental "I" that underlies all acts of consciousness. He therefore adopted a policy one might call *systematic suspicion* (to be distinguished from Cartesian systematic doubt), which takes into account that we may not be transparent to ourselves – that the "I" of the intentional act may be rather far from any proper self-understanding (for his critique of the givenness of the "I," see BT §25, 150 ff.). That the phenomena may be familiar to us but not

properly understood leads to the special approach Heidegger takes in *Being and Time*, that is, starting with a characterization of human beings in their *everydayness*. His approach has a twofold advantage. First of all, he can avoid "passing over" the peculiar nature of those ties we have with the world that get lost when we take the armchair philosopher's detached theoretical stance. Second, he can turn the distortions that we are prone to import in our "average everydayness" into the subject of his phenomenological investigation.

Since Heidegger disagreed with Husserl's assumption that there is an impersonal transcendental ego providing us with incontestable truths, he had to work out *who* that entity really is that in its very nature has a concern with the question of being. Because he did not want to foist yet another artificial construction on this entity in his own interpretation, Heidegger started his phenomenological investigation by capturing the phenomenon that all philosophers before him had "passed over" as trivial and not worth the theorist's attention, namely, everyday existence. The vocabulary he introduced to characterize the various features of everyday existence and its structure was designed to avoid all associations with common philosophical terminology; it was not designed to turn it into a secret doctrine open only to the initiate. His terminology, though often unusual in German, is much easier to understand than its English counterpart, because Heidegger plays with easily comprehensible etymological family relationships that often do not exist in English.

This method of suspicion explains the special methodological twist Heidegger gives to his phenomenology. While acknowledging his debt to Husserl (his teacher's painstaking analyses seem to have greatly sharpened his sensitivity to the importance of precision in phenomenological description), he did not think that phenomena can simply be read off from the way they are given in acts of consciousness. Rather, they have to be unearthed as that which might be only implicitly contained in our understanding. So Heidegger was looking at the phenomena behind the surface appearances – at what lies hidden behind what we find familiar and regard as natural "in the first approach and for the most part," as he expresses it. This method of suspicion explains Heidegger's predilection for an archaeological vocabulary in his depiction of the phenomenological method: that it is the task of his analysis to "uncover" the phenomena that have been covered up, buried, or hidden, so that they have to be "freed" or "laid bare." The same conception forms the background of his famous theory of truth as "unhiddenness" and of understanding as a form of "disclosedness" in general. Heidegger's method of "uncovering" proceeds on two levels. He distinguishes between (a) the "ontic" level of the factual (for human existence Heidegger introduces the special term "existenti*ell*") that is open to observation, the level of field studies for the phenomenologist, and (b) the "ontological" level, the phenomenological description of the deep structures that underlie and explain the ontic (for the structure of human existence Heidegger introduced the term "existenti*ale*"). Although Heidegger himself gives few examples on the ontic or existentiell level, he always stresses that all ontological claims must find their "ontic confirmation."

In spite of our tendencies to "cover up" the phenomena, Heidegger saw it as necessary to start with the analysis of human existence, since human understanding is the only entrance and key to the nature of being. For we are always already concerned with both ourselves and our whereabouts ("the world") and have always already an at least implicit understanding of the being of both ourselves and the world. Because of this self-awareness and world awareness, he introduced the technical term "Dasein" for human beings. Although the term "Da-sein" has become so customary in English that it needs no further introduction, it is useful to keep the literal meaning of the German "being-there" in mind, since it is designed to signify that the "disclosedness" of our whereabouts, and therefore a natural tendency to form at least a preontological understanding, is the most decisive characteristic of humans for Heidegger.

The aim of Heidegger's phenomenological description of our everydayness is to make explicit what basic structures underlie this preunderstanding. If the key to all understanding of being lies in Dasein's disclosedness of the world, then an analysis of Dasein must precede a general "fundamental ontology." As Heidegger indicates, it had been his original plan for *Being and Time* to proceed through a "preparatory fundamental analysis" of Dasein's being to an explication of how time provides a "transcendental horizon" for the question of being as such. He never finished this task (for the original outline, see BT 63–4); that is, he never got beyond the analysis of Dasein, for reasons to which we will have to return later. The publication of *Being and Time,* with its focus on the analysis of the conditions of human existence, made Heidegger instantly famous after 1927. It is this focus that justifies, within limits, calling him an *existentialist* philosopher, a label he always rejected since he regarded fundamental ontology as his real task.

(2) If the pure "I" is, then, an abstraction that permits a proper comprehension neither of Dasein nor of the embeddedness of all meaning and understanding in everydayness, it is also clear why Heidegger came to the conclusion that any *bracketing* of the factual *world* in phenomenology must be a crucial mistake. For Heidegger, who was concerned with a penetrating analysis of how we are related to the world and to ourselves as beings with a world, all abstraction from the way Dasein actually experiences the world must destroy the phenomenon of "having a world." For the world is precisely the context in which we encounter beings and *ourselves,* and it is this encounter that determines what they *are* for our understanding.

Heidegger's analysis of the *a priori* structure of our having a world therefore consists in displaying the way we deal with the world, with the entities in it, as we encounter them in our actual existence. As Heidegger saw it, we are not "thinking things" that may on different occasions entertain different relationships to different items in different intentional acts. Instead, our very being is defined by the fact that we are beings-in-a-world. This existential analysis consists of a two-pronged investigation that elucidates not only in what sense we encounter entities in the world and what makes them fit for such encounters, but also what *in us* constitutes such encounterings, what in our understanding makes it possible to disclose the entities to ourselves in this way. The analysis is transcendental in the Kantian sense that it unearths the conditions that make it possible for us to encounter whatever we do encounter in the way we make "sense" of the phenomena, because all such encounterings are ways of determining the being of the entities in the world. There is no other "sense" or "meaning of being" than the one we bestow on entities in our understanding. This is how Heidegger time and again defines how he understands "the *meaning* [or sense] of being": "Meaning is that wherein the intelligibility of something maintains itself" (BT 193).

This transcendental investigation is not supposed to supply us with new insights about the world, but to retrace and articulate the way in which we "always already" understand what we are dealing with. If "to be" means "to be already understood as," then a thorough investigation of all different kinds of *understanding* that underlie our dealing with the world is called for. This explains the importance that *interpretation* has for Heidegger, for in all interpretations we give in our activities, we draw on the implicit understanding of the meaning things have without being fully aware of it. The phenomenologist has to trace the different ways in which we deal with the "given" and bring them to articulation. So Heidegger is merely trying to bring to light what we always in a sense know "in our bones," as Ryle phrased it in his review of *Being and Time*.[13]

(3) Since our implicit understanding of being is not only the basis of Heidegger's own interpretation but, as he saw it, the all-pervasive feature that characterizes humankind in general, there has always been an at least dim understanding of the "question of being." Heidegger makes no claims to originality here. What needs an explanation is, rather, why this dim understanding was never fully developed before, and a good deal of Heidegger's originality consists in his explanation of what he calls our "forgetfulness" of being.

The forgetfulness is twofold. There is the forgetfulness of our everyday understanding, which does not even try to gain any authentic comprehension but takes over the ready-made interpretations that it finds in its environment, the explanations and evaluations of one's own society and time. For the most part we simply adopt our mode of living and self-understanding in compliance with the general standards: we behave, speak, and value as "one" speaks, behaves, and values. Heidegger's depiction of the all-embracing influence of the anonymous public "one" (the impersonal pronoun, not the numeral) is one of the most colorful sections of *Being and Time* (Div. I, Chap. 4). The English translation of *das Man* as "the They" is misleading, since it does not show that there is not usually any detachment from this basic mode of existence that "anyone" shares. It takes a special effort to shake off the yoke of this public interpretation in order to gain an authentic understanding; for Heidegger, the experience of coming to terms with our finitude in the *anxiety* of facing up to death is the crucial situation that forces us to wrench ourselves away from domination by the anonymous public understanding (Div. II, Chap. 1). As he repeatedly affirms, there is no way to live permanently in authenticity, since we have to take the everyday world and its routine for granted in all our practical concerns.

If the "forgetfulness of being" in our everyday absorption in the world seems natural, the special forgetfulness that Heidegger ascribes to philosophers seems much less so, since it is their task to reflect explicitly on this question, and they in fact have reflected on it ever since the Greeks first raised the question, What is being? If philosophers up to Heidegger's time missed the crucial point, there must be a definite reason for this monumental misunderstanding. And Heidegger thought indeed that he could put his finger on the crucial mistake: the mistake lies in the *theoretical* approach as such.

As mentioned earlier, the stance taken in theorizing allows the thinker to have a detached point of view. The thinker can treat the objects of his investigation as "indifferently occurring"[14] things that exist independent of observation, just as the observer in his turn is at liberty to fasten on any object. So observer and observed, thinker and the object of his thought, are regarded as "indifferently occurring" alongside one another. And this theoretical stance, according to Heidegger, was not overcome by the subject-centered ontology in the Kantian tradition; it was not even overcome by Husserl's insistence that all objects be treated as intentional objects, that is, as objects represented in consciousness. As Heidegger sees it, in Husserl's phenomenological analysis the objects in consciousness retain the status of mere occurrence, just as consciousness itself remains in an ontologically uninterpreted state, for it is treated as an entity that simply occurs. *Being* in Husserl would therefore have to be defined as the "occurrent" correlate of the series of meanings as they are determined separately by each act of intuiting an essence revealed by phenomenological analysis.

That the theoretical stance does have its justification for the theoretician himself Heidegger does not deny. It would in fact be quite innocuous if scientists, and particularly philosophers, had recognized it for what it is: a *derivative* mode of being, constituted by their special way of *viewing* the objects of their research. By mistaking it for *the* significant mode of being that underlies all entities, however, they become guilty of suppressing the discovery of the other modes of being that Heidegger takes great pains to work out. Besides the "mere occurrence" ("presence-at-hand") of theoretical understanding, there is also "readiness-at-hand" constituting our practical understanding of dealing with equipment, "being-with" other human beings, and "in-each-case-mineness," the relation to and concern for our own selves that we are and have to be.

For Heidegger, our everyday life is determined largely by our understanding of all entities in terms of our practical concerns, purposes, and designs, and this includes our dealings with other human beings and with ourselves. Among the four modes of being, therefore, the theoretical stance fastens on the least characteristic one, the one Heidegger calls "founded" or "derivative" because it comes into focus only when we disregard what he calls the "referential totality" of those practical and personal concerns that make up the everyday world (cf. BT §13).

The mode of being that we assign to different entities is not always fixed, at least not on the "ontic" level. One and the same "thing" can be treated as a piece of equipment with a practical meaning, or as a piece of art, or as the object of scientific investigation. Other human beings can be treated as "scientific objects" (as ciphers in statistics) or as mere tools (something ready-to-hand) instead of as "Dasein-withs." The context therefore determines their "being." There can even be (ontically) a certain indeterminacy as to which of the ontological possibilities will be seized upon in such treatments under a specific aspect. What is not open for decision in the particular context is the preexisting *structure* of these different possibilities, since it forms the ontological structure of our very nature.

HEIDEGGER'S TWOFOLD TASK

If Heidegger has found important supplementary modes of being that determine our existence in the world, one may wonder why he regards the age-old commitment to the ontology of *Vorhandenheit* (occurrence) as so fateful a mistake that he comes back to it again and again. If his predecessors omitted something of importance, is it not enough to supply what is omitted, without harping so much on the omission? The point, however, is that simply supplying what is omitted will not do. What is needed is rather a complete revision in two respects. The first concerns the intepretation of the history of philosophy; the second concerns the proper search for the conception of "being" itself, that is, Heidegger's actual enterprise. This is in fact the *twofold task* that Heidegger has set for himself in *Being and*

Time, the task he calls the "Ontological Analytic of Dasein as Laying Bare the Horizon for an Interpretation of the Meaning of Being in General" and the task of "Destroying the History of Ontology" (see BT 36–49).

A clarification of this twofold task, even if sketchy, will provide a better understanding of Heidegger's project as such. Let us start with the second task, the task of destroying the history of ontology. Heidegger is not out to do violence to history or to badger his predecessors for their blindness. The German word "*Destruktion*" is not as violent as its English counterpart. This "destruction" is not a *deconstruction,* as some people would have it nowadays, but an analysis intended to show where the decisive steps of the derailment took place in Kant, Descartes, and Aristotle. Heidegger does not have the deconstructionists' detachment from tradition: he thinks it can be mastered and rectified even while acknowledging that the "missteps" were inevitable. His emphasis on continuity in the history of being (through all historical vicissitudes) also speaks against recruiting him for the now fashionable "historicist" camp. A historicist Heidegger could not regard himself as the rightful heir of Parmenides, the discoverer of the tie between being and thinking; he could not look for any continued problems through different periods of history, but would only notice curious doxographical coincidences that are as external and as accidental as the resemblance between a triceratops and a rhinoceros.

Heidegger's concern is rather with "unravelling" the history of ontology to show the decisive steps that lead to the dominance of the ontology of *Vorhandenheit* and to the forgetfulness of "being," that is, to the prejudice that being has no concrete meaning because it is the "most general of generalities" (BT 29). If in the past this prejudice was derived in one way or another from Aristotelian ontology's view that *being* transcends the categories and can therefore have no "real" content, today it rests on the view that "being" applies indifferently to whatever we may introduce by the existential operator or include in our universe of discourse.

What Heidegger finds most fateful in the development of Western philosophy is, to repeat, the orientation toward being as "*re*ality" or "thinghood" (BT 96), for this makes the world a sum total of *independently* existing entities that exist for observing subjects insofar as those subjects manage to make contact with them. He blames this ontology for all the difficulties philosophers have been unable to solve through the many turns that philosophy has taken since its origin with the Greeks, difficulties that did not end when philosophy became "subject-centered" in the Cartesian–Kantian tradition. If there are basically two separate entities, subject and object, that occur side by side, the question of how contact is possible between the thinking subject and independently existing objects remains an insoluble problem, even if one grants that the subject somehow bestows the "form" or the "meaning" on the objects. For the question remains: How can there be truth if it is conceived of as the *correspondence* between our thoughts (or the content of our consciousness) and the outside world? In other words, what guarantees the objectivity of our subjective impressions? Even the critical realist remains saddled with the question of what we can know about the world and, most of all, with the problem of how we can even be sure of the existence of the "world outside us." In spite of his "Copernican turn" toward subjectivity, Kant left the main feature of ancient ontology intact: the centrality of substance, the *thinghood* of the thing, remained uncontested. That is to say, for Kant the independent substance that persists through time remains the fundamental building block of all reality. The independent "thing" that is dealt with and categorized in all our experience and determined by scientific thought remains in its very *being* separate from the subject. In particular, the attempt to prove the existence of the external world is treated by Heidegger as a clear indication that Kant had not questioned the basis of traditional ontology rigorously enough.[15]

The idealist, in turn, seems to be condemned to *immanentism*, the problem of explaining the "transcendence" of objects in relation to our minds such that it makes sense even to talk about the natural world outside us. All these problems arise, Heidegger tells us, only if one posits a fundamental *rift* between the isolated subject or "mind" and an independently existing realm of objects. Such a rift for Heidegger is not a necessary presupposition; it is rather the result of the philosopher's mistaken "theoretical stance" and leads to what Heidegger calls a "splitting asunder of the phenomena" (BT 170). There is no way to get beyond the split between what occurs inside us and what occurs outside so long as "occurrence alongside" is the only available ontological category.

Because in *theoria* we merely "gaze" at what appears as an isolated object, we are led to take this "reification" as the natural way of being of that "object." Such a dissociated perspective is quite justified for the "theoretical view" so long as we do not forget that it is an artificial isolating perspective and we fully realize that it is neither the only perspective nor one that is even capable of doing justice to the other ways in which things are "given" to us. Because for centuries the theoretical stance had been regarded as the only one worthy of the philosopher-scientist, no other way of understanding, and at the same time, therefore, no other way of *being* of objects, was ever taken into consideration. The ontology of "merely occurring things" is therefore cut back by Heidegger and relegated to the scientists' special point of view as a "founded mode" or derivative understanding of being. This derivative point of view, which treats us as initially *worldless* subjects who somehow establish cognitive contact with separate objects, ought rather to be understood as a special version of the more original way of understanding ourselves as beings *with a world* that is characterized as a "being-among" or involvement in the world of the ready-to-hand.

The promised "destruction" of the history of ontology, as Heidegger had initially planned it, was never carried out (see BT 64). Part II of *Being and Time,* which was to contain a discussion of "Kant's doctrine of schematism and time," "the ontological foundation of the 'cogito sum' of Descartes," and "Aristotle's essay on time, as providing a way of discriminating the phenomenal basis and limits of ancient ontology," never appeared and can be, at best, reconstructed from some of his later publications. It seems clear that the treatment of history itself was not the stumbling block. Heidegger found himself increasingly at a loss as to how to complete his first task, the "laying bare of the horizon for an interpretation of the meaning of being as such," for he never published the missing Division III of Part I of *Being and Time,* the division he claimed he had merely "held back" (BT 17) when he was forced to publish his manuscript sooner than planned. This division was to bring the "reversal" of *Being and Time,* that is, "Time and Being." Why Heidegger was so dissatisfied with this last part perhaps will never be known, since he did not consent to have it included in his posthumous edition. We will not try to enter into any speculations here, but will try to follow Heidegger in his initial project as far as he took it.

The gravest consequence of the omission of a proper understanding of "being" in the ontology of occurrence is that it does not permit the development of what one might call a *dynamic* rather than a *static* ontology. It cannot lead to a proper development of the conception of time or temporality as Heidegger envisages it. To work out this concept is the ultimate task of *Being and Time* as we have it. We have seen that for Heidegger a human being is never an isolated, worldless subject, but is an entity that in its very essence is constituted by its *world*. We have to see what is meant by this. So far, the modes of being of the occurrent, the ready-to-hand, being-with, and being-oneself do not seem to form a meaningful whole. Nor do they form a unity if one looks at the corresponding kinds of understanding in which they are grounded: theoretical understanding, practical concern, solicitude, and the many ways of comportment toward one's own self. All these modes of comportment are, as Heidegger explains, different kinds of "-sights," different kinds of "enlightenment" about the world.[16] Up to this point in his analysis they do not form any unity that would constitute anything like *the* meaning of being. We seem to have only different ways of understanding *beings*, just as in Husserl's phenomenological analysis. If Heidegger had gone no further, the only difference between him and Husserl would be that Heidegger fastened on different "root types" of understanding, with an emphasis on our direct involvement in the world rather than on "intuiting" the essences of beings in consciousness.

But Heidegger did not leave matters here. First of all, he introduced a unifying term – "care" – to designate the basic feature in us that constitutes all our involvements in the world (BT Div. I, Chap. 6). It is the analysis of the structure of care that allows him to claim that our being is at the same time "being-in-the-world" as an organic whole. This holistic conception of "care" must take account of the overall *sense* we give to our existence as being-in-the-world by virtue of which it is an integrated whole. The decisive characteristic in our relation to the world as such, which includes ourselves as our ultimate point of reference, is conditioned by the care that allows us to treat everything as part of our *project* in the largest sense of the word. This feature leads to the temporal interpretation of the structure of our being-in-the-world. We project ourselves, our whole existence, into the world and understand ourselves as well as everything in the world in terms of the *possibilities* within the design or "projection" that we make of ourselves. (Since the translation of *Entwurf* as "projection" [see BT 184] may suggest wrong associations with psychological projection, "design" in the sense of an architect's blueprint is perhaps a less misleading synonym.)

Everything we are dealing with finds its meaning within this projection, and things have a meaning only insofar as they form part of it. Within this "project" we make of ourselves, everything has its meaning and thereby its *being*. The design is, as the term suggests, directed into the future: we project ourselves into an anticipated future as the ultimate aim of our endeavors. But this is not the only temporal dimension that is at work in our projection, because our projection is not a free choice of the future. According to Heidegger, we cannot make any such projections without an existing understanding of the world and ourselves in it, an understanding determined by the past we have been and still are. Therefore, not only do we carry our past with us, as one carries weighty memories, but we always already understand ourselves and our projects in terms of the past and out of the past. Finally, in all our enterprises, whatever they may be, we are tied to the present, because we are in and with the world that absorbs us and ties us down to our everyday endeavors. The absorption by the here and now constitutes our (for the most part) inescapable involvement in the inauthentic, or "falling," way of understanding the world in terms of the One (BT §§27, 71).

This, in a nutshell, is the structure Heidegger calls our "temporality." By temporality he does not mean that we are, as are all other things, confined to time, nor that we have a sense of time, but rather that we exist as three temporal dimensions at once: it is being ahead of ourselves in the future, drawing on our past, while being concerned with the present that constitutes our being. The way we project ourselves into the future (*ahead of ourselves*) while taking with us our past (*being already in*) in our immersion into the present (*being at home with*) is what Heidegger designates as the "*ekstases*" of temporality. There is nothing "ecstatic" about this. All it means is that we are already "extended" outward in temporal dimensions and so are never contained in a "punctual" here and now (see BT 370 ff.).

Since we are neither static points in a preexisting indifferent universe nor confined to a segment of an infinite arrow of time, but are instead entities whose very understanding makes up the temporal dimensions of our existence, this temporality is the transcendental condition of Dasein's having a universe of meaningful beings. The "meaning of being" as it is constituted by our understanding is thus grounded in the temporal structure that underlies our understanding. Temporality in this sense was to provide the foundation for Heidegger's further analysis of the "transcendental horizon" of being as such, that is to say, of the being that goes beyond Dasein itself. Dasein provides access to being in understanding insofar as we disclose it, but our understanding neither is identical to being as such nor does it *create* it. How Heidegger had planned to complete this step toward an analysis of being as such is not clear. The published portion of *Being and Time* breaks off after the repetition of the analysis of everydayness in terms of temporality, the explanation of our concern with history, and the accounts of our "historicality" and of the everyday conception of time.

It would require a survey of Heidegger's later work, sailing out on the high sea of speculation, to find out why he did not take the last step from Dasein's temporality to being when he wrote *Being and Time.* At one point, he mentioned the difficulties language presented.[17] This would be a genuine problem, because the language and concepts that describe the "horizon of intelligibility" would necessarily be derived from the language and concepts we use to describe the realms of the beings that are contained within that horizon. We would have to describe the conditions of all understanding – of being as such – in terms of what is conditioned by the horizon, that is, the foundations in terms of what is founded on them. It is doubtful that this can be done in a nonmetaphoric way.

In later years, Heidegger seems to have become increasingly skeptical about the enterprise of a fundamental ontology that "lays bare" the structures of being as such, since this now seems to him a kind of "foundational" enterprise that reeks of metaphysics, the project of establishing an ultimate basis for all things. To make human understanding the key to such a transcendental investigation carries such dangers in itself, for it somehow suggests that we are in *control* of the "being" of all beings, if the sense of whatever is given depends on our understanding.

If Heidegger seems to develop a kind of transcendental anthropocentrism in *Being and Time,* as I have tried to show, we must also emphasize the fact that, for him, this can be only half the story. For it is only in a limited sense *up to us* how we understand the "being" of all beings. Heidegger's "light-" and "sight-metaphors," and such terminology as "disclosedness" and "unhiddenness," show that we do not create our own universe, not even its meaning. The intelligibility resides as much in the "things" encountered themselves as in the understanding residing in us, and this "fittingness" is not due to any merit of ours. *Enlightenment* (*Lichtung*) is something that simply *happens* to us, and in this sense "being" is quite out of our control. It is an "opening," a "free gift," as Heidegger liked to say later in his life; all we can try to do is "appropriate it" in an authentic understanding. Heidegger always insisted that there is "being" only as long as there is the understanding of being in Dasein, but that the entities themselves do not depend on that understanding (BT 269 ff.). That we are passive recipients of "being" seems to be a strong argument against recent attempts to interpret Heidegger as a predecessor of the "new pragmatism" that would make "being" a matter of social construction. Heidegger would agree that *ontically* every epoch articulates (constructs) its own interpretations, but that does not justify a pragmatist conception of *ontology* itself. He in fact warned against our present-day submission to the spirit of technology. What sense can such warnings and the wistful claim that "only a God can save us" make in the mouth of a pragmatist?[18]

Why we are enlightened entities, why being "speaks to us," is shrouded in mystery for Heidegger, a mystery he tended to express in increasingly mystifying terms in his later years. It is undeniable that his increasing skepticism about the feasibility of transcendental reasoning as such, and his conviction that Dasein is confined to the "receiving end" of being, represents a major shift in Heidegger's thinking after *Being and Time.* That this "turn" is a radical shift away from the project of *Being and Time* can nevertheless be doubted with good reasons. In his preface to the edition of 1953, Heidegger reaffirmed that "the road it has taken remains even today a necessary one, if our Dasein is to be stirred by the question of being" (BT 17). Who is to contradict this testimony?

NOTES

1 Heidegger's last comments on his lifework, found in his unfinished notes for a preface to the edition of his collected writings (*Gesamtausgabe letzter Hand*) written shortly before his death in 1976, in *Frühe Schriften* (GA 1 437). All translations or paraphrases are my own.

2 Since space is limited, this essay gives only a very rough sketch of Heidegger's development without any detailed discussion of the formative influence on him of the pre-Socratics, Plato, Aristotle, the Scholastics, Descartes, Kant, or Husserl. Nor does it deal with the question of whether his reading of these philosophers does justice to them.

3 *Von der mannigfachen Bedeutung des Seienden nach Aristoteles* (Freiburg: Herder, 1862), trans. Rolf George (Berkeley and Los Angeles: University of California Press, 1975). Brentano's book has remained a classic (he was the first in modern times to stress the importance of the special relationship of the "focal meaning" of being as centered around substantiality; see 56 ff.), and Heidegger was fully aware of its importance. He could not have come across a better introduction to Aristotle's metaphysics. For Heidegger's acknowledgment, see GA 1 56: "The question of the unity of the manifold of being that stirred then, darkly, unsteadily, helplessly, remained throughout many reversals, wanderings and indecisions, the persistent source leading up to *Being and Time,* which appeared two decades later." His early admiration for Brentano's work on Aristotle was not diminished by his critical stance toward Brentano's later work in the tradition of psychologism (see GA 1 155 ff.).

4 For a comprehensive discussion of the different meanings of "being" and the importance of the distinction between the copulative, existential, and veridical senses of "is" for the development of philosophy, see C. H. Kahn, *The Verb 'Be' in Ancient Greek* (Dordrecht: Reidel, 1973).

5 What Plato meant by his claim that "being" is the "kind that pervades everything or combines with everything" (*Sophist,* esp. 251d ff.) is still very much a matter of debate, so it is difficult to say whether the being that accrues to all that is has *one* definable meaning for Plato.

6 "So we say that not only animals and plants and their parts are substances, but also natural bodies such as fire and water and earth and everything of the sort" (*Metaphysics* Z 2, 1028b9 ff.). By the latter Aristotle does not mean "stuff" but individual "pieces" that actually exist and display their own characteristic functions.

7 The unreflected identification of "being" with "thinghood" or "reality" – derived from the Latin word *"res"* (the same etymology applies to the German term *"Realität"*) designating "thing" as an indifferently occurring independent entity or a carrier of attributes – is the main point of criticism of traditional ontology in *Being and Time* (see BT 245, passim). It is in this sense only that Heidegger refused to be called a "realist."

8 By "logical" Heidegger usually means *conceptual analysis,* in accordance with the German tradition that goes back to the scholastics; the same meaning is to be found in Kant and Hegel and is still presupposed

by Husserl. Formal logic is usually called "logistic" or "mathematical logic."

9 The theory itself can be called "Scotist" only in a qualified sense, for Heidegger (following the distinguished linguist H. Steinthal, *Einleitung in die Psychologie und Sprachwissenschaft;* see GA 1 303–4) uses as one of his main sources the *Grammatica speculativa,* now by common consent regarded as the work of Thomas of Erfurt, as well as the equally spurious *De rerum principio.* But Heidegger's interpretation is also based on genuine writings by Duns Scotus: extensive references are given to the *Quaestiones subtilissimae super libros Metaphysicorum Aristotelis,* the *Reportata,* and the *Ordinatio.* Heidegger is aware of the fact that his attempt to demarcate reality may go beyond the scope of what Scotus clearly saw and worked out systematically himself, but he claims that he is following at least Scotus's intentions (GA 1 211).

10 We find here already some of the terminology that Heidegger used later in *Being and Time,* e.g., "*Bewandtnis*" for "significance" (see GA 1 223, 346, 387).

11 He stresses the need to allow for "the peculiar mobility of meaning that is constituted through live speech and assertion" – "*eine durch die lebendige Rede und Aussage gegebene eigentümliche Beweglichkeit der Bedeutung*" (GA 1 336). This emphasis may have made Heidegger skeptical about Husserl's rather abstract phenomenological approach from early on.

12 Since Husserl worked and reworked his conception of phenomenology throughout his long life, there are quite differing accounts of it. For the uninitiated, the most accessible depiction is a short article that appeared in the *Encyclopaedia Britannica* in 1927. Husserl had prepared no less than four German versions, three of which are reprinted, with comments by Heidegger, at Husserl's request, in *Phänomenologische Psychologie, Husserliana,* Vol. 9, ed. W. Biemel (The Hague: Nijhoff, 1962), pp. 237–301.

13 "Review of *Sein und Zeit,*" *Mind* 38 (1929): 355–70. Rpt. in G. Ryle, *Collected Papers* (New York: Hutchinson, 1971), Vol. 1, pp. 197–214.

14 I prefer to translate "*Vorhandenheit*" as "occurrence", even though "presence-at-hand" (see BT 67) has become customary and preserves the etymological connotations as well as the parallel with the "readiness-at-hand" of equipment. But the parallel between "Vor*hand*enheit" and "Zu*hand*enheit" cannot be imitated in English. In German, "*Vorhandenheit,*" though originally signifying being "on hand," has lost all connotation of nearness (one can say of any distant star in the Milky Way that it is "*vorhanden*"), hence my preference for "occurrence." In contrast, "*Zuhandenheit*" signifies the "handiness" of equipment for use. "Ex-

tant" has replaced "present-at-hand" in some recent translations (e.g., *Basic Problems of Phenomenology*), but it might wrongly suggest a contrast to what has become extinct.

15 For a more extensive discussion of this problem see my "Heidegger and the Scandal of Philosophy," *Human Nature and Natural Knowledge*, ed. A. Donagan, A. Perovich, and M. Wedin (Dordrecht: Reidel, 1986), pp. 129–51.

16 It is impossible to render adequately in English all the terms Heidegger derives from the German roots "*Licht*" and "*Sicht*." There is the "sight" by which we deal with equipment (*Umsicht* = circumspection), or with others (*Rücksicht*), and the perspective of our projection into the future in foresight (*Vorsicht*). Light metaphors are used when Dasein is compared to a "clearing" (*Lichtung*) or is "lit up" (*gelichtet*). Heidegger sees himself in an old tradition, for he refers to the ancient *lumen naturale* theory as an anticipation of his own view of our natural disclosedness (see BT 171).

17 A revised later version of his lectures in 1927, *The Basic Problems of Phenomenology*, supplements *Being and Time* but does not carry the promised "reversal" or "turn" much further. Heidegger's late remarks, *On Time and Being*, trans. J. Stambaugh (New York: Harper & Row, 1972), contain some comments by the later Heidegger on the difficulties of the younger one: "[It] must still in a way speak the language of metaphysics."

18 "Nur noch ein Gott kann uns retten." Interview in *Der Spiegel* (May 1976): 193–219.

THOMAS SHEEHAN

2 Reading a life: Heidegger and hard times

THE END OF A CATHOLIC PHILOSOPHER

It was just before Christmas Eve – Monday, December 23, 1918 – when the young Mrs. Heidegger, eight months pregnant, decided to brave Freiburg's bitterly cold weather, travel across town, and break the bad news to Father Krebs. Engelbert Krebs, a Catholic priest and professor of theology at Freiburg University, was a close friend of her husband, the philosophy lecturer Martin Heidegger. In fact, Krebs had officiated at the Heideggers' Catholic wedding in Freiburg Cathedral on March 21, 1917.

At the time of that wedding Father Krebs had already been skeptical. It was a confessionally "mixed" marriage – Elfride Petri was a Lutheran, Martin Heidegger a Catholic – and even though the bride had solemnly declared her intention to convert to Catholicism and raise her children in the Roman faith, Father Krebs had had his doubts. Therefore, he was not entirely surprised when, a year and a half later, the 24-year-old mother-to-be sat across from him in his office and poured out her feelings:

> My husband has lost his church faith, and I have not found mine. At the time of our marriage, his faith was already undermined by doubts. But I insisted on the Catholic wedding, hoping that with his help I would find faith. We have read, spoken, thought, and prayed a great deal together, and the result is that both of us now think only as Protestants – that is: we believe in a personal God and pray to Him, but without any dogmatic ties and apart from Protestant or Catholic orthodoxy. Under these circumstances, we would consider it dishonest to let our child be baptized in the Catholic church. But I felt it was my duty to tell you this beforehand.[1]

Two weeks later, on January 9, 1919, Martin Heidegger himself decided to write to Father Krebs and explain the personal and philosophical transformation he had undergone in the past two years.

What had caused these changes in Heidegger? Was it the cataclysmic Great War, which had ended a few weeks earlier at a cost of 16 million lives? Or his own disastrous four months on the Western Front, which ended, as if symbolically, with his promotion to lance corporal on the day the German generals petitioned for an armistice? Or the role he played as a weatherman in preparing poison gas attacks on U.S. soldiers during their final push from Verdun to Sedan in early October?[2] Edmund Husserl would think so. "The war and ensuing difficulties drive men into mysticism," he said a dozen years later (August 13, 1931), after his bitter falling out with Heidegger.[3]

But in his 1919 letter to Father Krebs, Martin Heidegger did not refer at all to the world-shattering events that had transpired over the past two years – the war, for example, or the Bolshevik Revolution, or the end of the Hohenzollern dynasty and the proclamation of a socialist republic in Germany, or the outbreak in January 1919 of a virtual civil war between the left-wing Spartacus League and the reactionary Free Corps with their shadowy death squads, the Feme.

Yes, these were hard times for Germany, but in his letter Heidegger mentioned none of that. After all he was a philosopher, even something of a theologian – in any case, a deeply religious man – and in writing to Father Krebs he addressed what was presumably most important to him. Since 1916 Heidegger had been teaching Catholic philosophy at Freiburg University, occasionally in tandem with Krebs, and had built something of a reputation as a Catholic philosopher of the future. But now he had to tell Krebs that he had abandoned dogmatic Catholicism both in philosophy and in his personal life:

Freiburg
January 9, 1919

Esteemed Professor,

Over the last two years I have set aside all scientific work of a specialized nature and have struggled instead for a basic clarification of my philosophical position. This has led me to results that I could not be free to hold and teach if I were tied to positions that come from outside of philosophy.

Epistemological insights that pass over into the theory of historical knowledge have made the *system* of Catholicism problematic and unacceptable to me – but not Christianity and metaphysics, although I take the latter in a new sense.

I believe that I – perhaps more than those who work on the subject officially – have perceived the values that the Catholic Middle Ages bears within itself, values that we are still far from really exploiting. My investigations into the phenomenology of religion, which will draw heavily on the Middle Ages, should prove beyond dispute that in transforming my basic standpoint I have not let myself be dragged into abandoning my objective, high judgment of and esteem for the Catholic life-world, in favor of the empty polemics of an embittered apostate.

Therefore, it is especially important to me – and I wish to extend you my heartfelt thanks for this – that I not lose the benefit of your invaluable friendship. My wife, who first told you about this, and I too would like to preserve the very special confidence we share with you. It is hard to live as a philosopher – inner truthfulness toward oneself and those one is supposed to teach, demands sacrifice, renunciation and struggles that remain forever foreign to the academic "tradesman."

I believe that I have an inner call to philosophy and, by fulfilling it in research and teaching, a call to the eternal vocation of the inner man – *and for that alone* do I feel called to achieve what is in my powers and thus to justify, before God, my very existence and activity.

With cordial thanks, Yours,
Martin Heidegger

P.S. My wife sends her warmest greetings.[4]

We note that Heidegger does not say he has lost his religious faith or broken with the Catholic worldview and the values he perceives in it. Nor does he say he has abandoned the Catholic church, taken as a community of people with shared traditions and rituals. (Later in life he would tell a confidant that he had never left the Catholic church: "Ich bin niemals aus der Kirche getretten.")

Rather, Heidegger is announcing his break with the *system of dogmatic Catholicism* and in particular with its way of policing its members' freedom to research and teach as they see fit. Once liberated from ecclesiastical restrictions, Heidegger intends to continue working to retrieve the meaning he has found latent in Christianity and traditional metaphysics, although he says he now understands metaphysics in a different sense than before. And he proposes to present the positive results of his research in a study devoted to the phenomenology of religion.

This letter is a watershed in the philosophical and religious development of the 29-year-old Martin Heidegger. Firmly and decisively it marks the end of his budding career as the up-and-coming "Catholic philosopher," a reputation he had been carefully cultivating around Freiburg University ever since he took his doctorate in philosophy there in 1913.[5]

Martin Heidegger was born on September 26, 1889, in Messkirch, southwest Germany, the first child of a relatively poor Catholic couple, simple village people who had lived through the hard times of Bismarck's *Kulturkampf.* After grammar school, he spent seven and a half years of his academic curriculum studying for the Roman Catholic priesthood: six years as a high school seminarian (1903–9), two weeks in a Jesuit novitiate (September 30 to October 13, 1909; he was dismissed for reasons of health), followed by a year and a half of theology studies at Freiburg University.

However, in February 1911 a deteriorating heart condition forced Heidegger to leave the seminary and abandon all plans to become a priest. In October 1911 he took up studies in mathematics and, under the strong influence of Professor Heinrich Rickert, in philosophy. On July 26, 1913, Heidegger received the doctorate in philosophy with a dissertation entitled "The Doctrine of Judgment in Psychologism."

A few weeks later members of the Philosophy Faculty, particularly philosophy professor Arthur Schneider and history professor Heinrich Finke, began grooming the promising young scholar, then 23 years of age, to take over Freiburg University's Chair of Catholic Philosophy. A grant from the Catholic church was arranged to tide Heidegger over for two years while he wrote the requisite "qualifying dissertation" (*Habilitationsschrift*) that would win him a license to teach at the university as a *Privatdozent,* or unsalaried lecturer. The terms of the grant stipulated that in order to receive the stipend of 1,000 marks per year Heidegger had to promise to follow the church's line and "remain true to the spirit of Thomistic philosophy."

Moreover, Heidegger's mentors suggested that if he wanted the chair in Catholic philosophy, he should change the topic of his qualifying dissertation from his chosen subject, titled "The Logical Essence of the Concept of Number" (which reflected his interest in the philosophy of mathematics, inspired by reading Edmund Husserl and Heinrich Rickert), to a topic in medieval philosophy. Heidegger decided to write on Duns Scotus's doctrine of categories and meaning, basing himself on the *Tractatus de modis significandi,* which was later found to have been written not by Scotus (1266–1308) but by his follower, Thomas of Erfurt, around the year 1379.

These were hard times for Catholic intellectuals. For the better part of the preceding century the traditional Catholic worldview – especially but not exclusively its fundamentalist interpretation of the Bible – had been on the ropes, severely buffeted by the revolution in religious and philosophical thinking that the Vatican, tarring with a very broad brush, denounced as "Modernism." Launching his counterattack in the summer and fall of 1907, Pope Pius X lashed out against alleged Modernist tendencies in Catholic university circles, and in the process plunged the church into one of its darkest, most repressive periods. Among other things, the Vatican demanded (September 1910) that certain Catholic professors swear an anti-Modernist oath of fidelity to traditional formulations of doctrine on such things as miracles, the founding of the church, and the nature of faith.

Even Heidegger, when he was 20 years old and still a seminary student, had thrown in his lot with the Vatican on this one. He publicly condemned Modernism and defended the church's teaching authority both in a speech he gave in Hausen im Tal, near Messkirch, on September 6, 1909 (three weeks before entering the Jesuits), and in an article he published in the conservative Catholic weekly *Der Akademiker* in May 1910.[6]

Four years later, however, while in the throes of writing his qualifying dissertation, Heidegger apparently began to feel the pinch of the church's anti-Modernist crusade and changed his mind. In a letter to his friend Father Krebs (July 19, 1914, just two weeks before the Great War broke out) he remarked ironically how the Vatican might guarantee conformity among Catholic intellectuals: "Philosophical demand could be met by setting up vending machines in the train station (free of charge for the poor)" and "all who succumb to having independent thoughts could have their brains taken out and replaced with spaghetti."[7]

Nonetheless, Heidegger, in hot pursuit of the chair of Catholic philosophy, continued to assure the administrative offices of Freiburg's Catholic archdiocese, in writing and presumably with conviction, that his academic work would be devoted to "researching and teaching Christian-Scholastic philosophy" (September 20, 1914), that he saw himself as standing "in the service of Christian-Scholastic philosophy and the Catholic worldview" (November 23, 1914), and that his philosophical career would be dedicated to "making the intellectual riches stored up in Scholasticism available and usable for the spiritual battle of the future over the Christian-Catholic ideal of life" (December 13, 1915). Moreover, in a handwritten curriculum vitae that he presented to the philosophy department on July 2, 1915, he declared that his "basic philosophical convictions [remain] those of Aristotelian-Scholastic philosophy" and that his lifework would be taken up with (here we find a slight twist away from neo-Scholasticism and toward Husserl) "a comprehensive presentation of medieval logic and psychology in the light of modern phenomenology."[8]

Therefore, a year after he had successfully completed his dissertation on medieval philosophy, and after being told for three years that he was the inside favorite for Freiburg University's chair of Catholic philosophy, it came as a great shock and a bitter disappointment when in June 1916 Martin Heidegger saw the philosophy department give the chair to Josef Geyser, a second-rate neo-Scholastic professor from the University of Münster.

It seems that between June 1916 and March 1917 Heidegger underwent the personal and philosophical conversion that culminated in his abandonment of dogmatic Catholicism. Several factors, including a personal crisis of faith, contributed to this Protestantizing turn.

For one thing (and probably bound up with his disappointment at being passed over for the Catholic chair) there was the increasing tension that Heidegger felt between, on the one hand, the conformity to ecclesiastical authority that the Vatican's anti-Modernist campaign demanded and, on the other, the "inner truthfulness towards oneself and those one is supposed to teach" (as he would later put it to Father Krebs) that was demanded by his vocation to philosophy. It is significant that Privatdozent Heidegger, after a year of giving courses in Catholic philosophy, spent the summer of 1917 reading the Protestant theologian Friedrich Schleiermacher (1768–1834) and would soon be studying Martin Luther.

Another factor was Heidegger's encounter with Edmund Husserl, who had come to Freiburg University in April 1916 to take over the chair of non-Catholic philosophy. Heidegger's first personal meetings with Husserl, from late July 1916 through the fall of 1917, were disappointing. To be sure, Husserl was happy to help the young man get some part-time teaching at the university. However, he gave Heidegger's qualifying dissertation only a desultory reading and, in October 1917, sent to Professor Natorp of Marburg University an at best lackluster evaluation of Heidegger's promise as a scholar.[9]

Again, one of the major issues was religion. Husserl, who called himself a "free Christian" and a "non-dogmatic Protestant" and who once denounced what he termed the "Catholic International," vigorously opposed ecclesiastical interference with philosophical research. "Scientific work would be deprived of its freedom," he said on January 16, 1920, with explicit reference to the Vatican, "if one had to fear being censured by some learned commission." The point is that up through October 1917 Husserl, being unfamiliar with the religious transformation Heidegger was undergoing, thought that the young lecturer was still passing himself off around Freiburg as a Catholic philosopher.[10]

Only in November–December 1917 did Husserl learn from his student, Heinrich Ochsner, who was a close personal friend of Heidegger, how radically Heidegger's views on Catholicism had changed. That was the turning point. Husserl now began to open up to Heidegger both personally and professionally. However, after only a few weeks, their direct personal contacts were broken off when Heidegger was called up, on January 17, 1918, for active military duty and eventually, at the end of August, 1918, was sent to the Western Front.[11]

In any case, Husserl was clearly pleased when he could finally announce to Professor Natorp that by 1917 the young Dr. Heidegger had "freed himself from dogmatic Catholicism" and had "cut himself off – clearly, energetically, and yet tactfully – from the sure and easy career of a 'philosopher of the Catholic worldview.' " But the change had not come easily. In a letter to Professor Rudolf Otto, also of Marburg University, Husserl would recall – as if describing the conversion of a modern St. Augustine – the hard times Heidegger had gone through and the "difficult inner struggles" that had led him to "radical changes in [his] basic religious convictions." But the outcome, Husserl wrote, had been happy: Heidegger had "migrated over to the ground of Protestantism."[12]

No doubt aiding the troubled young scholar to chart his course through the crisis was his romantic encounter during the summer of

1916 with his Protestant student Thea Elfride Petri. An economics major, she had been following his philosophy courses since the fall of 1915. By the late summer of 1916 they were vacationing together at Reichenau; by Christmas they were engaged; and three months later – both of them in deep religious crisis – they were married.

THE RADICAL PHENOMENOLOGIST

On February 7, 1919, amid the social and political chaos of Germany's collapse and regeneration, Heidegger began his first lecture course after the war, and he hit the ground running. "Today we are not ready for *real* reform of the university," he announced to his students. "And just getting mature enough for the task will take a *whole generation*" (GA 56/57, 4).[13]

These were hard times for Germany, both economically and politically. Right-wing death squads had just murdered Rosa Luxemburg and Karl Liebknecht, and the bodies of other leftist victims were turning up by the scores. The reichsmark was falling in value and by November 1923 would exchange at 4.4 trillion to the dollar. The Versailles Peace Conference was busily paring away 10 percent of Germany's population, 13 percent of its national territory, and 100 percent of its colonies, as well as imposing (over and above Germany's war debt, which had set the national wealth back by 25 percent) a war reparations bill that was worth, in today's exchange rates, $220 billion.[14]

Renewing the nation in general and the university in particular, said Privatdozent Heidegger on the first day of class, would require a "return to the authentic origins of the spirit," and that meant not flights of rarified theory but a concrete immersion in the practical experiences of real life in order to get to the core of what it means to be authentically human. "Man, become essential!" he exclaimed, citing the German mystic Angelus Silesius (1624–77). And quoting a somewhat better known figure: "He who can grasp it, let him grasp it!" (5).

What was going on? Certainly the passionate intensity of Heidegger's lecture style announced that there was a new force to be reckoned with at Freiburg University. But something else was afoot. Just two weeks before, fresh from his "letter of resignation" to Father Krebs, Heidegger had been appointed Edmund Husserl's new teaching assistant, taking the place vacated by Edith Stein. And yet virtually everything the young lecturer had to say in his first course, "The Idea of Philosophy and the Problem of Worldview," seemed to undercut, or at least to reinterpret radically, Husserl's own positions on phenomenology.

Heidegger's main attack was on the primacy that Husserl attributed to theory over lived experience and to the pure transcendental ego over what Heidegger at this point called the "historical ego" and the "ego of the situation" (205–6) and that he would later term "Dasein." "We find ourselves at a methodological crossroads," he said on March 14, "where it will be decided whether philosophy shall live or die" (63). And everything depends on first getting clear what philosophy's true issue is. "What is messing up the real problematic is not just naturalism as some people think," he said with explicit reference to Husserl, "but the overall dominance and primacy of the *theoretical*" (87).

For Heidegger the theoretical orientation of the pure ego of Husserlian phenomenology sucks the blood out of the richly textured *Umwelt,* the firsthand world of lived experience (*Erleben*) in which one primarily exists and carries out practical tasks. In this firsthand world, things are not just "there," and they do not primarily have "value." They are not even just "things." They are "*the meaningful* – that's what's primary. . . . When you live in the firsthand world, everything comes at you loaded with meaning, all over the place and all the time, everything is enworlded, '*world happens.*' " (73). Here we do not know ourselves as egos who observe the entities lying around us. Rather (this was Heidegger's rereading of intentionality), we are the act of experientially "*living out unto something,*" which has "absolutely nothing to do with an *ego*" (68–9). And this primary level of experience is intensely personal: "Only in the resonances of one's own individual 'I' does a firsthand thing get experienced, only there does 'world happen,' and wherever and whenever world does happen for me, *I* am somehow entirely there" (73; for Heidegger's discussion of sociality, see 210).

But this richly textured firsthand world gets drained of all life, meaning, and history when it becomes infected by theory (89; *entlebt, ent-deutet, ent-geschichtlicht,* and *Infizierung*). The dynamic, personal, and historical "happening" of world (*Er-eignis*), which is intimately bound up with the living and appropriating of one's own life, gets flattened out to a "process" (*Vor-gang*) of objective knowledge. Ultimately the human being is reduced to a level of experience that is "absolutely without world, world-alien, a sphere where the breath is knocked out of you and you cannot live" (75, 78, 112; cf. 205). "In theoretical acts I leave my lived experience behind. To be sure, something of the experiential still comes along with me – but no one knows what to do with it, so they invent the convenient label of the 'irrational' for it" (117).

To preserve the firsthand world of lived experience, including the world of religious experience (207, 211), from the ravages of theorizing, Heidegger radically reinterpreted the "principle of all principles" that Husserl had laid down for phenomenology in Section 24 of his *Ideas for a Pure Phenomenology and a Phenomenological Philosophy* (1913). If, according to the Master, firsthand intuition is the starting point of phenomenology, that intuition ("even though Husserl doesn't say this in so many words") is not some theoretical comportment but an "understanding intuition, a *hermeneutic intuition*," from which theory is but a precipitate (117). This hermeneutic intuition, which already understands the world prior to any theorizing and which is the basis of all the rigor that phenomenology claims for itself, is

> the aboriginal intention of authentic living, the aboriginal comportment of lived experience and of life as such, the absolute *sympathy with life* that is identical with lived experience. Prior to anything else – that is, if we take this path away from theory and more and more free ourselves from theory – we *see* this basic comportment all the time, we have an orientation *to* it. This basic comportment is absolute, but only if we live in it directly. And no conceptual system, no matter how elaborately constructed, can reach it. Only phenomenological living, as it continually intensifies itself, can get to it. (110)

But this *Urhabitus*, or basic way-of-being, that Heidegger calls phenomenological living "cannot be acquired from one day to the next, like putting on a uniform." It is not a method and has nothing to do with adopting "standpoints" (that, he says, would be the "mortal sin" that ruins everything). Rather, phenomenology, like lived experience, "can authenticate and prove itself only through itself," that is, only in the *living* of it (110).

This was pretty gutsy stuff, but it did not promise a faithful adherence to traditional Husserlian phenomenology. In any case, Heidegger not only continued the attack during the following semester in his course "Phenomenology and the Transcendental Philosophy of Value" (May 9 to July 25, 1919), but even let Husserl in on what he was saying. In the middle of June in one of the Saturday morning discussions that Husserl used to hold at his Freiburg home with his close associates, Heidegger told Husserl publicly that the much vaunted pure ego of Husserlian phenomenology was "derived" from the historical ego by the "repression" of historicity and concretion, and that the pure ego was limited to the role of being the "subject" only of "theoretical acts."[15]

A dozen years later Husserl would say that in those early years he thought Heidegger actually did agree with him (Husserl used to tell Heidegger, "You and I are phenomenology") and that the only problem was that he did not understand Heidegger's language.[16] But clearly the game was up from the beginning, even though it took Husserl ten more years (until the summer of 1929) to realize how much Heidegger had gone off on his own.

Which way had Heidegger taken? From his doctoral studies onward, Heidegger had been captivated not by Husserl's *Ideas* with its neo-Kantian turn toward transcendental subjectivity, and even less so by his Cartesian turn in the twenties, but rather by the Master's earlier, ground-breaking work, *Logical Investigations* (1900–1). There Husserl had advanced Franz Brentano's notion of intentionality – the idea that all mental acts are characterized by directedness to a meant object – and solidified it into the fundamental problematic of the *phenomenological correlation* between intentional acts and the mental objects they reveal. And Husserl did so specifically with reference to acts of logical-theoretical intentionality and their logical-theoretical correlates. Heidegger, however, took at least seven important steps both behind and beneath Husserl's early work and its theoretical interests.

First, Heidegger went back to the ancient Greeks and came to see the intentional relatedness-to-the-meant of Husserlian phenomenology as only an imperfect carry-over of what Aristotle had already worked out in terms of human acts of "disclosing" entities (Greek: *aletheuein*). Thus, "What phenomenological investigations had recently discovered to be the underlying posture of thinking turns out to be the basic trait of Greek thinking, indeed of philosophy as such" (SD 87; TB 79).

Moreover, whereas Husserl's interests in intentionality remained focused primarily on theoretical comportment, Heidegger began probing the *pre*theoretical intentional acts operative in such everyday lived experience as work, talk, self-concern, and faith. He argued that we first encounter things within historical contexts of meaningfulness that first of all are bound up with our pretheoretical concerns and practical interests. And there a more primordial "hermeneutic" *logos* is at work: we know the present objects of practical concern by reaching "beyond" them to antecedently grasped purposes and goals. Heidegger claimed to find clues for this firsthand "hermeneutic" understanding in Aristotle's discussions of self-referential acting (*praxis–phronesis*) and creative making (*poiesis–techne*) in *Nicomachean Ethics* VI.[17]

Second, Husserl had already argued in *Logical Investigations* VI, 6, that intentionality or disclosive comportment reveals not just entities but also and primarily the *essence* of entities, their "being." Following Husserl, Heidegger interpreted this "being" (*Sein* or *Seiendheit*) no longer objectivistically as the whatness and thatness of entities, the way much of traditional metaphysics had done. Rather, he read it phenomenologically, that is, in correlation with acts of disclosive intentionality, as referring to the howness (*das Wie*) or hadness (*die Habe*) of entities: the way in which, at any given moment, they are disclosed to and "had" in the human acts that coperform that disclosure. But since practical activity entails prior anticipation of a goal or purpose, the primary modes of the being of an entity are not the presential modes of "being there" before a static subject but rather the future-oriented modes of "being for" the purposes posited by self-exceeding human existence.

Third, Heidegger's intense rereading of Greek philosophy in general and of *Metaphysics* IX 10 in particular led him to the major if implicit tenet of Greek thinking, namely, that entities, to the degree that they are "natural" (*physei on*), are intrinsically self-presentative, that is, accessible and intelligible – *on hos alethes* – even if that accessibility and intelligibility is always shot through with finitude.

Fourth, Heidegger conjugated this "aletheiological" insight of the Greeks with the phenomenological insights he had learned from

Husserl and Aristotle: entities are self-disclosive (*alethes*) only insofar as they are in *correlation* with the various modes of the human co-performance of disclosure (*aletheuein*), primarily the practical ones. Thus, the phenomenological correlation became the "aletheiological" correlation, and Heidegger found it already named in Heraclitus as *logos* (Frag. 50) and *physis* (Frag. 123), and in Parmenides as the "togetherness" (*to auto*) of thinking and being (Frag. 3). This "event" of intelligibility in its facticity became, for Heidegger, the "thing itself" that philosophy had to interrogate. It was, he thought, the ultimate *a priori*, the "first" of everything about the human world, and thus (for those with the sensitivity for it) the most obvious fact of all.[18] Yet it is generally overlooked, not primarily because of some human defect but above all because it "prefers to hide" (Heraclitus, Frag. 53) in the sense of being ultimately unfathomable. In any case, the "happening" of this correlation – the always-already operative empowering of the essential togetherness of disclosive human comportment and of entities *qua* accessible – is what Heidegger, both tentatively in his early courses and boldly in his final writings, called *Ereignis*.

Fifth, insofar as intentionality reveals the being of entities, phenomenology became for Heidegger only a method for probing more deeply metaphysics' unresolved question about the essence or meaning of being, that is, about the analogical unity underlying all the various modes of the being of entities. However, given his phenomenologizing reading of the tradition, Heidegger now reshaped the question about the meaning of being into the question about the essence of the phenomenological correlation, that is, about the analogical unity underlying all possible ways in which entities can present themselves and thus be humanly appropriated. If the human "world" is at bottom a matter of the disclosive correlation, or *aletheia*, then how come *aletheia*? What is the essence, provenance, and "cause" of the disclosure of entities that happens in and with human nature?

Sixth, in working out the essence of this phenomenological–aletheiological correlation from the side of human nature and its pretheoretical "hermeneutic" understanding of things (as he mainly did in the twenties), Heidegger burrowed beneath the Husserlian structures of pure intentional consciousness with its alleged immanence, self-transparency, and apodictic self-givenness and spelled out the more primordial elements of fallenness and finitude, mortality and temporality, which he saw as the *a priori* or "fated" essence of human existence and its hermeneutic understandings.

Seventh, in working out the question about the essence of the disclosive correlation with emphasis on how it happens at all (the question of *Ereignis,* which he took up explicitly in the thirties), Heidegger came to see that the *a priori,* factical, and inexplicable *givenness* of the correlation – its "fatedness," back behind which one cannot go – was itself bound up with the *a priori,* factical, and inexplicable finitude that is the essence of human existence. This state of affairs – the unfathomable fatedness of the phenomenological correlation in conjunction with the inexplicable fatedness of human finitude – he called the *lethe* at the heart of *aletheia.*

Heidegger gestated these issues for a period of seven years, first at Freiburg, where he continued as a *Privatdozent* and as Husserl's assistant from 1919 until 1923, and thereafter at Marburg, where he was appointed associate professor in the fall of 1923 and taught until the summer of 1928. Between 1916 and 1927 Heidegger published absolutely nothing, and in the eyes of some colleagues this stood in the way of his being appointed to the chair of philosophy that Nicolai Hartmann was about to vacate at Marburg University in the fall of 1925.

But Edmund Husserl came to Heidegger's defense. In a letter to Professor Jaensch of Marburg's Philosophy Faculty (June 30, 1925), he said that "in the new generation [Heidegger] is the only philosophical personality of such creative, resourceful originality." "In my eyes," Husserl wrote, "Heidegger is without a doubt the most significant of those on their way up" and is "predestined to be a philosopher of great style. . . . He has kept silent for years so as to be able to publish only what is completely mature and definitively compelling. His publications that are soon coming out will show just how much he has to say and how original it is."[19]

Despite Husserl's rousing recommendation, Heidegger failed to get the appointment. Nonetheless, his reputation as a radical phenomenologist continued to grow. In late April 1927 Heidegger's question about the essence of the phenomenological–aletheiological correlation came to birth – a bit prematurely, as he himself later admitted – in his most famous work, *Being and Time.* The fame of that book won him the appointment first to Hartmann's chair at Marburg in the fall of 1927 and then, in the fall of 1928, to the position he most coveted: Husserl's successor in the chair of philosophy at Freiburg University.

It would take two years before Husserl got around to reading *Being and Time,* and only then would he realize how much Heidegger's path had split off from his own. But even before that, personal tensions were building up between these two very different phenomenologists, now bottled up in the same provincial town of Freiburg, the one in retirement, the other at the height of his career. Husserl began to suspect his protégé; Heidegger began to avoid his old master; and, to make matters worse, their wives no longer seemed to get along.

But they kept up appearances. April 8, 1929, marked Husserl's seventieth birthday, and Heidegger, in the name of Husserl's closest collaborators, publicly presented him with a *Festschrift,* a collection of essays in his honor. But the brief speech Heidegger gave on this festive occasion was fraught with ambiguity and gave strong hints that Heidegger thought he was leaving the Master in the dust. He said in part:

> The works we are presenting to you are only a testimony that we *want* to follow your guidance, not a proof that we have succeeded in doing so. For is it not the case that your research has, in the first instance, created an entirely new space for philosophical inquiry, one with new demands, transformed assessments, a fresh regard for the hidden powers of the great tradition of Western philosophy? Yes, precisely that![20]

Heidegger's message was clear, and Husserl finally got it. Two months later, having at long last read through *Being and Time* while on vacation at Lago Como (July–August 1929), Husserl took a pencil and scrawled on the title page, no doubt sadly, "Amicus Plato, magis amica veritas": "Plato is my friend, but truth a greater friend."[21]

THE POLITICAL ACTIVIST

Four years later Germany was in revolution, and not for the better. On January 30, 1933, President Paul von Hindenburg had appointed Adolf Hitler chancellor of the German Republic. A month later, following the burning of the Reichstag building on February 27, 1933, Hitler got the Parliament to suspend the German Constitution and replace it with a permanent state of emergency, under which fundamental civil liberties such as freedom of speech and assembly and privacy of the mails were canceled. Within a week of that (March 7) Hitler arrested all eighty-one of the Communist deputies who had been duly elected to the Reichstag the day before and confined them to the newly opened concentration camps. On March 23, the Reichstag passed the Enabling Act, giving Hitler plenipotentiary lawmaking powers, and with that the Nazi dictatorship was born. This was followed on April 5 by the Nazi "cleansing laws" aimed at excluding Jews and Marxists from the civil service.

Then on Monday, May 1 – one day before Hitler would arrest hundreds of labor leaders and throw them into concentration camps – Martin Heidegger, the newly elected rector of Freiburg University, very ostentatiously joined the National Socialist German Workers Party.

That same day, Professor Emeritus Edmund Husserl and his wife Malvine, who were vacationing near Locarno, received a letter from Mrs. Elfride Heidegger, dated April 28. These were hard times for Jews. Because of the "cleansing laws," Husserl, who was born a Jew and converted to Protestantism in his youth, had been forced to resign from Freiburg University two weeks earlier. In these difficult times, Mrs. Heidegger wrote, she and her husband wanted to assure the Husserls of their continuing gratitude for all the help in the past.

Husserl was close to rage. On May 4 he wrote his old friend Professor Dietrick Mahnke of Marburg University to tell him what he felt. Many of his students and colleagues over the years had been a consolation to him, he wrote, but

> with others I have had to suffer the worst experiences – the final case (and it hit me the hardest) being Heidegger: hardest, because I had come to place a trust (which I can no longer understand) not just in his talent but in his character as well. The loveliest conclusion to this supposed bosom friendship between philosophers was his publicly enacted entrance into the Nazi party (very theatrical, indeed) on May 1. Before that there was his self-initiated break in relations with me (in fact, soon after his appointment [at Freiburg]) and, over the last few years, his anti-Semitism, which he came to express with increasing vigor – even against the coterie of his most enthusiastic students, as well as around the department. That was a hard thing to get over.[22]

Heidegger had been supporting the Nazi party at the ballot box at least since the spring of 1932, and in 1936 he told his former student Karl Löwith that the basis for his political engagement with the

Nazis was his very central philosophical concept of "historicity" (*Geschichtlichkeit*).[23] Although it seems he did not accept the party ideology in its entirety, Heidegger strongly supported its anticommunism. He saw Nazism as a force for crushing Marxism and as a vehicle for realizing the ultraconservative vision of one of his favorite political theorists, Friedrich Naumann (1860–1919), that of a strong nationalism combined with a militantly anticommunist "socialism" under the guidance of a charismatic leader. The goal was to fashion a middle European empire that preserved the spirit and traditions of Wilhelmian Germany against what Heidegger saw as the onslaught of global technology.[24]

From April 1933 through April 1934, Heidegger served as the heavy-handed and controversial rector of Freiburg University, and in the early months of his tenure he not only lent his name and efforts to the Nazi revolution but also became an outspoken propagandist for Hitler's foreign and domestic policies. During this period he rushed to establish the *Führer* principle at the university (October 1, 1933), thereby making himself the virtual dictator of the campus. He applied the Nazi "cleansing laws" to the Freiburg University student body (November 3) and thus ended financial aid for "Jewish or Marxist students" or anyone who fit the description of a "non-Aryan" in Nazi law. On the same day he told the assembled students that "the *Führer* himself and he alone *is* German reality and its law, today and for the future," and a week later (November 10) he took to the radio to urge ratification of Hitler's withdrawal of Germany from the League of Nations.[25]

In private he engaged in the more despicable work of a Nazi informer. On September 29, 1933, he secretly denounced a colleague, Professor Hermann Staudinger, for having been a pacifist during the Great War, and when the Gestapo confirmed his tip, Heidegger quietly urged the government to fire the man without a pension (February 10, 1934). He also wrote a secret and damning letter to the head of a Nazi organization against a former friend and colleague, Professor Eduard Baumgarten (who, he said, had "very actively frequented the Jew Fränkel"), and thereby helped get the man suspended from a teaching job (December 16, 1933). As late as 1938 he prevented the young Max Müller from getting an academic position by informing the administration of Freiburg University that Müller was "unfavorably disposed" to the Nazi regime.[26]

And always just under the surface, there was the odor of anti-Semitism. On October 2, 1929, some three years before Hitler came to power, he wrote a letter to the Society for the Support of German Science recommending his assistant, the same Eduard Baumgarten (when they still were friends), and he offered his reasons why the Society should give financial aid to this young scholar who was not a Jew:

> I would like to say more clearly in this letter what I could only hint at indirectly in my report: It is nothing less than the urgent consideration that we are faced with a choice, either to provide our *German* intellectual life once more with real talents and educators rooted in our own soil or to hand over that intellectual life once and for all to the growing influence of the Jews [*Verjudung*] in the broad and narrow sense. We will find our way back only if we are able, without baiting and without useless arguments, to assist budding talents in their development.
>
> Regarding this important objective I would be especially grateful if Mr. Baumgarten, whom I have selected to be my assistant, could be helped with a grant.[27]

And on July 1, 1933, in what would seem to be a typical expression of his mind, Heidegger announced his belief that "there is a dangerous international alliance of Jews" – this to Karl Jaspers, whose wife was Jewish.[28] Moreover, from 1934 on, Heidegger declined to direct the doctoral dissertations of Jewish students. Fifty years later Heidegger's close friend Heinrich Petzet wrote (as if no further explanation were needed) that Heidegger felt ill at ease with big-city life,

> and this was especially true of that mundane spirit of Jewish circles, which is at home in the metropolitan centers of the West. But this attitude of his should not be misunderstood as anti-Semitism, although it has often been interpreted that way.[29]

After Heidegger resigned the rectorate in April 1934, he continued to support the Nazi regime, though more quietly and perhaps more critically. In the spring and summer of 1936 he still thought that Hitler and National Socialism were the right path for Germany (although he did criticize some forms of Nazi bureaucracy), and he spoke positively of the achievements of both Mussolini and Hitler in the battle against nihilism (GA 42 40–1). And to judge from his public lectures, he apparently supported Hitler's war aims at least until the inevitability of an Allied victory became obvious.[30]

After the war the State Committee for Political Purification declared Heidegger a Nazi "fellow traveler" and prohibited him from teaching. But Freiburg University came to his defense, and in 1951 he was granted emeritus status and was allowed to teach and lecture again at the university.

In posthumously published texts – some prepared in 1946 for the denazification committee, one for eventual publication in *Der Spiegel*[31] – Heidegger tried to explain what he called his political "error." Otherwise he maintained a hermetic silence about the motives, responsibility, and particular forms of his involvement with National Socialism. But in 1953 he published the text of a 1935 lecture course in which he had attempted briefly to distinguish between, on the one hand, vulgar Nazism and, on the other, the "inner truth and greatness" of the Nazi movement, namely, its alleged effort to mediate between human beings and global technology. However, the paragraph was so shot through with ambiguity and even subterfuge that Heidegger himself tried, unsuccessfully, to get Yale University Press to drop it from the eventual English translation, *Introduction to Metaphysics*.[32]

In general, Heidegger put the blame (if we can call it that) for the tragedy of World War II and the Holocaust not on any individuals or political movement but on an impersonal planetary force, the Will to Power, which he thought lay beyond anyone's responsibility or control. This force had brought about a new and unfortunate form of human nature: the "worker" taken as technology-oriented, world-dominating subjectivity. Heidegger frequently affirmed that in the thirties and forties Ernst Jünger's book *Der Arbeiter* (The worker, 1932) had opened his eyes to a suprametaphysical vision of the true meaning of the modern social, political, and economic order: "From the standpoint of the reality of the Will to Power I saw even then [in 1939–40] what *is*," Heidegger wrote.[33] And he tried to capture that vision in a handwritten text, dating from the late thirties, which has recently been found among his papers at the Marbach Archives:

> The "form of the worker" is not *any one man* – not even primarily a type of man. Rather, as a type, it is only a form of *subjectivity*, whose essence consists in the *certitude* of calculation. As the Will to Power it is one form, the *last* form, of *the "truth" of beings as a whole*. Therefore, in essence it is *techne*, but a deeper essence than Jünger sees: he keeps turning around in a superficial circle but does not sense the whirlwind.

> The "worker" is the unconditional *menial* who has been expanded into the limitless *master,* i.e., the modern "free" enactor of *techne,* the latter taken as the planning, cultivating, calculating and finally the securing of entities as a whole (including human beings) within its own power to fabricate – a complete actualization of what lies at hand, but an actualization of its essence. The "worker" and the limitless subjectivity of such complete anthropomorphism consists in this: Being happens as power-to-make.[34]

It was this power to dominate everything that Heidegger, in his role as political philosopher, saw as infecting all modern political forms without differentiation. "Today everything stands within this reality, whether it is called communism or fascism or world democracy."[35]

To put it minimally, Heidegger was never a very strong supporter of democracy, whether before or after the war. He excoriated the "democratized decay" of Germany's postwar institutions and declared himself unconvinced that democracy was the best political system for the modern age.[36] He used to like to cite Homer (*Iliad* II 204): "The rule of the many is not good; let there be one ruler, one king," and at least for a while, whether he was finally happy with it or not, he apparently got his wish.

WHAT WILL HEIDEGGER HAVE BEEN?

The period after the war saw the spread of Heidegger's writings throughout the intellectual world in an explosion of interest that crossed lines of language, culture, and academic disciplines. By the time of his death on May 26, 1976, at the age of 86, his books and essays had been translated into all Western languages, as well as into Chinese, Japanese, and Arabic, and the voluminous *Collected Edition* of his works was already under way.

Yet throughout all those works Heidegger claimed to be the thinker of "one thought only," which took many forms of expression: What is the provenance of disclosure? What is the essence of "world"? What is the "cause" of the correlation that lets human beings have meaningful access to entities? In a word, How come *aletheia*?

Over the half-century of his philosophical career Heidegger largely succeeded in establishing the structures of human existence that are essential to this event-of-intelligibility, and he worked out as well the general lines of its historical forms and epochs. However, he insisted that the question about the originating source of this disclosive correlation – the "how-and-why-it-comes-about" – was finally unanswerable. We cannot say why, whence, or to what end there is disclosure (i.e., why *es gibt Sein*) without already presuming the fact of disclosure and thereby moving in a circle. Thus, the essence of *aletheia* is *lethe;* the provenance of disclosure is unfathomable.

Unfathomable, yes, but something can be said about this correlation insofar as it always affects human existence and remains its chief, if largely unheeded, concern. First, Heidegger calls the "origin" of disclosure *das Er-eignis,* which we can translate as "em-propriation": the event that brings disclosive comportment and disclosible entities together into their asymptotic "own" (*proprius, eigen*), that is, into the openness of disclosure.

Second, he speaks of the "origin" of disclosure as *difference* (Greek *diaphora,* German *Unterschied*), that is, that which is responsible for the fact that human existence and the human world are always nonimmediate and not self-coincident – right down to the non-self-coincidence that is dramatically registered in human mortality and that condemns us to ineluctably finite meanings derived from endless mediation.

Third, regarding the "origin" of disclosure, Heidegger insists on the simple fact that *es gibt Sein,* "disclosure just happens to happen." In this context there seems to be no real room for history in the usual sense. Instead, Heidegger calls the *a priori* happening of the correlation *das Geschick des Seins,* disclosure's inherent "fatedness" or givenness to human nature, on the basis of which alone entities are accessible. And when he considered this *a priori* givenness in its various epochal forms, he called it *die Geschichte des Seins,* the "dispensations" of disclosure.[37]

Fourth, the facticity of human existence is its condition of being ineluctably bound up with this *a priori* givenness of disclosure. Facticity is the human fate of being "thrown" into the endless, finite mediation necessitated by difference, without being able to know why this endless mediation is necessary.

And fifth, because disclosure is always-already operative everywhere in the human world, all entities are, in principle, open to human appropriation. That is, everything is endlessly accessible, except the *fact that* everything is endlessly accessible. This now achieved state of affairs, which is the gift of the intrinsic unfathomability of the aletheiological correlation, Heidegger termed "nihilism," and he suggested that human beings be not less nihilistic but more.[38]

Heidegger thought that the archaic Greek poets and thinkers implicitly understood the fact of this endless but finite accessibility of things, and he set it against all theological traditions that would root the comprehensibility of entities in the *full* comprehensibility of God. Yes, "the belonging-together of subject and object [arises] from something that first imports their nature to both . . . and hence is prior to the realm of their reciprocity." But no, this "wellspring" of the aletheiological reciprocity "does not want . . . to be called by the name Zeus" (Heraclitus, Frag. 32); that is,

> it does *not* properly admit of being named Zeus, and of being thereby degraded to the level of existing as one entity present among others – even if the "among" has the character of "above all other present entities."[39]

Heidegger thought that the "hiddenness" or "oblivion" of the disclosive correlation led to its being increasingly overlooked throughout Western history, to the point that in our own day it has become completely forgotten and counts for nothing. He took it as his mission to reawaken a new sense of the unfathomable mystery that, whether attended to or not, yawns like an abyss under the tidy little world of bourgeois certitude – all of this in the interests of helping to bring about a revolutionary transformation of human nature.

And somehow, he said, he came to see Hitler's National Socialism as a movement that might help with that reawakening, at least in Germany.

The degree to which Heidegger's political convictions and actions were a faithful reflection of his philosophy – and vice versa – is a matter of much debate today. Many of his most devoted followers believe that his intellectual work is in no way significantly related to, much less contaminated by, his support for Nazism, even though Heidegger himself rooted that support in his own very central notion of historicity. Other Heideggerians claim that "metaphysics made him do it"; that is, they explain his political "error" as the result of his being victimized by the intrinsic hiddenness of disclosure, which, in the form of "errancy" (*Irre*), inevitably tends to lead people astray, almost like a secularized form of Original Sin. Still others claim that Heidegger got trapped for a period of time in the nightmare of metaphysical "humanism" from which he was struggling to awake – with the corollaries, first, that Heidegger's political blunder is in fact very concrete proof of everything he had to say about the dark side of the forgottenness of disclosure and, second, that the alleged "overcoming" of metaphysics in his later thought is a guarantee that such an error would not happen again.

Others, however, argue that the reasons for Heidegger's support of Hitler and the Nazis were much more simple – and much more base – than these rather high-flown explanations would have it, and that in order to understand his political motives and despicable actions during the Third Reich one must start by investigating the hard times he lived through and specifically the concrete economic and social factors that conditioned his decisions.

If Heidegger himself insisted that his engagement with Nazism came from the very essence of his philosophy, perhaps his followers should believe him on this point. If Heidegger himself felt free, even for a while, to put not just his person but also the major categories of his philosophical thought at the service of Nazi foreign and domestic policy, then one would do well to ask whether those categories are really as free of economic, social, and political interests as most Heideggerians contend.[40]

The point is not to condemn a man for his past but to learn something about oneself in the present, not to dismiss Heidegger's philosophical work out of hand but likewise not to join the Perpetual Adoration Societies that currently thrive among the Heideggerian faithful in Europe and America. The task, for those who care to take something from Heidegger, is to learn how to read him critically, both his life and his works, not to swallow his philosophy whole but to sift it for what is still of value and what not.

That would entail asking whether Heidegger's dogged pursuit of the *essence* of disclosure did not blind him to crucial problems bound up with *specific modes* of disclosure, particularly in the economic, social, and political orders. It would entail asking whether one risks perpetuating that same blindness to the very degree that one remains faithful to Heidegger's metaontological line of questioning. Maybe it is not wise – whether the times are hard or easy – to be the thinker of "one thought only."

As Derrida puts it, the task of critically rereading Heidegger requires "showing – without limit, if possible – the profound attachment of Heidegger's texts (both writings and deeds) to the possibility and actuality of all nazisms,"[41] even, one might suggest, those that pass themselves off in the guise of furthering "Western democracy," preserving the "American way of life," or instituting various kinds of "World Order," whether old or new.

Heidegger has been dead for some years now, and it is still not entirely clear who he was or what he meant to say. His works lie there, some seventy-odd volumes of them, and it is not entirely clear what they mean either. The hermeneutic principle that Heidegger himself suggested for reading texts, be they books or lives, was: "Possibility is higher than actuality." The way we read his life and his works in our own hard times can help determine, in some far-distant future, who and what Heidegger will have been.

NOTES

1 Hugo Ott, *Martin Heidegger: Unterwegs zu seiner Biographie* (Frankfurt: Campus, 1988), p. 108.
2 Ibid., pp. 104–5. For anecdotal accounts of the effects of these gas attacks on U.S. soldiers see Elaine George Collins, ed., *If Not for War* (Redwood City, Calif.: Collins, 1989), pp. 86–7, 123–4.
3 Dorion Cairns, *Conversations with Husserl and Fink* (The Hague: Nijhoff, 1976), p. 9.
4 Ott, *Martin Heidegger,* 106–7.
5 On Heidegger's education and career up to July 1915 see Thomas Sheehan, "Heidegger's *Lehrjahre,*" in *The Collegium Phaenomenologicum: The First Ten Years,* ed. John Sallis, Giuseppina Moneta, and Jacques Taminiaux (Amsterdam: Kluwer, 1988): 77–137.
6 Victor Farias, *Heidegger et le nazisme,* trans. Myriam Benarroch and Jean-Baptiste Grasset (Lagrasse: Verdier, 1987), pp. 51–2. Also see Ott, *Martin Heidegger,* pp. 63–4.
7 The entire letter is translated in Sheehan, "Heidegger's *Lehrjahre,*" p. 113.
8 Ibid., pp 114, 137 n. 178, and 80–1.
9 See Thomas Sheehan, ed., *Heidegger, the Man and the Thinker* (Chicago: Precedent, 1981), pp. 7–8.
10 For the quotations in this paragraph see Thomas Sheehan, "Heidegger's 'Introduction to the Phenomenology of Religion,' 1920–1921," *Personalist* 60 (July 1979): 312–24, p. 314, and Ott, *Martin Heidegger,* pp. 113, 110.

11 According to written statements he made in 1915 and 1928, Heidegger had already been in the army three times before, once as a volunteer (August 2–10, 1914) and twice as a draftee (October 2–10, 1914, and August 18 to October 16, 1915), and each time had been dismissed for reasons of health. See the documentation in Sheehan, "Heidegger's *Lehrjahre*," pp. 119, n. 2, 121 n. 13.

12 See Sheehan, "Heidegger's 'Introduction to the Phenomenology of Religion,' " pp. 313–14.

13 Unless otherwise noted, in this section all page references within parentheses are to GA 56/57.

14 V. R. Berghahn, *Modern Germany: Society, Economy and Politics in the Twentieth Century*, 2d ed. (Cambridge: Cambridge University Press, 1987), p. 72.

15 See Gerda Walther's letter to Alexander Pfänder, June 20, 1919, Husserl Archives, Leuven, cited in "Introductory Note" to Martin Heidegger, "The Understanding of Time in Phenomenology and in the Thinking of the Being-Question," *Southwestern Journal of Philosophy*, 10 (Summer 1979): 199–200, p. 199.

16 Cairns, *Conversations with Husserl and Fink*, pp. 9, 106.

17 Heidegger treated the issue at length in the first half of his course "Interpretation platonischer Dialoge (Sophistes, Philebus)," winter semester, 1924–5, and summarized it in his lecture "Dasein und Wahrsein nach Aristoteles: Interpretationen von Buch VI der Nikomachischen Ethik" delivered at Cologne University on December 2, 1924, at the invitation of Max Scheler.

18 See *Physics* B 1 193 b 3–6, and *Metaphysics* 1006 a 5–11. See also the quote from GA 56/57 110, cited above on page 79, where Heidegger says that "we *see* this basic comportment all the time. . . ."

19 Husserl's handwritten letter from Freiburg, dated Tuesday, June 30, 1925, in response to Jaensch's letter of June 24, was intended to answer the question Professor Wedekind had raised at the Marburg Philosophy Faculty meeting of June 24 about how little Heidegger had published. Husserl's letter and other documentation relating to Heidegger's application for Hartmann's chair are found in the Staatsarchiv Marburg, "Akten der Philipps-Universität Marburg: Philosophie und Pädagogik, 1922–1943" (Bestand 307d: Acc. 1966/10, No. 28) and "Akten Universität Marburg betreffend die Professoren der philosophischen Fakultät. . ." (305a: Acc. 1950/9, No. 646). See Thomas Sheehan, " 'Time and Being,' 1925–1927," in *Thinking about Being: Aspects of Heidegger's Thought*, ed. Robert W. Shahan and J. N. Mohanty (Norman: University of Oklahoma Press, 1984), pp. 180–3, and Theodore Kisiel, "Why the First Draft

of *Being and Time* Was Never Published," *Journal of the British Society for Phenomenology,* 20 (January 1989): 3–22, p. 31.

20 Martin Heidegger, "Edmund Husserl zum 70. Geburtstag," *Akademische Mitteilung: Organ für die gesamten Interessen der Studentschaft an der Albert-Ludwigs-Universität in Freiburg/Br.,* 4. Folge, 9. Semester, No. 4 (May 14, 1929): 46–7, p. 46.

21 Cf. *Nichomachean Ethics,* A 6 1096 a 14–17.

22 The German text appears in Bernd Martin, ed., *Martin Heidegger und das "Dritte Reich": Ein Kompendium* (Darmstadt: Wissenschaftliche Buchgesellschaft, 1989), p. 149.

23 Karl Löwith, *Mein Leben in Deutschland vor und nach 1933* (Stuttgart: Metzler, 1986), p. 57.

24 See Thomas Sheehan, "Heidegger and the Nazis," *New York Review of Books,* June 16, 1988, p. 44.

25 These texts are printed in Guido Schneeberger, *Nachlese zur Heidegger: Dokumente zu seinem Leben und Denken* (Bern: Suhr, 1962), pp. 136–7, 144–6.

26 Bernd Martin and Gottfried Schramm, "Ein Gespräch mit Max Müller," *Freiburger Universitätsblätter,* 92 (June 1986): 13–31, pp. 27–9.

27 The German text appears in Ulrich Sieg, "Die Verjudung des deutschen Geistes," *Die Zeit,* "Feuilleton," December 22, 1989, p. 50. The term "*Verjudung*" became a Nazi term of contempt ("Jewification") in the thirties.

28 Karl Jaspers, *Philosophische Biographie,* expanded ed. (Munich: Piper, 1977), p. 101; also his *Notizien zu Martin Heidegger,* ed. Hans Saner (Munich: Piper, 1978), pp. 15, 257, 284.

29 Heinrich Wiegand Petzet, *Auf einen Stern zugehen* (Frankfurt: Societät, 1983), p. 40.

30 Heidegger's criticism of the Nazi bureaucracy is mentioned in Löwith, *Mein Leben in Deutschland,* p. 57. Heidegger's positive statement about Hitler and Mussolini was intentionally omitted from the first German edition of his 1936 course *Schellings Abhandlung "Ueber das Wesen der menschlichen Freiheit" (1809)* (Tübingen: Niemeyer, 1971), and therefore is absent from the English translation by Joan Stambaugh, *Schelling's Treatise on the Essence of Human Freedom* (Athens: Ohio University Press, 1985). It has been restored in the *Gesamtausgabe* edition of the work, GA 42 40–1.

31 The *Der Spiegel* interview appears in English translation by William J. Richardson: "Only a God Can Save Us," in Sheehan, ed., *Heidegger, the Man and the Thinker,* pp. 45–67.

32 The disputed text appears in Martin Heidegger, *Einführung in die*

Metaphysik (originally published in 1953), republished in 1983 as GA 40 208; English translation by Ralph Manheim, *Introduction to Metaphysics* (New Haven, Conn.: Yale University Press, 1959), p. 199; it is discussed in Sheehan, "Heidegger and the Nazis," pp. 42–3. Regarding the Yale incident see Elisabeth Young-Bruehl, *Hannah Arendt: For Love of the World* (New Haven, Conn.: Yale University Press, 1982), p. 443.

33 Martin Heidegger, "The Rectorate 1933/34: Facts and Thoughts," trans. Karsten Harries, *Review of Metaphysics,* 38 (March 1985): 481–502, p. 485.

34 The transcribed text, with a photograph of the original, appears in Heimo Schwilk, ed., *Ernst Jünger: Leben und Werk in Bildern und Texten* (Stuttgart: Klett Cotta, 1988), p. 131.

35 Heidegger, "The Rectorate," p. 485.

36 Petzet, *Auf einen Stern zugehen,* p. 82; cf. p. 232.

37 The German verb *schicken,* as transitive, means to send or dispatch and, as reflexive, to happen. From the transitive sense comes the noun *das Geschick:* destiny, fate, fortune. From the reflexive sense comes the noun *die Geschichte:* event or happening; history; story. The Latin deponent verb *fari* means to say or speak something to someone. The past participle *fatum,* taken as a substantive, means that which is "spoken" (destined, fated) to someone.

38 See Thomas Sheehan, "Nihilism, Facticity, and the Economized *Lethe,*" in *Heidegger: A Centenary Appraisal,* ed. Edward S. Casey, Samuel IJsseling, Thomas Sheehan, and Jacques Taminiaux (Pittsburgh, Pa.: Duquesne University, Simon Silverman Center, 1990), pp. 28–61.

39 Martin Heidegger, *Early Greek Thinking,* trans. David Krell and Frank Capuzzi (New York: Harper & Row, 1984): finite comprehensibility, pp. 107–8; "belonging-together," p. 103; "wellspring," p. 102; Zeus, p. 74.

40 See, e.g., the text from November 11, 1933, in Schneeberger, *Nachlese,* pp. 148–50.

41 Jacques Derrida, "Heidegger, l'enfer des philosophes," *Nouvel Observateur,* November 6–12, 1987, p. 173.

FREDERICK A. OLAFSON

3 The unity of Heidegger's thought

In 1975, just a year before his death, the publication of a complete edition of Heidegger's works began. This edition will eventually comprise not only all of his previously published writings, but also a considerable number of unpublished manuscripts from various periods in his philosophical career and the lecture series that he presented at the universities of Marburg and Freiburg in the twenties, thirties, and forties. Since the first volume of this edition appeared, a considerable number of these lecture series have been published, and they constitute a resource of the first importance for anyone interested in the evolution of Heidegger's thought. This is especially the case for those lecture series that fall into the period in which Heidegger was working out the position he presented in *Being and Time* (1927), as well as those presented in the years immediately thereafter. In a recent study of Heidegger's thought I draw extensively on these new publications, and it is the main thesis of that study that I present in this essay.[1]

As my title indicates, that thesis has to do with the unity of Heidegger's thought; by this I mean the unity of his thought through the "turning," or *Kehre*, that is usually supposed to separate the thought of the later period from that of *Being and Time*. It has become common practice among interpreters of Heidegger's philosophy to base themselves mainly on the writings that follow this turning, and even to push the divorce of the later from the earlier writings to the point of consigning *Being and Time* to a suppositious "Cartesian and Kantian" period in Heidegger's philosophical career.

This essay was first presented as the Alfred Schutz Memorial Lecture under the auspices of the American Philosophical Association at Northwestern University, April 17, 1986.

There was, however, no such period; and it will be my contention that if we misconstrue *Being and Time* by assimilating its distinctive theses to those of modern transcendental subjectivism, we will not be able to understand the character of the reorientation of Heidegger's thought that did in fact take place from the mid-thirties onward. In asserting the unity of Heidegger's thought, I am not, therefore, denying that such a reorientation took place. What I am saying is that the discontinuity that this reorientation involves can be understood only against the background of an even deeper continuity that runs through all the periods of Heidegger's thought. I will also try to show that the central concepts of *Being and Time* survive that reorientation instead of simply being replaced, as is now often assumed, and that it is the way the relationship between certain of these concepts is reconstrued that accounts for the sharply different tonalities of the later writings. There were, I will argue, serious difficulties connected with the ontological theses of *Being and Time;* and Heidegger, who was certainly never very open about the emendations of his own theses that he undertook, appears to have responded to these tensions within his own conceptual scheme by shifting the weight of emphasis from one term to another within his central distinctions. He did not, however, abandon the distinctions themselves or – what would have amounted to much the same thing – the requirement that each term in these distinctions be linked to the other. It is this fact that obliges us to reject prevailing interpretations of the *Kehre* as a replacement of one set of concepts by another.

I

Being and Time begins with an evocation of the question of being, and it is made clear that it is the concept of being as such that the book as a whole is to be concerned with. In the portions of the book that were published, however, Heidegger was concerned mainly with another matter that was said to be a necessary preliminary to the question of being, and this was the question about the character of the entity that asks the question of being. This was the entity to which Heidegger gave the generic name "Dasein." The analysis of Dasein is the topic with which the first of the two sections of Part I that we have deals. Even the second, which is entitled "Dasein and

Temporality" and in which the concept of temporality was to prepare the transition from Dasein to being as such, really extends that analysis without making it at all clear how the transition itself would take place. It is hardly surprising, therefore, that Heidegger's references to being as such in *Being and Time* have been treated as unredeemed promissory notes, or that many commentators have concluded that the concept of being could not be reached by the route through Dasein that Heidegger chose to follow in *Being and Time*. Once this conclusion is accepted, it is taken to explain Heidegger's failure to complete that work; and his subsequent writings come to be viewed as setting forth a conception of being that is altogether independent of Dasein and that can be approached only by a quite different route of thought. The trouble with this view is that by treating being as something that lies beyond the horizon of *Being and Time* as we have it, it runs the risk of confusing what Heidegger means by "being" with various traditional concepts of being that he explicitly repudiates. In fact, there are a number of characterizations of being as such in *Being and Time*, and these make it quite clear that what Heidegger has in mind when he speaks of being as such is something radically different from the traditional notions that the term is most likely to bring to our minds.

The distinctive features of Heidegger's construal of being as such in *Being and Time* can best be delineated in terms of the contrast between being and entities that he establishes there. He tells us that, for his purposes at least, being is always the being of entities, but that it is not itself an entity. When he says that being is always the being of entities and amplifies this statement by saying that being is what determines entities as entities, it would be natural to suppose that being must be the defining and thus essential property of entities – that which *makes* them entities. It seems quite clear, however, that when Heidegger denies that being itself is an entity, he is also excluding the possibility of its being understood as what we ordinarily mean by the notion of a property of an entity. From the lectures of the period we also know that being as such is prior to the fateful distinction that Western philosophy has made between being as essence and being as existence – a distinction that, in Heidegger's view, preempts any further inquiry into the unitary sense of being as such that it presupposes.

But if being as such is not itself an entity or a property of an entity, in what sense can it be the being of entities as Heidegger insists it is? *Being and Time* does not contain an explicit answer to this question. What Heidegger does say is that we must approach being as such through an inquiry into a certain kind of entity that is privileged in its relation to it. This entity is Dasein; and it is extremely important to understand that while this is the generic name for a kind of entity, there are indefinitely many entities that belong to this kind. These are the same entities – extensionally – that we ordinarily refer to as human beings. If there ever was any real question about the plurality and individuality of the entities to which Heidegger applies the term "Dasein," that question is unequivocally settled in the lectures by the many locutions – among them *ein Dasein* – that Heidegger uses there and that make sense only on the assumption that there are many such entities.[2] What is of most immediate relevance with respect to the character of this entity, however, is the fact that it not only asks the question of being, but does so out of a prior inarticulate familiarity that it has, Heidegger tells us, with being as such.

This claim on his part is subject to serious misconstrual if we assume that "being" here is to be taken in some traditional sense as essence and that Heidegger is therefore asserting that we have a preconceptual understanding of the *summum genus* under which the entities that make up the world – ourselves included – fall as so many kinds. What he is really saying is quite different, and it is something that is both logically prior to and presupposed by any such typically metaphysical claim as this. What is distinctive of the kind of entity that Dasein is, is in the first instance the fact that other entities are there for it in a way in which no entity – Heidegger's example is a chair and a wall – is ever there for another such entity that is not of the Dasein type. His way of expressing this foundational fact about Dasein – itself an expression that means "being-there" – is to say that Dasein is in the world in the mode of having a world as other kinds of entities that are in the world in the mode of spatial inclusion do not. To this, it should be added that the entities that are there for Dasein are there *as entities*, and it is this fact that is of primary importance for any effort to understand the sense in which being as such is the being of entities. The fact that they are there as entities is something that can be understood only by reference to the special character of Dasein, which is such that it "uncovers" or "clears" entities, and it is as so uncovered or cleared that they become part of the world in the very special sense of that term that Heidegger employs. The world in this sense is not just the totality of entities as it is ordinarily held to be. It is the totality of entities as uncovered or "present." This notion of presence is the most general term that Heidegger uses to convey the status that accrues to entities that are uncovered or cleared, and in his lectures from the period of *Being and Time* he uses the terms *Praesenz* and *Anwesen/Anwesenheit* for this purpose. The first of these later drops out of use, but the latter was to remain a central concept of Heidegger's philosophy in all its periods and, it must also be said, a prime source of confusion as to his intentions in his use of the concept of being as such.

The formulation that I have found most helpful in trying to express what I take to be the main thesis of *Being and Time* is to say that existence as the mode of being of Dasein is the ground of presence as the mode of being of the world and of entities understood as forming part of the world in Heidegger's sense of that term. The term "existence" is also being used here in a very special sense that draws heavily on its Greek etymology, which has to do with standing out or outside. In this sense of "to exist," not all actual entities can be said to exist. Only those entities that have a world and uncover entities other than themselves and also uncover themselves as so uncovering other entities can be said to exist in this sense, a sense that is substantially the same as that of the concept of transcendence, which Heidegger also introduces in this context. Just how this dependence of presence upon existence is to be understood is a complex matter, and it is made more so by the active and free character of the entity that is Dasein. The world of Dasein is the milieu not just of presence but of possibility as well and, more specifically, of the possibilities that correspond to the choices a particular Dasein can make and to the actions it can perform. Precisely because Dasein is conceived in these terms, it might seem tempting to suppose that among the other things that it does is its grounding of presence. Such a claim, however, would invite a dangerous confusion between the ontic and the ontological levels of Dasein's agency – the kind of confusion in fact that makes it seem proper to speak of that grounding as a kind of creation or production of presence by Dasein. The point here is that Dasein has no choice at all about its being-in-the-world or about its active character – its unavoidably having to do this or that if only through inaction – and so, although choice and action are central to the way existence grounds presence, Dasein grounds presence no matter what it does. It does not, in other words, have the option of *not* being in the world and thus of not choosing or acting and not grounding presence, so it is inappropriate to speak of these ontological features of Dasein as though they were ontic matters and as though grounding presence were comparable to this or that action which it undertakes or not as it pleases. Or to make the same point in still another way, it is made quite clear in *Being and Time* that a certain kind of entity – Dasein – is always and necessarily linked to something that is not an entity at all, namely, presence.

In *Being and Time* it was already evident that being, as Heidegger interprets it there, is tied to Dasein and thus to existence in much the same way as the world, again in Heidegger's sense of the terms, is. As he puts it, "Being is only in the understanding of those entities to which an understanding of something like being belongs"; and these entities are, of course, those to which the concept of Dasein applies (BT 228; BP 19; GA 24 25). This thesis is asserted with the greatest possible emphasis in the lectures of the period; in fact, Heidegger goes so far as to speak of being itself as "existing," that is, as having the mode of being of Dasein. He even declares that "being is grounded in an entity, namely Dasein" (BP 229; GA 24 318). It is also made explicit in the lectures that being itself is presence, the presence of entities to the kind of entity whose mode of being is existence and that therefore grounds the presence of those entities. Now this thesis that equates being with presence has given rise to a good deal of confusion, because it has not been distinguished from another formulation of what sounds very much like the same thesis but in fact is not and serves quite different purposes. I am referring here to the fact that Heidegger on occasion cites the equating of being with presence (*Anwesenheit*) as a misconception of being that he accordingly rejects. Thanks to the publication of the lectures from 1927, which contain the substance of what Heidegger evidently intended to include in the crucially important third section of Part I of *Being and Time* – the section called "Time and Being" that was never published – we are now in a position to understand how both these positions taken by Heidegger are compatible. The equating of being with presence on the part of the Greeks was faulty because they did not have any understanding of the temporal character of being. They simply equated presence with the present tense and the Now; and the conception of time that was worked out by Aristotle, and that determined the course of all subsequent Western thinking about time, construed time as a manifold of Nows. As Heidegger tries to show in a long analysis of the Aristotelian theory of time that introduces his own treatment of time and being, this altogether obscures the distinctive character of the Now, which is at once a "having been" and an "about to be," and is thus closely bound up with both the past and the future.

I will not try to do justice here to the richness of Heidegger's constructive account of what he calls the "phenomenological chronology of being." What is of fundamental importance in it for the purposes of this discussion is the notion that being cannot be identified with the "is" of the present tense, no matter how disguised, or with the mode of presence that corresponds to it. Instead, being is complexly articulated in the way that the system of tenses expresses, and there is no possibility of simplifying this complex ordering in favor of a single one of its modalities. The analysis of this articulation of being into its various modalities is ontology; and perhaps the most radical claim that Heidegger makes is that ontology has an essentially temporal character. This is because the distinctions it explicates among the modalities of being – between the "is" and the "is not" and between "is possible" and "not possibly" – have to be understood in temporal terms. The articulated structures of being are thus inextricably bound up with the distinctions of past, present, and future that are comprised in our own temporality as this was characterized in *Being and Time*. What "is," is thus necessarily what will have been; and what is, is also what has or has not been and what will or will not be. But these temporal qualifications of the articulations of being also articulate presence, which is, therefore, not just a matter of the static immediacy of the present tense. To put this point in a maximally paradoxical way, presence also comprises absence. It takes the form of the "has been" and the "will be" as well as of the "is," and the being of the entities that form part of the world of Dasein is understood in just this ecstatic mode that characterizes the temporality of Dasein. In psychological terms, we would speak here of "memory" and "expectation," but it is just this psychological mode of description that Heidegger avoids because it obscures what most needs attention for the purposes of ontology. Instead, he speaks of the presence of such entities as their presence-to the entity – Dasein – which is itself temporal in the way that makes this presence possible. This presence is also declared to be the *being* of those entities, once it is accepted that the concept of being is complexly articulated in the manner that has been described and that corresponds to the set of temporal distinctions that Dasein itself deploys.

It may be helpful at this point to relate these theses of Heidegger to a controversy that has been going on for a good many years in our own philosophical province. This concerns the issue as to whether the world is made up of things or of facts. The more widely accepted view at the present time is, I think, that the world is an aggregate of things or, as Heidegger would say, of entities, and that facts or states of affairs are not to be included among the contents of the world but rather viewed as being in some sense the artifacts of language. Since the "is" that is an essential constituent of facts and states of affairs is assumed to belong most naturally in a proposition, and propositions, for these purposes at least, are taken to be somehow outside the world that is an aggregate of things, it is thought proper to deny any such propositional character to the world and to the things that make it up. There is reason to think that the notion of "language" as it occurs in this context may be a pseudonaturalistic stand-in for the transcendental and thus extramundane subject that philosophers are now unwilling to acknowledge as such but nevertheless continue to cultivate under more discreet terms of reference such as these. However that may be, it is clear that Heidegger holds just the opposite view, namely, that the world is made up of states of affairs, usually of a highly pragmatic character, and that the very possibility of presence is bound up with something's *being* something or other. He also denies with great vigor any suggestion that this "is"-character is in any way a projection, linguistic or otherwise, of a subject that would thus have to be understood as having a prior familiarity with mere things; and he does so in a way that is somewhat reminiscent of Sellars's insistence on the rock-bottom propositional character of the datum.[3]

Whatever one's stand on this issue, it must be acknowledged that it is extremely difficult to adhere with absolute consistency to one or the other of the two rival views. There are, after all, considerations on both sides that cannot be simply dismissed. Even Heidegger himself turns out in the lectures to be less than completely consistent in his espousal of the view that the world is the totality of pragmatic involvements (*Bewandtnisse*) – these are surely states of affairs – and he goes so far as to speak of entities or things as coming into the world and taking on the character of instrumentality, or *Zuhandenheit*, that is, as becoming part of states of affairs. Clearly no one could speak in this way without some kind of understanding of entities as independent of any being – any "is" – that may supervene upon them. But if we so understand them, they can hardly be denied a place, if not in "the world" as Heidegger wants to use that term, then in the world as it is ordinarily understood. It should also be noted that if he wants to speak in this way, Heidegger must be using both concepts of world without acknowledging that this is the case, and that would amount to a grave incoherency in his scheme.

A discussion of these matters occurs in a lecture series from 1929–30 published as *The Fundamental Concepts of Metaphysics: World, Finitude, Solitariness.* This discussion is of quite exceptional interest because in it Heidegger takes up the question of the independence of being from, and its dependence on, Dasein in terms of just this contrast between entities and entities qualified by the "is." This contrast itself is first placed in the closest possible relationship to what Heidegger calls "'is'-saying" ("*ist*"-*Sagen*), that is, to saying that "this is such and such, [that] that is, [that] that is not so and that is" (GA 29/30 518). This "is"-saying expressly includes both saying *what* something is and saying *that* it is, and the "is" occurring in both is therefore more fundamental than the distinction of essence and existence that emerges from it. The distinction between being and entities is thus constantly made use of by us, but without our having any explicit understanding of what this distinction really involves. From this Heidegger concludes that "it is not *we* [who] bring about [*vollziehen*] this distinction; instead it happens [*geschieht*] with us as the primal happening [*Grundgeschehen*] of our Dasein" (GA 29/30 518–19):

If this distinction did not happen, then we could not even, in obliviousness to the distinction, devote ourselves, initially and for the most part, to entities alone. For precisely in order to experience *what* and *how* an entity in each case *is* in itself as the entity that it is, we have to understand already, even though not conceptually, matters like the What-ness [*Was-sein*] and the That-ness [*Dass-sein*] of entities. This distinction not only happens continuously; but it must [also] have already happened if we desire to experience entities in their being-such-and-such [*So-und-so-sein*]. We do not learn – and certainly not subsequently – anything about being from entities; instead entities, wherever and however we come at them, stand *already in the light of being.* Taken metaphysically, the distinction thus stands at the beginning of Dasein itself. . . . Man thus always stands in the possibility of asking: What is that? and Is it really or is it not? (GA 29/30 519)

The essential point these passages make is that being, in the distinction between being and entities, is coordinate and coeval with Dasein and that Dasein is accordingly always already conversant with the What and the That as implicit articulations (*Gliederungen*) of entities and thereby of its world. Plainly, being, so understood, is in no sense the creature or the handiwork (*Gemächte*) of Dasein or man, and in this sense being may be said to enjoy the independence vis-à-vis Dasein that Heidegger is so concerned to preserve. The status thus accorded to being, moreover, does not require any duplication of the presence or clearing that is constituted by Dasein. It is also evident that within the one clearing – the one world – that is effected by the "happening" of this distinction between being and entities, the truth character of being stands in an intimate relationship to the articulation that the "is" in all its modalities brings to entities. This is not because, as might ordinarily be supposed, truth is a property of propositions and thus presupposes the logical form of the latter. Heidegger's claim is rather that, in the world as the milieu of presence in which we have to do with them, entities always already *are,* in the several modalities of which the verb "to be" that eventually expresses them is susceptible. Truth, as the presence of entities in what might appropriately be called their "be-ing," is thus both prepredicative and prelogical in the sense of being prior to language and judgment. It is not, in other words, as though, apart from language, presence could only be a beam of light playing over an unstructured entity or thing. What is present is always an entity as a such and such, and it is as be-ing such and such that it is understood. This apple, for example, is understood as being here in front of me and not in the bag I left in my car, and this pencil as not making a dark enough mark. The difference between an entity and an entity's be-ing, whether in the mode of the What or the That, is thus not one that arises with the insertion of entities into propositions by language. It is one that is implicit in any form of presence as such. In presence, something is *there* and it is there as a such and such. Neither its being there nor its being such and such – what we eventually conceptualize as its existence and its essence – can be simply identified with the entity in question itself. The picture of a presence to which "logical form" would have to be subsequently added with the advent of language is therefore mistaken, at least in the sense that it treats such form as something wholly new for which there is no analogon in presence as such.

What I find so impressive in this discussion is the sensitivity Heidegger shows to the considerations that motivate both sides in the controversy about being and entities or, in our dialect, between facts and things. The view he defends here is essentially the same one that he formulated in *Being and Time,* but it is expressed with more care and with a notable avoidance of those adaptations of ontic verbs like "to project" (*entwerfen*) to ontological purposes that tended to give a Nietzschean flavor to so much of what was said about the various functions of Dasein in that work. I, for one, could wish that Heidegger had persevered in this kind of ontological analysis rather than resorting to the quite different strategies he was to adopt in his later period for avoiding just these excesses and the ambiguities to which they give rise. I will say more on this point later, and I will try to show what the significance of these considerations was for the evolution of Heidegger's later manner. What I want to emphasize first, however, is the fact that, quite apart from this source of potential difficulty, and even if Heidegger had maintained the eminently balanced style of the lectures I have just referred to, there were serious difficulties in the way of the position he had set forth in the period of *Being and Time.* The source of these difficulties lies in the fact that in the period of *Being and Time* the rapprochement of being as such with existence, and thus with Dasein as the entity whose mode of being is existence, had become so close as to be virtually complete. The extent of that rapprochement is indicated not only by the fact that both being and truth are declared to *exist* and are thereby assimilated to the mode of being of Dasein, but also by the fact that they are both characterized as finite and so akin to Dasein in this fundamental respect as well. It is, in other words, quite possible that there should not be any being or any truth; and if there were no Dasein, there could not be. But if there is no gap between being as such and Dasein, how can it any longer be maintained that being is not an entity as Dasein is? Notice, by the way, that the same question arises in the case of Heidegger's treatment of the concept of the world, which is also said not to be an entity and nevertheless is explicitly made an ontological appendage of Dasein – that is, dependent upon the existence of the latter as a kind of entity. It is important to note in just this connection, where the dependence of the world upon Dasein is so unambiguously asserted, that Heidegger is at some pains in his lectures to make it clear that the dependence runs the other way as well, and that man (*der Mensch*) would not be man in the sense of Dasein unless he had a world.

Even so, in the period of *Being and Time* it is the dependence of being as presence upon Dasein – an entity – that is far more emphatically insisted upon, and what that emphasis does is to endanger the status of being as not itself an entity. More specifically, the source of the difficulty in both these cases is the fact that being as such is singular and common (*koinon*) as the world also is, while Dasein is plural and particular; and if being is to retain these characters, it quite obviously cannot be identified with each individual Dasein. If each Dasein itself constituted being as such and thus its own milieu of presence, there would be a plurality of such milieus and the sense in which singularity and commonness could qualify being as presence would become wholly mysterious. One alternative here would be to say that being in Heidegger's sense is independent of each particular Dasein but not independent of Dasein as such. Being as presence does not, after all, begin to exist with the birth of a particular human being, and it survives the death of each one of us, as long as we are replaced by others. It is a real question, however, whether in *Being and Time* Heidegger had developed the conceptual instruments he would need in order to give an account of the dual status of being as both independent of individual Dasein and dependent on Dasein generically or collectively. Such an account would have to rest on a much more strongly developed theory of *Mitsein*, or "being-with," than Heidegger ever actually developed, and though I have tried to show that the elements of such a theory are in fact present in the writings and lectures of that period, they were not developed in this direction.

II

It thus appears that the fundamental difficulty facing Heidegger in attempting to effect the turn to the theory of being as such was that he had associated being too closely with individual Dasein and as a result was unable to reconcile the singularity and unity of the one with the plurality of the other. But to this difficulty there was added another, to which I have already alluded. The Heidegger of *Being and Time* had made the world and thus being as presence a space of possibilities and of possibilities that were coordinate with the *Selbstheit* – the "selfness" – of Dasein, and being as such therefore had to be understood in the closest possible connection with the projects of individual Dasein. The freedom in which such projects are generated, and the indefinitely extensive variety of content by which these are characterized, unquestionably add a further dimension to the problem of safeguarding the unity and singularity of being as presence, although it does not seem to me that this would be an insuperable difficulty for a deeply conceived theory of *Mitsein.*

As things turned out, however, Heidegger dealt with this difficulty by simply dropping the active and projective character of Dasein from his theory of being as presence from the mid-thirties onward. This profound and fateful shift was never acknowledged or explained, and this circumstance makes it very difficult not to conclude that the reasons for it lay in Heidegger's life as it intersected the events of the time rather than in any necessity revealed by philosophical reflection. It is certainly significant that the shift toward the quietism of the later period came immediately after the one deplorable sortie that Heidegger made into the public world; and it has seemed obvious to those who, like Hannah Arendt, were close to Heidegger that this new quietism was his reaction to the inevitable disappointment of his naive expectations that the Nazi revolution would somehow proceed under the banners of resoluteness and authenticity. In philosophical terms, however, his way of dealing with the difficulties generated by his conception of presence as grounded in existence was to distance the former from the latter. This meant reorienting his conception of being in such a way as to assert as complete an independence of being from entities as possible. More specifically, it meant making being as presence independent of the kind of entity – Dasein – in whose mode of being – existence – it had been grounded.

If this is the way the turning through which Heidegger's thought passed is to be understood, then one could appropriately formulate its import as the thesis that presence is the ground of existence rather than the other way around. What is of the most fundamental importance, however, although it seems to have been largely missed in the critical literature, is the fact that the concept of being does not itself change. From the *Introduction to Metaphysics* in 1935 to *Time and Being* in 1962, being as such is identified with presence. It follows that the whole picture of Heidegger's philosophical evolution that represents him as having tried to reach being as such by the route of Dasein in *Being and Time,* and then, after failing in that effort, setting out again by another route, is simply wrong. The change that in fact occurs is that Heidegger from the mid-thirties on tries to conceive being as presence in such a way as to keep it clear of just those features of entities – that is, of Dasein – that would endanger its unity and singularity and commonness. This is a momentous shift, but one that is compatible with and in fact ensures the kind of continuity in his thought that I have in mind in speaking of the unity of Heidegger's thought.

One of the things that makes it harder to discern what is going on in Heidegger's later writings and often effectively obscures the central difficulty that I have just described is the philosopher's preoccupation with another related but nevertheless quite different theme. In *Being and Time* it was argued that there is a constitutional disposition on the part of Dasein to avoid acknowledging the distinctive character of its own mode of being, and to do so by assimilating itself to the mode of being of entities within the world. As Heidegger puts it, Dasein understands itself as a special kind of "spiritual thing." This effort of self-obscuration is associated with an ontology of substance, and especially of mental substance, that has the serious disadvantage of making the existence of an "external" world problematic, since the only immediate objects of "consciousness" – another concept that goes with the contrast between the outer and the inner that this ontology generates – are the inner states of this mental substance, which are supposed to represent that external world, but without our ever being able to be sure whether or not they really do. What has just been described is, of course, the Cartesian scheme of which the cornerstone is the "worldless subject." It is this "interpretation of the being of consciousness" that *Being and Time* criticized and replaced with a radically different conception of the subject – the "existing subject," as Heidegger puts it – as Dasein. There was, however, nothing in this powerful critique of Cartesian subjectivism to suggest that human agency was in any way the source or the special locus of this kind of subjectivism; as has already been pointed out, in *Being and Time* such agency in fact plays a central role in the project character of being as presence.

From the mid-thirties onward Heidegger greatly expands his conception of philosophical subjectivism, and he does so in such a way as to include within it every conception of human agency as having any such role in the constitution of the being of entities. Such conceptions are now associated with the modern aspiration to be the final judge of what is and of what is not, and thus to create or produce being itself. Heidegger does not, of course, say that this is what he himself came close to doing in *Being and Time,* but in some of his rather cryptic remarks about the reasons for not completing that work he seems to imply as much. It looks very much as though Heidegger, in a period of sharp disillusionment with human agency, resorted to quite drastic expedients to avoid these ambiguities. Instead of working out more carefully the relevant distinctions within a theory of Dasein as coeval with being as presence along the lines sketched in his lectures entitled *The Fundamental Concepts of Metaphysics,* he appears to have simply severed the ties that link agency to the understanding of being and to have made the relationship of human beings to being as presence entirely a matter of receiving something that agency has no part in constituting. Moreover, human agency in almost all its forms – especially those of modern technology – is now described in a way that associates it with the obscuration of being as such through the substitution for it of all the many surrogates that modern thought has proposed: the Will to Power, the World Spirit, and so on. Characteristically, even this perverse exercise of human agency is not finally allowed to retain the character of an action imputable to human beings. Instead, Heidegger insists that it is itself a part of the history not of man (*Mensch*) but of being itself, which in a certain epoch – our own – announces itself by withholding itself; and it does so in a way that is quite beyond our control.

Although all of these matters – especially the many facets that the eclipse of being assumes – dominate most of the later writings, they by no means exhaust the philosophical significance of the later writings. It is evident that Heidegger was still struggling with the problem of the unity and singularity of being as presence in its relation to the plurality of the entities that understand being or, in the language he favored in his later period, *think* it. There are immense problems associated with any attempt to conceive being as presence as somehow radically independent of and prior to the entities that are now held to receive it; a careful study of the language Heidegger devises for the purpose of rendering the character of this relationship clearly shows the strain that this task imposes on his language. One famous crux for such inquiries is the passage in the "Introduction" to *What Is Metaphysics?* which Heidegger first published in 1944, long after the work to which it was an introduction had appeared (GA 9 306, nn. 2, 3). In the first edition of the "Introduction," in the course of a discussion of the relation of being as such to entities (which of course include Dasein, although it is not explicitly mentioned) Heidegger stated that being might well be (*west*) without entities, and that would mean without Dasein as one such entity. In subsequent editions, however, this was changed to its opposite, and it was said that being *never* is without entities. This is only an especially dramatic example of the difficulty that Heidegger was quite evidently having in replacing the thesis that existence is the ground of presence with the thesis that presence is the ground of existence. The evidence for this is so pervasive that it seems to me that one can say that in these works Heidegger is testing the limits of the independence of being as presence from Dasein – a term that in this period tends to be replaced by *Mensch* – even though the semiprophetic tonalities of many of these writings do not exactly suggest that any kind of experiment is going forward. The pattern that emerges from a close analysis of these writings is one in which a strong initial assertion of the independence of being as presence is subsequently qualified in quite substantial ways which in effect reintroduce the element of dependence upon Dasein that was initially denied. These qualifications are very similar to those that, in the period of *Being and Time,* limited the independence of Dasein by showing that it was as dependent upon being as presence and upon the world as they were upon it. It is as though two radically different metaphors – neither wholly satisfactory for its purpose – were both being qualified in a way that points to an eventual equivalence of what is to be said by means of them although there is no linguistic instrument that expresses the convergence itself.

III

By way of illustrating and justifying the claim I have just made, I want to take up one central theme of Heidegger's later thought and show how the continuing tensions of which I have spoken manifest themselves in that domain. The theme I have chosen is that of language. Although language was a dominant interest of Heidegger's throughout his career, it unquestionably assumed a special importance in the later period. It is, moreover, this aspect of his later thought that has commanded the widest interest among our contemporaries. Some of the theses about language attributed to Heidegger have been taken up by critics and theorists of literature and are still central to the controversies going on in that area of thought. The theory of literature has recently been passing through a period of pronounced revulsion from the concept of the subject in all its classical manifestations. Just as in contemporary philosophy, from which this attitude seems to have passed to literature, language has come to be regarded as the one medium in which the matters that have traditionally been dealt with in the vocabulary of the subject can be treated without incurring unwelcome philosophical commitments. Language, after all, has the advantage of not being private in principle as so many mental functions have been supposed to be, and because it is not controlled by purely individual decisions and preferences, it lends itself to a form of generalizing description of the rules to which individual speakers must be subject if they are to use language at all. In a sense, one could say that in language a kind of reconciliation is effected between the plurality of speakers and the singularity of the medium in which, as speakers, they move. It also appears that this takes place in a way that accords to the latter a marked precedence over the former – a precedence that would be, at least superficially, in keeping with the orientation of Heidegger's later thought. In what follows, I will try to show that in spite of its great importance in Heidegger's later thought, it is by no means the case that language simply replaces existence or Dasein, as is often assumed to be the case. What happens is rather that in the shift from existence as the ground of presence to presence as the ground of existence, language comes to be incorporated into Heidegger's ontology in a different way that corresponds to this new order of priority. It can be shown, however, that even in this new ordering the tensions between existence and presence maintain themselves, and that any thought of a complete independence of the one from the other – of presence from existence or of language from speech – is not something that one can attribute to Heidegger.

The question that Heidegger raises again and again in his later discussions of language is whether we really understand at all adequately what language is. We assume that we do and that language is a kind of datum with which everyone is familiar at the outset. The words for language in the Western European languages show that the understanding we claim to have is one that associates language primarily with the production of speech (*stimmliche Verlautbarung*) by certain parts of our bodies and with the communication that is thereby achieved. Understood in this way as a certain form of human activity, language quite naturally comes to be thought of as something that we bring into being or create. It is this view of language that Heidegger is most concerned to discredit. It is therefore essential that he show that language has some status other than that of the "utteredness" (*Hinausgesprochenheit*) of discourse or speech, which he had declared it to be in *Being and Time*. This might suggest that it is Heidegger's own earlier views of language that are being corrected, but this is true only up to a point. Discourse, and derivatively language, were unambiguously described in *Being and Time* as a modality of the uncovering of entities as entities. The whole strategy of the treatment of language there was to show that at every point it is embedded in and presupposes existence as the mode of being of the entity – Dasein – that is itself conversant with being understood as the uncoveredness or presence of entities as entities. There is no reason to suppose that in his later writings on language Heidegger wanted to repudiate these theses of *Being and Time* or to conflate them with crudely naturalistic conceptions of language. It looks, instead, as though within this general conception of the uncovering character of discourse and language, it was the earlier notion of the way discourse and language are related to one another that was found to be in need of revision.

It is true that the term "discourse" (*Rede*) drops out of the later writings in favor of the word "language" (*Sprache*). With the former, the picture of the individual human speaker and of language as what he produces by his speech or discourse also disappears, and it is replaced by a picture of language as that out of which such an individual speaker speaks and upon which he depends in multiple ways that need describing. This might seem to be itself a conventional enough picture; but any notion of language as a syntactic or semantic system that has to be in place if individual speech acts are to be performed would fall far short of Heidegger's conception of language as the background against which the latter take place. Language understood as that upon which discourse depends is described by him as a "showing" (*Zeige*) that "reaches into all regions of presence and lets what is in each case present appear and mis-appear [*verscheinen*] out of them" (GA 12 243). This is in marked contrast to the view taken in *Being and Time* that discourse contributes to uncovering entities as entities but only as a further articulation of an uncoveredness that has already been realized independently of it. In behalf of language as contrasted with discourse, Heidegger now makes the much stronger claim that it is "the word" that "first brings a thing into its 'is' " and "lets a thing be as a thing" (GA 12 177, 220).

This conception of language as realizing our primary access to being is one that contemporary thought finds deeply congenial in the many contrasting versions in which it has been proposed. But this apparent consonance of Heidegger's position with current predilections can prove very misleading. This is because the language that Heidegger characterizes in this way is not, in the first instance, a language with a grammar and a vocabulary such as English or Chinese is; and it is not, therefore, to the constraining influence of such features of language that Heidegger is attributing our apprehension of being. Instead, the enlarged significance that he now attributes to language is due primarily to the fact that although he seems to be describing presence and thus being in terms that assimilate both to language, it is also and equally language itself that is being understood in terms of presence. What this comes to is a claim that the unitary presence of entities as entities is best understood as a kind of "saying" (*Sagen*) and that, as this "saying," language is, in its unitary essence, prior to all individual speakers and all natural (and artificial) languages in the same way that presence itself is prior to all particular perceptions, memories, choices, and so on. Extravagant as such a claim will inevitably seem, it has been anticipated by remarks that were made earlier about presence as having, not to be sure a propositional character, but one that might be called proto-propositional in the sense that it constitutes the milieu of truth within which what an entity *is* can eventually find expression in an assertion of some kind.

At the same time, it must be conceded that the mistrust with which this dramatic expansion of the domain of language meets is understandable. There have been so many naive theories of the identity of word and thing, and of a natural language that is somehow laid down in the order of creation, that one inevitably approaches with a good deal of caution any theory that, like Heidegger's, may sound as though it were invoking conceptions of this order. It may be helpful, therefore, to approach Heidegger's later treatment of language via theses from the earlier period that prepare the ground for the much closer association of presence with language in the later period. One clue is provided by the thesis defended in *Being and Time* that meaning is an essential character of the world and that, as such, meaning is prior to both discourse and language understood as deriving from discourse. If, independently of any act of interpretation (in Heidegger's sense) or discourse, we understand how to ride a bicycle or to catch a fish, our world to that extent bears the instrumental meaning that corresponds to these forms of understanding and competence on our part. This meaningful character of the world can then be expressed as its "saying" something to us. Such a "saying" is obviously silent or mute because there is no speaker in the ordinary sense and that is no "act" of expression or communication. But if it is admissible to speak of the meaningfulness of the world as a kind of silent "saying," then it will also be appropriate to describe the relationship of human beings to that "saying" as one of "hearing." In his later writings on language, Heidegger assigns great importance to this notion of hearing and goes so far as to assert that the speaking of human beings is always and necessarily preceded by a "hearing" in this sense. This is a "hearing" of the "saying" in which presence is realized; and because language in the widest sense is just this presence and this saying, Heidegger can say not only that "language itself speaks" but that "we hear the speaking of language" (*das Sprechen der Sprache*) (GA 12 243).

The difficulty for this way of understanding Heidegger's conception of a language as in some radical way prior to expression and communication on the part of human beings is that in the later writings where this conception is put forward, the notion of *Zuhandenheit* as the instrumental meaningfulness of the world is in abeyance. Indeed, the notion itself of the world, on the occasions when it is employed at all, is understood as what Heidegger now calls "the Fourfold" (*das Geviert*) or "World-Fourfold" that is made up of "the earth," "the sky," "man," and "the gods." This conception is developed in a way that one can only call mythic, and its philosophical import is therefore far from clear. The pairing of sky and earth would seem to correspond to the contrast between the openness of being as presence and the closure of things, and "man" who defines himself as such in some sort of relationship to "the gods" is, instead of being the ground of the world, incorporated into the "play" of all these elements in the Fourfold with one another. There is no reason to suppose that Heidegger no longer recognizes the kind of prior instrumental meaningfulness of the world that was so central to his account of Dasein, but it now appears to be encompassed within the wider "play" of the elements of the Fourfold. Heidegger also describes the latter as *Gegeneinander-über* – a reciprocity of linkages in which "each of the regions of the World-Fourfold is open for the others – open as if hiding itself" (GA 12 199). In the later writings, it is this play of reciprocity among the regions of the Fourfold that is understood as the "saying" by which man is addressed and to which any utterance of his must be understood as responding. This is really another way of saying that man is addressed not just by the world in the earlier sense of that term in which he was its ground, but by being as that which lets what is present be present and, in the case of "the earth," present precisely as that which closes itself off from presence. It is as though man, instead of being spoken to only by the ontic (but implicitly ontological) instrumentalities of his world, were also being addressed by the explicitly ontological "saying" of the world – the Fourfold – as such. To say "explicitly ontological" here does not mean that this "saying" is a bit of philosophical ventriloquism in which man is the real speaker. The case is rather that the elements in what is said themselves do the "saying." It is what they "say" that man "hears," and he can hear what they say because he can understand being as that which "lets-be-present." He does not himself organize the world as a Fourfold any more than he constitutes the distinction between being and entities. Instead, because "we human beings have been admitted to the domain of language [*das Sprachwesen*]," we cannot step out of it so as to view it from some other standpoint; as a result "we catch sight of [*erblicken*] language only insofar as we are regarded [*angeblickt*] by it" (GA 12 254).

Although there is much that is unclear and problematic in this notion of the Fourfold, it is only the notion of language as prior to human utterance as such that will be examined here. In evaluating that claim, there can be no doubt that in speaking of our understanding of language as having to shift from language as something we do to language as something by which we are sustained and in some sense encompassed, Heidegger is expressing in his own way the sense that all students of language must have of the element of dependency that characterizes the relationship between the individual speaker and the language he speaks. This dependency is usually associated with the rule-governed character of language, and our sense of submitting "blindly" to those rules can become so strong that it is as though our language were speaking us rather than we, the language. That is an idiom that Heidegger himself uses, but he does not do so as a way of testifying to the rule-governed character of language. The language that itself speaks is not one that is ordered by syntactical and semantic rules; it would be a serious mistake as well as an encouragement to mystification to apply what Heidegger says about language as the play of the Fourfold to natural languages as conceived in naturalistic terms. As he uses it, the notion of language as that out of which we speak expresses the fact that our utterance is possible only within a milieu of presence, and that the structure of presence as the Fourfold forms the indispensable context for every natural or constructed language and thus for the utterances of those who speak each such language. Indeed, Heidegger is even willing to go so far as to declare that "language is the house of being and it is by dwelling (in this house) that man ek-sists" (GA 9 333). He adds that this house of being has also "come to pass [*ereignet*] and been fitted together [*gefügt*]" by being itself. Although the priority of language to man thus appears to be asserted in the strongest possible form, it is notable that in the same context man is spoken of as the "shepherd of being," and it is stated that as he dwells within language as the house of being, he also "protects the truth of being to which he belongs" (GA 9 333). Since the notion of protection immediately suggests that of a need – in this case, as before, a need on the part of being for man – it is evident once again that the relationship between being as presence and existence, which, in the course of Heidegger's discussion of language, may appear to be so one-sidedly a dependency of the former on the latter, is a good deal more ambiguous than at first appeared.

The question is thus whether, if language is somehow prior to human utterance, it must also follow that language and its "saying" are independent of man. This in turn is really just a new version of the question about the possible independence of presence from existence. In this new form that ties it to language, it sounds more than usually strange because, as has been pointed out, we imagine that the language that might be prior to or independent of man is a language like English or French or some common distillate of all such natural languages, and this idea of there being such a language independently of the existence of human beings seems too incongruous to be taken seriously. But even when we are clear that the "language" we are talking about here is not a language in this sense, but rather the ontological context of presence that is required for language as more familiarly understood, the question still remains. Fortunately, it is one to which Heidegger directly addressed himself:

> And the saying itself? Is it something separated from our speaking [*Sprechen*] [and] which we could reach only by throwing a bridge over to it? Or is the saying rather the stream of silence that itself connects its banks – its saying and our resaying – as it forms them? Our usual conceptions of language fall short here. Aren't we running the danger, if we try to conceive the nature of language [*das Sprachwesen*] on the basis of "saying," that we will raise language up into a fantastic being that exists in itself but that we can find nowhere as long as we reflect soberly on language? After all, language remains unmistakably bound to human speech. Certainly. But of what type is this bond? Whence and how does its binding character obtain? Language requires [*braucht*] human speech and it is nevertheless not the mere creature [*Gemächte*] of our speech-activity. (GA 12 244)

This passage makes clear that although Heidegger's way of describing language often makes it sound as though some stronger kind of independence of language from human speech were intended, the kind he is really talking about is consistent with language's being bound to human speech. We have here, in other words, much the same pattern as before of an apparent assertion of a radical form of priority – in this case, of language, as formerly of being as presence – that is then qualified by an acknowledgment of a dependence on something human. It thus emerges that what is really important is the special character of the dependence that is only apparently being denied. It is, in the first place, reciprocal, since without language man could not be man any more than language could be language. This is also a dependence that is such that what is dependent – in this case language – is nonetheless not created by that on which it is dependent and is not subject to any arbitrary form of control that the latter would like to assert over it. The fundamental articulation of the World-Fourfold is one that all speech and every natural language necessarily register and preserve just as, according to the Heidegger of *Being and Time,* discourse and thus language presupposed the structure of being-in-the-world. Just how this independence within dependence is to be understood may not be altogether clear, but it is not to be explained by any notion of language as a thing in itself. It is interesting in this connection that Heidegger says that not just language as the silent play of the World-Fourfold, but language as what is uttered by human beings can come to *look* as though it were separated from speaking and speakers and did not belong to them. In both cases, however, this appearance is misleading and there can no more be a language without speakers than there can be a Fourfold without man.

What I have been trying to suggest in the course of this brief examination of the way Heidegger deals with language in his later writings is that it is in terms of an interdependence of language and speech that we should understand the distinctive difference between these writings and those of the period of *Being and Time.* Writ large, this would also be the interdependence of presence and existence, and the thesis of this essay is that the unity of Heidegger's thought must be understood as his continuing effort to find a satisfactory way of bringing that interdependence to conceptual expression. Whether he was successful in this effort is another question. Clearly, the unity of which I speak is more a matter of philosophical intention than it is of full realization, and it is constantly threatened by the sharp incompatibilities between the antithetical strategies that he deployed at different times. It also has to be conceded that matters are not made easier by Heidegger's rooted unwillingness to acknowledge the revisionary character of some of his successive approaches to this matter. In my view, one of the main sources of the difficulties he encounters is his failure to follow up some of the clues that suggest a much stronger role for intersubjectivity – for *Mitsein* – in the way the interdependence of existence and presence is to be conceived. But that is a topic for another essay. What I have proposed here is a way of understanding Heidegger's philosophical career in terms of a kind of unity that we will inevitably fail to grasp as long as his concept of being is construed otherwise than in terms of the concept of presence with which he in fact associated it from the beginning. I would also venture to suggest that if this unitary interpretation of the problematic of Heidegger's thought were to inform our understanding of what he represents within philosophy, both we and philosophy would stand to gain.

NOTES

1 Frederick A. Olafson, *Heidegger and the Philosophy of Mind* (New Haven, Conn.: Yale University Press, 1987).
2 Textual references illustrating Heidegger's use of "Dasein" as the name of a particular can be found in ibid., pp. 62, 269.
3 See, e.g., his essay, "Empiricism and the Philosophy of Mind," in Wilfrid Sellars, *Science, Perception and Reality*, (New York: Humanities Press, 1963).

HARRISON HALL

4 Intentionality and world: Division I of *Being and Time*

Division I of *Being and Time* contains the complete account of early Heidegger's quarrel with and departure from the philosophical tradition. In spite of the attempts by many, beginning with Husserl,[1] to incorporate Heidegger's insights into a more traditional framework, that departure was a radical one. For Heidegger the tradition that began in ancient Greece finds what may be its ultimate expression in Husserl's phenomenology.

As Føllesdal and his successors have argued,[2] Husserl's phenomenology can be understood as the joint product of two influences. From Brentano he took the insight that the defining characteristic of consciousness is its intentionality – that is, its "of-ness" or directedness toward some object. But the model he uses for understanding this intentionality or directedness is essentially the same as Frege's model of linguistic reference, with the basic notion of meaning or sense (*Sinn*) suitably generalized so as to apply to all acts of consciousness, linguistic and nonlinguistic.[3] As Figures 1 and 2 suggest, just as Frege distinguishes the sense of a linguistic expression from its referent, so Husserl distinguishes the meaning of a conscious act from the object it is *about*. For both, the meaning is that in virtue of which we can refer to or intend objects.

The result is a Fregean account of intentionality that avoids the obvious problems facing Brentano's theory. If the directedness of consciousness is accounted for in terms of its relation to real objects, the perceptual equivalents of failure of reference (hallucinations, illusions) defy explanation. But if this directedness is explained in terms of perceived mental contents (images, percepts), the distinction between veridical and nonveridical perception seems to disappear. Husserl avoids this dilemma by accounting for the inten-

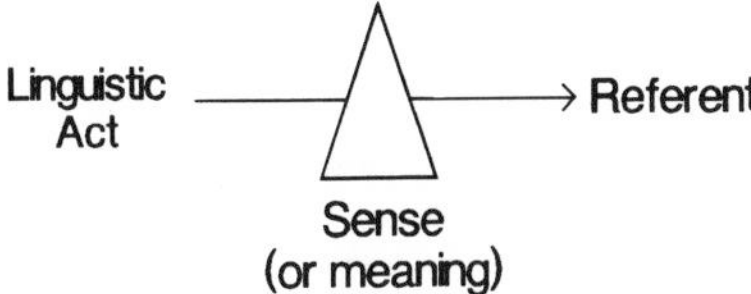

Figure 1. Frege's model of linguistic intentionality.

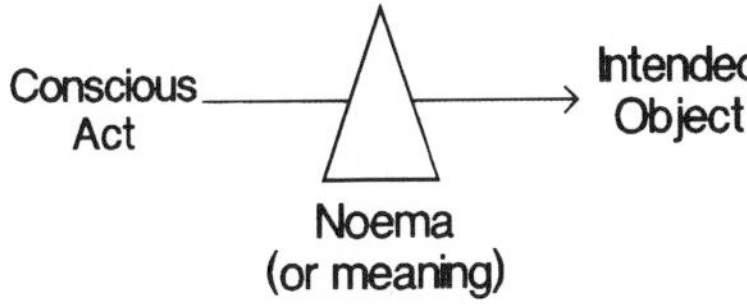

Figure 2. Husserl's model of intentionality in general.

tionality of consciousness in terms of abstract intensional (with an "s") structures (analogous to linguistic meanings) through which consciousness is directed, rather than in terms of objects toward which it is directed or the actual mental contents that accompany its directed acts. Husserl uses the term *noema* to refer to these intensional structures or meanings. Thus, Brentano's thesis that every act has an object is transformed into the thesis that every act has a *noema,* or meaning. It is by virtue of such meanings that consciousness is directed toward or intends an object under a particular description and with an appropriate set of structured anticipations, past associations, and so on.

Since Heidegger places Husserl's theory of the intentionality of consciousness squarely within the philosophical tradition he seeks to criticize and correct, the notion of intentionality might seem a strange choice for explicating Heidegger's thought. And this would be reinforced by the virtual absence of the term in *Being and Time* and by Heidegger's refusal to characterize human experience in terms of the relation of consciousness to its objects. Nonetheless, Heidegger's lectures and notes from the period of *Being and Time* contain many references to and discussions of intentionality, and understanding the various senses of intentionality and the corresponding senses of the world for Heidegger is one way to make sense of Division I of *Being and Time.*

Before getting down to the important details of Heidegger's story, let me go straight to the bottom line and try to block the most common misunderstanding of *Being and Time.* There are at least three crucially important and crucially different notions of intentionality and world for Heidegger. There is (1) the intentionality and world of the theoretical subject (the passive observer or traditional knower and the objects observed or known), (2) the intentionality and world of the practical subject (the active, involved participant and the objects utilized), and (3) a more primordial intentionality and world (Heidegger would prefer "worldhood"), which precludes any use of the subject–object model and without which the understanding of the other two sorts of intentionality and world are necessarily misunderstandings. The most common misinterpretation of Heidegger's thinking here is to stop short of this more radical understanding of intentionality and world and to see him as simply drawing special attention to and asserting the special importance of the world of practical activity with its skillful subjects and useful objects. It is important to avoid this misunderstanding if we are to grasp Heidegger's departure from Husserl and the tradition.

I

Husserl shares with the tradition the desire to turn philosophy into a strict science. It is no accident that the most concise presentation of his philosophical method is titled *Cartesian Meditations.* And Husserl believed the key to the transformation of philosophy into such a science (phenomenology), and to its separation from the other sciences as well, was the exclusive focus of its attention toward the meanings (*noemata*) that mediate our experience of objects. Husserl's phenomenology sought to explain how consciousness was directed in various ways (e.g., perceiving or remembering) toward objects of various kinds (e.g., ordinary material objects or other people). Like Descartes's, Husserl's primary interest lay in what we would today refer to as the cognitive: acts of perception or observation and their relation to beliefs about the world.

On Husserl's account, even though not all of the aspects of a perceptual object are sensuously presented to the perceiver, such objects are completely intended in each conscious experience of them. He describes the meanings that mediate such experience as made up of both filled and unfilled components, corresponding respectively to the aspects of an object that are presented and appresented (Husserl's term for the co-intended but not sensuously presented aspects of an object from a particular perceptual point of view). Perceptual consciousness is of objects by virtue of systems of such meanings, and belief or knowledge is a matter of the consistency of our experience over time with such systems.

To this story about how meanings function to organize our experience of the world and provide us with the necessary epistemic credentials, Husserl added a story about the priority relations the various components of meanings have among themselves. This second story is a natural sequel to the first. The most basic or fundamental part of our sense of things consists of those characteristics needed in an account of perceptual objects. Value and relational predicates that go beyond the description of objects as simply perceived or observed are secondary, added to, and dependent upon the more fundamental components of perceptual meaning.

What Heidegger shares with Husserl's "philosophy as rigorous science" is the desire to get at things as they really are, free of any philosophical or other assumptions that could distort our point of view. And, like Husserl, he believes that such access is to be found by paying very careful attention to our actual experience of the world and of ourselves. He uses the term "phenomenology" to capture this getting things to reveal themselves to us in this way. But all the details of Heidegger's story differ markedly from Husserl's, and Husserl's priorities of meaning, which Heidegger identifies with the entire philosophical tradition, are simply reversed.

In Division I of *Being and Time* Heidegger discovers that our fundamental sense of things is not as objects of perception and knowledge, but rather as instrumental objects (equipment) that fit naturally into our ordinary practical activity:

> The kind of dealing which is closest to us is as we have shown, not a bare perceptual cognition, but rather that kind of concern which manipulates things and puts them to use. (BT 95)

> The less we just stare at the hammer-thing, and the more we seize hold of it and use it, the more primordial does our relationship to it become, and the more unveiledly is it encountered as that which it is – as equipment. (BT 98)

And our fundamental sense of ourselves in the midst of such activity is not as passive observers, but rather as purposively involved participants at home in the practical world:

> Dasein finds "itself" proximally in *what* it does, uses, expects, avoids – in those things environmentally ready-to-hand with which it is proximally *concerned.* (BT 155)

> Proximally and for the most part, Dasein *is* in terms of *what* it is concerned with. (BT 181)

Heidegger makes these discoveries by getting things to show themselves to us as they really are in our ordinary dealings with them. And this turns out, according to Heidegger, to be rather difficult, since in our ordinary dealings with things they hardly show up at all in the traditional sense of being explicitly noticed or perceived. In ordinary practical activity we make use of things, but we do not typically notice or attend to them. When we use the doorknob to open the door and get into the next office, we do not attend to its perceptual characteristics. Our attention instead is directed toward where we are going and what we are doing, and the doorknob is used so automatically in familiar surroundings like these that it withdraws from view and serves its instrumental function invisibly:

> The peculiarity of what is proximally ready-to-hand is that, in its readiness-to-hand, it must, as it were, withdraw in order to be ready-to-hand quite authentically. That with which our everyday dealings proximally dwell is not the tools themselves. On the contrary, that with which we concern ourselves primarily is the work. (BT 99)

Practical intentions seem to go through the things we use toward the goals or purposes of our activity. The famous hammer of *Being and Time* has its perceivable properties, of course, but for the most part they are not explicitly noticed when the hammer is being skillfully employed. The skilled carpenter uses the hammer to drive the nails to build the house to shelter a family, thereby providing for her family either directly or indirectly. Explicit attention is typically directed toward the work (nail driving and house building) rather than the equipment used to accomplish it. It is this invisible functioning of equipmental things that is definitive of their being in the world of practical activity according to Heidegger. His claim is that the hammer and doorknob really are what they are as practically employed. The trick is to see what they are without changing them from instrumental to perceptual objects and breaking down the network of relations essential to their instrumental nature.

This trick can be accomplished when things go wrong in the right sort of way. When practical activity is interrupted by the failure of an instrumental thing, we suddenly see the network of relations in which that instrumental functioning was embedded. When the doorknob comes off in our hand or the head falls off the hammer, the transparent functioning ceases and the relation of that functioning to complexes of instruments (latches, doors, and hallways or nails, lumber, and the rest of the carpenter's tools and materials) and to our ongoing purposes and projects (getting into our office and finding a book to prepare a lecture or assembling boards and runners to repair some deteriorated stairs) comes suddenly into view.

Heidegger labels the ordinary way that objects are for us in the midst of practical activity "ready-to-hand." The way that such objects are for us during breakdowns in their normal functioning he calls "unready-to-hand." The complexes of instruments just referred to he calls "equipmental totalities." And the system of ongoing purposes and projects he refers to as hierarchical "toward-which," "in-order-to," and "for-the-sake-of" relations between our activities and our short- and long-term goals. What shows up when our normal activity is interrupted, when things we are using become unready-to-hand, is the world of practical activity (BT 105–6). This world *just is* the network of relations into which can be fitted the systems of equipmental totalities with their internal relations ("references") among the tools they contain and their external relations ("assignments") to the purposes of the humans who use them, and human beings with their practical ties to one another and to the objects they deal with. Ready-to-hand things *just are* their place in such a world. To be a hammer is to be related in the right way to nails and boards, to house repairing and parental caring or providing, and so on.

The intentionality of practical activity is typically directed through the objects we use toward the immediate purposes for which we use them. The space of practical experience is neither Euclidean nor perceptual in nature. Instead, it has dimensions of accessibility and interest. Things are "near" in the former dimension when they are accessible, in their assigned spots and available for use when needed; and they are "distant" when they are unavailable for use even if they are right under our noses. Things are "near" in the latter dimension when our interests make the activity of using them essential; and they are "distant" when they play no part in our current projects (BT 135–6, 140–2).

Heidegger is careful to avoid the term "perception" even when discussing the kind of looking around that is sometimes necessary in practical contexts. The term he prefers is "circumspection," a term referring to the kind of looking around that makes sense only against the practical background or world, and that is always guided by our practical interests and concerns (BT 98). The carpenter looks to see that the nail is going in straight when the confined space in which she works alters the skillful movements with which she would routinely drive the nail. Or she searches the parts of the workshop most likely to contain an object of the appropriate size and weight to substitute temporarily for the broken hammer. At no point in such circumspection is she just looking at the environment and noting disinterestedly the objective characteristics of the items perceived. Circumspection is itself a worldly activity, one that is purposive, skillful, and no less practical in its structural relations than the rest of the normal activity of daily life.

Heidegger argues that this practical world, the intentionality appropriate to it, and the sense things have for us within it are more fundamental than the traditional sense of the world as a collection of things in objective space, the intentionality of cognitive acts, and the sense things have for us within such acts. That priority or fundamentality comes to at least the following:

(1) The practical world is the one we inhabit first, before philosophizing or engaging in scientific investigation – in Heidegger's words, it is where we find ourselves "proximally and for the most part."

(2) The world in the traditional sense can be understood as derivative from the practical world, but not the other way around – that is, starting from Heidegger's account of the practical world we can make sense of how the traditional sense of the world arises, whereas any attempt to take objective perception and cognition as basic and construct the practical world out of the resources traditionally available is doomed to failure (BT 122, 146–7).

Heidegger's critique of the world as interpreted by the philosophical tradition occurs in the context of his discussion of the Cartesian picture of mental and material (or "corporeal") reality and their interrelationship. The ingredients of this world are a mind whose contents are mental representations (ideas) and an independent substantial reality (typically material) capable of being represented. The goal of philosophy and science within this tradition is to get at reality as it is in itself and then to find ways to guarantee that our mental representation of it is accurate. Getting at things as they are independent of our purposes and projects requires that we depart from the practical attitude and world and adopt the theoretical standpoint. Heidegger thinks of this standpoint as that of the disinterested spectator whose observation is motivated only by a kind of pure curiosity about the true nature of things. To adopt this standpoint is equivalent to just looking ("staring") at things and encountering those properties they present to us simply as perceivers. Heidegger calls things as they are encountered in this way "present-at-hand." Traditional ontology is thus the ontology of the present-at-hand, the theory that takes the things that figure in perception and traditional cognition rather than those that are the objects of circumspection and practical utilization as most basic (BT 127–30).

Heidegger offers a number of reasons to think that the traditional view is a mistake. I can only summarize them, since the arguments in each case would be too lengthy to reproduce here. First, he believes that the picture of subjects with their internal (private) representations confronting a world of independent (public) objects is the source of the traditional problem of knowledge (skepticism). We can avoid the problem only by avoiding the theoretical picture of reality that gives rise to it (BT 247–50). Second, the traditional account has no way to explain how things have value. Starting with present-at-hand objects that are independent of us, there seems to be no satisfactory account of the transition to objects with value predicates that seem to depend on the relations of the object to us. Heidegger attributes the traditional fact–value dichotomy and its associated problems to the traditional construal of the present-at-hand as most real or basic (BT 132).

At this point we have returned to the second and more important sense in which the practical world is primary or basic for Heidegger, the "you can't get there from here" challenge to traditional ontology. It is clear that we have access to both worlds, the theoretical and the practical, and that we encounter both present-at-hand and ready-to-hand objects. In Heidegger's view, Husserl's attempted explanation of how we add layers of meaning to our mental representations in order to get from bare things to the culturally useful and valuable objects of the world of everyday life is about the best that can be done given the traditional framework, and it is an obvious and complete failure. The practical (social, cultural) world is not the world of the present-at-hand plus some relations and relational predicates. We cannot get to the everyday world that Heidegger describes in that way.

But we *can* get from the ready-to-hand to the present-at-hand by something like subtraction of interest and involvement from ordinary practical activity. If the carpenter cannot find anything to substitute for the broken hammer and abandons her efforts to get on with the work, she may eventually reach the point of just looking at the things around her in the workshop, a condition that puts out of play the network of practical relations that make the ready-to-hand what it is. This breakdown of practical activity is not our only access to the present-at-hand. We are not always at work or in the midst of practical activity, not always characterizable in terms of making use of equipment in order to, and so on. And there are special kinds of practice, such as those involved in science, which seem to require a kind of just looking and seeing in order to achieve their own special purposes. The point is, however, that if we take the relational context of practical activity as basic, the modifications required to reach the theoretical point of view are intelligible in terms of a lessening of practical interest and concern or the substitution of special limited interests and concerns for the ordinary everyday ones, and the resulting decontextualization (or minimal contextualization) of the everyday world. Heidegger not only traces the route from the ready-to-hand to the present-at-hand in this way, he also shows how the space ("existential space") of practical activity can undergo a similar transformation and become objective space (BT 146–7). In Division II of *Being and Time* he attempts to tell the same story with respect to "existential" and objective time. If all of this is correct, the ready-to-hand and its practical world enjoy a priority over the present-at-hand and the theoretical world in terms of intelligibility or explanatory self-sufficiency, and Heidegger takes this to be equivalent to priority in the logical, ontological, and epistemological senses.

II

The third and most important sort of intentionality and world for Heidegger is much more difficult to get hold of than either the practical or the theoretical. The best way to do so is to return to the fundamental intentionality and world of practical activity and look for something even more fundamental that they presuppose – not in the direction of the present-at-hand, but in something like the opposite direction. The hammer "refers," according to Heidegger, to the nails and boards with which it is used. In fact, the "being" of equipment consists of such "reference" relations to other equipment in the same equipmental totality, as well as of "assignments" to the typical purposes for which it is used. But the hammer does not wear such relations "on its sleeve" or present them in the way that it seems to present its color or shape to any observer. To someone entirely unfamiliar with the tools and activity of the carpenter, the hammer is at best a present-at-hand object to be observed or thought about. The hammer is what it is as ready-to-hand – it is a piece of equipment with the appropriate practical relations – only for those familiar with the workshop and work of the carpenter. And it is fully ready-to-hand in the sense of functioning transparently and smoothly as equipment only for those skillfully coping with the carpenter's tools and tasks, those who are truly at home in the workshop.

Readiness-to-hand is tied in this way to specific familiarities and skills for coping in specific practical environments. And if we stopped with this insight, we could make sense of much of Heidegger's case against the philosophical tradition. This familiarity with specific practical environments certainly does not involve explicit mental contents or representations. There are no Husserlian systems of meanings, or *noemata,* that mediate practical expertise. Nor is such expertise a matter of beliefs or cognitions.[4] The traditional emphasis on the cognitive, the attempt to explain all human behavior in terms of what we believe and how we consciously represent things to ourselves, cannot account for the implicit familiarity and competence that are the hallmarks of everyday practical activity. Explicit representations of things in the practical world and conscious beliefs we form within practical contexts always presuppose this nonrepresented and, for Heidegger, nonrepresentable background of familiarity and expertise.

There is, however, a background of familiarity and associated competence for dealing with things and with others that is even broader and more basic than those associated with specific practical activities and settings. Just as we have a specific familiarity with the carpenter's workshop and specific skills for coping with things in the carpenter's environment enabling us to encounter the hammer as a hammer, so we have a general familiarity with things and others and a set of implicit skills for dealing with them that form the necessary background for our encountering anything at all. Heidegger's discussion of practical activity and the relations that constitute the practical world were meant to prepare us for grasping the more general "activity" of being human and the "worldly" structure it presupposes.

This sense of the world as the most general structure of involvements that enables and "calls forth" all human "comportment" is probably the central contribution of *Being and Time,* and it is the link between *Being and Time* and Heidegger's later writings. For Heidegger, specific ready-to-hand and present-at-hand environments are just particular cases of this general worldhood, and the skills and familiarity involved are just particular cases of the general familiarity and ways of coping that constitute our human way of being in the broadest sense. Dealing with hammers is just a specific case of the more general skilled "comportment" of dealing with objects – identifying them, drawing near to them, picking them up, and so on – and our familiarity with the workshop is just a specific case of our more general being at home or "dwelling" in everyday environments – knowing (in the sense of possessing the skill or competence, not in the sense of having the right sort of beliefs) how to position and move ourselves, what to do and say, and so on.

These most general skills and familiarity are even more transparent and invisible than specific practical ones. Not only do we not normally attend to them (because we attend to the activities in which we are involved through them), but the very notion of attending to them flies in the face of Heidegger's account of human being and world. The point of that account is that things show up for us or are encountered as what they are only against a background of familiarity, competence, and concern that carves out a system of related roles into which things fit. Equipmental things *are* the roles into which they are cast by skilled users of them, and skilled users *are* the practical roles into which they cast themselves. Breakdowns of practical activity can give us an opportunity to grasp the background of practical familiarity, competence, and concern associated with specific systems of practical relations and roles because the world of the carpenter, for example, is not the entire human world and being a carpenter is not the whole of being human. We have a broader and more basic background to fall back on. Attending to or grasping is a human activity. All human activity is worldly; that is, it requires a background of implicit familiarity, competence, and concern or involvement. But when it comes to our broadest and most basic sense of things, our sense of human being and world, there is no broader context from which we could attend to or grasp it. We cannot abandon our most general skills for dealing with things in order to make them reveal themselves as we can with the skills of the carpenter. Human being is skillful coping all the way down, and this broadest level of familiarity, competence, and involvement is rock bottom. We do not even consciously acquire such things. We grow up into them through socialization or enculturation. They are what we are, not what we are aware of.

It is this last point that Heidegger seeks to capture when he says that human being is its world ("existingly") and that the world has our ("Dasein's") way of being (BT 92, 416). We just *are* our most general and fundamental way of "comporting" ourselves toward things and human beings, and these same manners of "comportment" are the background without which things and others could not be encountered, namely, the world.

This third and most fundamental sense of intentionality and world provides another insight into the priority of practical intentionality and the practical world over theoretical intentionality and the world of the present-at-hand. The practical world adds some specialized ways of coping, together with their correlative familiarity relations, to the full-blown general background skills and familiar ways of dealing with things and others that make up *the* world. The theoretical world, however, is accessed by methodologically constraining our full range of general background skills and our range of specialized practical skills and purposes so that only those relevant to theoretical observation and cognition are "in play." The theoretical world has its own background skills and familiar ways of coping with things – it is still a "world" in Heidegger's language – and it uses the general competence and familiarity of *the* world as its background. Nevertheless, it is incomplete, deficient, or derived in relation to the practical world.

Values are built into both the world as the general background of all encountering and the world of practical activity. Values are implicit in the operation of our most general skills for dealing with things and others. The particular cultural form of this coping will tend to make certain kinds of things and relations stand out as important to the exclusion of others. One might think of the difference in the general ways of dealing with everyday things in Eastern and modern Western cultures as illustrative of this point. Until very recent Westernization, the Japanese and Chinese treated things like teacups and dishes with a reverence we in the West tend to reserve for works of art. These objects were crafted with great care, passed on through generations, and valued for their beauty and intricacy of design. Comparably useful Western items could be made of anything from mass-produced unbreakable ceramic material to styrofoam or paper, and they are valued for the economy and speed of their manufacture and the ease and efficiency of obtaining, using, and reusing or disposing of them. The different background practices and perspectives lead to equally different styles of encountering and dealing with the things involved, and they make different features of the things relevant or irrelevant, important or unimportant. In addition, cultural background practices and perspectives embody tacit norms of appropriateness. Some of these may find expression as public norms of conduct, what one ("*das Man*") does or does not do or say in certain situations (BT 164–8). But for the most part they remain unexpressed, as do the cultural norms that govern how close to people it is appropriate to stand to engage in casual conversation, the conduct of business, and so on. There is a felt correctness, of getting things "right," when our particular dealings with things and others are consistent with the implicit norms of our cultural background.

In the practical world there are obvious sources of value. Since the practical world includes human purposes and projects, things will take on value in relation to their potential positive or negative contributions to the achievement of those purposes and the success of those projects. The practical world consists primarily of practical activity in pursuit of such purposes, and the norms attached to specific activities will generate value judgments. There will be right and wrong ways to hammer, appropriate and inappropriate nails for a given purpose, and hammers that can be too light or too heavy for the task at hand.

III

In addition to covering intentionality and world in all its senses and parting ways with the philosophical tradition as indicated above, Division I of *Being and Time* lays the foundation for the discussion of authenticity and temporality in Division II. A sense of the overall project of *Being and Time* will help to make the connection between the previous discussion of human being and world and Heidegger's account of the various aspects of "inauthentic" human being toward the end of Division I. The overall project of *Being and Time* was to discover the meaning of being. The first half (the only part written) of the complete work as projected is an analysis of human being (or "Dasein"). The reason for starting with human being in the quest for being in general has already emerged (though not clearly) in our discussion of the world. Every human project is a taking up of a culturally available possibility and presupposes the culturally determined background of skills and familiarity that Heidegger calls the world. This world makes possible the encountering of specific entities ("beings"), and it embodies our implicit sense of what it is for them to be. So human being, by virtue of its inseparability from the world (human being is "being-in-the-world") necessarily includes a sense ("understanding") of what is to be, that is, of being. Division II argues that this understanding of being that we are is essentially temporal or historical ("temporality"), and the second (never written) half of *Being and Time* was to trace the historical development of our understanding of being in search of its transhistorical meaning, the meaning present but hidden in the history of Western metaphysics.

Getting back to Division I, it turns out that human beings can "understand" what it is to be in two different ways, authentically and inauthentically, and that the authentic way, not surprisingly, is the one that gives us the best access to the meaning of being. So Heidegger begins the analysis of inauthentic human being to prepare the way for the eventual understanding of authentic human temporality ("historicity") and the approach to the essential meaning of being through our historical (mis)understandings of it.

Practical projects or purposes are typically arranged in a hierarchical order. I hammer the nail to assemble the boards in order to build the house so that my family will have a suitable place in which to live. The hammering may be invisible to the skilled carpenter engaged in this hierarchy of purposes, but the other pieces of this purposive hierarchy are not. Awareness is directed toward the task at hand and its place in the larger project toward which it contributes. There are, however, invisible purposes ("for-the-sake-ofs") on the far end of this chain. I am concerned about housing my family "because" I strive to be a good spouse and parent "because" I strive to be a good human being. These most ultimate purposes are not typically things of which we are aware. They are bound up inextricably with the invisible general background of all of our intentional relations, that is, with the world. It is the culturally determined background of experience that gives us our implicit sense of what it is like to get things like family relationships or being human "right."

In taking up particular practical projects and human purposes, we also take up or take over a variant of our cultural understanding of being. According to Heidegger we typically do so either in an undifferentiated way or in the inauthentic manner. Here is what he has in mind. The current cultural understanding of being includes a sense of the appropriateness of human purposes and projects and of the manners in which we engage in them. This sense is mostly implicit, especially the deepest or most fundamental parts of it, but not entirely so. Much of it resides in public or social norms of comportment, at least some of which can be made explicit. These are the norms captured by such expressions as "One [*das Man*] just doesn't do that," "One doesn't do that here, in that manner . . . ," or "One always . . . ," and so on. These norms are the typical vehicles of peer control during adolescence. But Heidegger's point is that such norms are not limited to the world of adolescence but are everywhere, at least implicitly, as the potential expressions of the cultural sense of what it is appropriate to do when or where, and of the appropriate and inappropriate ways of doing it.

Heidegger identifies three aspects of our relation to being, to the cultural sense of appropriateness, the general skills for coping with entities, and the familiarity associated with them: mood, understanding, and discourse. In Division II these are associated with the three aspects of time – past, future, and present. By "mood" Heidegger means something like our sense of how we find ourselves to be. It is our implicit or felt sense of the brute facticity of the cultural sense of being that we inherit rather than choose, our "thrownness" into a world that was not of our making but with which we are nonetheless stuck (BT 174–6). By "understanding" Heidegger means literally taking a stand on. We take a stand on our own being whenever we choose a particular possibility or project. Every purposive, future-directed choice from among the culturally determined alternative possibilities expresses an understanding, in Heidegger's sense, of what it is to be a human being (BT 185–6). In addition, every circumspective encountering of the ready-to-hand in the course of our projects involves understanding in the full sense, the interpretation of something *as* what it is by virtue of its equipmental relations (BT 189–90). It is important to note that interpretation in Heidegger's sense need not be verbal at all. Finally, "discourse" for Heidegger is the articulation of the intelligibility (i.e., the being) of things (BT 204–5). Discourse involves communication and it makes use of language as its tool, but it is not necessarily a matter of speaking. We can sometimes communicate an understanding of something most effectively by keeping silent. And silence is essential to hearkening to and grasping the understandings communicated to us (BT 208–9).

For Heidegger, we are always choosing from among the cultural possibilities and against the cultural background of intelligibility into which we have been thrown. That is, we are always understanding ("taking a stand on") our being on the basis of our thrownness or facticity. Human being is essentially self-interpreting being ("-in-the-world"). But for the most part this self-interpreting is not only implicit – it is anonymous ("public" in Kierkegaard's sense). We choose, frequently without realizing we are choosing, to do "what one does." When these choices are virtually unconscious, we are existing in what Heidegger calls an undifferentiated mode vis-à-vis authenticity and inauthenticity. But when we *choose* to interpret our being in the public way – living in the world of the one (*das Man*), doing "what one does" because it is either the "right" or the comfortable thing to do – we "fall" into the inauthentic way of being (BT 221–4).

We have a tendency toward the inauthentic understanding of our being because of some facts of (human) life that are hard to take.

These all have to do with the lack of ground, foundation, or objective justification for our being. The general background of intelligibility or world that gives us our most basic sense of things, others, and ourselves is itself without any ultimate source of intelligibility or ground. It is the deepest level for us or of us. It is that according to which we must interpret everything, but is itself nothing more than further interpretation. We are, and the world is, interpretation all the way down. What is rock bottom in terms of basic skills and felt familiarity is only contingently so – there is no further sense of correctness or final justification for the way we are. Even the choices we make from among the possible interpretations (purposes, projects) culturally available to us are utterly contingent – determined if at all by more fundamental implicit choices that are themselves contingent. In both directions our understanding of being is in this sense groundless. The sense of ourselves and our world that our cultural past sticks us with has no ultimate claim to validity, and the future-directed projects and practices that constitute our taking over of this cultural facticity and our interpretation of ourselves in terms of it are equally incapable of objective validation. Our practices, skills, and familiarity are grounded in nothing firmer than further practices, skills, and familiarity. And all of these facts of life can be brought vividly home to us by an attack of the mood Heidegger calls anxiety (BT 230–5).

Anxiety for human beings is analogous to breaking down for pieces of equipment. Just as the breaking down of equipment can show its worldly character by revealing its place in a network of relations in which it has become dysfunctional, so anxiety can show the groundless character of human being by revealing the contingency of the network of purposes and projects and their background of intelligibility in which we are no longer involved by virtue of our having become "dysfunctional." The details of exactly how that works and exactly what Heidegger thinks is revealed are best left to a discussion of Division II. What we have said in this section is sufficient to complete this brief sketch of inauthenticity: it is that into which we flee or fall to avoid anxiety and its unsettling revelations.

The inauthentic form of understanding is (idle) "curiosity" (BT 216–17). In order to avoid coming to grips with the unsettling deep truths about our being and world, we occupy ourselves with the kind of questioning of our being and world that can be satisfied by the superficial sense of things that (every) one has and by the kinds of irrelevant information that is the stuff of superficial conversation and gossip. And it is just such superficial conversation and gossip, "idle talk" for Heidegger, that makes up the inauthentic version of discourse (BT 213–14). Having no deep understanding of things to communicate authentically to others, and afraid of being silent for fear of "hearing" the deeper truth about our being (the "call of conscience"), we engage in the kind of noisy chatter that never questions or gets below the anonymous public understanding of things and, hence, never really says anything.

Heidegger believes that this inauthentic understanding of human being represents more than just an unfortunate failure of self-knowledge into which many of us fall. Toward the end of Division I of *Being and Time* he attempts to tie this misunderstanding to traditional metaphysics and its fundamental ontological mistake (BT 245–7). The claim is that inauthentic self-understanding is the first step toward the traditional misunderstanding of being. The story is as follows.

Falling into the inauthentic understanding of our being is equivalent to "absorption" in the public world (the world of *das Man*). This world is objective and is treated as such. It is essentially a world of objects. More important, the inauthentic understanding of this world seeks to ground or validate the norms that constitute it, and hence construes them as objective facts dictated by an underlying independent reality. It is but a short step from here to the (mis)understanding of ourselves as "real" objects of a special kind. This makes objectivity the fundamental category of being, our being as well as that of the rest of reality. At this point we arrive at the ontology of the present-at-hand and join Husserl and the rest of the philosophical tradition.

NOTES

1 See, e.g., *The Crisis of European Sciences and Transcendental Phenomenology* (Evanston, Ill.: Northwestern University Press, 1970), pp. 123–48, 173–83.

2 See D. Føllesdal, "Husserl's Notion of Noema," *Journal of Philosophy*, 66 (1969): 680–7; idem, "Husserl's Theory of Perception" in *Handbook of Perception*, Vol. 1, ed. E. Carterette and M. Friedman (New York: Aca-

demic Press, 1974), pp. 377–85; and D. Smith and R. McIntyre, "Intentionality via Intensions," *Journal of Philosophy,* 68 (1971): 541–61.

3 I should note at this point that although Brentano clearly influenced Husserl, it is quite likely that Frege was *not* instrumental in the actual development of either Husserl's general theory of consciousness or his more specific account of linguistic experience. See J. Mohanty, "Husserl and Frege: A New Look at Their Relationship," *Research in Phenomenology,* 4 (1974): 51–62. The reason for *understanding* Husserl's theory in terms of Frege's model is that Husserl explicitly acknowledges the parallel with his own theory, and it moves the point of possible confusion back one important step. There may still be very serious problems involved in making the Fregean distinctions across the entire range of conscious experience, but thinking in terms of Frege's model at least makes clear the kinds of distinctions Husserl is trying to make.

4 For an extended defense of this Heideggerian claim, see H. L. Dreyfus and S. Dreyfus, *Mind over Machine,* (New York: Macmillan, 1986).

ROBERT J. DOSTAL

5 Time and phenomenology in Husserl and Heidegger

One common view of the history of twentieth-century Continental philosophy is as follows. At the beginning of the century Edmund Husserl, disturbed by what he saw as the increasing relativism and historicism of Western culture, introduced the phenomenological method as a way to ensure that philosophy would arrive at final, incontrovertible truths. Phenomenology means primarily description – description of the things presented in our experience and description of our experience of them. The phenomenological movement was heralded by Husserl's cry, "Back to the things themselves!" Because phenomenology "brackets," or suspends belief in, all metaphysical constructs in order to focus solely on what shows up *as* it presents itself in our experience, its findings are supposed to be apodictic, beyond all possible doubt.

According to the standard story, the early Heidegger came along and raised questions about the viability of Husserlian phenomenology by taking an "interpretive" turn. What is most important about Heidegger's hermeneutic ontology, so the story goes, is his recognition of the significance of the finitude, worldliness, and historicity of our human predicament – the recognition that our access to things is always colored and preshaped by the sense of things circulating in our historical culture. The story then concludes with poststructuralists and various postmodern thinkers detecting a nostalgia for metaphysics even in such Heideggerian concepts as worldliness, finitude, and history. Jacques Derrida especially points out that Heidegger still seems to be trapped in essentialism and totalization, twin sins of the very "metaphysics of presence" that his hermeneutic approach was supposed to displace.

Critical to this story is the assumption that Heidegger's ontological hermeneutics succeeded in undercutting Husserl's phenomenology. Yet a closer look at Heidegger's early work suggests that the real story is not so simple. Thinkers such as Hans-Georg Gadamer and Paul Ricoeur, who build on Heideggerian hermeneutics, make it clear that their own thought presupposes phenomenology.[1] And Heidegger himself, who is supposed to have broken with Husserl, bases his hermeneutics on an account of time that not only parallels Husserl's account in many ways but seems to have been arrived at through the same phenomenological method as was used by Husserl. So important is the phenomenological account of time to recent Continental philosophy that even Derrida's well-known critique of the metaphysics of presence was initially formulated through a reflection on the Husserlian account of temporality.[2] The phenomenology of time, then, can serve as a key for understanding not only the relation of Husserl and Heidegger, but the development of Continental thought throughout this century as well. The differences between Husserl and Heidegger are significant, but if we do not see how much it is the case that Husserlian phenomenology provides the framework for Heidegger's approach, we will not be able to appreciate the exact nature of Heidegger's project in *Being and Time* or why he left it unfinished.

In this essay I will focus on Heidegger's early phenomenological account of time and its roots in the work of Husserl. It was Husserl himself who first undertook the project of phenomenological ontology – that is, the attempt to clarify the being of entities in general – and, as we shall see, he saw the phenomenological account of time as central to this project. Heidegger's *Being and Time,* with its explicit task of relating being to time, follows in the footsteps of Husserl's project. By showing the relation of Heidegger's thought to Husserl's, and by showing the similarities of both to the transcendental philosophy of Kant, I hope to show why time has such a central role in Continental thought. But it will also become clear that serious problems arise for the accounts of time in both Husserl and Heidegger. These problems can help us understand why *Being and Time* was never completed. But they also point to deep questions about the possibility of phenomenology generally, and they can clarify the motivation for some of the recent moves made by poststructuralists, postmodernists, and (to use Richard Rorty's self-descriptive oxymoron) postphilosophical philosophers.

HUSSERL AND TIME

Let us look first briefly at Husserl's project. Husserl hoped to provide a formal ontology linked with material ontologies of the various regions, or sorts, of entities. Ontology, as we have already noted, is the account of being in general and concerns essences and fundamental categories. A "formal" ontology treats the basic "forms" or structures of being in general, while a "material" ontology considers how these more general forms are filled out "materially," so to speak, in the various main types of entities. Husserl uses the geographic metaphor of "region" for these main divisions of entities – hence, the expression "regional" ontology, which is interchangeable with "material" ontology. In *Formal and Transcendental Logic* (1929) Husserl writes that the task of formal ontology is to "state what holds good for any objects whatever, any object-provinces whatever, with formal universality, in what forms they exist or merely can exist."[3] What the phenomenologist asserts in formal ontology must be true of any entity whatever. Sometimes Husserl speaks of formal ontology as treating the basic concepts (*Grundbegriffe*) or categories of objectivity as such. He thinks of being as objectivity. The notion of "object" and "objectivity" is a broad one, for "object" means more than the objects of perception. There are higher objectivities for Husserl such as those established in mathematics or the social sciences.

Husserl also refers to his project of phenomenological ontology as transcendental. We have just noted that phenomenology describes "objects" (in a broad sense). In order to justify these descriptions and in order to understand ourselves as describers, phenomenological description requires, in addition to careful and methodical description, a consideration of what description is and how it is made possible – that is, phenomenology considers the condition of the possibility not only of objects but of the description of objects. Thus, Husserlian phenomenology is "transcendental" in much the same sense as this term is defined in Immanuel Kant's introduction to the *Critique of Pure Reason,* the work that inaugurates the tradition of transcendental philosophy: "I entitle *transcendental* all knowledge which is occupied not so much with objects as with the mode of our knowledge of objects in so far as this mode of knowledge is to be possible a priori."[4] By *a priori* is meant knowledge gained of objects, as well as of the knower or subject, by way of rigorous philosophical reflection and not through the empirical sciences or generalization from everyday experience. *A priori* literally means "prior to experience." Such knowledge is said by Kant to be "necessary," while Husserl calls it "essential." According to the above citation, transcendental philosophy is particularly concerned with the self or subject who carries on this rigorous reflection. Kant was so much concerned with the subjective conditions of objective knowledge that he came to assert that we can never know things as they are in themselves, but only as they appear to us conditioned as we are by certain subjective cognitive structures. Here we find the most important disagreement of Husserl with Kant, for Husserl thinks we can know things as they are in themselves. How Husserl squares this commitment with his own version of "transcendental idealism" is something we cannot consider here. Many of his closest students did not think he could; others defended his attempt. In any case, it is important to note that not only objectivity, but also subjectivity must come under scrutiny for a fully justified philosophy. The bare rational self or ego considered only in terms of its basic cognitive structures (or forms) is called the "transcendental ego" by both Kant and Husserl.

Further comparison with Kant's *Critique of Pure Reason* might be helpful here. Formal ontology corresponds to what Kant attempted to accomplish in the Transcendental Analytic, that is, the *a priori* knowledge of an "object in general." For Husserl and Kant, the key to the discovery of the basic forms of objectivity is formal logic. Kant in the metaphysical deduction held that any formal logical law can be converted into an equivalent formal ontological law. Like Kant in the *Critique,* Husserl in *Formal and Transcendental Logic* begins with formal logic and moves on to "transcendental logic," which is formal ontology, though Husserl wants to avoid what he thinks is Kant's naive acceptance of traditional logic as a ground from which to derive the forms of objectivity. Formal logic for Husserl serves rather as a starting point and clue for the development of a formal ontology. For Kant, the regional or material ontology based on the "formal ontology" of the *Critique* would be the metaphysics of nature. According to Husserl's *Ideas II* and *Ideas III,* the task is somewhat more variegated since there are three primary regions: material nature, animate nature, and souls (or persons), and accordingly three regional ontologies: physics, somatology, and psychology.[5]

If we pursue the Kantian analogy further, we find that Husserl's *Formal and Transcendental Logic* also requires a supplementary transcendental aesthetic and a schematism, two other important components of Kant's *Critique.* The intelligible aspect of experience, treated in formal and transcendental logic, needs to be related to the sensible aspect of experience. In the conclusion of this work Husserl acknowledges this need. Recall that the Transcendental Analytic of the *Critique* is preceded by the Transcendental Aesthetic, which is an account of space and time. Recall further that after the argument of the metaphysical and transcendental deductions establishing the basic categories, there follows a section entitled "Schematism," which shows how each of the categories, initially presented independent of time, is in the end nothing other than a form or configuration of time. The categories are temporalized, though they are not "spatialized" because, for Kant, all experience is temporal but not all experience is spatial. Time has priority for Kant as it does for Husserl and, as we shall see, for Heidegger. Another way to express this is to say that the categories are nothing other than rules of temporal configuration (or schematization). To give two Kantian examples, the category "substance" is the "permanence of the real in time" and the category "cause" is "succession subject to a rule."[6]

Husserl had long been involved in the attempt to provide a phenomenological account of space and time, of the spatial and the temporal, but these accounts were never adequately integrated into the larger project.[7] As we have just noted, time has an important priority for reasons similar to those given by Kant. Husserl, however, never shows us how his formal objectivities or categories are temporalized. But he does return again and again throughout his life to the theme of time because he becomes convinced that time is the basic form of all experience. One might not infer the importance of this topic for Husserl from his publications, since his only publication in this regard is *The Phenomenology of Internal Time Consciousness,* lectures from 1905 with addenda. These lectures first appeared in 1928 (the year after the publication of *Being and Time*) under Heidegger's editorship. Husserl had asked Heidegger to publish his 1905 lectures some time earlier, and Heidegger agreed on the condition that he first complete *Being and Time.* It seems that this was Husserl's last attempt to remind Heidegger of Husserl's account of time and Heidegger's debt, as a phenomenologist, to this account. In the introduction to the first English translation of these lectures (1964), Calvin Schrag comments that the materials of the volume were "compiled and published" by Heidegger.[8] Though Heidegger did edit and publish them, it has become clear that he did not "compile" them. Husserl's assistant, Edith Stein, had compiled the manuscript, and Heidegger did relatively little but pass it on to the publisher. After 1928 the only further publication of Husserl's work on time was the republication of that edition together with extensive addenda that doubled the size of the volume.[9] But from approximately 1917 on Husserl returned in his writing again and again to time as his central and most basic theme. In the early twenties, Stein compiled another manuscript dedicated to the theme of time, and Husserl touted it at one point as his most important work. He attempted unsuccessfully to get first Roman Ingarden and then Eugen Fink to publish it.[10] This manuscript, usually referred to as the "Bernauer" or "L" manuscripts, remains unpublished, as does a later collection of manuscripts on the phenomenology of time from the late twenties and early thirties called the "C" manuscripts.

The phenomenology of time requires, of course, that we ignore our ordinary or scientific assumptions about time and attend rigorously to the lived experience of time. We must bracket "objective" time, as Husserl calls it in those lectures, to see how time is constituted immanently in experience – hence the title "inner time consciousness." On this account, we experience time primarily as the present "now." Yet it is important to see how fundamentally significant for Husserl is the rejection of the "objective" view of time as a punctilinear row of "nows" that stretch both back and forward to infinity and constitute a one-dimensional line, the objective time line. In contrast with this one-dimensional view of time, Husserl offers us a three-dimensional view. The present, for him, is not the nondimensional point of the instantaneous now. Rather, we might say that the present is "thick" to the extent that, *within* the present, we find both the past and the future; that is, we find all three dimensions of time. Any present moment, according to Husserl, has what he calls "retentive" and "protentive" aspects. In other words, any moment is what it is in virtue of what it retains of the past (retention) and what it anticipates of the future (protention). Every present moment carries these two aspects as essential to its being what it is *as* present. Crudely expressed, they are part of the present. The past is retained *as* past in the present, and the future is anticipated *as* future in the present. Husserl says that these three dimensions constitute the present. As time passes, each present (this "thick" present with three dimensions internal to it) is retained in the succeeding moment – retentionally. This retention and anticipation is, in our everyday experience, unconscious, but philosophical reflection shows it to be constitutive of the structure of any moment. Husserl distinguishes retention from memory, for in memory the past moment is experienced simply as past and not as part of the present. In similar fashion, he distinguishes protention from hopes and expectations, the conscious focusing on some imagined future event as future and not as a constitutive aspect of the present. There is a certain symmetry in the constitution of the lived experience of time; both protention and retention are essential to the account and both are distinguished, respectively, from memory and hope. Yet there is at least one other important element of Husserl's account: the flow of time is directional. Time flows ineluctably toward the future; it is not reversible. This understanding of the present as constituted by retention and protention is the core of Husserl's contribution toward a philosophy of time.

The centrality of "the present" for this analysis has led to Derrida's criticism of Husserl's phenomenology as a "metaphysics of presence." The primary point of this critique is that the Husserlian account suppresses absence. Rudolf Bernet, who has developed Derrida's critique, writes, for example, that absence cannot so easily be disposed of and that it returns to haunt Husserl – in his words, "the repressed element returns."[11] I would suggest on the contrary that absence is not ignored in Husserl's account, but is considered an essential element of the present. Retention and protention are modes of the presence of the absent (the past and the future) as well as the absence of the present (the past as no longer present and the future as not yet present). Husserl's thickening of the moment is just the attempt, I would argue, to render the temporal character of human experience as the ineluctable interplay of presence and absence.

When, in his *Ideas I* of 1913, Husserl comes to reflect on the phenomenological approach of the time lectures and of his earlier ground-breaking work, *Logical Investigations* (1900–1), he defends his method in the problematic terms of "transcendental idealism."

Here as before, Husserl distinguishes phenomenological time and objective (or cosmic) time. Phenomenological time, he writes, is "the unitary form of all lived experience (*Erlebnisse*) within *one* stream of lived experience (*Erlebnisstrom*), i.e., within *one* pure Ego."[12] "Phenomenological" or subjective inner time is given methodological precedence over "cosmic" or "objective" time, which is said to be constituted in inner time.

Husserl's form of idealism follows from the methodological precedence of subjectivity. In the words of *Formal and Transcendental Logic,* "The whole of phenomenology is nothing more than the self-examination on the part of transcendental subjectivity."[13] Only transcendental subjectivity, Husserl claims in the concluding sections of this book, exists "in and for itself." And so he writes that "the ultimate grounding of all truth is a branch of the universal self-examination that, when carried through radically, is absolute. In other words, it is a self-examination . . . which leads me to the grasping of my absolute self, my transcendental ego."[14] This egological self-interpretation of phenomenology Husserl calls the Cartesian way into phenomenology.[15]

When we turn to the question of time, we find that instead of time being just another object constituted in the thematic field of transcendental subjectivity, subjectivity is itself radically temporal. Frequently Husserl simply identifies time with subjectivity (much as Kant sometimes identifies "inner sense" with the subject). At other times it seems as though Husserl is arguing that the ego, as absolute, is not itself temporal but is the source of temporality. He speaks of the ego as the origin (*Ursprung*) and the source (*Quelle*) of time.[16] As the *Quelle,* which also means "spring," the ego is the spring of the stream of time. The spring itself does not flow but is constantly in the same place. Thus, in these same manuscripts Husserl often refers to the ego, which is this source or spring, as the *nunc stans,* or "standing now," a phrase that goes back to medieval scholasticism. It is the now that originates the flow of time but is not itself in time – hence its "standing" character. The standing now is the ego's primal form of being. As "standing," it constitutes the flow of time.

We have just noted how one approach of Husserl is to say that subjectivity (or the ego) is radically temporal. Taken this way, it is just the flow of time. A second approach sees the ego as somehow outside of time constituting time. But as Husserl develops his treatment of time in the late C manuscripts, he comes to think of time in relation to the subject in a third way – that is, neither (1) as subjective, nor (2) as originating in atemporal subjectivity, but (3) as somehow prior to the distinction between subject and object. In this third way time itself comes to be understood as that primordial source (*Ursprung*) out of which the ego and object poles emerge. The ground of the ego is time; time itself is "radically pre-egological." It is "a temporalizing-temporal primal occurring [*Urgeschehen*] which does not spring from egological sources (*aus Quellen des Ichs*); it therefore occurs without participation of the ego."[17] Again and again Husserl here takes up the notion of the "standing and perduring primal now," which itself is not in time but temporalizes – which is to say that it is the source of time. What is flowing and ephemeral is grounded in what is permanent. The permanent standing now is the absolute, which has its own ground in itself and is not grounded in anything else. It is, he writes, without ground (*grundlos*); as constituting, it is not itself constituted. We could say of time, seen in this way, what Heidegger later comes to say: "Temporality temporalizes" (BT 377).[18]

Thus we can see that when Husserl develops his treatment of time, he is ambivalent about the relation of transcendental subjectivity and temporality. Are subjectivity and temporality identical? Or is temporality prior to subjectivity and its objective correlate, that is, is it a pre-egological source out of which subjects and objects are constituted in time? If it is, then it is no longer appropriate to characterize the most important level of phenomenological analysis as egology. The egological project breaks down. The paradox of subjectivity (being both a subject for the world and an object in the world) becomes the paradox of time (being both a nontemporal source of the world and a temporal objective characteristic of the world). Further, we are led to ask whether phenomenology can resolve these questions. Is Husserl still maintaining a phenomenological standpoint when he discusses the primal ego as a monad or when he develops the concept of the standing now? That is, is this still a description of what is immanent in consciousness? Another way to see this difficulty is to recall the title of the early lectures on time: "Inner Time Consciousness." Time on the later account just discussed is neither "inner" nor a function of "consciousness." These two closely related sorts of questions – the ontological and the methodological – are two aspects of what might be called Husserl's deep problem with time.

There is a second important complex of ontological problems with respect to time that we should note here, if only briefly. It concerns not the deep question of the nature of time itself, but the "higher-level" question of the temporal constitution of different sorts of entities. As we have seen, Husserl is committed to the thesis that human experience is radically temporal. All aspects of experience have a temporal genesis – hence the importance of *genetic* (as opposed to static) phenomenology. But what are the relations between (1) time as such, (2) natural time (which Husserl sometimes calls "space-time" [*Raum-Zeit*]), and (3) historical time? Husserl never treats this question extensively, though he does distinguish natural and historical time as different modes of time. Sometimes Husserl seems to be working toward a treatment of natural and historical time that would render them equally fundamental, each with its own basis in the temporality of transcendental subjectivity. More often he seems to be working toward the view that historical time is founded on natural time. That which mediates the two is human bodiliness. We historical beings are also natural and bodily beings.

To sum up, we have seen how the transcendental phenomenology of Husserl was confounded by the problem of time in at least two ways. The deeper ontological problem of time concerns the relation of temporality and subjectivity, and it leads us to the limits of an egological phenomenology. The higher-level difficulty concerns the relation of natural time and historical time to each other, and to time as such. We can find parallel problems concerning time in Heidegger's ontology, problems both methodological and substantive.

THE EARLY HEIDEGGER AND TIME

Some of the disagreements between Husserl and his protégé Heidegger result from a fundamental misunderstanding on the side of Husserl as to the nature of Heidegger's project. Husserl had established a phenomenological research program in the early twenties in Freiburg. Based on his method, this research program was to be a cooperative one. Husserl, as founder of the method, understood his own task as doing the ground-breaking work in formal ontology and methodology. He hoped his followers and students would develop the regional ontologies. His journal, the *Yearbook of Philosophy and Phenomenological Research,* would publish the results of their research.[19] He hoped that Heidegger, whom he considered his most able follower, would provide the regional ontology for history and the historical sciences.[20] Sometimes Heidegger himself presented his own project in this way, but in fact what Heidegger chose to do instead was to pursue the ontology of time itself (what I have called the deeper ontological question) rather than the regional ontology of the historical realm. From Husserl's perspective, however, Heidegger asserts of time itself and being as such what might well be appropriate of the historical region. For Husserl, such a move historicizes being in such a way that we are left only with anthropology, historicism, and relativism. It seems that he understands Heidegger this way because Heidegger's starting point is Dasein, defined as being-in-the-world, a being-in-the-world that is thoroughly historical.

Whatever Husserl's assessment of Heidegger's attempt, a careful look at Heidegger's early project shows that he gets caught up in methodological and ontological problems similar to those of Husserl. Heidegger never completed this project and later abandoned it. We can find it developed in *Being and Time* (1927) and in the early published works that immediately follow it: *Kant and the Problem of Metaphysics* (1928) and *On the Essence of Reasons* (1928), as well as in the recently published lectures delivered when he was at Marburg from 1922 to 1928. Though we cannot here examine the problems and the parallels in detail, we can provide a short sketch.

Heidegger's early project: ontological, phenomenological, transcendental, and hermeneutic

The question for *Being and Time* is the question of being. In the Introduction, Heidegger tells us that he seeks to clarify the meaning of being (BT 31). This is his question, he tells us further, because it is the most basic question. All other questions presuppose that there is being, and all the sciences make assumptions about being. Since the work is about being and not about this or that sort of being or entity, his task is, in the first place, ontology. He calls the work "fundamental ontology" because it is concerned with the most basic question and because ontologies of the various sorts of entities necessarily presuppose it:

> The question of Being aims therefore at ascertaining the a priori conditions not only for the possibility of the sciences, which examine entities as entities of such and such a type, and, in so doing, already operate with an understanding of Being, but also for the possibility of those ontologies themselves which are prior to the ontical sciences and which provide their foundations. (BT 31)

We find here a clear parallel with Husserl's project. Fundamental ontology concerns the meaning of being as such. It establishes the basis for the ontologies of various regions of being, which, in turn, provide the philosophical basis for the sciences, clarifying the assumptions and basic concepts of the sciences. By "ontical" in the passage just quoted Heidegger means that which is concerned primarily with entities and not with being as such. The regions that Heidegger has in mind are those of history and nature. The regional ontology of each would provide the appropriate philosophical basis, respectively, for the human sciences and for the natural sciences. It is not clear whether Heidegger ever intended for himself to develop the regional ontologies, but it is clear that it is in relation to possible regional ontologies that Heidegger conceived of his task in *Being and Time* as fundamental ontology.[21]

Being and Time is also a work in transcendental phenomenology in much the same sense as the philosophy of Husserl. Phenomenology, Heidegger writes in the Introduction, "signifies primarily a *methodological conception.* This expression does not characterize the *what* of the objects of philosophical research as subject-matter, but rather the *how* of that research" (BT 50). It is a descriptive method that allows things to show themselves for what they are. To call it "transcendental" is to adopt terminology from Kant and Husserl, which means, as we saw earlier, "*a priori*" or necessary knowledge. As the preceding quotation states, fundamental ontology hopes to establish the *a priori* or necessary conditions for the regional ontologies and the sciences. In other words, fundamental ontology would develop the background required for the regional ontologies to proceed. It should establish the basic concepts and assumptions of these fields by making clear the basic or "formal" structures of being. Heidegger expresses his debt to Husserl in a footnote about the *a priori,* in which he writes that "Husserl has given us the necessary tools" (i.e., a method) for discovering the *a priori*. Here Heidegger asserts, "A-priorism is the method of every scientific philosophy which understands itself" (BT 490).

Heidegger's phenomenological method is also transcendental in the further related sense discussed earlier that such a method is as much concerned with the structures of subjectivity as it is with the structure of objectivity. In the Introduction Heidegger, self-consciously using Kantian language, criticizes Kant for not adequately treating the "subjectivity of the subject" (BT 45). Heidegger sets out to deal with this aspect in a better way than his predecessors Kant and Husserl. Important to Heidegger's improved approach is to drop the language of subject and subjectivity, object and objectivity. When Heidegger uses these terms, they are almost always in quotation marks to indicate that he is referring to the way things have been discussed in the philosophical tradition. One of the chief reasons Heidegger is so keen on avoiding this language is that to start with this duality of subject and object seems inevitably to lead to an unbridgeable gap between them, so that the logical outcome is subjectivism in some form or other. One prominent form of subjectivism related to the question of knowledge is representationalism, the view that the subject makes the world available to itself by means of representations. Since these representations are inevitably of its own making, there is no way of knowing in the end whether the representations mirror nature truthfully or are "merely" useful fictions. Kant's denial of any knowledge of the way things are in themselves is a good example of one such view. For Kant, neither the transcendental ego nor things in themselves are in time. Rather, time is a function of our subjective capacity to represent things to ourselves, so that the things we experience are shaped by our activity of representing. Though Heidegger did not regard Husserlian phenomenology as a form of representationalism, he did think that Husserl's language, particularly the language of subjectivity and objectivity, often betrayed Husserl's best insights.

So Heidegger sets the stage for his own attempt to clarify the meaning of being by giving an account of what he calls *Dasein*, the "there" (*Da*) where being (*Sein*) shows itself. Before directly addressing the central theme, being, we are to consider first where it is that being shows itself. And this means examining ourselves, since being is "an issue" for us in a way that it is not for other entities. To consider this is to consider the conditions that hold for there to be meaning. *Being and Time* sets for itself the task of establishing the meaning of being, and it addresses the question of meaning before it directly addresses being. Much like Kantian transcendental philosophy, Heidegger's fundamental ontology asks about the conditions of the possibility of knowing the subject matter of the inquiry before it takes up the subject matter, though Heidegger focuses on "understanding" instead of "knowing" with its implied relation of a subject to an object.

It is important to note that Heidegger's study of Dasein is a study of us *insofar as* we can come to terms with being. Heidegger's study or phenomenological account is about Dasein, being-there, and not about human being or human nature. Thus, it is not an attempt to give a full account of what it means to be human. According to Heidegger, his account in *Being and Time* should provide the appropriate basis or background for such an account, but this work is intended to be fundamental ontology, not philosophical anthropology.

The most important single fact about *Being and Time* is that it is unfinished. This work, as envisaged at the end of its introduction (BT 63–4), was to have two parts, each with three sections. The published text provides only the first two sections of Part I, which means that only the preparatory treatment of Dasein is accomplished. The third section, which is entitled "Time and Being" and which was to elucidate directly the concept of being, was never satisfactorily completed. In the end we have only the account of Dasein.

Time and the analysis of Dasein

Let us look at what is accomplished in the published text, that is, the analysis of Dasein, and notice the centrality of the theme of time. In the Introduction Heidegger declares that

> in contrast to all this [the history of philosophy], our treatment of the question of the meaning of Being must enable us to show that *the central problematic of all ontology is rooted in the phenomenon of time, if rightly seen and rightly explained,* and we must show *how* this is the case. (BT 40)

Heidegger shows "how" time is central through the description, or "Interpretation," of Dasein. Because we are temporal beings, our ability to encounter things *as* such and such is also temporal. Dasein is thoroughly temporal, and thus Dasein's understanding is temporal. And so must be our understanding of being. Thus, to cite the Introduction once again, "the Interpretation of Dasein" is to be accomplished "in terms of temporality (*Zeitlichkeit*)" (BT 63). In this way time comes to serve "as the transcendental horizon [or context] for the question of Being" (BT 63). Accordingly, it is clear that the phenomenology of time is at the heart of Heidegger's ontological project.

The first half of the text ("Preparatory Fundamental Analysis of Dasein") provides what could be called a "static" structural or "formal" account of Dasein. The second half ("Dasein and Temporality") then shows how these structures must be understood as temporal structures. Heidegger himself calls the analysis formal but explicitly rejects calling it categorial. Categories, as we will see later, pertain to nature but not to Dasein. Heidegger names the formal structures and defining concepts of Dasein "existentialia." Dasein, as already noted, is defined as being-in-the-world. The hyphens, almost as awkward in German as they are in English, are indicative of the fact that, as Dasein, self and world are a unity. The world is not something external but is constitutive of Dasein. We are born into a world whose history and culture help make us who we are. The Christian view that "we are in the world, but not of the world" is transformed. We are both in and of the world. "Worldliness" is an ontological property of Dasein; it is our context of involvements.

The preparatory analysis of Dasein is concerned primarily with an explication of what it means to be in the world, of how we find ourselves in relation to things in the world in "average everydayness." This "being in relation" is our worldliness. Being-in is seen to have two principal structures: understanding and state of mind. We understand ourselves and our world in terms of our practical involvements and projects. In understanding, we are ahead of ourselves, writes Heidegger. State of mind is the way we find ourselves already disposed toward things in this way or that. ("Disposition" might be a better translation for *Befindlichkeit* than is "state of mind.") The analysis concludes with an attempt to show how both of these are aspects of care (*Sorge*), which best captures not just one aspect of Dasein but Dasein in its entirety. Heidegger defines care as "ahead-of-itself-Being-already-in-(the world)-as Being-alongside-(entities encountered within the world)" (BT 237). This is a tripartite definition which says that Dasein has the following structures: (1) ahead of itself (understanding), (2) already in (disposition), and (3) alongside. Heidegger often refers to these three structures as existentiality, facticity, and fallenness.

For our purposes here it is most important to note that these three aspects of Dasein are given a temporal interpretation in the second half of *Being and Time:* "The primordial unity of the structure of care lies in temporality" (BT 375). The three aspects of care correspond to the three dimensions of time: the future (ahead of itself), the past (facticity), and the present (fallenness). The unity of Dasein is founded on care, whose unity in turn is founded on temporality. Any moment of human experience has these three dimensions. Heidegger talks about this three-dimensionality of the lived experience of time as the "ecstatic" unity of time. By this he means how each of these three dimensions is distinctive and distinguishable from the other two, that is, how each dimension "stands out" from the others. "Standing out" is the literal meaning of "ecstasy." By the ecstatic character of time Heidegger also means to describe how any moment is a crossing point of past and future. The present bears within it the past and the future. Past and future make it up. This connectedness and ecstatic unity he sometimes refers to as the "transcendence" of time and the transcendence of Dasein, which is essentially temporal in just this way. The present moment goes beyond, or "transcends," the merely present in the way that it, as present, is at the same time future and past. In this way Heidegger recovers and maintains in the context of his own work the Husserlian insight about what I have called the thick unity of time. He follows Husserl as well in criticizing the view of time that thinks of it as an infinite series of points, of nows – what Heidegger calls "now-time" (*Jetzt-Zeit;* see BT §81).[22]

What most obviously distinguishes Heidegger's account from Husserl's is the way, on Heidegger's account, Dasein can live out its temporality as authentic or inauthentic. Thus, there are authentic and inauthentic modes of understanding and disposition.[23] For the most part, according to Heidegger, Dasein is inauthentic and fallen, caught up and lost in the present in a way that cuts it off from its authentic future (its "ownmost possibility") and its past. What the future holds for any and every Dasein is death. Another definition of Dasein is therefore provided: being-toward-death. In the authentic moment, we recognize and accept our mortality. Heidegger's story of Dasein is, in this regard, not so unlike the Christian story of fallen human nature (though Heidegger denies that his story is just another version of original sin). While the present has priority for the inauthentic, the future has priority for the authentic life. Notice that this gives priority to understanding over disposition, since Heidegger connects the understanding with the future and disposition with the past.

Time and the meaning of being

Being and Time, as we have already noted, never gets so far as to address directly the meaning of being, but instead concludes with the question: "Is there a way which leads from primordial *time* to the meaning of *Being?*" (BT 488). Approximately a year after his completion of the text of *Being and Time,* in the lectures of the summer semester of 1927, *Basic Problems of Phenomenology,* Heidegger explicitly sets for himself the task of finding this way from time to the meaning of being and so of completing Part I of *Being and Time* with a full-fledged ontology.[24] Yet the reader (and the student in the lecture hall) is disappointed, because the lectures break off just before the designated treatment.[25] We can find in these lectures, nonetheless, indications of the approach Heidegger was taking and the problems he faced. As required, he approaches the question of being through time. The shift from the analysis of the temporality of Dasein to the temporality of being is marked terminologically by the shift from the standard German *Zeitlichkeit* (temporality) to the Latinate *Temporalität* (temporality). The temporality of Dasein is *Zeitlichkeit;* the temporality of Being is *Temporalität.* A question the text does not answer concerns what the consequences of this shift might be. Is the analysis of the temporality of being merely an extension of the account of time in *Being and Time,* or are there important differences in the two accounts? Heidegger's comment in the *Letter on Humanism* makes us wonder about the shift when he says of the third section of Part I, "Time and Being": "Here everything is reversed" (BW 208). This comment, however, comes after the great turn in Heidegger's thought and his abandonment of the project of fundamental ontology. There is no talk of "reversal" in *Basic Problems.*

What we do find Heidegger doing in *Basic Problems* is giving an account of being in terms of its regions that is consistent with the stated project of developing a fundamental and regional ontology. The regions are divided according to their type of temporality. There are two main regions, each with two subdivisions: (1) that within time (*das Innerzeitige;* subdivisions: nature and history) and (2) the atemporal (*das Unzeitige;* subdivisions: extratemporal and supra-temporal). We might be inclined to object to these divisions of being and the notion of the atemporal, since Heidegger has rejected eternal truths and asserted that we are to understand being only through temporality. Yet the discussion here in *Basic Problems* does not deny the temporality of all understanding. It insists, rather, that the atemporal can be understood only in terms of temporality. Being and time are not simply equivalent, though the understood meaning of being must, in some way, be temporal.

Working out these divisions while at the same time maintaining the unity of being clearly posed serious problems for Heidegger. This is indicated directly in the title of the lecture series, *The Basic Problems of Phenomenology,* and by the introductory outline for the lectures, which indicates that Part II was to be concerned with thematic problems in laying out the basic structures of being, while Part III was to be concerned with the methodological problems of Heidegger's phenomenological approach to the question of being. Heidegger's designation of these problems for his fundamental ontology reminds us of what we have called Husserl's "deep" ontological problems of theme and method. Though we can distinguish the problems this way, that is, as thematic and methodological problems, they are closely related. Their close relationship can best be seen if we ask how the method allows us to make this thematic distinction of regions within being. Does the method take us outside both regions such that from the perspective of being we view these regions and differentiate them? In other words, is the distinction made "externally"? Yet if we are speaking from the perspective of Dasein, are we not making the distinction from "within time"?

In *Basic Problems* as well as in *The Metaphysical Foundations of Logic,* lectures of a year later (the last lectures at Marburg, summer semester, 1928), Heidegger is clearly concerned with the methodology of phenomenology and its specifically scientific character. As scientific, phenomenology according to Heidegger is necessarily neutral and indifferent with respect to its subject matter or themes.[26] In other terms, phenomenological methodology is inevitably objectifying. In the context of his discussion of the regions of being according to time as "in time," "out of time," and "above time," we must wonder about the justification of the distinctions and how it is that these regions become objects of study. This is particularly problematic if we recall Heidegger's oft-stated criticism of objectivism and his treatment of "indifference" in *Being and Time* as an inauthentic quality of Dasein. Were we simply and straightforwardly to follow Heidegger's suggestion that indifference is inauthentic, it would seem that phenomenology must be inauthentic. This is, of course, absurd in the context of Heidegger's project. We are left to wonder if, in the projected last part of *Basic Problems,* where Heidegger was to have addressed these questions of methodology at length, he would not have reinterpreted indifference for the philosophical attitude. Perhaps the indifference and neutrality of philosophy are significantly different from the indifference of inauthentic everyday experience. But nowhere in Heidegger's early work is a satisfying account to be found.

The ontological difference between nature and history

Another major problem with the project of *Being and Time* that becomes quite apparent in *Basic Problems* concerns the distinction within the temporal region of being, the distinction we have referred to as that between nature and history. Earlier we referred to Husserl's treatment of this distinction as his "higher-level difficulty." Anyone who has attended to Heidegger at all knows how important for his work – early, middle, and late – is the ontological difference (*ontologische Differenz*), the difference between being and beings. But there is another ontological difference that plays an equally significant but systematically quite different role for the early Heidegger. In German he calls this the ontological *Unterschied,* as opposed to the ontological *Differenz.* This less discussed difference, the *Unterschied,* is the difference, just mentioned, between nature and history. Heidegger charges the philosophical tradition with indifference to this ontological difference (*Unterschied*) and rests much of his own claim to philosophical originality on just this distinction.

He recognizes, of course, that something like this distinction has commonly been made in modern philosophy. Kant's distinction between persons and nature is the most pertinent example because of Kant's lasting influence in philosophy. Heidegger objects to the way that Kant handles the distinction, because, according to Heidegger, the distinction implicitly collapses inasmuch as persons (historical beings for Heidegger) are treated much like natural entities. Though Kant means to present the person as quite different from natural entities (most importantly different, since persons are free and morally responsible), he does not, according to Heidegger, adequately sustain the distinction. Ultimately the person is treated as a different sort of natural entity. It is worth noting here that Heidegger is almost never critical of the Kantian treatment of nature. In fact, he sometimes affirms it. The mistake he sees being made is the dominance of the treatment of nature over the treatment of persons. Kant's first *Critique* is a regional ontology of nature for Heidegger, and it is within this frame that persons are presented. Thus, for Heidegger the Kantian account undermines the distinctiveness of Dasein even though it hopes to affirm it. Heidegger would succeed where Kant had failed. The difference (*Unterschied*) between history and nature, as Heidegger hopes to develop it, is so great that it is, he asserts, far greater than the traditional ontological difference drawn between God and man, between creator and creation.[27] His distinction is so radical that it would obviously disallow the Husserlian understanding of ourselves as natural beings.

Inasmuch as this distinction between two regions of beings is developed and prepared in fundamental ontology, that is, in the treatment of the meaning of being, we could say that with this ontological distinction Heidegger is attempting to drive the Kantian distinction of person and nature (implicit even in Descartes's *res cogitans–res extensa* distinction) back into the very treatment of being as such. But if the difference between the two is so great, then working out a unitary concept of being will become exceedingly difficult. And Heidegger explicitly set himself the task of working out a unitary concept of being, though he never succeeded in developing it. The "higher-level" problem of the relation of Dasein and nature in terms of temporality is at the same time a "deep" problem in the basic account of the meaning of being as such. We should recall that the immediate context for establishing this unitary concept of being is the account of temporality that Heidegger begins in the *Basic Prob-*

lems lectures. Let us look a little more closely at this distinction, which is so important to Heidegger's project.

First of all, we should note that Heidegger abandons, for the most part, the term "nature," presumably because both in ordinary and in philosophical usage the term has received interpretations that cover over the distinction Heidegger wants to make. Thus, the distinction that Heidegger draws in the temporal region "within time" is that between Dasein (which we have used here as a technical term and have not translated) and *Vorhandensein* (translated as "presence-at-hand" in *Being and Time* and "being-extant" in *Basic Problems*). According to Heidegger's sketchy account of the distinction in *Basic Problems* (for which we can find the ground laid in *Being and Time*), Dasein is a "who," not a "what." The formal structures laid out in the phenomenological account of it are "existentialia" (a term coined by Heidegger), and not "categories." Presence-at-hand (or extantness) is appropriately considered a "what," and the appropriate philosophical treatment of it is by way of categories. That is, the philosophy of nature was treated appropriately in modern philosophy (and particularly in Kant) by way of categories.[28] Methodologically the accounts of the two regions are parallel (who/what; existentiale/category), but we might ask about their intersection. That is, how is it that Dasein knows or uses the extant? In more traditional terms, we might wonder how it is that we, as persons, find ourselves in a world not only of persons (and history) but of nature as well.

It would be helpful here to look back at the treatment of extantness in Section 15 of *Being and Time* (and again later in §69 b), where Heidegger treats our encounter with things in the world as exemplified by work in a workshop. In the first place, according to the account given there, we experience things practically as equipment (*Zeug*). The equipment of the workplace is either "handy" (*zuhanden*, translated as "ready-to-hand" in *Being and Time*) or "not handy." Only when the tool breaks down or cannot be found do we "theoretically" attend to it as being present in a certain way, that is, as having certain properties, or as not being present at all. Heidegger insists here that "handiness is the way in which entities as they are 'in themselves' are defined ontologico-categorially" (BT 101). With this assertion he also rejects the suggestion that handiness be understood merely as "a way of taking them, . . . a subjective coloring." Nonetheless, he also says that "yet only by reason of something present-at-hand [or "extant"] 'is there' anything handy" (BT 101). He then asks a question he does not answer: "Does it follow . . . that handiness is ontologically founded upon presence-at-hand?" At stake in this question is the question as to which is ontologically prior – our practical approach to things or our theoretical approach.

It is telling that the opening scene of *Being and Time* is that of the craftsman at his workbench surrounded by his tools, and not a scene in a more "natural" setting. Tools, like the hammer or turn signals of an automobile (Heidegger's examples), are human constructs and are defined, as Heidegger points out, by a network of (human) involvements. But when Heidegger turns to another example and another scene, the scene of a farmer in Swabia (where Heidegger was born and grew up) surveying the sky for signs of rain, it seems to be an example of a different kind, since we should ask whether the wind can be understood as equipment in the same way that the hammer can. If it cannot be, it is hard to accept the claim that Heidegger makes here: "Only by the circumspection with which one takes account of things in farming is the south wind discovered in its Being," that is, as the herald of rain and good crops (BT 112).

The workshop and the fields are part of Dasein's world. Dasein is ontologically defined as worldly, as we have already seen; it is being-in-the-world. On the other hand, nature, or extantness, Heidegger tells us, does not belong ontologically to the world. Worldliness (*Weltlichkeit*) is not an ontological property of nature. Yet Dasein encounters nature only in the world. Accordingly, Heidegger calls nature (or the extant) as encountered in the world "intraworldly" (*innerweltlich*, translated as "innerworldly" in *Being and Time*). Yet to cite Heidegger once again: "Intraworldliness does not belong to nature's Being" (BP 169). We are left to ask, If nature is encountered only as intraworldly, yet intraworldliness does not belong to nature's being, do we encounter nature as it is in itself? This question is promoted by Heidegger himself when he insists with the example of the south wind in Swabia that only through farming do we discover it "in its Being." With the difference between Dasein and nature as great as it is, how can nature be what it is "in its Being" in Dasein's world?

This great difference between Dasein and nature is most starkly asserted in terms of time in the concluding paragraph of *History of the Concept of Time* lectures, where Heidegger simply states that "they [the movements of nature] are as such completely *time-free.*" He also says here, consistent with what we have already noted, that nature is "encountered 'in' the time which we ourselves are" (HCT 320). But we must recall the assignment of nature as a subdivision to the region "within time" in *Basic Problems.* Nature is "within time" only *as encountered* in Dasein's world. As encountered, it becomes a part of history and culture. Accordingly, in *Being and Time* we can find Heidegger saying that "even nature is historical." He quickly adds, however, that "it is *not* historical, to be sure, in so far as we speak of 'natural history' " (BT 440). The examples of nature as historical are cultural: the battlefield and the site of a cult. It is in the sense referred to as "natural history" that Heidegger later says in *Basic Problems* that "culture *is* not the way that nature is" (BP 169). We are left to wonder how Heidegger can say in *Basic Problems* that nature (or the extant), if it is indeed "time-free" and so different from Dasein, can together with Dasein constitute the region of being that is within time.

Their difference is emphasized in still another way in the *History of the Concept of Time,* where Heidegger utilizes Wilhelm Dilthey's distinction between understanding and explanation in saying that nature is explainable (*erklärbar*) but not understandable (not *verständlich*). Nature is "the incomprehensible [*Unverständliche*] pure and simple" (HCT 217). Yet to say that nature is not to be understood runs against the claim that the Swabian farmer knows the south wind "in its Being." We might wonder about the less practical, and more theoretical, knowledge of weather of the natural sciences. Presumably meteorology is derived from the more primordial experience of living with the weather. Clearly for Heidegger both the natural sciences and farming are aspects of culture; they have their place in the world and are historical. But nature is not "worldly," as we have just seen. This is made clear when Heidegger asserts that, though there is no world without Dasein, there would be nature without Dasein: "Nature can also be when no Dasein exists" (BP 170). Nature, then, is not merely a projection of the natural sciences or of our practical involvements with it. But it seems that our understanding of it, such as it is, comes from our practical involvements. This raises the question as to whether nature for Heidegger can be encountered only instrumentally. It also suggests a parallel with the Kantian view that we cannot know things as they are in themselves, but only insofar as they appear to us.

On this reading of Heidegger's claims, it is tempting to sever the question of being (ontology) from the question of knowledge (epistemology). Yet the central motive of phenomenology for both Husserl and Heidegger was to overcome this break and to make the claim that in some important sense we can know things in themselves. Heidegger thinks that Husserl's transcendental idealism does not succeed, and that Husserl falls back into a version of Kant's idealism. As a result, Heidegger set out to develop a phenomenology that would not give precedence to the subject in the way that Kant and Husserl (in his egological approach) did. Yet he finds himself in a position with important parallels to Husserl and Kant. In one sense, Heidegger's problem is greater than Husserl's insofar as the difference between Dasein and nature is so much greater. Whereas Husserl thinks we are natural beings, this does not seem to be the case according to Heidegger.

CONCLUSION

Our discussion may seem to have taken us away from the theme of time. Yet we should recall that Heidegger (like Husserl before him) draws the distinction between extantness (or nature) and Dasein within the context of a treatment of the temporality of being. The boundaries of the regions of being are, in the first place, temporal boundaries, and the problems this creates parallel what I have called Husserl's "higher-level" problem of time. Both Dasein and extantness are "within time," yet we have just seen some of the problems that Heidegger faces in this regard.

Perhaps the clearest indication of Heidegger's initial orientation and its problems is his statement in the conclusion of the *History of the Concept of Time* lectures that "Dasein . . . temporalizes" (HCT 319). This is like Husserl's according time to the function of transcendental subjectivity. Dasein (in the case of Heidegger) or the transcendental ego (in the case of Husserl) originates time. Yet in *Being and Time* Heidegger writes that "temporality (*Zeitlichkeit*) temporalizes" (BT 377). And, further, he summarizes his position in *Being and Time* with the statement, "Time is primordial as the temporalizing of temporality, and as such it makes possible the Constitution of the structure of care" (BT 380). We can note again here the Husserlian language of "constitution" and "structure." But, more important, we see that it is time that makes care and Dasein possible. Time is somehow prior to Dasein. We are reminded of the priority of time over subjectivity in Husserl's late manuscripts. In *Basic Problems* Heidegger talks similarly about the temporalization of temporality (BP 319).

We might want to consider a later remark that seems to demand a basic reappraisal of Heidegger's approach, though we cannot fully address it here. In the late lecture "Time and Being" (1962), Heidegger tells us that "the attempt in *Being and Time,* section 70, to derive human spatiality from temporality is untenable" (TB 23). What Heidegger means by this largely unexplained comment is not entirely clear. But insofar as it challenges the Kantian precedent followed by both Husserl and the early Heidegger of giving both methodological and ontological priority to the temporality of inner sense, this comment challenges substantively the phenomenology of both Husserl and the early Heidegger. Husserl had considered the consciousness of temporality as the fundament of all experience of ourselves and the world. The early Heidegger rejects the language of consciousness, yet he follows Husserl in considering time to be primordial. If spatiality were, to use the Heideggerian term, equiprimordial, the phenomenological project would require substantial revision. The early Heidegger clearly does accord priority to time and does, in the words of the later Heidegger cited earlier, attempt "to derive human spatiality from temporality." It is hard to envision what shape an ontology based as much on spatiality as temporality would take. Perhaps the later Heidegger is attempting this in some way or other. Notions like "region" (*Gegend,* not *Region*) and "nearness" are clearly prominent, and the concept of *Zeit-Spiel-Raum* accords equal prominence to space and time.

Thus, we can say of Heidegger's early phenomenological attempt that his way of starting with Dasein and not transcendental subjectivity does not resolve adequately the problems that Husserl faced concerning temporality, but instead leads him to correlative ones. Methodologically, his account of being seems to require an indifference that is unjustifiable on his own account of Dasein. Thematically, his attempt at a unitary concept of being is made hopelessly difficult by the great difference between Dasein and extantness. This difficulty is related to the first insofar as the methodological priority of Dasein makes it difficult to make sense of the extant as independent of Dasein, though such independence is ontologically, if not epistemologically, required. It is perhaps these difficulties that led Heidegger later to write that "the ecstatic-horizonal temporality delineated in *Being and Time* is not by any means already the most proper attribute of time that must be sought in answer to the Being-question."[29]

As a consequence, the planned shift or reversal from Dasein's temporality (*Zeitlichkeit*) to the temporality of being (*Temporalität*) cannot be satisfactorily carried out. Another turn is needed – one that leaves behind the project of a phenomenology that is transcendental, ontological, and hermeneutic. In his later writings Heidegger abandons the planned defense of the necessary apriorism of "scientific" philosophy. He abandons "philosophy" for "thought."

Yet it is precisely the central role given to time by Husserl and Heidegger that has brought about our current insight into the historicity and finitude of all human experience and all philosophical inquiry. Whether one sees this as ground for further philosophizing, or, with the later Heidegger, as leading us to a postphilosophical project of "thinking," or as a warrant for a new stance of postmodern "playfulness" and "decentering," it is clear that the phenomenology of time, with all its problems, has redefined our understanding of what philosophy can be.

NOTES

1 Gadamer tells us that one of his goals in *Truth and Method* (New York: Seabury Press, 1975) was to measure up to the "conscientiousness of phenomenological description which Husserl has made a duty for us all" (p. xv). He also says that "it is true that my book is phenomenological in its method" (p. xxiv). Ricoeur explicitly asserts that hermeneutics presupposes phenomenology in his essay "Phenomenology and Hermeneutics" in *Hermeneutics and the Human Sciences,* ed. and trans. John B. Thompson (Cambridge: Cambridge University Press, 1981), pp. 101–28. Moreover, time is a theme central to both Ricoeur and Gadamer. Note Ricoeur's recent three-volume work *Time and Narrative* (Chicago: University of Chicago Press, 1988). I have shown the significance of an understanding of temporality for Gadamer's hermeneutics in my essay

"Philosophical Discourse and the Ethics of Hermeneutics," in *Festivals of Interpretation*, ed. Kathleen Wright (Albany: State University of New York Press, 1990), pp. 63–88.

2 See *Speech and Phenomena*, trans. David Allison (Evanston, Ill.: Northwestern University Press, 1973).

3 Edmund Husserl, *Formal and Transcendental Logic*, trans. Dorion Cairns (The Hague: Nijhoff, 1969), p. 120. For the discussion of formal ontology in Husserl's earlier work of 1913, *Ideas I*, see §10, "Region and Category." This is available in English translation as Vol. 2 of *Edmund Husserl: Collected Works*, trans. F. Kersten (The Hague: Nijhoff, 1982).

4 Immanuel Kant, *The Critique of Pure Reason*, trans. Norman Kemp Smith (New York: St. Martin's Press, 1965), p. 59 (B 25 according to the standard pagination of the second edition of the *Critique*).

5 *Ideas II* and *Ideas III* are available in English translation in *Edmund Husserl: Collected Works*, respectively as Vol. 3 (trans. Richard Rojcewicz and André Schuwer) and Vol. 1 (trans. Ted Klein and William Pohl). These two volumes were never published by Husserl and were first published in German in 1952 and 1971 (*Husserliana*, Vols. IV and V [The Hague: Nijhoff]). In a footnote in *Being and Time* Heidegger gratefully acknowledges his familiarity with these then-unpublished manuscripts (BT 489).

6 See the end of the chapter on the schematism in the *Critique of Pure Reason*, pp. 184–7.

7 For Husserl's treatment of space and spatiality see his lectures from 1907, *Ding and Raum*, Vol. 16 of his collected works, *Husserliana* (The Hague: Nijhoff, 1973) – not available in English translation.

8 See Schrag's Introduction to *The Phenomenology of Internal Time Consciousness*, trans. James S. Churchill (Bloomington: Indiana University Press, 1964), p. 12.

9 Edmund Husserl, *Husserliana*, Vol. 10: *Zur Phänomenologie des inneren Zeitbewusstseins (1893–1917)*, ed. Rudolf Boehm (The Hague: Nijhoff, 1966). This has recently been translated by John Brough (with a complete retranslation of the 1905 lectures) as Vol. 4 of *Edmund Husserl: Collected Works – On the Phenomenology of the Consciousness of Internal Time (1893–1917)* (The Hague: Nijhoff, 1991). See Brough's helpful introduction concerning the history of the edition.

10 See Karl Schumann, *Husserl Chronik* (The Hague: Nijhoff, 1977), p. 325.

11 See his "Is the Present Ever Present?" *Research in Phenomenology*, 12 (1982): 85–112, p. 87.

12 *Ideas I*, p. 192; translation revised.

13 Husserl, *Formal and Transcendental Logic*, p. 273.

14 Ibid., p. 274.

15 See §13 of Husserl's *Cartesian Meditations* (1931), trans. Dorion Cairns (The Hague: Nijhoff, 1960): "We are envisaging a science that is absolutely subjective. . . . It begins in pure egology." It should also be noted here, however, that the Cartesian approach is not the only way into phenomenology. The "way in" attempted in the *Crisis of the European Sciences* (1936) is through everyday experience, what Husserl calls the "life-world." Even when adopting the Cartesian mode, Husserl is substantially critical of Descartes.

16 There are many examples of this in the unpublished C manuscripts. For example, in No. 71, p. 5 of the typed transcription, Husserl writes that "the ego in its most original originality is not in time." And in No. 7 II, pp. 11–12, he discusses the absolute ego as the source or spring (*Quelle*) of all phenomena. Husserl wrote almost daily in shorthand, returning always to the theme of time. These manuscripts from the late twenties and early thirties are repetitive and sometimes contradictory, since Husserl is carrying out thought experiments trying to find out where different approaches might lead him. For example, Husserl sometimes comes close to identifying this "standing now" with God – Leibniz's God – as a way to consider the higher-level subjectivity that is not temporal but constitutes the temporality of subjectivity. In other contexts, he considers the possibility of an ultimate unconscious behind consciousness – e.g., *On the Phenomenology of the Consciousness of Internal Time,* p. 394.

17 C Manuscript No. 10, p. 25.

18 *"Die Zeitlichkeit . . . zeitigt sich"* (SZ 328). It is important to note that what is the subject and agent here is temporality, not the ego (as it is sometimes for Husserl) or Dasein (as it is for Heidegger in the earlier lectures, *History of the Concept of Time*). In the same context as this quote concerning *Zeitlichkeit,* Heidegger asserts that "primordial temporality" is prior to Dasein (BT 380–2).

19 *Being and Time* first appeared in Vol. 8 (1927) of this yearbook, together with Oskar Becker's phenomenological account of mathematics. Becker was another of Husserl's assistants.

20 In the twenties Husserl often made the comment to Heidegger: "You and I are phenomenology." See Dorion Cairns, *Conversations with Husserl and Fink* (The Hague: Nijhoff, 1976), p. 9.

21 Note the comment about the possibility of working up a philosophical anthropology on the basis of *Being and Time* (BT 169–70). Philosophical anthropology is to be understood as a regional ontology. See the discussion of this in *Kant and the Problem of Metaphysics* §37. In *History of the Concept of Time,* lectures from 1925 that are an earlier version of *Being and Time,* Heidegger begins and ends with a discussion of the distinction of nature and history. The subtitle of the published edition

and the announced title of the lecture series is "Prolegomena to a Phenomenology of History and Nature."

22 In *The Metaphysical Foundations of Logic* (lectures of 1928) Heidegger acknowledges the importance of Husserl's account for his own view of time and temporality: "With regard to all previous interpretations, it was Husserl's service to have seen these phenomena [the unity of time and its various aspects] for the first time" (MFL 204).

23 The attentive reader is rightly puzzled about the modes of Dasein in *Being and Time.* Usually Heidegger writes as though there are two modes of Dasein, authentic and inauthentic, but sometimes he suggests that there are three. The third is neither authentic nor inauthentic but indifferent. I discuss this puzzle in "The Problem of *Indifferenz* in *Sein und Zeit," Philosophy and Phenomenological Research,* 43 (September 1982): 43–58. I show how Heidegger's ambivalence between two or three modes is related to the methodological problems of the phenomenological method that are discussed briefly later.

24 A footnote to the first sentence of the lectures reads simply, "A new elaboration [*Ausarbeitung;* more literally, "working out"] of division 3 of part 1 of *Being and Time."*

25 The outline of the projected lectures in the introduction has three parts, each with four chapters: Part 1, a historical introduction; Part 2, the direct discussion of being; and Part 3, a treatment of phenomenology and its method. The lectures go only as far as the first chapter of Part 2, which discusses the ontological difference. The next (and undelivered and unpublished) chapter was entitled "The Problem of the Basic Articulation of Being." And the successive two chapters were to treat the unity of being and the truth of being.

26 See the discussion of thematization and objectification in science in *Being and Time* (BT 412–15). In *Being and Time* Heidegger never discusses the "scientific" and objective status of fundamental ontology, but he does discuss it briefly in *Basic Problems* (BP 281–2, 320–4). See also my "Problem of *Indifferenz."*

27 "Existence (*Existenz*) and extantness (*Vorhandensein*) are more disparate than, say, the determinations of the God's being and man's being in traditional ontology" (BP 176).

28 See the treatment of categories and existentialia in *Being and Time,* §9.

29 See the letter to William Richardson of 1962 published as the preface to Richardson's book, *Heidegger: Through Phenomenology to Thought* (The Hague: Nijhoff, 1963), p. xiii.

DAVID COUZENS HOY

6 Heidegger and the hermeneutic turn

The closing decades of this century have been marked by a wide-ranging, multidisciplinary exploration of the theory of interpretation and its practical implications. To speak of a revolution in the history of thought is perhaps too grand, but certainly there has been a general movement that can be called the "hermeneutic turn." This turn has taken various forms, including poststructuralist cultural studies, deconstructive literary studies, interpretive anthropology and social science, and critical legal studies. Of course, the specific turns taken in each of these fields are reactions to older ways of practicing each discipline. But in each case the emphasis on interpretation is used as an antidote, usually to objectivistic conceptions of the discipline's methods. However, none of these particular turns would have been imaginable without a dramatic change earlier in this century, the change brought about in philosophy by Martin Heidegger in 1927 in *Being and Time.* Heidegger's hermeneutic turn is taken most explicitly in Sections 31 and 32 of that book, where Heidegger makes interpretive understanding the central mode of human existence (or Dasein).

In 1927 Heidegger himself could not have foreseen the diverse effects of his theory on later thought, and in the final section of this essay I will describe his influence on the hermeneutic and deconstructive philosophies that emerged in the latter half of the century. But at the time Heidegger did see his account of understanding as a revolutionary break from the traditional philosophical emphasis on problems about knowledge and on the dichotomy between subjectivity and objectivity. To explain this break I will begin by working through the details of Heidegger's account of understanding and interpretation in *Being and Time,* situating this material against the background of traditional hermeneutics as well as of Cartesian and Kantian philosophy.

THE METAHERMENEUTIC TURN IN PHILOSOPHY'S SELF-CONCEPTION

Hans-Georg Gadamer, who in *Truth and Method* (1960) was the first philosopher to develop Heidegger's account of interpretation into a general hermeneutics, defines hermeneutics as the philosophical enterprise for which the central question is, How is understanding possible?[1] This formulation is a reasonably straightforward way to characterize the hermeneutic philosophy that Gadamer himself has contributed to twentieth-century thought. However, before Heidegger, or to anyone who has not read Heidegger, the question would be misleading, since hermeneutics might thereby seem to be merely one branch of philosophy, the one that analyzes the phenomenon of understanding in contrast to other human activities such as knowledge or language. Hermeneutic philosophers before Heidegger did think of understanding in this way, and they therefore distinguished disciplines that could acquire knowledge in an objective way, as in the natural sciences, from those that could not give lawlike explanations but instead offered interpretations, as in the humanities (or *Geisteswissenschaften*).

So classified, since the humanistic disciplines like history, law, literary and cultural studies (and perhaps philosophy itself) rarely or never give explanations emulating the causal laws of natural science, they seem to be poor cousins in the family of knowledge. One defense of these *Geisteswissenschaften* is to claim a separate status for them and to take them as examples of a distinct cognitive operation called understanding. This move, which ran through traditional hermeneutics from Friedrich Schleiermacher (1768–1834) to Wilhelm Dilthey (1833–1911), has a weakness in that it seems to leave understanding as a derivative and deficient subspecies of knowledge.

A central part of Heidegger's legacy comes from his strikingly different conception of hermeneutics. Heidegger's analysis of Dasein as being-in-the-world changes our understanding of understanding from a derivative phenomenon to the central feature, the keystone, of human experience. As Gadamer remarks, "Heidegger's temporal analytics of Dasein has, I think, shown convincingly that understanding is not just one of the various possible behaviors of the subject but the mode of being of Dasein itself . . . and hence embraces the whole of its experience of the world."[2] When understanding becomes the central phenomenon for philosophy, hermeneutics is no longer conceived of as simply one minor branch of philosophy. Instead, philosophy itself becomes hermeneutic. Or at least one can now speak of a distinctively hermeneutic approach to philosophy in contrast to the traditional approach running from Descartes through Kant to Husserl. This traditional approach conceived of the human being as a "subject," a knower disengaged from the world and from practical activity in the world.

Heidegger's hermeneutic turn is more radical than earlier philosophy, then, in that it avoids the traditional model of the subject as the knower standing over against what is to be known, the objective world. His hermeneutic turn shows both that the mentalistic vocabulary of the subject–object model is not the only possible starting point for philosophy and that this vocabulary is derivative from the more basic starting point where Dasein and world are coterminous in understanding. Heidegger conceives of Dasein and world as forming a circle, and he thus extends the traditional hermeneutic circle between a text and its reading down to the most primordial level of human existence. Traditionally the paradigm for the hermeneutic circle is the reading of a text, where the parts cannot be interpreted without an understanding of the whole, but the whole cannot be grasped without an understanding of the parts. As I shall explain, in Heidegger's deeper conception of the hermeneutic circle as a feature of human existence in general, the relation of knowledge and understanding is one neither of antagonism nor of indifference, but one in which the legitimate task of achieving knowledge is a *subspecies* of the more general phenomenon of human understanding.

Heidegger begins his radicalization of the hermeneutic turn in Section 31 of *Being and Time* by distinguishing his conception of understanding from a different conception of how a philosopher might be interested in analyzing understanding: " 'Understanding' in the sense of *one* possible kind of cognizing among others (as distinguished, for instance, from 'explaining') must, like explaining, be Interpreted as an existential derivative of that primary understanding which is one of the constituents of the Being of the 'there' in general" (BT 182). Traditional, pre-Heideggerian hermeneutics distinguished humanistic understanding and interpretation from the lawlike explanations of the natural sciences, and it thus put itself in a weak position when the metaquestion was raised, What is the status of the knowledge claimed by hermeneutic philosophy itself? Is hermeneutic philosophy itself the one right explanation, or is it only one possible interpretation? Obviously, hermeneutics is not itself giving causal explanations, so it appears to be at best only one possible interpretation, not the definitive explanation, of human inquiry and existence. Traditional hermeneutics, and Dilthey especially, was thus plagued by the threat of relativism, particularly by the relativism of its own philosophical status.

Now Heidegger too will want to say that *Being and Time* is an interpretation. But because he has a deeper conception of what understanding is, he will have a different conception of interpretation, and a different account of how interpretation arises from understanding. What he means by understanding is not simply one form of cognition among others, but our most basic ability to live in and cope skillfully with our world. Of course, this ability must take into account that the ways in which features of the world show up are constantly changing, and this constant change requires us to form particular interpretations. As our projects and needs change, we will change our interpretations. For instance, sometimes we must interpret ourselves as students, sometimes as family members, sometimes as consumers, and perhaps sometimes as philosophers. Yet Heidegger suggests that all these interpretations presuppose a primary understanding of the world that runs through them. Our shift from one interpretation to another at the appropriate moment is a sign that we do understand the world. So a change in interpretation is not necessarily a sign of lack of understanding, since in these cases the change of interpretation shows that we can cope with the various demands the world places on us.

Heidegger is describing the "primary understanding" that runs through our various ways of existing in and interpreting the world. What is the status, then, of this philosophical activity of description? The philosophical description is itself an interpretation, but it is on a plane different from the interpretations that flow naturally from our everyday ways of coping with the world. Heidegger thus distinguishes between *Auslegung* and *Interpretierung*. *Auslegung*, the standard translation of which is "interpretation" with a lower-case "i," includes the everyday phenomena of ordinary skills like hammering, typing, or driving. *Interpretierung*, translated as "Interpretation" with an upper case "I," includes thematized, discursive articulation and theorization. *Interpretierung* is itself said to be a derived form of *Auslegung*, but Heidegger obviously does not mean to denigrate *Interpretierung* since that is what *Being and Time* is. An *Interpretierung* is a reflective working through of phenomena, such as is done in philosophy and philology. So Heidegger claims the status of philosophical *Interpretierung* and not "knowledge" or "explanation" as a description for what he is doing.

Whereas the ordinary interpretations are more or less automatic, philosophical Interpretation of these ordinary interpretations is reflective in two senses. First, it is reflective in that it must explicitly articulate or thematize what goes on more immediately and less explicitly in everyday coping. Second, it is logically self-reflective in that it must itself be one possible manifestation among others of primary understanding; it will not be a representation of something that is of a different order from it, but it will be of the same kind as what it captures. Philosophical Interpretation can be "true to" the phenomenal activity of ordinary world interpretations because it is itself a form of the same phenomenon, although a more articulated or explicit form. So philosophical Interpretation is not simply arbitrary, and not threatened by the problem of relativism, because it is a case of the primary understanding that it is trying to capture. Philosophical Interpretation may be refined, or it may be supplanted by later redescriptions of what philosophy should be, but if it is agreed that there is a primary understanding of the world, then the philosophical articulation of that understanding will be binding to the degree that it is adequate to phenomenal manifestations of understanding, which include philosophy itself.

Is there any way to *test* Heidegger's philosophical Interpretation? Such an Interpretation will aim not merely to clarify ordinary usages of terms like "understanding," "explanation," and "knowledge," but will *reinterpret* or *reorder* them. This reordering is what goes on when Heidegger argues that something is *derived* from something else. If Heidegger can argue successfully that explanatory knowledge is a derived case of understanding, he will thus be in a stronger philosophical position than traditional hermeneutics, where understanding is simply an alternative mode of cognition. Heidegger's "derivations" are reminiscent of Kant's "transcendental deduction" in the *Critique of Pure Reason,* where Kant claims to demonstrate and justify our assumption that our experiences are not simply subjective but objective. Heidegger points to Section 31 as an attempt to go deeper than Kant did by explaining what Kant left unexplained (BT 184). One metaproblem with Kant's attempt to explain the possibility for our scientific knowledge of nature is the status of the synthetic a priori knowledge claimed by the *Critique* itself. That is, Kant is often accused of trying to give philosophical explanations of scientific explanation without reflecting sufficiently on whether the philosophical knowledge propounded in the first *Critique* had the same conditions as scientific knowledge.

Heidegger can avoid this problem by consistently claiming that *Being and Time* is an Interpretation. This Interpretation does not eliminate ratiocinative operations like explaining, deliberating, reflecting, and deciding, but situates them within a more general account of how they fit together in a primary understanding that also includes our everyday interactions in and with the world. Heidegger's account tells a story about how cognitive explanation always inheres in a context of intelligibility that is projected in understanding. Heidegger's account is thus properly construed not as a single, decisive transcendental argument, but as an Interpretation, that is, a reasonably complete and plausible reconstruction of the conditions that obtain if the things of the world make sense, and if beings like ourselves are also part of the world. Understanding is among these conditions and is the projection of an inclusive context or pattern of intelligibility as the background against which particular instances of sense making succeed.

In sum, contrary both to Kant and to traditional hermeneutics, Heidegger is trying to show us that we need not take "knowledge" as primary and see "understanding" and "interpretation" as derived, but that we can reverse this derivation. Even if the reversal is successful, however, a further problem arises if this result tells us simply that either direction of derivation is equally valid. The entire strategy of reordering or deriving would be undermined if that were the only conclusion, and relativism would again threaten. But Heidegger thinks that since traditional philosophy has come up against unsolvable antinomies and unbridgeable dichotomies, his reordering acquires greater plausibility to the degree that it avoids such difficulties. Also, Heidegger can urge that by starting from the more primary phenomenon of understanding, he can make better sense than the tradition of how knowledge is really possible. Traditional philosophy from Descartes to Kant wanted to offer not only a definition of knowledge (for instance, as correct representation of the real world), but also an account of how the knower is connected to the known. Heidegger's strategy is different from the Cartesian strategy, which starts by assuming a basic ontological disconnection (e.g., between mental and physical substance) and then looks for instances of epistemological connection that cannot be doubted (e.g., the knowledge of the existence of a thinking subject). Heidegger's strategy is to see Dasein as already in the world, which suggests that what needs to be explained is not the connection, which is the basis, but the disconnection. Instances of disconnection happen obviously and frequently, as when humans make mistakes, not only cognitively but practically. The Cartesian strategy runs into difficulty when it fails to explain (e.g., to skeptics) connection. The Heideggerian strategy must show that it does not run into similar problems when it tries to explain how apparent disconnections could arise, as in the breakdown of a ready-to-hand tool and its transformation into a merely present-at-hand object or piece of junk. A crucial part of Heidegger's account of the connection of Dasein and world is the section on understanding as the projection of possibilities, and I will now focus on how the details of that section contribute to the hermeneutic turn.

UNDERSTANDING, PROJECTION, AND POSSIBILITY

One question that arises if philosophy is itself a mode of interpretation is, How can one such Interpretation be said to be better than others? Is it "true"? Are there other such Interpretations that could be "true" in the same sense? To clarify these questions Heidegger distinguishes two senses of truth. One is the ordinary philosophical sense of truth, where an assertion uncovers or discovers some fact about the world. Heidegger usually describes truth in this sense as being about things that do not have the character of Dasein (BT 118), using the term *Entdecktheit* (discoveredness). The contrasting term, "disclosedness" (*Erschlossenheit*), suggests that the total context is opened up through understanding. Understanding thus does not consist only of making assertions about the world, but also of grasping the entire mode of being-in-the-world. Understanding grasps the world as such, without which the discovery of particular features of the world would not be possible. However, understanding grasps not only the world, but also Dasein's way of being in the world. So an understanding of the world is always also a self-understanding.

To speak of self-understanding can be misleading, however, if it suggests a Cartesian or Kantian ego, which stands at a remove from the objective world as if it occupied a different, subjective world. Heidegger says instead that disclosure involves both the world and Dasein at the same time. Dasein's understanding of its world is thus not distinct from its understanding of itself, but is at the same time an interpretation of itself. This self-interpretation thus does not discover facts about the properties of a mental substance or a noumenal self, but discloses how Dasein has dealt with and is dealing with the question or "issue" of its own existence. A student of physics, for instance, is not simply learning some facts about the physical world, but is learning how to do physics. The student is thus becoming a physicist, at least to some degree. Being a student is generally best described neither as finding innate abilities in oneself nor as acquiring a mass of facts about the world. Instead, being a student on Heidegger's account is learning how to go about in the world in a certain way, for instance, as a physicist or as a philosopher, where who one is and what one does are inseparable.

Understanding involves, therefore, more than the discovery of facts about particular features of the world. Understanding is more primordially the disclosure of what Heidegger calls possibilities. Heidegger suggests that the disclosure of possibilities could not be derived from the discovery of factual features. His philosophical Interpretation is trying to show that both discovery and disclosure are necessary to human activity. Focusing on the discovery of facts alone (e.g., as empiricist philosophers might) will obscure the dimension of disclosure. So Heidegger's Interpretation shows that if the dimension of disclosure is recognized, then both discovery and disclosure can be accounted for, since disclosure makes the phenomenon of discovery intelligible. The isolated, atomistic discovery of one fact after another would not generate an understanding of a world that was significant and intelligible, but only of a disconnected aggregate. An interpretation is precisely not a heap of facts but an account of how these facts are *possible.*

Possibility for Heidegger is not simply logical possibility, since understanding is of real relations and situations. Possibility also does not mean not-yet-actual, since Dasein is itself currently one possible way of existing and understanding. Dasein exists as "definite" or concrete possibilities (BT 183), which it does not choose arbitrarily. Dasein finds itself as already having these possibilities. We can begin to see what Heidegger means by returning to my example of what it is to be a student. Heidegger is not describing the process of explicitly planning to be, say, a physicist or a philosopher, and possibilities are not the abstract thoughts a student might have about what it would be like to be a physicist or a philosopher. Possibilities are recognized only in the concrete activity of doing physics or philosophy and are what limit the range of what it makes sense to do or to try to do in those activities. What it is sensible to do in a particular situation is already laid out in advance in a genuine understanding of the concrete possibilities. Dasein may not be explicitly aware of those possibilities it has let go by, or even of the ones that currently characterize it. Dasein can also be mistaken about its possibilities, for instance, by trying to fix them so rigidly that it takes them as necessities instead of as possibilities, thereby misunderstanding itself and becoming disconnected from a more primary understanding of itself (BT 183).

Dasein's understanding of itself as possibility, and its "knowledge" of those possibilities of which it is capable, is thus a matter of degree. This "knowledge" is often more implicit "know-how" than explicit "knowing-that," and it is more a grasp of the worldly situation than a reflective turn inward. Insofar as Dasein finds itself already thrown into a situation that is not of its own making, it has "in every case already gone astray and failed to recognize itself" (BT 184). Dasein thus does not "know" itself from the start, but if it is to recover or "find itself," it must come to understand what it can do given its own possibilities in its particular worldly situation.

Understanding thus involves possibilities, and these are not simply subjective or inner phenomena, but are always tied to worldly situations. Heidegger wishes to distance himself from the traditional idea that these possibilities should be thought of as spontaneously free choices, and he rejects the "liberty of indifference" (BT 183). So he avoids making "choosing" the starting point for his analysis of primary understanding, and instead starts from what he calls "projecting." Projection involves an understanding of what matters, and there will always be two sides to what matters. First, there must be a context of significance, of meanings that are really possible in the "current world." Second, nothing could matter or make a difference unless it mattered or made a difference to beings who cared, so Heidegger suggests that Dasein's own being is also projected as that "for-the-sake-of-which" whatever matters or makes a difference.

Projection is not simply reasoning from a list of all the particular possible choices that one has, as well as the pros and cons for each choice, to some decision. Listing all the "facts" about oneself and one's situation would be an interminable process, and the idea of specifying all that could be known about anything may even be unintelligible. Furthermore, "facts" about humans are always already meaning-laden and interpretive. Heidegger thus draws a distinction between "factuality" and "facticity." Factuality has to do with nonhuman things, discrete facts about which could be entered in a list. Trying to draw up such a list for any particular instance of Dasein would always fall short of characterizing that Dasein, and thus Dasein itself always is something "more" than it is (factually). But a central aim of Heidegger's account of understanding is to show Dasein's inherence in the world, which is to say that Dasein is not some free-floating spirit that transcends its material situation. As a projection (*Entwurf,* from the German stem "to throw"), Dasein finds itself "thrown" into a world, and it finds itself as already projected or "thrown" into a situation with concrete possibilities. Possibilities that are concrete (or definite, *bestimmte*) differ from purely logical possibilities in that they come with concrete limitations. So Heidegger speaks of these limitations as Dasein's "facticity," in contradistinction to the other kind of fact that he calls "factuality."

Now exactly *why* something matters or makes a difference may be difficult to say or explain, either to oneself or to others. Hence, Heidegger wants to distance his concept of projective understanding not only from spontaneous choice, but also from deliberate decisions, conscious planning, or the weighing of alternatives. He denies that projection consists of making explicit plans or of grasping its possibilities "thematically" as explicit contents of the mind. Does explicit planning or conscious weighing of alternatives and deciding *never* enter human action? In *Being and Nothingness* Jean-Paul Sartre takes the strong position that conscious reflection (or deliberation) has little to do with real choice, and that one is really just fooling oneself by such reflection to put off the inevitable need to act. As Sartre says, "a voluntary deliberation is always a deception," one that really postpones a choice that has already been made; so conscious decision always comes too late, and "les jeux sont faits" (the dice are cast).[3]

Heidegger need not make such a strong claim, precisely because he has a different Interpretation of what understanding is. Understanding involves a holistic projection of a context in which particular possibilities first become intelligible. Much of what we understand thus remains largely inexplicit. However, it does not follow that when Heidegger says that understanding does not grasp its possibilities "thematically" that he must be denying that understanding is ever thematic in any way. Unlike Sartre, he need not assert that thematizing (deliberating and deciding) is only ever a way of postponing the need to take action and is thus inefficacious. The point is instead that more reflective operations such as explaining, deliberating, or deciding would ever be possible only by supervening on a larger background of features that could never be explicitly thematized, but that nevertheless were part of the understanding and thus of the concrete possibilities.

In contrast to Sartre's claim that "les jeux sont faits" Heidegger's argument is focused on a different claim, "Become what you are" (BT 186). This slogan has an ancient tradition, going back to the Greeks, but it also features famously in Nietzsche. The imperative that one should become who one is seems paradoxical, for one would seem able to become only what one was not (yet), and a being that already was what it was could not even try to become that way. Heidegger's solution is to say that the paradox may indeed hold for beings that do not have the character of Dasein. But he asserts that not only can Dasein become what it is, it can also fail to become what it is. The facticity–factuality distinction thus clarifies how "Become what you are" expresses an imperative that is genuine. Dasein is not its factuality, so it is not what it is *factually.* However, because Dasein is understanding, and understanding involves projection into a concrete "current world," Dasein is what it is *factically.*

But because the projection also involves concrete possibilities, Dasein can *become* what it is by becoming what it is already possible for it to be. There is a genuine alternative here, for Dasein can equally well fail to face these possibilities, and thus it can become disconnected from itself by failing to own up to all that it has been and can be.

INTERPRETATION

Becoming who we are requires interpretation for two reasons. First, we cannot become who we are unless we have an interpretation both of who we are and of how we can continue to be who we want to be. Second, what we are interpreting is already interpretive. How we get to be who we are is through interpretations, not only of ourselves but also of the possibilities inherent in the public world, which is already interpreted meaningfully for us. A question that has plagued hermeneutics, however, is, What makes some interpretations better than others? Are some interpretations true and others false?

Since interpretations involve possibilities and not simply facts, the true–false distinction may not be the most pertinent one to use when judging interpretations. If an interpretation of any sort can be said to be "true," one must be using truth in a different sense from that in which a statement is said to be true. Interpretations typically contain or imply many statements, so in speaking of the truth of the set of statements, the sense of truth is extended. One might say that an interpretation is true only if all its assertions are true, but this reductive claim seems to misconstrue what is meant by calling an interpretation true. An interpretation may consist of more than simply those assertions that are uttered, since a good interpretation frees up the possibility of uttering many other significant assertions. There is also no reason to think that the set of possible assertions generated by an interpretation is closed. Furthermore, two interpretations could conflict with each other on some central claims while each one contained many other claims that either interpretation would grant to be true. In sum, interpretive understandings may be better judged by labels other than true or false, and Heidegger invokes such contrasting normative terms as authentic or inauthentic, genuine or not genuine, and transparent or opaque.[4]

Already this traditional philosophical obsession with the truth or falsity of interpretive claims may be on the wrong track in trying to understand Heidegger's account. In Section 32 of *Being and Time* Heidegger is not primarily concerned with explicit, deliberate Interpretation (*Interpretierung*) but with the phenomenon of *Auslegung*, that is, with interpretation of a practical sort that may not always involve articulated judgments or thematizing. Contrary to present tendencies to think of the reading of texts as the paradigm case of interpretation, Heidegger's paradigm cases are everyday activities like opening a door or hammering. Even Heidegger's philosophical Interpretation is an interpretation not of a text, but of Dasein. But these cases are analogues of texts insofar as Heidegger's point is that even the most obvious ordinary objects taken by themselves do not have their characteristics inscribed in them. Instead, the characteristics of the tools come into being in the concrete interpretation manifested in the activity of using them.

Contrary to an empiricist epistemology that presupposes that we first "perceive" objects with their particular properties and only secondarily apply or use them, Heidegger's suggestion is that this type of perception is not primary. Seeing is not simply perceiving the properties of external objects with the bodily eyes (BT 187). Instead of construing seeing as seeing *that* an object has such and such a property, Heidegger construes seeing as already interpreting something *as* something (e.g., seeing something as a hammer, as a door, or as a table). Another example of such "seeing-as" (not Heidegger's own) is found in the hermeneutic phenomenon of reading. When we read a text, we do not first perceive black marks on a white page and then construe their meaning. Instead, the meaning of the text, and indeed the text itself, comes to be only in the reading. Hence, for later hermeneutic theory the text and the reading form the paradigm case of the hermeneutic circle. While the early Heidegger does not emphasize textuality to the same degree, his account does underwrite the shift of philosophical attention from the epistemological model of perception to the hermeneutic model of reading.

Since reading involves grasping the meaning of the text, it is appropriate that Heidegger features the notion of meaning (*Sinn*) centrally. He does so in a way that will be congruent with this hermeneutic model and that will block some traditional problems that arise from construing meanings as private, internal, mental states. Meaning for

Heidegger is not something that one imposes on an object, and it is neither a distinctive object of perception nor an intermediary between the subject and the object. Strictly speaking, says Heidegger, what is understood is not the meaning but the entity. There is thus a sense in which Heidegger eliminates the traditional philosophical notion of meaning from his vocabulary. He thinks that we grasp entities as entities in their webs of relations with other entities, not as aggregates of perceptual qualities. Thus, we do not first see some colors or hear some noises and only secondarily infer that we are seeing or hearing a motorcycle. Instead, we first encounter a motorcycle, and only secondarily (if at all) do we abstract its properties (perhaps to hear its "noise").

"Meaning" for Heidegger thus involves the holistic way in which something can become intelligible *as* something in a web of relations (BT 193). Independent of the web of meanings, entities are not meaningful (in this special sense). Since this web of meaning requires Dasein, only Dasein can be said to be meaningful or meaningless, as Heidegger understands the notions. In other words, unless objects inhere in an interpretive context, they could not be understood. So they cannot be said to have meanings that are prior to and independent of their interpretive uses.

The context of meaningfulness is thus what makes it possible to interpret something *as* something. For the most part this context is not explicit, but makes up the background of understanding, or what Heidegger calls the "fore-structure" of understanding. For an explicit interpretation of something as something to occur (e.g., in picking up the hammer and hammering), there are three levels at which understanding must be running in the background. First, there must be a general grasp of the whole situation (e.g., of the workshop as a whole). Heidegger calls this the "fore-having" (*Vorhabe*), where, before making any particular object explicit, we *have* a background grasp of the totality of possible practices involved. But to have a grasp of the whole is not yet to make any particular feature explicit, so the second level required before anything can become explicit is "fore-sight" (*Vorsicht*), where we *see* in advance the appropriate way in which things can appear. But for something to become fully explicit in an act of interpretation there would have to be some particular concepts under which it would be appropriate even to begin interpreting it. So the third level required before an explicit interpretation can occur is the "fore-conception" (*Vorgriff*), where we grasp conceptually in advance the appropriate way to interpret something.

Each of these levels brings the interpretation closer to being explicit, but none of them is fully explicit. Should we infer from this insistence on the fore-structure of understanding that it is "prior to," whether genetically or logically, the explicit articulation of an interpretation? That Heidegger might be giving a priority to the prereflective and prelinguistic levels is perhaps reinforced by his examples, which come from everyday activities such as using hammers and opening doors, not from more explicitly cognitive activities like reading texts. Heidegger warns us, however, not to break interpretation up "into pieces" (BT 192), and we should not infer that the implicit levels of the fore-structure of the understanding would function independently of explicit interpretations. The fore-structure of understanding goes together with the as-structure of interpretation, and the levels of *Vorhabe, Vorsicht,* and *Vorgriff* are all in play at once in any given act of interpretation.

Furthermore, while Heidegger wants to show that interpretation takes place in areas of activity other than those where language is involved, he would not need to claim that understanding is more essentially prelinguistic than linguistic. While not all interpretation involves uttering sentences or making assertions, Heidegger's point is not to deny but to affirm that asserting is itself an interpretive practice. He will have a separate argument in later sections that although not all interpretation involves explicit linguistic thematization, the being who is Dasein and is able to interpret would also need to be a being who could thematize and assert. In this section, moreover, he does include textual interpretation as a case of interpretation. If he says that philological Interpretation is a derivative case, he is not making a derogatory claim about textual interpretation (BT 194). On the contrary, he objects to the philosophical tendency to contrast the "textual" disciplines like historiography and literary studies with the natural sciences and to conclude that the former are "less rigorous" than the latter. While he recognizes that natural science is a "legitimate task" (BT 194), as we have seen, he thinks that science is a subspecies of understanding. So instead of thinking that science is a separate domain of knowledge, and then puzzling about whether history and literature should count as knowledge, Heidegger is giving an account of human understanding that will accommodate these different disciplines as subspecies. Hence, he does not see them either as unrelated enterprises or as a family in which the humanities are poor cousins of the natural sciences.

To make this case he need not privilege the textual disciplines over the sciences. So he does not invert the hierarchy and privilege historiography over mathematics. Mathematics is "narrower," he says (BT 195), which is not to say that it is poorer, but simply that it has defined its limits in a different way than the humanities. Historiography on his model is not criticized because it is incapable of precise definitions and rigorous demonstrations. Instead, when properly practiced, it can highlight the possibilities, and not simply the factual consequences, of human action. Historiographic understanding is circular, but this circle is not the vicious one of an allegedly rigorous deduction that succeeded only in proving what it already presupposed. Instead, all understanding is circular, says Heidegger, in the sense that "any interpretation which is to contribute understanding must already have understood what is to be interpreted" (BT 194). This "hermeneutic circle" thus characterizes all understanding, for there must already be a context of intelligibility for any discovery to be made, or for any conclusion to be proved.

This insistence on the circularity of understanding raises the problem of whether one is always trapped within one's own assumptions, or whether there is some way to get out of the circle. The solution to this problem will depend on how "getting out" is construed. Heidegger, of course, believes that interpretations can make discoveries and that they can correct their own inadequacies. Heidegger grants that we do not simply prove things that we already know, or limit ourselves to "popular conceptions." *Genuine, primordial* understanding will see that these popular conceptions or standard assumptions are hindrances to better ways of interpreting (BT 195). However, Heidegger's way of explaining how fanciful interpretations and popular conceptions are to be avoided may confuse some readers. He says that the task is to check our prior understanding of the subject matter against "the things themselves" (BT 195). This phrase "the things themselves" might suggest that there is a domain outside the circle against which our beliefs can be tested. However, Heidegger's main point is to undermine this strong philosophical assertion of a radically independent "outside." His point is instead that beliefs can be checked only against other beliefs. Understanding is holistic and includes a dense pattern of interlocking beliefs and skillful know-how, so the idea of "getting out" of it is not really intelligible. Heidegger thus insists that interpretation is never a "presuppositionless apprehending" of some *given* (BT 191).

Even if one is willing to abandon the idea of an independent given "outside" the circle of understanding, one still might object to the holism in the thesis that all understanding is interpretive.[5] That is, one might think that understanding is *prior to* interpretation. This claim could mean that there is an understanding of something, and that this understanding then gets "interpreted," for instance, by applying that understanding to a particular situation (as when a judge interprets a statute by applying it to a case not explicitly covered by the abstract legal language). Or the claim might be that when we really understand something we do not describe ourselves as interpreting it, since to say that we were interpreting would suggest that there were features that we had not yet grasped correctly or adequately. Either way expresses the feeling that there must be something "beneath" interpretation, such that interpretation is not a circle but an "arch" that remains firmly grounded in its object.[6] Behind this insistence on the priority of understanding over interpretation would be an *epistemological* intuition, since the worry would be that understanding needs to be adequate to its object, which somehow anchors interpretation.[7]

Although many philosophers before Heidegger started from this epistemological worry, Heidegger's own project is to show that this problem can only arise *within* the circle of understanding. To start from the problem is already to disconnect the interpretation and that which is being interpreted to such a degree that it becomes impossible to reconnect them. Heidegger's insistence on the circle sees a particular misunderstanding arising only against a tacit background of shared understanding. While any interpretation may involve particular points of misunderstanding, it would be a mistake to infer that all readings are misreadings or that, as Jonathan Culler characterizes the literary theories of Paul de Man and Harold Bloom (but not Jacques Derrida), "understanding is a special case of misunderstanding."[8] Understanding must generally be a successful practice before particular aspects of the interpretive understanding could even emerge as mistakes or misunderstandings. Of course, in the process of interpretive understanding, the interpreter has the sense that there is something "out there" that is to be understood. Heidegger himself insists on this phenomenon and gives the following explanation of what is really happening: "If, when one is engaged in a particular concrete kind of interpretation, in the sense of exact textual Interpretation, one likes to appeal to what 'stands there,' then one finds that what 'stands there' in the first instance is nothing other than the obvious (*selbstverständliche*), undiscussed assumption (*Vormeinung*) of the interpreter, which necessarily lies in every interpretive approach as that which has already been 'taken for granted' in interpretation as such, that is, as that which is pre-given through the fore-having, fore-sight, and fore-conception" (BT 192; translation modified). So Heidegger does not deny that interpretations include some apparent givens, commitments, or purchase points. However, these points do not lie outside the circle of understanding, but are already at play within the circle as tacit aspects of our prior understanding of our world and ourselves. The world is itself in the circle, both in general as its horizon and also concretely as the commitments of any successful practice of understanding. Any particular assumption may become problematic, and therefore move from being tacitly taken for granted to being explicitly called into question. Then the assumption may show itself to be merely a popular misconception or a fanciful, superficial glossing over of difficulties. But any challenge to any particular assumption can be made only by appeal to other commitments that the interpretation is not willing to give up. So the challenge is from within the circle and is not to some independent given "outside" or "beneath" the circle.

If there is no outside to the circle, understanding should not itself be taken as a mental operation that is distinct from interpretation. Understanding is itself always realized in interpretation and is not a separate, prior operation that then gets reprocessed in a secondary operation of interpretation. Understanding functions concretely only as interpretation: "In interpretation, understanding does not become something different, but instead it becomes itself" (BT 188). Interpretation is the concrete working through of the possibilities projected by the understanding. That is, the context of intelligibility that is tacitly understood provides the background against which specific interpretive actions make sense. The tacit background and the explicit interpretive action are integral functions of any instance of interpretive understanding.

AFTER HEIDEGGER

If the pieces of Heidegger's account of understanding and interpretation are now in place, some concluding reflections on the outcome of the hermeneutic turn later in the twentieth century are in order. Two thinkers in the second half of the twentieth century whose work would not have been possible without these sections of *Being and Time* are Hans-Georg Gadamer and Jacques Derrida. Yet the hermeneutic theory developed by Gadamer and the deconstructive movement fathered by Derrida take the Heideggerian account in different and apparently opposed directions. Gadamerian hermeneutics appear to deconstructionists to harbor the hidden assumption that the text has an internal unity of meaning, and that meaning is a single thing that interpretation must aim at *reconstructing.* The deconstructionists see this faith in the unity and the coherence of the text as a vestige of metaphysical faith, which they aim to *deconstruct.* In contrast to the hermeneutic move to recover and reconstruct *the* meaning of the text, deconstruction is the operation of questioning this faith in the meaning of the text by finding in the rhetoric and style of the language of the text moments where the assumption of the unity of meaning fails.

At least two problems, then, are raised by these two different ways of developing Heidegger's analysis of the circle of understanding. One problem is whether interpretation should be reconstructive or deconstructive in intent. The other is whether the interpretation's account of the meaning of the interpreted entails a metabelief that the interpretation is approximating the ideal of the one right interpretation. I will call the position that believes that this ideal is posited in all interpretation *monism,* and the denial of monism I will label *pluralism.*

The debate about deconstruction is too complex to be summarized here, and I will therefore limit myself to the issue of what follows directly from Sections 31 and 32 of *Being and Time* for this controversy. The issue has two sides, a methodological one and a political one. The methodological one turns on the question whether Heidegger's insistence on the circle of understanding does not simply imprison us in our own outlook, blocking us from recognizing the otherness or alterity of the text. The political issue arises from Heidegger's further insistence that the fore-structure of understanding forms our interpretations *in advance.* Thus, interpreters inherit from their tradition much of the background of their readings. From the deconstructive point of view the hermeneutic position that accepts Heidegger's analysis is too traditionalist and thus politically suspect because it seems unable to challenge the cultural and political status quo.

The countercharges against deconstruction are easy to imagine. Methodologically, deconstruction will appear to be fantasizing an escape from the circle of understanding by its dalliance with an impossible "outside" where meaning is undecidable and thus hopelessly multiple and fractured. Politically, its critique will seem pointless, since the fantasy of a complete break with tradition can lead nowhere. Deconstruction will seem to be neglecting Heidegger's insistence that we find ourselves already thrown into a social situation, which has specific concrete possibilities but also real limitations. Deconstruction's own faith that any construction can be deconstructed will lead to an undirected resistance that will be ineffectual because of its inability to generate a positive construction of its own.[9]

Unfortunately, these charges and countercharges may obscure the reach of Heidegger's original account of the hermeneutic circle. That account did not envision the specific controversy that I have sketched. Without minimizing this controversy, which is stimulating much current work in literary theory and social philosophy, I will outline some ways in which Heidegger's account can accommodate central features of both the reconstructive and the deconstructive enterprises.

Before this reconciliation can begin, however, the issue of monism versus pluralism must be clarified. Part of the deconstructive worry about the hermeneutic recovery of meaning may be caused by a suspicion that this recovery presupposes the monistic ideal of the one final, right interpretation. Much can be said for that ideal, yet in the exposition that I have given of Heidegger's account I have deliberately stressed the elements in it that I find pointing toward an antimonistic pluralism. Heidegger's account of "meaning" in his technical sense may seem monistic because it posits a whole, a totality of involvements, a single context in which interpretation may take place. My insistence on the holistic nature of meaning in this special sense suggests, however, that the context is always revisable, and that revision will come from within the context of belief itself. This holism implies, therefore, that while the task of understanding strives to be coherent and unified, it must always recognize that there are elements in it that have not been worked through explicitly and that may be inconsistent with other central commitments. So the context can always turn out to include inadequate elements. The drive of understanding toward a single coherent position is thus compatible with its allowance for the inevitability of hidden error and bias, and the recognition that no interpretation is final.

Other aspects of Heidegger's account that support the metaposition of pluralism include his revision of the ordinary conception of truth and his description of the fore-structure of projective understanding. While interpretations contain true statements, one cannot adjudicate between two conflicting interpretations simply by counting the true statements that would be entailed by each one. Other criteria (such as richness, relevance to the present, genuineness, or authenticity) come into play, and these more normative considerations can lead us to prefer some interpretations to others. But the criteria are themselves interpretable and do not obviously support the monistic belief in a single exclusive interpretation. Furthermore, Heidegger's account of understanding as projection suggests that explicit interpretations always arise from implicit needs. The appearance of a new interpretation is likely to generate new needs, and these will in turn stimulate further interpretation. That the circle of understanding is never closed need not raise the specter of epistemological relativism. The nihilistic conclusion that our present interpretations are mostly false does not follow from the pluralistic thought that they will be altered by future generations, for whom the context and the background conditions will have changed.

Heidegger himself may not have fully accepted this pluralistic conclusion about his own theory of Dasein in *Being and Time.* I noted Heidegger's apparent desire to outdo Kant with Heidegger's own suggestion that Section 31 rivals Kant's transcendental deduction. But I also pointed out another reading of Heidegger's enterprise, one that takes seriously his claim that the account of Dasein has the metastatus of an interpretation, in the sense of an *Interpretierung.* Taking seriously this metaposition of interpretive pluralism allows us to imagine ways in which Heidegger's account of understanding could be expanded and modified. One way it can be modified is to take the hermeneutic turn more radically than Heidegger did in 1927, allowing language a more central role by modeling the account of understanding more explicitly on reading, as Gadamer did in 1960. Another way would be to recognize more explicitly and strategically how understanding can directly challenge meaning and how much more conscious the rhetorical play of language can become. The latter way was the achievement of Derrida and the deconstructive movement from the late sixties to the present.

If these modifications are granted, it must also be recognized that they are prefigured in *Being and Time* itself. Whatever Heidegger's personal politics were, the text of *Being and Time* allows for the deconstructivist suspicion of simply recovering the tradition. Heidegger insists that the tradition may need to be criticized, and he reminds us that the "tradition" is not simply the "past." The past is finished, and there would be no point in criticizing it since the criticism could have no effect on the past. What we (and poststructuralists like Derrida and Michel Foucault) may need to criticize is the present, or more specifically, the present's interpretation of how it has come to be what it is, which is what "tradition" is. The criticism of the "traditional" in the present need not be presented as a complete break with tradition, but more reasonably as a break with a prevalent but mistaken understanding of the tradition's possibilities. So an effective criticism will see places where the present has misconstrued the possibilities inherited from the tradition, and it will also draw our attention to concrete possibilities in the tradition that have currently been lost from sight.[10]

If political, social, and historical criticism is to be genuinely possible on the Heideggerian account, however, there must be some resolution of the methodological question that I raised about whether we are not always imprisoned in our own cognitive and normative standpoint. This problem seems to follow from Heidegger's general claim that we can understand something only from within a context that we bring with us already. If the circle of understanding were static, this worry would be justified. But close attention to Heidegger's text shows that he thinks of the circle as a dynamic process of making aspects of the implicit background explicit and then testing standard assumptions to see if they really hold up, given the rest of what we believe and do. Hence, he speaks of testing assumptions against the "things themselves" to make "the scientific theme secure" (BT 195).

Gadamer's own theory in *Truth and Method* (see pp. 254–71) is built around an explication of these sections of *Being and Time.* Gadamer replies to the charge that, on the hermeneutic account, understanding is always imprisoned in its own standpoint by pointing out that in interpreting a text our own preconceptions often do not work out. The text may give us a shock by showing us a side of the subject matter that we had not anticipated. So the circle of understanding is a dynamic one where preconceptions will either work out or fail. Heidegger himself had spoken of genuine understanding as that which gets beyond "fancies" and "popular conceptions," and these are precisely what come to nothing when the interpreter tries explicitly to work them out.

Gadamer thus insists that it is false to conclude that the hermeneutic circle cannot recognize the alterity of the text. I would add that deconstruction could indeed be a crucial moment in the circle of interpretation, for its techniques could be used to ensure that the alterity of the text was taken seriously enough. The circle of understanding should not be purely reconstructive, if by that is meant either that the interpreter reads only what is already familiar back into the text or that in the effort to find a unity of meaning the interpreter should overlook tensions and contradictions that are also at play. But the circle could also not be purely deconstructive, since there must first be an assumed meaning that is deconstructed, and the discovery of tension and contradiction is itself a projection of an understanding of what is really going on in the text.

Heidegger's model of projective understanding can therefore recognize both reconstruction and deconstruction as necessary moments of interpretation. How these are balanced in particular cases is itself a matter of judgment and may be part of what makes interpretations interestingly different. What makes some interpretations more interesting or insightful than others is a question that I suggested at the beginning of this essay and is an appropriate one with which to conclude. While the question is a large one, there is at least the outline of an answer in these sections of *Being and Time.* At least one central aspect of what makes an interpretation better will be whether it understands not only its object and subject matter, but also itself. Interpretations that are methodologically more self-aware are therefore better if they bring to light unnoticed features not only of the object of interpretation, but also of the conditions and procedures of interpretation. A good interpretation, on Heidegger's model, will show something about the possibilities of interpretation as such. An interpretation presupposes a self-understanding, and bringing crucial features of this implicit self-understanding to light will make the interpretation insightful (in Heidegger's special sense of sight, which is not simply the perception of present-at-hand objects, but the disclosure of the total background or context).

As I have suggested, however, self-understanding is not to be taken in the traditional sense in which it might suggest grasping some inner, private self. In German, "self-understanding" (*Sichverstehen*) has to do with knowing one's way around. So for Heidegger, who construes Dasein as being-in-the-world, self-understanding thus has to do with knowing one's way around in the world or in some specific worldly subject matter. That Heidegger was himself interpreting Dasein and not simply a text does not signify a conflict with later hermeneutic theory. Instead, his *Interpretierung* of Dasein brings out a double-sided possibility of interpretation. On the one side, genuine interpretation will reflect the being who is interpreting. So there must be some dimension of the interpreter's context that is itself brought into focus. On the other side, who this being is will itself depend on its interpretations of the world, including its beliefs and its activities. So on the Heideggerian account any good interpretation should disclose something about both Dasein and the world. Interpretation is, after all, the way that both meaningful human existence and a significant world become what they are.

NOTES

1 Hans-Georg Gadamer, *Truth and Method,* 2d rev. ed., trans. Joel Weinsheimer and Donald G. Marshall (New York: Crossroad, 1989), p. xxx.

2 Ibid.

3 Jean-Paul Sartre, *Being and Nothingness,* trans. Hazel E. Barnes (New York: Washington Square Press, 1956), p. 581.

4 For a detailed account of these terms see Hubert L. Dreyfus, *Being-in-the-World: A Commentary on Heidegger's "Being and Time," Division I* (Cambridge, Mass.: MIT Press, 1991), Chap. 11.

5 Or at least, all understanding is interpretive in the sense of *Auslegung,* not necessarily in the sense of *Interpretierung.* Richard Shusterman raises the objection under discussion here in his article "Beneath Interpretation: Against Hermeneutic Holism," *Monist* 73, No. 2 (1990): 181–204.

6 Paul Ricoeur appeals to the metaphor of the arch in the account of interpretation in "Qu'est-ce qu'un Texte? Expliquer et comprendre," in *Hermeneutik und Dialektik: Aufsätze II,* ed. Rüdiger Bubner, Konrad Cramer, and Reiner Wiehl (Tübingen: Mohr, 1970), pp. 181–200.

7 For the Heideggerian critique of epistemological foundationalism see Charles Guignon, *Heidegger and the Problem of Knowledge* (Indianapolis, Ind.: Hackett, 1983), esp. pp. 150–82.

8 Jonathan Culler, *On Deconstruction: Theory and Criticism after Structuralism* (Ithaca, N.Y.: Cornell University Press, 1982), p. 176. Jacques Derrida explicitly rejects this thesis in *Limited Inc* (Evanston, Ill.: Northwestern University Press, 1988), p. 157.

9 Jürgen Habermas advances this line of attack on deconstruction in Chapter 7 of *The Philosophical Discourse of Modernity: Twelve Lectures,* trans. Frederick Lawrence (Cambridge, Mass.: MIT Press, 1987). For a response see my article, "Splitting the Difference: Habermas's Critique of Derrida," *Praxis International,* 8, No. 4 (1989): 447–64.

10 See Section 74 of *Being and Time,* especially BT 438, and my article, "History, Historicity, and Historiography in *Being and Time,*" in *Heidegger and Modern Philosophy: Critical Essays,* ed. Michael Murray (New Haven, Conn.: Yale University Press, 1978), pp. 329–53.

PIOTR HOFFMAN

7 Death, time, history: Division II of *Being and Time*

> This certainty, that "I myself am in that I will die," is *the basic certainty of Dasein itself*. . . . The MORIBUNDUS *first gives the SUM its sense.* (HCT 316–17)
>
> Only in dying can I to some extent say absolutely, "I am." (HCT 318)

Modern philosophy turns away from things in the world and zeroes in on the human self that grasps them in thought and transforms them in action. The self becomes the repository of both their truth and their ultimate purposes. By the same token, the human self is given the status of the self-grounding ground of reality. In this new and exalted status, the self ceases to be viewed as part and parcel of some independent order of things. Beginning with Descartes's *cogito,* the self withdraws from the world and falls back on its own experiences and thoughts. The subjectivity of the self supplies both the point of departure and the validating ground for various philosophical attempts at a reconstruction of our knowledge of the world.

One of Heidegger's aims in *Being and Time* was to question and to overcome this subjectivist tradition of modern philosophy. I hope to show, however, that in Division II of *Being and Time* Heidegger reveals himself as an heir to that tradition and to its model of the human self.

THE HUMAN SELF

In the very first section of Division II (BT 274–8) Heidegger makes two claims whose importance to the entire philosophical project he is pursuing in his opus magnum cannot be overestimated. In the first place, since the aim of this project is to investigate the meaning of being in general, and since the meaning of being in general is disclosed by Dasein, the ultimate clarification of the meaning of being demands an appropriately ultimate ("primordial") interpretation of Dasein. In other terms, we cannot be satisfied with this or that partial or approximate view of Dasein; we must achieve the grasp of Dasein *as a whole.* In the second place, and as we shall see more clearly later, from the present vantage point "one thing has become unmistakable: *our existential analysis of Dasein up till now cannot lay claim to primordiality.* Its fore-having never included more than the *inauthentic* Being of Dasein, and of Dasein as less than a *whole* [*als unganzes*]" (BT 276). The entire Division I, then, must now be considered profoundly incomplete, since it failed to give us the required insight into both the *totality* and the *authenticity* of Dasein (BT 276).

Even at this, still provisional and still quite general stage of Heidegger's analysis, the joint appearance of "totality" and "authenticity" can be given some justification. For the authentic life (in contrast to the inauthentic life) is one in which not just this or that aspect of Dasein, but Dasein *as a whole,* comes to expression. And if, as it will soon become clear, Dasein's authenticity requires the lucid acceptance of one's own death, it is precisely because Dasein's totality can be revealed only in its being-toward-death.

This last statement can first be taken in its obvious and least controversial sense. As long as a human individual is alive – as long as he continues to take a stand on what it means to be – his identity is not a settled matter, for it is open to constant revision and reinterpretation. At every stage of my life I can always take this rather than that option open to me – and, in so doing, not only do I determine what the course of my life will be from now on, but I also reshape and redefine the meaning of what my life was all about until now. This is so because the options that I take shed light on what was important to me all along, on the endurance and the strength of my commitments (or lack thereof), and so on. To shift back to Heidegger's terminology: as long as Dasein is, it can choose its possibilities; hence, as long as this "ahead-of-itself" item in the structure of Dasein is not extinguished, Dasein will be characterized by a "lack of totality" (BT 279). And since death does extinguish – ultimately and irrevocably – man's ability to choose his possibilities, death puts to rest the ongoing process of reshaping and redefining an individual's identity. What his life was all about becomes now a settled matter.

So far, however, this characterization of death has been offered from a third-person standpoint, and this cannot be satisfying to Heidegger. We must ask about "the ontological meaning of dying of the person who dies, as a possibility-of-Being which belongs to *his* Being" (BT 283). Elsewhere (HCT 308–9), Heidegger spells out in more detail both the thinking behind this requirement and the difficulty it immediately leads to. Since Dasein is defined as being in each instance *mine*, the emergence of death as totalizing my life must appear from within *my own* first-person standpoint. But this requirement seems impossible to satisfy, for as long as I envision things from my own standpoint, I have *not* yet reached my totality, and, conversely, when I *have* reached my totality, there is no standpoint of mine from which to gain the experience of that totality. To put it plainly, if my identity is in principle incomplete while I am alive, then I cannot see what it would even *mean* to say, "This is what my life was all about," unless I construe my death as an event witnessed and interpreted by other people. But by doing this I *eo ipso* abandon the first-person account of my own death.

But the dilemma we have just noted – *either* I am, and then any talk about the completion of my identity is meaningless from my own standpoint, *or* such talk is meaningful, but then it is not conducted from my own standpoint – is a false alternative. It results entirely from our conception of death as a present-at-hand item, that is, as an event within the world (BT 280). I have assumed that in order to gain the first-person sense of what it would mean to say (irrevocably), "This is what my life was all about," I would have to *wait* until that event of my death actually takes place; the insurmountable alternative we have seen to emerge is then a foregone conclusion. But this need not be so. To be sure, I cannot grasp just *what* my complete identity will be. But I nevertheless know, even from within my own standpoint, *how* to view my life as something I have the potential to realize.

In effect, I do not have to wait until my life runs its course to gain a sense of being exposed to, and defined by, the power of death. For the *cogito sum*, we remember from the epigraph, must be restated as *moribundus sum:* I *am* only in that I find myself, at every moment of my life, powerless to escape the possibility of dying at precisely that particular moment (and not only tomorrow, or the day after tomorrow, etc.). As will be shown later, *this* is the one truth that I cannot doubt, though I may try to conceal it and cover it up. And as we shall see shortly, my ability to doubt all truths is itself dependent on that unshakable truth about my being always totally vulnerable to the power of death.

At the same time – and due to the very same circumstance of my total vulnerability to death – the complete identity that I envision as attributable to me remains *my* identity. For my first-person sense of death establishes my life not only as a *totality*, but also as uniquely *mine* – that is, not as an intersection of social and natural roles and functions that I share, or may share, with others.

Heidegger's justification of this important connection – death gives my life its "totality" and its "mineness" (*Jemeinigkeit*) as well – is simple (BT 283–4). Being a member of the public world I can be easily replaced ("represented") by another person. Somebody else could have filled the position I occupy in society; somebody else could have been the husband of the woman I married, the father of her children, and so on. Now this possibility of being "represented" by another individual breaks down in one case and in one case only: in the case of my death. It is true, of course, that when we speak loosely we can easily point to a number of other cases in which, apparently, our personal presence is indispensable; no one, it seems, can replace me at that operating table when the surgeon is about to perform an operation on me, or in that imposing office of the dean, who expects from me an explanation of my repeated absences from the university functions, and so on. But it is also easy to see why such counterexamples can have no bearing whatsoever on Heidegger's point about death, for I can always avoid the experiences I have just described: I can decide to take my chances without the surgery, or I can fail to appear at the dean's office, and so on. My presence or absence on those occasions is a matter of my own choice: if I think that I have lived long enough anyway, or if I don't care much about keeping my job, I will not find it difficult, and certainly not impossible, to miss my appointments with both surgeon and the dean. But in no case can I avoid appearing before the tribunal of death. In all other cases where it seems that no one can replace me, changing my own goals will make me capable of avoiding those experiences. But there is no goal and no strategy that would allow me to maneuver myself out of my rendezvous with death.

We can understand now why Heidegger attributes to death the power of *both* totalizing and individualizing Dasein. Death totalizes me, for due to death my identity will become complete. Death individualizes me, for it imposes upon me the one and only experience that is inescapably mine. Thus, "if 'ending,' as dying, is constitutive for Dasein's *totality,* then the Being of this wholeness itself must be conceived as an existential phenomenon which is in each case *one's own*" (BT 284, my emphasis). But although these two functions of death – to *complete* my identity and to establish it as uniquely *mine* – are inseparable, they nevertheless remain distinct. Since somebody else could have filled in for me with each and every one of the experiences making up my life history, all of these experiences are uniquely mine only because that life history as a whole is individuated *independently* of them by its ultimate term: by death. Of the latter, it can only be said that it is "in every case mine insofar as it is at all" (BT 284). Thus, our first-person encounter with the menace of death, demands the *repudiation of the principle of the identity of indiscernibles:* I am *this* particular person not on account of the totality of determinations attributable to me, but due to the "mineness" of death, where the mineness at issue is an underived and primitive term distinguished only by its sheer "thisness," and not by any property or set of properties.

We can now see with more clarity Heidegger's reliance on the modern idea of subjectivity, indeed his profound kinship with Descartes. For both philosophers, the human individual is thrown back upon *his own* self by a sense of *total powerlessness and vulnerability* in the face of an ultimate threat (of, respectively, the evil demon and death). I shall return to this idea later.[1] But there is an immediate difficulty standing in the way of that parallel, just noted, between Descartes and Heidegger. If in Descartes the threat of the evil demon seems indeed inescapable (at least before the self's discovery of God), it is because the demon is said to deceive me constantly.[2] Thus, the demon gives me no respite and no escape; his power holds me in its grip without the slightest letup or slackening. And it seems equally obvious, at least to common sense, that death does *not* have this sort of power over me. I can be said to be under death's real threat when I wake up in a hospital bed, after a complicated and dangerous operation. But I seem to confront no such threat at all when, healthy, vigorous, and fresh from my yearly medical checkup, I find myself walking leisurely on a sandy beach. Death does not seem to threaten me "constantly." And so it follows that the "mineness" I was said to acquire through the exposure to death's menace cannot be one of the core characteristics of human selfhood. Yet such was precisely the status attributed to this characteristic at the very beginning of Heidegger's analytic of Dasein.[3]

The difficulty is genuine, but it stems from a misunderstanding of Heidegger's interpretation of death. The difficulty is raised from within the *commonsensical* view of death, while for Heidegger, the commonsensical view of death is a gross distortion of the actual state of affairs. When that actual state of affairs – that is, the true face of death – is brought out and articulated, the threat of death reveals itself as being indeed constant and all-pervasive.

Heidegger's analytic of death takes off with a reminder that "care is the basic state of Dasein" (BT 293). For if death is to have the constancy and the all-pervasiveness required by its function of individualizing the human self, that status of death must be made clear in terms of the very basic state of Dasein. This is indeed the route Heidegger now takes. He has already, at the earlier stages of his analytic of human finitude, defined care as composed of "existence," "facticity," and "falling." He will now show how all these three aspects of care reveal the constancy and the all-pervasiveness of man's exposure to the threat of death.

But the essential connection between care and death can be grasped on a more general level as well. Dasein is care, for Dasein is always concerned about its being. My life (both in its "that" and in its "what") is not something indifferent to me, something that leaves me cold, as it were; on the contrary, it is something that *matters* to me. Now my life matters to me – indeed *must* matter to me – only because I am aware that I don't have it "forever" and "once for all"; life matters only because I am aware that it can be snatched away from me by the power of death. And so care is Dasein's basic state only because Dasein is, and understands itself as being, a mortal creature: "I am this 'I can die at any moment.' . . . *I myself am this constant and utmost possibility of myself,* namely, to be no more. Care, which is essentially care about the being of Dasein, at its innermost is nothing but this being-ahead-of-itself in the uttermost possibility of its own can-be" (HCT 313). Conversely, just as Dasein's (basic) state of care is dependent on Dasein's sense of being a mortal creature so, too, *"as regards its ontological possibility, dying is grounded in care"* (BT 296). In other terms, the mere conception of a mortal creature that would remain unaffected by, and indifferent to, its own perishability is not at all logically contradictory. If death moves us to show concern about our life, it is because man's "basic state" is indeed care – and not some sort of total obliviousness to his own finitude. To summarize, if we were not threatened by death, our basic state would not be care; but if our basic state were not care, our death would not be felt as threatening. Care and the sense of one's mortality are thus, to use one of Heidegger's favorite terms, "equiprimordial."

Now since care is the *basic* state of Dasein – that is, the state in which Dasein *always* is, the state that underlies *all* of Dasein's experiences – and since care implies one's exposure to the menace of death, this exposure must be just as constant and all-pervasive as care itself. For if I could remove the menace of death from a certain stretch of my life, then at least within *that* stretch I would not have to worry about my life being snatched away from me (I could say, "I will think about crossing that bridge when I get to it – when I get sick, old, and so on.") and thus care would cease to permeate *all* of my experiences. If, then, care is to remain the "basic state" of Dasein, the threat of death must be constant to Dasein.

Now the constancy of death's threat to Dasein reveals itself with a particular clarity in the first and most fundamental aspect of care: in Dasein's being-ahead-of-itself, projected toward a field of its possibilities. Death is constant insofar as it is the only *pure* possibility of Dasein, that is, the sort of possibility free of any admixture of actuality (and of necessity as well). Ordinarily, Heidegger argues (BT 305–7), we lack any understanding of such a pure possibility – including the possibility of our own dying – for our control-oriented stance toward the world is bent on reducing every possibility to a predictable and manageable event or process. Owing to this stance, possibility loses its character of possibility and it becomes possible only "relatively to" certain circumstances and conditions. A possibility whose occurrence is thus made dependent on the *actuality* of such and such conditions becomes something less than a possibility to the precise degree to which it becomes more connected with actuality. To appear in all the purity of its character *qua* possibility, a possibility must thus be equally possible under any conditions whatever.

But this does not mean that such a possibility becomes transformed into a *necessity.* There are two kinds of necessity to be considered, and rejected, in this connection. If we try to connect (or, worse still, to reduce) the possibility of dying to some *real* necessity produced by the operation of causal laws in our universe, then we are once again on our way to depriving possibility of its quality of possibility by making it dependent on something foreign and external to it. If it is necessary that I die at some point given certain facts and laws of human biology then, by the same token, I will not die unless and until all the required conditions have actually taken place. But then I can anticipate (at least to some degree) when and how I am likely to die and I can make my plans accordingly. So if death is viewed as occurring due to a real necessity, then death is not always equally possible – and then its character of pure possibility is, once again, glossed over. On the other hand – and this is the second sense of necessity to be considered here and rejected – the constancy and the all-pervasiveness of the threat of death to us is not a matter of *logical* necessity either. Given certain general facts about the human condition, the threat of death must indeed shadow every individual at every stage of his life. But it is not logically necessary that these general facts about the human condition be such as they are.

The all-pervasiveness and omnipresence of death's threat to an individual is captured by Heidegger with the term "indefiniteness" (*Unbestimmtheit*). The possibility of death is indefinite, for it is not confined to any particular moment or time span. The possibility of death can materialize at any moment. Furthermore, since Heidegger argues (in § 70 of *Being and Time*) that space is encountered from within the temporal project of Dasein, the indefiniteness of death's "when" (BT 302) implies its lack of connection with any particular "here" or "there." This is why the threat disclosed in anxiety – the threat of death (BT 310) – is perceived as coming at us from *"nowhere"* (BT 231). Now, since due to its indefiniteness, the possibility of death is disclosed to us as a "constant threat" (BT 310), the parallel we have drawn between the threat of the evil demon in Descartes and the threat of death in Heidegger is vindicated. Both threats are indeed constant and all-pervasive; both threats reveal to the individual the powerlessness and the vulnerability of his condition.

But there is an even stronger kinship to be discovered between the *cogito sum* of Descartes and the existential *moribundus sum* of Heidegger. Insofar as I view myself in the light of the possibility of being misled by the evil demon, I suspend my reliance on the truths of everyday life; but at the same time, I discover the unshakable truth of my subjectivity: "There is some deceiver or other, very powerful and very cunning, who ever employs his ingenuity in deceiving me. Then without doubt I exist also if he deceives me, and let him deceive me as much as he will, he can never cause me to be nothing so long as I think I am something."[4] In a similar vein, my coming face to face with the (indefinite) possibility of death not only forces me to abandon the ordinary, everyday framework of intelligibility and truth, but at the same time leads me to discover the unshakable certainty and truth of my *sum*. Let us consider these two steps one by one.

In the first place, then, insofar as anxiety brings an individual face to face with the indefiniteness of death's threat to him, his public world is suddenly discovered as failing him. For the public world cannot protect an individual against death, and so this world *as a whole* proves to be unreliable. The tie between the individual and his public world is broken; the individual does not "find" himself in the latter; the meanings and the truths making up the fabric of the world become alien to the individual: "anxiety . . . takes away from Dasein the possibility of understanding itself, as it falls, in terms of the world and the way things have been publicly interpreted" (BT 232).

But – in the second place – insofar as the individual thus withdraws his assent to the intelligibility and truth of the public interpretation of reality, he discovers and falls back upon the unshakable evidence of the existential *moribundus sum*. Not only is this evidence subjectively "certain" (BT 309) but – just as in the case of the Cartesian *cogito* – it has "truth" as well (BT 309). To be sure, Heidegger warns us explicitly (BT 309) not to attribute to the certainty and truth of death the character of "apodictic evidence." But it is even more important to pay close attention to what he means by this warning, and how he justifies it. The passage is worth quoting in full:

Dasein must first have lost itself in the factual circumstances [*Sachverhalte*] (this can be one of care's own tasks and possibilities) if it is to obtain the pure objectivity – that is to say, the indifference – of apodictic evidence. If being certain in relation to death does not have this character, this does not mean that it is of a lower grade, but that *it does not belong at all to the graded order of the kinds of evidence we can have about the present-at-hand.*

Holding death for true (death *is* just one's own) shows another kind of certainty, and is more primordial than any certainty which relates to entities encountered within-the-world, or to formal objects; for it is certain of Being-in-the-world. As such, holding death for true does not demand just *one* definite kind of behavior in Dasein, but demands Dasein itself in the full authenticity of its existence. (BT 309–10)

In this crucial passage, Heidegger clearly spells out several things. In the first place, whereas the certainty and the truth of death should not indeed be confused with the "apodictic evidence" that characterizes our mental grasp of "formal objects" – that is, of objects of pure mathematics or else of the pure essences of things – death's omnipresent threat to us does not have, for that reason, a "lower" kind of evidence and truth. Quite the contrary, as Heidegger leads us to understand in the last part of the passage, our "holding death for true" permeates *all* of our attitudes and stances, while the truth attributed to, say, the axioms and theorems of mathematics is attributed in a special "theoretical" attitude, which – Heidegger argues in *Being and Time* – is not even basic and primordial to Dasein. To put it plainly, under certain circumstances, Dasein *can* withdraw its endorsement of the intelligibility and truth of "formal objects," while under no circumstances whatever is it possible for Dasein to liberate itself from the gnawing sense of its mortality.[5] And, in effect, the very same anxiety that alienates Dasein from the meanings and the truths of the public world – and hence also from the meaning and truth of "formal objects" – brings Dasein face to face with its *moribundus sum.* The evidence and the truth of that proposition are unique in that all other forms of evidence and truth are objects of assent or doubt performed by a creature that, throughout all those acts of assent and doubt, continues to acknowledge (authentically or inauthentically) its own mortality.

Now insofar as the evidence of Descartes's *cogito* is interpreted as a case of "apodictic evidence" accompanying our mental grasp of a present-at-hand item – of our own ego – then indeed there can be no analogy between Descartes's *cogito sum* and Heidegger's *moribundus sum*. In addition, there can be no doubt that this is how Descartes's claims were often understood and developed; and it is also true that there is ample support for this sort of interpretation in Descartes's own writings. Not only is the "ego" of the *ego cogito* interpreted as a (mental) substance, but our cognitive mode of access to that substance often exhibits the character of an "apodictic evidence" enjoyed by mathematical entities.

But there is another, and more correct, way of analyzing Descartes's *cogito*, and this analysis brings him very close to Heidegger's thinking on the *sum*. Jaakko Hintikka argued that Descartes's fundamental and self-founding principle has in fact a *performatory character*.[6] The "I am" is neither deduced from the "I think" nor logically true all by itself. Rather, when I say, "I do not exist," this sentence (or thought) is "existentially inconsistent" with my uttering this sentence or entertaining that thought.[7] What implies my existence, then, is not the thought itself, but my performance of the act of thinking that particular thought (or any other thought denying my being). Similarly, if we are prepared to agree with Heidegger's dictum "The MORIBUNDUS *first gives* the SUM *its sense*," then every attitude and stance of mine – including my very attempts, in whatever form, to deny my mortality – testifies to my existence as a mortal self. The structure of the argument is the same in both Descartes and Heidegger.

TIME AND HISTORY

Our endorsement of that Heideggerian dictum "The MORIBUNDUS *first gives* the SUM *its sense*" allows us to see why the instantaneity of the Cartesian *cogito* must be replaced with the inherently temporal character of Dasein. Mine is a finite, limited existence – the sort of existence that, inevitably, must meet its ultimate end. And this is another way of saying that I am aware of having a certain definite destiny ahead of me. Furthermore, my sense of that future destiny is instrumental in bringing me face to face with my past. For when I say that my life is bound to come to its end, I imply that I am a *determinate* self, a self endowed with a particular life history, with such and such social and cultural background, and so on. All of these items refer to my past and all of them come alive for me as making up my identity when I confront the finite future. This is why my sense of my past is dependent on my sense of that finite future (BT 373, 435).

Since death is revealed in anxiety and since my sense of death as my ultimate end imposes upon my experiences their temporal structure, it is only to be expected that the latter, too, will have its roots in anxiety. And, in effect, Heidegger speaks explicitly of the *temporality of anxiety,* which he carefully distinguishes from both the inauthentic and authentic forms of temporality:

> In contrast to this making-present which is not held on to [this is the inauthentic present, the present in which Dasein loses and disperses itself], the Present of anxiety is *held on to*. . . . But even though the Present of anxiety is *held on to,* it does not as yet have the character of the moment of vision which temporalizes itself in a resolution. (BT 394)

> This bringing-back has neither the character of an evasive forgetting nor that of a remembering. But just as little does anxiety imply that one has already taken over one's existence into one's resolution and done so by a repeating. (BT 394)

In the first of these passages Heidegger opposes both the inauthentic present (the "making-present") and the authentic present (the "moment of vision") to the present of anxiety. In the second passage, he draws a similar contrast between the inauthentic past (evasive forgetting, remembering) and the authentic past (repeating), on the one hand, and the past of anxiety, on the other hand.

The temporality of anxiety is the underlying ground of both authentic and inauthentic temporality. Whereas inauthentic temporality expresses Dasein's flight from its anxious anticipation of death, authentic temporality is built upon a stance in which one confronts what is revealed in the temporality of anxiety and expresses this in one's attitude toward one's entire life, from birth to death.

Let us try to get some grip on the basic concepts with the aid of which Heidegger attempts to articulate the structure of human temporalizing. Let us begin with inauthentic temporality, for this form of temporalizing represents the understanding of time characteristic of the ordinary, commonsensical Dasein. Since the entire commonsensical way of life expresses Dasein's attempt to turn away from the ever-present menace of death, the inauthentic future takes the form of a (hopeful, fearful, etc.) "awaiting" and "expecting" (BT 386–7). In the general strategy of an inauthentic Dasein, our sense of radical vulnerability and powerlessness becomes glossed over and made manageable by being projected onto the world. Whatever threats to our existence there may be, they are now viewed as threatening us from *within* the world. In conformity with this overall strategy, our entire future is seen as a pursuit of a secure acceptance by the world of the "they" (*das Man*). This understanding of the future entails a selective, highly utilitarian attitude toward one's past. Since successes and failures on the road of the inauthentic future are defined by the trends and pressures of the public world, an inauthentic Dasein's past will be disclosed through "forgetting." An individual will repress and relegate into oblivion such parts of his past as may prove detrimental to his search for success in the rapidly changing world of the "they" with all of this world's trends, fashions, and cliches. Conversely, whatever it is that this type of individual will remember will be remembered on the basis of forgetting (BT 389). Since an inauthentic individual retains from his past only what serves his pursuit of a secure acceptance by the public world, he remembers *A* only insofar as he forgets *B*, or *C*, or *D*. Finally, the overall attitude of "expecting" one's future and of "forgetting" one's past shapes one's inauthentic stance toward the present, the stance of "making-present." The inauthentic Dasein's search for security is reflected in a collection of entities – of persons, things, goods, and so on – with which this sort of Dasein surrounds itself (and thus "makes present" these entities) in order to gain a sense of having a place within the reassuring world of the "they."

In authentic temporality, the temporality of anxiety is incorporated into Dasein's self-interpretation. In the "anticipated" (authentic) future, an individual faces up to the ever-threatening menace of death as the meaning of what lies ahead. By thus confronting the limitedness and the finiteness of his existence, he finds himself brought back to his past. This authentic sense of acknowledging one's past is gained in "repetition." Finally, in the authentic present's "moment of vision" (*Augenblick*) an individual can open up to the present realities of his life, since his abandonment of the single-minded pursuit of social acceptance allows him to adopt a free, nonmanipulative attitude toward his present situation.

Viewed merely as items in the temporality of Dasein, the future, past, and present are disclosed in "ecstases" – in Dasein's ways of reaching out toward its death, its roots, and its surroundings. The *ordering* of these ecstases is prior to and independent of any temporal chronology (BT 375–6). The ecstatic future is not "later" than the ecstatic present, for at any moment of my life I am equally vulnerable to the power of death, and hence that vulnerability of mine is always an actual, live issue for me. My past, too, is not something that has simply elapsed and is now left behind, something existing "no longer now – but earlier" (BT 375). This is so because my past is nothing other than my "thrownness" – that is, my rootedness in a culture, my already established preferences, skills, habits, and so on – and it is precisely in terms of this thrownness that my present experiences get to be organized and endowed with a meaning. Nor does the ecstasis of the present derive its name from its position within a chronological order. In this ecstasis, in this "being-alongside (entities encountered within-the-world)," I am "present" to those entities and I thus allow them to "have presence" to me – in the sense of being available to me, of being at my disposal.

Just as the *ordering* of the ecstases is independent of any chronological relations, so too the *becoming* of the ecstases (thus, the present becomes the past, the future becomes the present, etc.) is not a chronologically determinable alteration either. Indeed, temporality's "essence is a *process* of temporalizing in the unity of the ecstases" (BT 377, my emphasis). And this dynamic, process-like character of temporality both precedes and conditions all our notions of temporal flow as chronologically understood.

But then how can Heidegger derive our ordinary, chronologically understood notion of time from the temporality of Dasein? We have already seen how the temporality of anxiety gets perverted into inauthentic temporality – into the temporality of a Dasein unwilling to confront its ontological powerlessness and vulnerability. This form of temporality is at the source of time as ordinarily understood: " 'Time' as ordinarily understood . . . arises from inauthentic temporality" (BT 374). We must now try to understand this claim in more detail.

Human temporality in general is mapped onto the world through the *horizonal schemata* of the three temporal ecstases. We have already noted that the ecstases are Dasein's ways of being "outside itself." This last expression includes an implicit reference to the horizonal-schematic structure of the ecstases: "There belongs to each ecstasis a 'whither' to which one is carried away" (BT 416). Now this "whither" is nothing other than the worldly counterpart of each ecstasis. For example, the horizonal schema of the past is defined as "that *in the face of which*" Dasein has been thrown. This means that my relationship to my past presupposes a reference to a certain condition of the world: to the society and the institutions within which I was born and raised, to my family environment, to my childhood friends, and so on. My past is thus mirrored in the past of the world. Heidegger gives a similar account of the link between the ecstases of the present and the future, on the one hand, and their own worldly counterparts, on the other hand.

Due to its grounding in human temporality, the world gains a temporal structure of its own. However, we are still one step short of accounting for the emergence of the temporal chronology. For example, "that *in the face of which* Dasein has been thrown" (the horizonal schema of the past) does not yet mean "earlier" than the horizonal schema of the present. But this still outstanding gap is rendered irrelevant within the context of the existential analytic of Dasein. For Dasein's temporality is schematized onto the world due to Dasein's practical, everyday absorption within the world, and this practical, everyday stance of Dasein imposes on it the necessity of "reckoning" with time, of taking time into account in all of our daily plans and projects (BT 456–7). And in order to respond to that necessity of reckoning with time we must *date* actions and events that take place in it. This is why the horizons and the schemata of the ecstases must be assigned a chronological standing vis-à-vis one another. And this is also why the origin of the temporal chronology must be looked for in the commonsensical, inauthentic temporality of Dasein. "In the 'then' concern expresses itself as awaiting [i.e., as the inauthentic future], in the 'on that former occasion,' as retaining [as the inauthentic past]" (BT 458). Only now can the horizons and the schemata of temporality receive the chronological significance they have been lacking so far: "The horizon for the retaining which expresses itself in the 'on that former occasion' is the *'earlier'*; the horizon for the 'now' is the *'today'* " (BT 459). From this stage on, when I think of the circumstances and conditions in the face of which I was thrown (the horizonal schema of the past), I think of them as being "earlier" than such and such circumstances and conditions that I confront right now or am about to confront in the near future, and so on.

The substitution of the *moribundus sum* for Descartes's *cogito sum* had proved to be instrumental in replacing the instantaneity of the Cartesian *cogito* with the temporality of Dasein. A further implication of this substitution is the rediscovery of the *historical* dimension of the human self. The reason is still the same: when I anticipate and endure the menace of death I find myself to be a limited, determinate self, and this means also a self with certain definite historical roots, a self with a "heritage" and a "fate" (BT 435). But in thus imposing upon Dasein a historical dimension, death works jointly with several other items in the structure of Dasein. "Only if death, guilt, conscience, freedom and finitude reside together equiprimordially in the Being of an entity as they do in care, can that entity exist in the mode of fate, that is to say only then can it be historical in the very depths of its existence" (BT 437).

Let us first say something about the "call of conscience" (*Ruf des Gewissens*), which imposes on the plain, ordinary Dasein a "demand" (BT 311) to turn away from the conformisms of the "they" and to live up to its authenticity and wholeness. What does the ordinary, everyday Dasein *hear* in the message delivered in the call of conscience? The answer to this question represents the next stage in Heidegger's deepening hermeneutics of conscience. In the message delivered in the call, the ordinary Dasein is told about its own *guilt*.

But while Dasein, as the addressee and the bearer of this message of guilt, is indeed the ordinary Dasein, the guilt in question is not ordinary guilt. The latter is always specific and determinate: I am guilty of having crossed that intersection at the red light, guilty of not having lived up to my administrative duties at the university, and so on. But the guilt addressed to the ordinary Dasein in the call of conscience is general and unconditional. It does not concern this or that, and it is not conditional upon my having (or not having) done this or that. What, then, am I guilty of according to the accusation raised against me through the call of conscience?

This "primordial existential meaning" (BT 326) of my guilt can be gathered "from the fact that this 'Guilty' turns up as a predicate for the 'I am' " (BT 326). If the "guilty" is to be taken as the predicate of the mere "I am," it's because my mere existence is discovered as making me guilty. If it were otherwise, I would have to refer to myself (at least implicitly) through some additional and still other predicates; I would have to say, "I *as* the father of a child am guilty of not paying child support," or "I *as* a driver am guilty of violating traffic regulations," and so on. Under such circumstances the predicate "guilty" would not apply to me *qua* merely being, but *qua* being only this or that. But the call of conscience tells me I am guilty insofar as I (merely) am.

Now Dasein is guilty in its (mere) being, for, to begin with, "Dasein is not itself the basis of being" (BT 300). While I can achieve a measure of mastery and control over various items making up my environment, I can achieve no mastery and no control at all over the basis of my life. Thus, for Dasein to exist means "*never* to have power over one's ownmost Being from the ground up. This '*not*' belongs to the existential meaning of 'thrownness' " (BT 330); and therefore our thrownness is shot through with "nullity" (*Nichtigkeit*). This connection of thrownness with nullity is also discovered through one's anxious anticipation of death: "The 'nothing' with which anxiety brings us face to face, unveils the nullity by which Dasein, in its very *basis*, is defined; and this basis itself is as thrownness into death" (BT 356).

In effect, in order to recognize myself as being thrown into death, I must come to see myself as a finite, limited, and hence a *determinate* self. What makes me such a determinate, concrete self is my social and historical background, my personal life history, my habits, and so on. Thrownness encompasses all of these established characteristics of mine, that is, my entire past (BT 373). And if my thrownness is the source of guilt, I must be guilty for having adopted the wrong attitude toward my entire past self. This does not mean that there is something *special* about my past that makes me guilty (if such were the case we would be back to the ordinary sense of guilt), but this does imply that I am guilty not as some empty form of a mortal self "in general," but as a determinate self.

But how *can* my thrownness represent a source of guilt for me? Where have I failed – where *can* I fail – in taking up an attitude toward my thrownness?

But I *can* fail and, as an ordinary Dasein, I *have* failed in my attitude toward my thrownness. "The Self, which as such has to lay the basis for itself, can *never* get that basis into its power; and yet, as existing, it must take over Being-a-basis" (BT 330). The accusation of guilt understood in that "primordial ontological meaning" is addressed to me insofar as I fail to respond to that task of shaping my life within a thrownness that I can never master and control.

The groundwork is now laid for man's acceptance of his historical roots. Once again, and quite predictably, the strategy of denial – the strategy of the inauthentic Dasein – will be brought to its end by Dasein's anxious encounter with the same menace of death:

> As a way of Being for Dasein, history has its roots so essentially in the future that death, as that possibility of Dasein which we have already characterized, throws anticipatory existence back upon its *factical* thrownness, and so for the first time imparts to *having-been* its peculiarly privileged position in the historical. *Authentic being-towards-death – that is to say, the finitude of temporality – is the hidden basis of Dasein's historicality.* (BT 438)

What is still required is man's active response – in anticipatory resoluteness – to the call of conscience, to his *guilt* vis-à-vis his thrownness. Through such an active response an individual situates himself within the historical background of his life. In addition, this historical background – the individual's "heritage" – now ceases to be viewed as open either to one's attempts at control or to ("detached" and "objective") justification. As of now, the individual is ready to accept his heritage in the latter's full contingency and groundlessness ("nullity"). This stance toward one's historical past is its "repetition."

Now to find himself free *for* such a repetition of his heritage, an individual must first free himself *from* the conformism and the pressures of the "they" world. In this respect, too, death plays the pivotal role. First, death "shatters all one's tenaciousness to whatever existence one has reached" (BT 308): insofar as I find myself exposed to the indefinite and constant threat of death, all of my ordinary ties and attachments cease to offer me any security and they thus lose their hold over me. Second, death gives me a "freedom which has been released from the illusions of the 'they' " (BT 311), for due to my anxious grasp of death I come to see the everyday world as a stage dominated by impersonal pressures and conformism.

Repetition allows Dasein to have a "fate" (*Schicksal*), a "destiny" (*Geschick*), as well as a "hero" (*Held*). In repeating my heritage I find myself endowed with a fate, for I acknowledge that my life can express itself only within a certain spectrum of values and traditions. I now realize that I cannot be "anything and everything," since my life is bound up with such and such (and not any other) historical roots. For the same reason, I have a destiny: my life is part and parcel of a broader current of life of the historical community to which I belong. And since both my fate and my destiny must be lived in a concrete possibility of existence, my historical past will provide me with a pool of role models ("heroes") to choose from. Whereas by having a fate, a destiny, and a hero, I can act with *loyalty* toward my historical past, the inauthentic Dasein – a Dasein bent on finding secure acceptance within the ever-shifting trends of the "they" world – will remain disloyal to its past and helpless to resist the tyranny of the "they."

But Dasein's linkup with a historical community does not remove from Dasein's structure its dimension of subjectivity. On the contrary, Dasein reveals itself as rooted in its historical community only by exploring the full depths of its own subjectivity – of its finitude, its freedom, its guilt, and so on. And these themes – the key themes of Division II of *Being and Time* – can be found not only in the classical writers of the subjectivist tradition (in Descartes, Kant, Fichte), but indeed, in its final and most radical version, in existentialism. One is thus perfectly legitimate in drawing parallels between Heidegger and such radically subjectivistic writers as Kierkegaard, Sartre, and Camus. In fact, one of the tasks of Heidegger scholarship remains the task of coming to terms with the tension between those individualistic and subjectivistic aspects of Heidegger's philosophy, on the one hand, and his simultaneous stress on the inevitably public character of intelligibility and significance, on the other.[8]

NOTES

1 For more detail, the reader may consult my book *Doubt, Time, Violence* (Chicago: University of Chicago Press, 1986).

2 R. Descartes, *Meditations on First Philosophy*, in *The Philosophical Works of Descartes*, 2 vols., ed. E. S. Haldane and G. R. T. Ross (Cambridge: Cambridge University Press, 1972), Vol. 1, p. 150.

3 "We are ourselves the entities to be analysed. The being of any such entity is *in each case mine*" (BT 67).

4 Descartes, *Meditations,* Vol. 1, p. 150.

5 For this reason alone our certainty of death cannot be an *empirical* certainty either (BT 301–2).

6 J. Hintikka, "Cogito, Ergo Sum: Inference or Performance," *Philosophical Review,* 71 (January 1962): 3–32.

7 Ibid., p. 25.

8 Here I must refer the reader again to my *Doubt, Time, Violence.* See also Charles B. Guignon's paper "Heidegger's 'Authenticity' Revisited," *Review of Metaphysics,* 37 (December 1984): 321–39.

CHARLES B. GUIGNON

8 Authenticity, moral values, and psychotherapy

PSYCHOTHERAPY AND THE QUESTION OF THE GOOD LIFE

Heidegger's influence on psychotherapy in the English-speaking world has followed a convoluted path. The Swiss physician and therapist Medard Boss tells us that Heidegger expressed the hope that "his thinking would escape the confines of the philosopher's study and become of benefit to wider circles, in particular to a large number of suffering human beings."[1] His participation in Boss's seminars for medical students and therapists from 1946 on was motivated by this concern.[2] Yet when his writings became more widely known among professionals in the field, it was less through this route than through the impact of existentialism in the fifties and sixties. As a result, though Heidegger's thought is often treated as the cornerstone of existential psychotherapy,[3] what one usually finds is a Heidegger refracted through the lens of the far more accessible writings of Sartre, de Beauvoir, and Camus. In the mouth of this "existentialized" Heidegger, the ideal of authenticity is pictured as the stance of the rugged individualist who, upon experiencing anxiety in the face of the ultimate absurdity of life, lives intensely in the present and creates his or her own world through leaps of radical freedom.

As the enthusiasm for existentialism has waned over the past two decades, however, so has the initial motivation for thinking that Heidegger has something important to contribute to therapy. The decline of existentialism can be attributed, I believe, to the growing suspicion that its image of the human condition is too limited to capture the concrete realities of actual existence. The conception of "terrible freedom" found in the French existentialists, for instance, seems to conceal the sense we have of being embedded in a world where not all things are possible. Idealizing this notion of freedom runs the risk of glorifying sheer capriciousness, the kind of "do-your-own-thing" willfulness that created such misery for the "me-generation." Moreover, when authenticity is equated with the existentialist vision of freely creating one's life as a work of art, it is quite natural to conclude that this idea is consistent with an amoral or even immoral way of life.[4] Existentialist psychology, allied in the sixties with "humanistic" movements, was supposed to provide a "third force" to serve as an alternative to Freudian and empirical approaches.[5] Opposing what it perceived to be the scientific "mechanism" and "determinism" of standard theories, this movement sought to protect the dignity of humans by insisting on human freedom. But, in the end, its overblown notion of freedom came to seem as unrealistic and pernicious as the view it sought to replace.

At the same time, however, many therapists and mental health professionals continue to feel that the mainstream "scientific" theories designed to explain and guide psychotherapy fail to capture much of what actually goes on in the practice of therapy. One way to describe this gap between theory and practice is to say that standard theories fail to make sense of the rich and complex forms of moral discourse that characterize therapeutic dialogue. We can see why moral discourse is essential to therapy if we reflect on the events that created the need for psychotherapy in the first place. Ira Progoff describes how the rise of modern technological civilization first *generated* contemporary psychological problems. In earlier, preindustrial societies, according to Progoff, "individuals experienced the meaning of their lives in terms of local religious orthodoxies and accustomed national or tribal ways of life" of their communities. These traditional practices and institutions "provided built-in psychic security for the individual." When faith in these commonalities broke down, however, the individual was left unprotected. With no recourse to a spiritual past shared with others, the individual "was isolated and cut adrift; and it is this situation of the lone individual no longer sustained by the cultural resources of his ancestors that is the main root of the psychological problems that have arisen in modern times."[6]

As a result of these changes, therapists are now asked to serve as moral authorities, filling the vacuum left by the loss of older sources of guidance. C. Marshall Lowe observes that since "the theological priesthood has lost much of its authority, . . . the scientist practicing counseling and psychotherapy assumes a new moral authority. He is asked to make moral pronouncements in the name of science in the way the clergy was called upon for religious directives."[7] Because of this demand placed on therapists, a central part of what goes on in helping people in the modern world will consist in addressing questions about what constitutes the good life and how we can be at home in the world. And these are clearly *moral* questions in the broad sense, where "morality" includes not just questions about right actions, but "questions about how I am going to live my life" – questions "which touch on the issue of what kind of life is worth living, . . . or of what constitutes a rich, meaningful life – as against one concerned with secondary matters or trivia."[8]

The need for moral guidance is all the more pressing given the kinds of problems therapists are asked to treat today. Morris Eagle points out that people currently seeking professional help suffer less often from the classical neuroses Freudian theory was designed to treat and more often from problems of self "experienced as feelings of meaninglessness, feelings of emptiness, pervasive depression, lack of sustaining interests, goals, ideals and values, and feelings of unrelatedness." Often quite successful in their careers, these individuals feel purposeless, adrift, and deeply dissatisfied with life. Although the immediate cause of such "self disorders" may be faulty parenting, Eagle suggests that they ultimately spring from such social factors as "the lack of stable ideologies and values . . . or an atmosphere of disillusionment and cynicism in the surrounding society." These disorders of the self reveal more than ever "the importance of goals and guiding values as both a reflection of and a maintainer of psychic health."[9]

Nevertheless, therapists may feel poorly equipped by their training to take on this task. For, to the extent that psychotherapy thinks of itself as an "applied behavioral science," it seems to embody assumptions that cloud any attempt to think of the therapist as a "moral authority." This is so because scientific endeavor from the outset has aimed at being value-free and objective, basing its findings solely on observation and causal explanation. The result is a deep distrust of authoritarian pronouncements and value judgments. Such distrust is evident, for example, in Freud's initial vision of psychoanalysis as a science concerned primarily with devising explanatory models for psychic conflict. For Freud, morality is treated as part of the workings of a harsh and punitive superego, more a source of conflict than its potential cure. Though newer approaches may take a less jaundiced view of morality, they still tend to treat moral concerns either as the personal business of the client or as reducible to whatever principles of procedural justice are currently accepted as "self-evident" in its own academic and professional community.

This situation points to the need for a way of understanding the human condition that can make sense of its irreducible moral dimension. In what follows, I will suggest that Heidegger's early concept of authenticity, properly understood, has a great deal to offer for this purpose. I will first sketch out some of the assumptions in the modern scientific outlook that make it difficult to grasp the moral dimension of psychotherapy. What is most interesting here is the way even the early approaches influenced by Heidegger, despite their hopes of escaping from "scientism," tended to slip back into the same assumptions and problems. By working out Heidegger's alternative view of human existence and authenticity, I hope to show that moral concerns are an inescapable part of any project of understanding humans, and that they quite naturally will be central to any meaningful therapeutic dialogue. In trying to display the evaluative dimension of psychotherapy, my aim is not to propose a new technique, but to provide an ontological basis for understanding what always goes on in therapy though it is never fully comprehended in standard theories.

UNDERLYING ASSUMPTIONS OF PSYCHOTHERAPY THEORIES

Much of contemporary psychotherapy theory draws its conception of humans from a view of reality shaped by the natural sciences, a view now commonly called "naturalism." Naturalism, the common ground for both Freudian and empirical approaches, holds that because humans are a part of nature, we understand them by applying the same canons of explanation used for other parts of nature. We might distinguish three assumptions drawn from naturalism that underlie the conception of humans found in most psychotherapy theories. The first concerns the nature of the self. Part of the achievement of the new science of the seventeenth century was to dispel the traditional image of reality as a value-laden, meaningful cosmos in favor of our modern naturalistic view of the "universe" as a vast aggregate of objects in causal interactions. Correlative with this objectifying view of the universe is a picture of the self as a *thing* or *object* of a particular sort. Humans are physical objects among others in the natural order, but they are distinctive insofar as they have a consciousness and so can freely act on the world. Despite the presence of the mind, however, humans are still conceived of as objects only contingently related to other items in the world. The self understood as a thing – as a "subject of inwardness" or a self-encapsulated center of action – has been central to most psychotherapy theories.

The second assumption has to do with the nature of agency and the proper conduct of life. With the tremendous success of instrumental reason in achieving technological control over the world, a conception of action as based on means–ends calculations became widely accepted. Through a formalizable procedure, it seems, we can work things over in order to achieve our goals. This capacity for strategic calculation and technical control was quite naturally expanded to include a psychotechnology for self-improvement. With the guidance of experts, we should be able to reengineer our own lives according to a rational blueprint. Thus, one finds, in self-help programs and popularized workshops, procedures of self-transformation described in a vocabulary of reworking the self to achieve particular ends – vocabulary of "strengthening the ego," "restructuring cognitive strategies," "instilling hardiness," "learning coping skills," or "managing stress."

What is most striking about this calculative-instrumentalist approach, of course, is its inability to reflect on the question of which *ends* are truly worth pursuing. Older views of life generally made a distinction between (1) "mere living," just functioning and satisfying needs, and (2) a "higher" or "better" form of existence that we could achieve if we realized our proper aim in life. In contrast, the modern naturalistic outlook tries to free itself from such a two-tiered view of life. The aims of living are now thought of either as the satisfaction of those basic needs dictated by our biosocial makeup or as matters of personal preference. Psychotherapy, seen as a technique designed to help people attain their ends, remains indifferent to the ends themselves so long as they are realistic and consistent.

The third assumption concerns the nature of human relations. Given what has been called the "ontological individualism" of modernity – the view that human reality is to be understood in terms of self-encapsulated individuals who are only contingently aggregated into social systems – a conflictual model of humans seems inevitable. When I see myself as a strategic calculator competing for limited resources, I tend to see others either as aids or as obstacles to my pursuits. Relationships are then experienced as temporary alliances entered into in order to secure our mutual benefit. The outcome is a kind of "therapeutic contractualism" that treats marriage, friendships, and love relations as means to individual self-enhancement, that is, as contractual arrangements to be maintained only so long as I "continue to grow" or "still feel good about myself" in the relationship.[10]

The humanistic and existentialist approaches of the fifties and sixties arose as a backlash against the objectification and instrumentalism they perceived in naturalistic theories. Turning away from science, they generally drew their understanding of the self from the "expressivist" ways of thinking that characterized nineteenth-century romanticism. According to this expressivist view, the self contains an inner seed of potential that is capable of self-fulfillment through artistic creativity, communion with nature, and intense relationships with others. The image of self-realization through the expression of one's innermost feelings and capacities seemed to offer an alternative to the "dehumanizing" effects of the naturalistic outlook. Nonetheless, to the extent that these approaches still bought into the assumptions of ontological individualism, they tended to perpetuate the very view of human reality they sought to overcome.

Some examples will show how this problem arises. Rollo May's writings display a refined moral sensibility and a commitment to making moral concerns central to the understanding of human existence. We can understand who we are, May writes, only through a "search for our values and purposes. . . . Without values there would be only barren despair." The two-tiered view of life, with its distinction of "mere life" and a "higher life," is indispensable to being fully human. Humans just are the beings who make certain values "more important than pleasure and even more important than survival itself."[11] It is because mainstream theorizing fails to account for the role of values in human life that psychotherapy risks becoming "part of the neurosis of our day rather than part of the cure."[12]

Yet May is less convincing when it comes to formulating his own positive account of moral values. The only ideal he seems to endorse is *commitment,* that is, a "decisive attitude toward existence," "the attitude of . . . the self-aware being taking his own existence seriously."[13] Indeed, commitment to values is necessary if one "is to attain integration," for values are needed to serve "as a psychological center, a kind of core of integration which draws together [one's] powers as the core of a magnet draws the magnet's lines of force together." Values make possible freedom and maturity: "The mark of the mature man is that his living is integrated around self-chosen goals"; such a person "plans and works toward a creative love relationship or toward business achievement or what not."[14]

It goes without saying, however, that the question here is precisely this "what not." When values and goals are chosen solely in order to attain integration and maturity, they are being treated as mere means to ends. The result, then, is that values come to be regarded as adventitious, presumably dispensable in favor of other means (perhaps brutality or destructiveness) if those would do the job better. In this respect May's writings display a paradox common to a wide range of psychotherapy theories.[15] On the one hand, theorists recognize the deep-felt need in the modern world for authoritative values to provide guidance and a sense of purpose to life. On the other hand, the deep distrust of authority in our culture leads them to feel that values can be justified only if they are treated as means to achieving such nonmoral ends as personal satisfaction or fulfillment or "empowerment." When looked at in this way, however, moral discourse is reduced to the very calculative-instrumentalist thinking May rightly sees as so debilitating. Moreover, this conception of values as tools on hand for our use threatens to reinforce the objectifying view of the self May wants to eliminate. For when values are thought of as items on hand for our free choice, we will tend to think of ourselves as dimensionless points of raw will, not attached in advance to anything, who can freely pick and choose among the smorgasbord of values set before us.[16] Thus, though May is right to say that "the degree of an individual's inner strength and integrity will depend on how much he himself believes in the values he lives by,"[17] he seems unable to account for how the autonomous, disengaged chooser of values could ever come to regard any values as genuinely binding in the first place.

Medard Boss and Ludwig Binswanger, two theorists profoundly influenced by Heidegger, try to give us a richer grasp of our "being-in-the-world" as embracing a wide range of possibilities of self-understanding and self-appraisal. Boss, for example, rejects Freud's notion of "guilt *feelings,*" claiming that it conceals the deeper phenomenon of "existential guilt." "Man's existential guilt consists in his failing to carry out the mandate to fulfill all his possibilities," a failure exacerbated by a tendency to follow "acquired moral concepts," the "foreign and crippling mentality which his educators forced upon him." To overcome this form of inauthenticity, Boss envisions the ideal of an "authentic" individual who, "accept[ing] all his life-possibilities," can "appropriate and assemble them to a free, authentic own self no longer caught in the narrowed-down mentality of an anonymous, inauthentic 'everybody.' "[18] And Binswanger, though less critical of the "everybody," agrees with Boss in regarding psychological problems as resulting from an overly constricted "world-design." Problems arise when the individual's *Eigenwelt* (own world) "is narrowed and constricted to such a degree [that] the self, too, is constricted and prevented from maturing." The aim of therapy, then, is to help people recover "the *freedom* of letting 'world' occur."[19]

Boss is confident that, once genuine freedom is achieved, "mankind's ethics becomes self-evident" and we will be able to "define man's basic morality."[20] Behind this confidence, I suspect, is the romantic faith that we have something deep within us, a "child within," who is truer, purer, and somehow "better" than the dreary, rigid, duty-bound self imposed on us by our socialization. The belief in this "authentic self" – an idea that has become common currency through the writings of such theorists as D. W. Winnicott, Alice Miller, and John Bradshaw – is tremendously appealing. But it is not at all obvious that "carrying out the mandate to fulfill all our possibilities" will help clarify our basic morality or make us better people. One thing Freud taught us is to be suspicious of such ideas as the "noble savage" and the "child within." Today we cannot avoid facing the fact that our "possibilities" include not just love and compassion, but also hostility, selfishness, and aggression. Does the "mandate to fulfill all our possibilities" include these as well? And, if not, what moral map guides us in distinguishing the possibilities we ought to fulfill from those we should not?[21]

Central to both Boss and Binswanger is their belief in what is the core value of modern individualism: freedom understood negatively as freedom *from* constraints. It may be the case, however, that this ideal of unbounded freedom is self-defeating. For where all things are equally possible, nothing is really binding, and so no choice is superior to any others. Freedom then becomes, in Rieff's classic line, the "absurdity of being freed to choose and then having no choice worth making."[22] What these criticisms show is that "third-force" approaches tend to slip back into the very naturalistic assumptions they set out to overcome. To get beyond these assumptions, I believe, we need a fresh way of thinking about human existence.

EVERYDAYNESS AND INAUTHENTICITY

Heidegger proposes that we bracket the presuppositions of modern naturalism and turn directly to a phenomenology of our pretheoretical sense of ourselves as we are in "average everydayness." In our ordinary agency, according to Heidegger's description, the self is not so much an object as an unfolding *event* or *happening* – the "movement" of a life course "stretched out between birth and death" (BT 427). From this standpoint, it is wrong to think of oneself as a mind or a center of consciousness with its own *Eigenwelt:* "Even one's *own* Dasein [is] something it can itself proximally 'come across' only when it *looks away* from 'experiences' and the 'center of its actions,' or does not yet 'see' them at all. Dasein finds 'itself' proximally in *what* it does" (BT 155). Because we are generally outside our "selves," caught up in equipmental contexts in a shared world, Heidegger can say that being a "self" is "'only' . . . a *way of being* of this entity" (BT 153, my emphasis).

In Heidegger's view, there is no pregiven "human nature" that determines what we are. Instead, we *are* what we make of ourselves in the course of living out our active lives. This is what it means to say that the "*'essence' of Dasein lies in its existence*" (BT 67). We can clarify this conception of humans as self-constituting beings by contrasting it with the kind of romantic expressivist view found in third-force psychotherapy theories. We saw that, for the expressivist, each person is endowed with deep, inner feelings, talents, and potentialities definitive of his or her "true self." A person's actions, then, are regarded as a more or less genuine outward display or expression of this inner germinal seed. Actions are physical movements to be explained in terms of inner beliefs, desires, and feelings. Here there is a sharp distinction between mind and body: the inner, mental realm is distinguished from the realm of mere physical movement.

When we look at our "average everydayness," however, we are led to what might be called a "manifestationist" view of human agency. For the manifestationist, there is no way to draw a clear distinction between an inner, core self and what is merely outward show. Instead, to say that we *are* what we *do* is to say that our very identity as agents – our *being* – is defined and realized only through our ways of becoming manifest in the world. We can clarify this conception of human agency by considering how we encounter a person who is particularly blunt and forthright. Her snappy responses, her no-nonsense style, her firmness in confusing situations – her ways of doing things – present themselves directly as her *being* the straight, unpretentious person she is. What she *is* is "written on the face" of things; for her, what you see is what you get. It is pointless here to think of such a person's actions as only outward representations of some hidden, inner mental acts, for what she does *presents* her being as the honest and direct person she is. Her agency is the "emerging-into-presence" or "coming-into-being" of her identity as a person of a particular sort, just as my wearing loafers and old sweatshirts *is* my being a casual or informal dresser. For the most part, the idea of an inner, mental source of actions has no role here. Suspicions about "what is really going on in her mind" make sense only when there are breaks in the otherwise smooth flow of her agency in familiar contexts.

From the manifestationist perspective, the mental remains inchoate and ephemeral until it is given shape in action. Even my *own* feelings and beliefs usually come to be defined for me only through the ways they show forth in the course of my actions. For this reason Heidegger locates human existence not in the mind, but in the unfolding "happening" or "event" of a life: as he says, "being-a-self *is* . . . only in its process of realization" (MFL 139, my emphasis). Understood as a "happening" that unfolds throughout a lifetime, a person's identity can be grasped only in terms of his or her life story as a whole. The temporal unfolding of life, as Ricoeur has pointed out, has the structure of a narrative.[23] We can understand who a person *is* only in terms of where that person is coming from and where he or she is going. From a narrativist perspective, actions in the present are fully intelligible only in terms of their place within the narrative unfolding of the person's life – in terms of what has happened up to this point and where things are headed in general.

Regarded as a temporal unfolding with both cumulativeness and purposiveness, Dasein's life course exhibits certain essential structures. First, Dasein is always "ahead of itself": it is a projection into the future insofar as its actions involve a commitment as to what sort of person it will be as a totality. What this means is that, in taking a stand on its own life, Dasein takes over some range of possibilities as definitive of its identity – some set of personality traits, life-styles, roles, or attitudes – and exists as a "being-toward" the realization of a final configuration of possibilities for its life overall. Since we will *be* something once and for all only at the culmination of our lives, Heidegger calls this futurity the "bringing itself to fruition" (*sich zeitigen*) of Dasein. We are "being-toward-the-end" or "being-*toward*-death" not in the sense of facing our demise or fulfilling a potential, but in the sense that everything we do contributes to making us people of a particular sort. Thus, whether I realize it or not, my ways of relating to my children involve a commitment toward the future: through my actions, I am making myself a parent who is neglectful or supportive or unavailable. Although I may always change the identity I have formed up to now by a radical shift in my ways of acting, so long as I continue acting the way I do, I am making myself into this sort of parent.

Where "projection" grasps the future-directedness of a life happening, "thrownness" refers to our being already enmeshed in a particular context. As a parent, for example, I find myself stuck with obligations rooted in my past undertakings that I must take up in my current actions. At the same time I also find myself enmeshed in a particular historical culture that predefines the range of possibilities of action that will make sense in my situation. For the most part, Heidegger says, Dasein is the "they" or the "anyone." Our everyday actions make sense only because they instantiate or exemplify the taken-for-granted patterns and norms of the shared life-world. In this respect, the public context provides the medium of intelligibility we draw on in making something of our lives. Or, to restate this idea in the narrativist mode, it is in terms of the plot lines made accessible in the anecdotes, tales, and stories circulating in our public language that we come to see what is at stake in situations, what is worth shooting for, and what courses of action will be appropriate. This rootedness of our personal life stories in the wider drama of our community's history is expressed in the claim that Dasein's "historicity" is embedded in the "co-happening" of a "community, of a people" (BT 436). Our participation in a social context is therefore a fundamental dimension of our existence as humans. Because we can *be* human agents only against the backdrop of such a shared medium of intelligibility, Heidegger says that the "they" is "*a primordial phenomenon* [which] *belongs to Dasein's positive constitution*" (BT 167).

As is well known, however, the "they" as Heidegger describes it is Janus-faced. On the one hand, our participation in the "they" is an enabling condition that first opens us onto a world and gives us the resources we need for *being* human. From the outset, Dasein draws its possibilities for self-understanding and action from the way things are interpreted by the "they." On the other hand, this involvement in public forms of life can have a pernicious effect. It threatens to level all decisions to the lowest common denominator of what is acceptable and well adjusted; it restricts "the possible options of choice to what lies within the range of the familiar, the attainable, the respectable – that which is fitting and proper" (BT 239). There is an inveterate tendency, then, to go along with the flow, content with "satisfying the easily handled rules and public norms of the 'they,' " and thereby being disburdened of all "responsibility" for ourselves (BT 334). "Dasein, as a they-self, gets 'lived' by the commonsense ambiguity of that publicness in which nobody resolves upon anything but which has already made its decision" (BT 345). The result is a "dimming down of the possible as such" (BT 239). Inauthentic Dasein is dispersed into a multiplicity of humdrum routines, drifting with the latest fads, tranquilly assured that "everything is 'in the best of order' and all doors are open" (BT 222). This "leveling down" of all possibilities obliterates the kind of two-tiered sense of life that lets us distinguish higher from lower, crucial from trivial, central from peripheral. Taking the familiar demands of the public world as of consummate importance – as "the only game in town" – we can become highly effective strategic calculators, convinced that everything is possible, yet lacking any overarching sense of what makes life worth living.

Inauthenticity is characterized by "falling" and "forgetting." In the ordinary busy-ness of handling daily affairs, Dasein tends to become ensnared in its immediate concerns and to drift along with the taken-for-granted practices of average everydayness. We hide behind social roles, enacting parts in familiar dramas and following the rules of socially approved games. This tendency to fall into mundane activities catches us up in the "turbulence" of life and tears us away from the possibility of taking hold of our existence in a coherent, integrated way. Our falling absorption in the public world is coupled with "forgetfulness." Although some degree of forgetting is unavoidable if we are to be agents in the world – "The self must forget itself if, lost in the world of equipment, it is to be able 'actually' to go to work and manipulate something" (BT 405) – what is insidious is the way this first-order forgetting is compounded by a second-order forgetting in which one "not only forgets the forgotten but forgets the forgetting itself" (BP 290). In other words, we become so mired down in ordinary chores that we forget that we are called upon to take a coherent stand in a world where things are genuinely at stake. This self-forgetfulness, paradoxically, tends to aggravate our own self-preoccupation and self-absorption. Constantly concerned with checking its performance against public criteria, Dasein becomes "entangled in itself," sinking into "the most exaggerated 'self-dissection' " (BT 222), into an "extravagant grubbing about in one's own soul which can be in the highest degree counterfeit" (BP 160).

An inauthentic life comes to have the warped temporal structure Heidegger calls "making-present." Absorbed in the demands of the moment, we understand ourselves in terms of what "is determined by the success or failure, the feasibility or unfeasibility, of [our] commerce with things" (BP 289). Everyday existence is fragmented into a series of means–ends strategies governed by the latest public attitudes about what constitutes success. Inauthentic Dasein "dwells with things, gets entangled in its own self, and lets itself be drawn along by things," with the result that it "loses itself within itself, so that the past becomes a forgetting and the future a mere expecting of what is just coming on" (BP 287). Making-present retains only what is relevant to the current context, and it merely awaits expected outcomes. As a series of strategies for coping with practical concerns, our everyday lives are contracted into a succession of episodes – the "one damned thing after another" of mere functioning or "getting by." The ends of living are seen as fixed, not themselves in question. They are the well-deserved rewards we expect for having performed well: the martini at the end of the day or the weekend in front of the television. Life is experienced, in Aristotle's terminology, as *techne* rather than as *praxis:* it is a matter of "production," which has its end outside itself, rather than "activity," whose "end is doing well itself," and so is internal to the practice.[24] The outcome of this disjointed way of living is alienation from oneself, an inability to see anything as really mattering, and feelings of futility only partially alleviated by occasional intense "peak experiences" that are supposed to "make it all worthwhile." The inauthentic form of life, as Heidegger describes it, seems to be a perfect breeding ground for the kinds of demoralization and self disorders found among current candidates for psychotherapy.

AUTHENTICITY

Heidegger's concept of "authenticity" is supposed to point to a way of life that is higher than that of average everydayness. It is important to keep in mind that authenticity has nothing to do with such romantic ideals as getting in touch with a deep inner self or rising above the herd. Heidegger says that authenticity "does not detach Dasein from its world"; the world "does not become another one 'in its content,' nor does the circle of Others get exchanged for a new one" (BT 344). Indeed, since our own life stories are inseparable from the wider text of a shared we-world, authenticity can be nothing other than a fuller and richer form of participation in the public context. Thus, we find that authentic understanding "is so far from extricating itself from the way of interpreting Dasein which has come down to us [from the 'they'], that in each case it is in terms of this interpretation, against it, and yet again for it, that any possibility one has chosen is seized upon in one's resolution" (BT 435).

Yet as Heidegger describes it, the *path* to this deeper involvement in the public world passes through a radical breakdown of our complacent absorption in everydayness. In his well-known description of anxiety, Heidegger suggests that our ordinary preoccupations in the busy-ness of the world are actually a form of "evasion" or "fleeing." We throw ourselves into the turbulence of day-to-day chores and they-roles in order to avoid facing up to something we find threatening. What we are fleeing from in everydayness is our own "thrownness toward death": the fact that we are finite beings and that we are "delivered over to ourselves" in the sense of being responsible for the task of making something of our lives. In the experience of anxiety, we are forced to confront our own finitude. Heidegger says that anxiety brings Dasein "face to face with the 'nothingness' of the possible impossibility of existence" (BT 310). Confronted with our being-toward-death, the roles we have been playing suddenly seem anonymous, and we are faced with the demand to own up to our lives.

If we can take a stand on our being-toward-death, our lives will be transformed. Facing death, one is pulled back from the dispersal, distraction, and forgetfulness of everydayness. The result is the ability to live with a clear-sighted grasp of the temporal continuity and future-directedness of one's own life-happening. This lucidity leads to a way of living we might call "self-focusing." The authentic Dasein, recognizing that not everything is possible, is "snatched back from the endless multiplicity of possibilities which offer themselves as closest to one" and focuses itself into a range of possibilities "which are determined by the *end* and so are understood as *finite*" (BT 435, 308). Such directedness into a coherent range of possibilities brings about a change in the way we relate to our thrownness and our being as projections toward the future. We take over our situatedness with "resoluteness" – a decisive dedication to what we want to accomplish for our lives. And our stance toward the future is that of "anticipation" or "forward-directedness": a clear-sighted and unwavering commitment to those overriding aims taken as definitive of one's existence as a whole.

Authentic self-focusing, understood as a resolute reaching forward into a finite range of possibilities, gives coherence, cohesiveness, and integrity to a life course. Authenticity is characterized by a distinctive temporal structure. Where inauthentic existence is lost in the dispersal of making-present, an authentic life is lived as a unified flow characterized by cumulativeness and direction. It involves taking over the possibilities made accessible by the past and acting in the present in order to accomplish something for the future. Or to rephrase this in the narrativist mode, such a life is lived as a coherent story. It is a life that is given focus by its future-directedness – what Hans-Georg Gadamer calls an "anticipation of completion" or Frank Kermode calls a "sense of an ending." This directedness toward the culmination of our lives lets us appropriate what has already happened as resources or assets whose latent significance is brought to realization through action in the present. Achieving the narrative continuity of authentic existence is what first makes possible personal identity understood as the "constancy of the self" – its "steadiness" and "steadfastness" – stretched out across a life span (BT 369). According to Heidegger, it is by taking a stand on one's life as a whole that one satisfies Pindar's counsel to "become what you are" (BT 186; cf. IM 101).

Heidegger's notion of "authentic temporality" might become clearer if we contrast two different ways of understanding the relation of actions to the whole of life.[25] The first is found in the "instrumentalist" approach to living we saw in discussing Rollo May. This stance treats life as a matter of finding the means to achieving ends, where the ends are usually goods external to the activities themselves – such "positive reinforcements" as what "feels good" or satisfies a need. In this instrumentalist, means–ends living, actions are done *in order to* get something; for example, I run everyday in order to get healthy, or I help a friend in order to get him in my debt. In contrast to this means–ends approach, the second way of living might be called a "constituent–ends" way of living. Here actions are not just routes to achieving extrinsic ends, but instead are experienced as central to *constituting* a particular way of life, a way of life that is good *because* it consists of this and comparable sorts of activities. Action here is undertaken *for the sake of being* such and such: I run as a part of being a healthy person, or I help someone for the sake of being a good friend.

It should be obvious that although the actions performed are the same in both cases, the *quality of life* will be quite different. In the means–ends case, life tends to be experienced as an episodic sequence of calculative strategies lacking any cumulative significance or overriding purpose. The activities themselves might well seem to be tedious chores I would rather avoid if I could find other means to the same ends. For example, running can feel like a grim imposition, and the quid pro quo, contractual approach to friendship can begin to feel cynical and manipulative. In contrast, the constituent–ends case reflects an experience of life in which one's actions are an integral part of *being* a person of a certain sort. Where the means–ends attitude trivializes the present by keeping us preoccupied with the carrot at the end of the stick, the constituent–end approach, by making us realize that what we are doing at this moment just *is* realizing the goals of living, throws us intensely into the present moment as the arena in which our coming-to-fruition is fulfilled. Running and being a friend are not just impositions I could as well do without; they make me the person I am. What is important is building myself *as* this kind of person, not scoring points or getting rewards "down the road." When life is lived as an ongoing process of self-building or self-composing, it has the kind of cumulativeness and continuity that makes up authentic temporality.

THE SELF AS A MORAL AGENT: IMPLICATIONS FOR PSYCHOTHERAPY

According to Heidegger's description of human existence, to know what we *are* is at the same time to know what we *can and should be* if we are to achieve coherence and unity in our lives. The idea that there is an unbridgeable gap between facts and values, an idea tied to the naturalistic outlook, seems less obvious on this account of humans. It may very well be true, as Hume claimed, that there is no way to *deduce* an "ought" from an "is" – no way to derive motivations from statements of fact alone. Yet the connections Heidegger is pointing to are not so much matters of logical entailment as connections whose overwhelming plausibility is rooted in our deepest understanding of life itself. To the extent that intelligibility and a sense of direction are tied to unity, cohesiveness, and future-directedness, it is hard to see how anyone could want the former and nevertheless not care about the latter. In contrast to naturalistic theories, then, Heidegger's account of life gives us a way of seeing substantive moral questions as an unavoidable part of any attempt to understand human beings.

One might object, however, that Heidegger's approach does not really represent much of an advance over traditional theorizing, for one might claim that merely acknowledging the inevitable presence of moral concerns does not yet give us any clue to *how* these concerns are to be dealt with in the therapeutic setting. Insofar as our culture is devoted to respecting diversity and freedom, the objection goes, any attempt to advocate some particular set of moral values would be dogmatic and so intolerable. In the therapeutic context, as in an open society generally, an "anything-goes" relativism seems preferable to *any* form of moral suasion. And so once again it appears that morality is the client's personal business, off-limits to the therapist.

The first thing to note about this objection is that it is itself based on a set of unargued-for, and so by its own standards "dogmatic," moral assumptions about the value of pluralism, tolerance, and individual rights. What this shows is that psychotherapy, and the human sciences generally, have always operated with a set of value assumptions they kept concealed under the guise of "value-neutrality." What is more important to note, however, is that the specific set of value assumptions underlying this objection – the glorification of "do-your-own-thing" individualism with its rejection of all binding authority – is very often the *source* of those problems that therapy is, by general consent, supposed to cure. If this is so, however, then standard approaches are in a deep sense self-defeating: they exacerbate the conditions they set out to cure, and they conceal in advance any alternative approaches that might be able to do what they fail to do.

These observations suggest that it will be worthwhile to explore Heidegger's alternative account of life to see if it can make better sense of what actually goes on in therapy. In this final section, I will look at some of the ways Heidegger's image of human existence might enrich our understanding of the role of moral discourse within professional counseling. First, though Heidegger is not concerned with proving that any one moral outlook is superior to all others, his description of authenticity does point to certain character ideals – what we might call "metavalues" – which provide a basis for being able to take a meaningful stand on whatever first-order moral commitments we make. Authentic self-focusing is said to require such traits as resoluteness, steadiness, courage, and, above all, clear-sightedness about one's own life as a finite, thrown projection. It calls for integrity and a lucid openness about what is relevant to one's actions. The authentic stance toward life makes us face up to the fact that to the extent that we are building our own lives in all we do, we are "answerable" for the choices we make. Heidegger tries to capture this by saying that the authentic person "chooses to choose." At the same time, however, to be authentic is to recognize that circumstances may arise that force us to take back our basic decisions. Thus, authentic Dasein "resolves to keep repeating itself" (BT 355); that is, it keeps renewing its commitments knowing that it might have to change its course. Repetition imparts "constancy" to one's life, making it clear that, in the end, we *are* what we *do.* For an authentic person, self-deceptive hiding behind roles and blaming others are ruled out. Heidegger also speaks of the "sober joy" of an authentic existence: when one seizes hold of one's life with decisiveness and clarity, one lives with intensity, openness, and exuberance.

Second, Heidegger's account of human existence points to a way of understanding why substantive moral reflection must play a crucial role in our self-understanding. This role becomes evident only when we consider a dimension of Heidegger's thought that is generally overlooked in the older existentialist interpretations: his concept of "authentic historicity." The concept of historicity grows out of the description of the embeddedness of Dasein in a wider context. We saw earlier that Dasein's possibilities of self-interpretation and self-evaluation are drawn from the background of intelligibility of the public world into which it is "thrown." As we become initiated into the practices of our community, we soak up the tacit sense of what is important that circulates in our world. This "attunement" to shared commitments and ideals cannot be regarded simply as a matter of having certain "life-style options" on hand for our choice. For these understandings and normative commitments are definitive for the kinds of people we are. They provide us with the possibilities of assessment and aspiration that first give us an orientation toward our own lives and a window onto the world. Given that we have become the kind of people we are – people who, for example, care about children and believe in justice – there is now no way to drop these commitments without ceasing to be who we are.

Now Heidegger wants us to see that these core, defining possibilities of understanding embodied in our everyday practices are themselves products of history. We react in knee-jerk ways to hate crimes and to cruelty because certain concerns have become fundamental to us in our heritage. The commitments to natural rights and the dignity of persons so dear to the humanistic enlightenment, for example, were opened up by earlier Greco-Roman and Judeo-Christian traditions that saw order in the cosmos or experienced all souls as equal before God. In this sense, our lives are, so to speak, commentaries on the wider "clearing" of stories and interpretations passed down in our historical community. Long before we can engage in detached critical reflection, we have absorbed a tacit sense of what life is all about by becoming attuned to the patterns of living in our surroundings. Thus, though we are all composing our own autobiographies throughout our lives, we are doing so by falling into step with the sense of reality built into our practices. Our moral understanding is shaped by these practices and by the familiar folktales, stories, anecdotes, and histories that articulate and sustain those practices. As agents, then, each of us appropriates, transmits, and transmutes a sense of what is important that we have inherited from our historical tradition.

What is distinctive about authentic existence is the way it takes over this historical embeddedness. Where inauthentic Dasein just drifts along with the latest trends, authentic Dasein "remembers" its rootedness in the wider unfolding of its culture, and it experiences its life as indebted to the larger drama of a shared history. As a result, authenticity involves encountering one's possibilities as drawn from the "wellsprings" of a "heritage" and living one's life as part of the "mission" or "destiny" definitive of one's historical community as a whole (BT 435–6). The temporality of an authentic existence is therefore a matter of "retrieving" the possibilities of the "Dasein who came before." This is why Heidegger says that authentic Dasein "chooses its hero" and is "free for the struggle of loyally following in the footsteps of that which can be repeated" (BT 437). To be authentic, then, is not to rise above the crowd by discovering one's own personal morality. Rather, it calls for "revering the sole authority which a free existing can have, . . . the repeatable possibilities of existence" (BT 443).

The idea of choosing a hero, together with the vocabulary of "loyalty," "reverence," and "authority," suggests that to be authentic is to find guidance for the conduct of one's own life in terms of the lives of models or exemplars drawn from history. Or putting this into the narrativist mode, we might say that authentic Dasein achieves self-focusing by articulating its existence in terms of the guidelines laid out by certain paradigmatic stories circulating in our cultural world – the stories of such heroes and heroines as Abraham

Lincoln, Martin Luther King, Mother Teresa, Helen Keller, and Malcolm X. The lives of these cultural exemplars sketch out plot lines or *mythoi* for composing one's own life story – for "following in the footsteps" of those who have come before. Such paradigmatic stories generally show how strengths and weaknesses, assets and liabilities can be integrated into a coherent, meaningful life that succeeds in contributing something to the world. Because these stories already prestructure our self-understanding, making explicit the tacit commitments we all have in common can play a central role in therapeutic dialogue.

The recognition of our embeddedness in and indebtedness to the wider context of our culture leads to a third observation about the moral significance of the ideal of authenticity. Authentic historicity brings about a strong sense of our solidarity with others. "Our fates have already been guided in advance in our being with one another in the same world," Heidegger says; "Dasein's fateful destiny in and with its 'generation' goes to make up the full authentic happening of Dasein" (BT 436). Authentic existence involves a clear-sighted recognition that human reality at the deepest level consists not of self-encapsulated individuals in unavoidable conflict, but of a "we" or a "co-Dasein" already attuned in the shared quest for goods definitive of a community – such goods, for us, as fairness, honesty, dignity, benevolence, achievement, and so on. Because we first find ourselves and become the people we are in the space of aspiration and assessment opened up by our shared historical practices, the goods that define our community cannot be treated as luxury items to be carried on board or left behind at our discretion. On the contrary, our very ability to live coherent, meaningful lives presupposes that we operate within the range of possibilities opened up by this background of shared intelligibility.

It follows, then, that genuine freedom is to be found not in the absence of all constraints, but in clarity and depth about the constitutive stories that lay out the guidelines along which we already shape our lives. We are free to the extent that we find ourselves enmeshed in contexts of shared meaningfulness that make it possible for us to grasp what situations demand from us and which options make sense. Heidegger's language of "loyalty" and "authority" shows that his concept of authentic freedom, far from pointing to some existentialist conception of "terrible freedom," is designed to bring out the role of those bedrock loyalties and commitments that already *inhabit* our lives, though often in a form distorted by ontological individualism.

Finally, the account of authentic existence can clarify and expand the conception, found in certain recent theorists, of therapy as the renarrativizing of a person's life story.[26] If it is true, as we have seen, that action makes sense only in the context of an ongoing story, and if greater narrative continuity implies greater intelligibility, then much of what goes on in therapy can be thought of as the joint composition of a more coherent and clear-sighted narrative. Understood as narrativizing, however, therapy must involve moral reflection. For insofar as composing a story always draws on the background of communal stories of trials, struggles, conquests, and defeats, such storyizing has a moral dimension: the narratives constructed have a "moral" to the extent that their resolution implies the achievement of some goods taken as normative by our historical culture – the worth of sacrifice, for instance, or the nobility of great strivings. This is why Jerome Bruner says, "Stories must necessarily . . . relate to what is morally valued, morally appropriate, or morally uncertain. . . . To tell a story is inescapably to take a moral stance."[27] Imparting narrative structure to a life involves emplotting events along the guidelines of a moral map of aspiration and evaluation that is rooted in the tacit background understanding of our moral heritage. Because narrative has this inescapable moral dimension, it is different from the explanations found in naturalistic approaches. Stanley Hauerwas points to the difference between stories and explanations when he says that a narrative is "not told to explain as a theory explains, but to involve the agent in a way of life. . . . I cannot make the story true by how I use it, but the story must make me true to its own demands of how the world should be."[28] Thus, narratives always have a normative dimension: they spring from and feed back into an understanding of the world not only as it is, but as it can and should be.

We began by looking at how naturalistic and third-force psychotherapy theories tend to presuppose a picture of the self as an essentially isolated individual in a morally neutral, objectified universe. What is troubling about such theories is the possibility that their picture of the self might be a major *source* of the emotional and behavioral problems that many people bring to therapists today. If this is so, then modern therapy risks perpetuating the problem in the cure. Heidegger's conception of authenticity, in contrast, can help us make sense of dimensions of therapeutic practice not fully accounted for in most forms of theorizing. Its value lies not in offering recipes for new types of technique, but in providing a basis for understanding our embeddedness in a wider context of meaning, the role of constraints in genuine freedom, and the fundamental role of moral commitments in our ability to be humans in any meaningful sense. In this way it provides a counterweight to conventional therapeutic ideals of effective behavior and self-actualization, and it can open up therapeutic practice to an understanding of life that is left unintelligible by prevailing theories.[29]

NOTES

1 Medard Boss, "Martin Heidegger's Zollikon Seminars," trans. Brian Kenny, in *Heidegger and Psychology*, special issue of *Review of Existential Psychology and Psychiatry*, ed. Keith Hoeller, 1988 reprint of Vol. 16, Nos. 1, 2, and 3 (1978–9): 7–20, p. 7.

2 A record of this collaboration is available as the *Zollikoner Seminare: Protokolle, Gespräche, Briefe*, ed. Medard Boss (Frankfurt: Vittorio Klostermann, 1987). For an excellent overview of the key ideas in this work, see Fred Dallmayr, *Between Freiburg and Frankfurt: Toward a Critical Ontology* (Amherst: University of Massachusetts Press, 1991), Chap. 8.

3 Irvin D. Yalom, in his *Existential Psychotherapy* (New York: Basic Books, 1980), describes *Being and Time* as the "single most important philosophical text in the field" (p. 16).

4 I discuss these criticisms of existentialism in my "Existentialist Ethics," in *New Directions in Ethics: The Challenge of Applied Ethics*, ed. J. P. DeMarco and R. M. Fox (New York: Routledge & Kegan Paul, 1986), pp. 73–91.

5 The classic works of existentialist psychology in English are Rollo May, Ernest Angel, and Henri F. Ellenberger, eds., *Existence: A New Dimension in Psychiatry and Psychology* (New York: Basic Books, 1958); Ludwig Binswanger, *Being-in-the-World: Selected Papers of Ludwig Binswanger*, ed. Jacob Needleman (New York: Basic Books, 1963); and Medard Boss, *Psychoanalysis and Daseinsanalysis*, trans. L. B. Lefebre (New York: Basic Books, 1963). Newer works include Rollo May, *The Discovery of Being: Writings in Existential Psychology* (New York: Norton, 1983), and Yalom's *Existential Psychotherapy*. Additional works are listed in Maurice Friedman, ed., *The Worlds of Existentialism: A Critical Reader* (Atlantic Highlands, N.J.: Humanities Press, 1991), Pt. 6 and

p. xvii. Louis A. Sass provides a bibliography of recent works in humanistic psychology in "Humanism, Hermeneutics, and the Concept of the Subject," in *Hermeneutics and Psychological Theory: Interpretive Perspectives on Personality, Psychotherapy and Psychopathology*, ed. Stanley B. Messer, Louis A. Sass, and Robert L. Woolfolk (New Brunswick, N.J.: Rutgers University Press, 1988), pp. 222–71.

6 Ira Progoff, *The Death and Rebirth of Psychology* (New York: McGraw-Hill, 1956), p. 5.

7 C. Marshall Lowe, *Value Orientations in Counseling and Psychotherapy: The Meaning of Mental Health* (Cranston, R. I.: Carroll Press, 1969), pp. 16–17.

8 Charles Taylor, *Sources of the Self: The Making of the Modern Identity* (Cambridge, Mass.: Harvard University Press, 1989), p. 14.

9 Morris N. Eagle, *Recent Developments in Psychoanalysis: A Critical Evaluation* (New York: McGraw-Hill, 1984), pp. 72–3.

10 Robert N. Bellah, Richard Madsen, William M. Sullivan, Ann Swidler, and Steven M. Tipton, *Habits of the Heart: Individualism and Commitment in American Life* (New York: Harper & Row, 1985), pp. 128–30.

11 May, *The Discovery of Being*, pp. 10, 17.

12 Ibid., p. 87.

13 Ibid., pp. 166–7.

14 May, *Man's Search for Himself* (New York: Dell, 1953), pp. 175–6.

15 Frank C. Richardson, "Freedom and Commitment in Modern Psychotherapy," *Journal of Integrative and Eclectic Psychotherapy*, 8 (1989): 303–19.

16 This was part of Heidegger's criticism of the notion of "values" (a word first imported into German moral philosophy from economics in the nineteenth century). Because values are usually thought of as present-at-hand objects, Heidegger abjured the concept altogether.

17 May, *Man's Search for Himself*, p. 176.

18 Boss, *Psychoanalysis and Daseinsanalysis*, pp. 271, 47.

19 Binswanger, "The Existential Analysis School of Thought," in *Existence*, May et al., eds., pp. 204, 194, my emphasis.

20 Boss, *Psychoanalysis and Daseinsanalysis*, p. 271.

21 David Hiley and I have discussed these problems in connection with Richard Rorty's glorification of "self-enlargement" as the post-Freudian character ideal. See "Biting the Bullet: Rorty on Private and Public Morality," in *Reading Rorty: Critical Responses to "Philosophy and the Mirror of Nature" (and Beyond)*, ed. Alan R. Malachowski (Oxford: Blackwell, 1990), pp. 339–64.

22 Philip Rieff, *The Triumph of the Therapeutic: Uses of Faith after Freud* (New York: Harper, 1966), p. 93.

23 Paul Ricoeur, "Narrative Time," in *On Narrative*, ed. W. J. T. Mitchell, (Chicago: University of Chicago Press, 1980), pp. 169–90; idem, *Time and Narrative*, trans. K. McLaughlin and D. Pellaner (Chicago: University of Chicago Press, 1984–6).

24 *Nicomachean Ethics*, trans. Terence Irwin (Indianapolis, Ind.: Hackett, 1985), 1140b.

25 In making this distinction I draw on David Wiggins, "Deliberation and Practical Reason," in *Essays on Aristotle's Ethics*, ed. Amélie O. Rorty (Berkeley and Los Angeles: University of California, 1980), pp. 221–40.

26 The key works are those of Roy Schafer: "Action and Narration in Psychoanalysis," *New Literary History*, 12 (1980): 61–85; "Narration in the Psychoanalytic Dialogue," in *On Narrative*, ed. Mitchell, pp. 29–53; and *Narrative Actions in Psychoanalysis* (Worcester, Mass.: Clark University Press, 1981). See also Donald Spence, *Narrative Truth and Historical Truth: Meaning and Interpretation in Psychoanalysis* (New York: Norton, 1984).

27 Jerome Bruner, *Acts of Meaning* (Cambridge, Mass.: Harvard University Press, 1990), pp. 50–1.

28 Stanley Hauerwas, *Truthfulness and Tragedy: Further Investigations in Christian Ethics* (Notre Dame, Ind.: University of Notre Dame Press, 1977), pp. 73, 80.

29 I am grateful to David Hoy, Frank Richardson, and Peter Tumulty for helpful comments on an earlier draft of this essay.

MICHAEL E. ZIMMERMAN

9 Heidegger, Buddhism, and deep ecology

Many commentators have remarked on the affinities between Heidegger's thought and East Asian traditions such as Vedanta, Mahayana Buddhism, and Taoism.[1] In this essay, I shall examine critically some aspects of the apparent rapport between Heidegger's thought and Mahayana Buddhism.[2] One reason for recent interest in Heidegger's thought and in Buddhism is that both are critical of and claim to offer an alternative to the anthropocentrism and dualism that some critics say is responsible for today's environmental crisis.[3] According to such critics, Western humankind is particularly anthropocentric. Regarding humanity as the source of all meaning, purpose, and value, humans justify doing anything they want with the natural world. Western humanity also thinks in terms of dualisms and binary oppositions, such as mind versus body, reason versus feeling, man versus nature, male versus female. Those possessing the "privileged" properties (mind, reason, man, male) allegedly have the right to dominate those possessing the "inferior" properties (body, feeling, nature, female). In an attempt to gain godlike security and power for humankind, modern Western ideologies call for transforming the earth into a titanic factory, thereby threatening to destroy the biosphere on which all life depends.

In my critical examination of the presumed similarities between Heidegger and Mahayana Buddhism, I shall focus particular attention on the claim advanced both by Heidegger and by Buddhism: that humans can learn to "let beings be" only by gaining insight into the nothingness that pervades all things. Such insight, we are told, spontaneously leads to the overcoming of anthropocentrism and dualism. In what follows, I first touch on the mystical origins of Heidegger's idea of nothingness; then I examine, in turn, his early and later accounts of the role of nothingness in authentic human existence. After some preliminary remarks about Heidegger's interest in Eastern thought, I examine the Buddhist conception of the relation between enlightenment and the revelation of nothingness. Then I compare what Heidegger and Mahayana Buddhism have to say about the relation between authenticity or enlightenment and insight into one's own "nothingness." Finally, I explore briefly the extent to which these Heideggerean and Buddhist ideas are congruent with the claims advanced by deep ecology, a version of radical environmentalism.

EARLY HEIDEGGER ON NOTHINGNESS

The reader may be wondering how there can possibly be any philosophical importance to the idea of nothingness. For the most part, when we think of nothingness, we simply think of . . . nothing at all! Nothingness, to our minds, is merely the absence of anything: sheer lack, emptiness in a negative sense. Western thinkers who emphasized the importance of nothingness have been primarily mystics such as Meister Eckhart, the latter of whom greatly influenced Heidegger's writings. Eckhart insisted that "God" is far beyond our conceptual categories, which are appropriate only for understanding *creatures*. Instead of speaking of God in positive terms, it is better to speak of Divine Nothingness.[4] The Divine cannot be regarded as a super entity existing somewhere else, but instead constitutes the unconditioned openness or emptiness in which all things appear. Meister Eckhart argued that humans are at one with this openness. So lacking is any distinction between one's soul and the Divine, in fact, that one who is awakened to Divine Nothingness forgets all about "God" and lives a life of releasement (*Gelassenheit*), moved by compassion to free things from suffering.

Heidegger's interest in mystics such as Eckhart was reflected in his hopes of becoming a priest. After these hopes were dashed for health reasons, Heidegger became a professional philosopher. Although increasingly antagonistic toward Christianity, he nevertheless continued to draw upon the insights of Christian mystics in his philosophical writings. In particular, his notion that human existence is the openness, clearing, or nothingness in which things can manifest themselves is deeply indebted to mysticism. For mystics, the "self" is not an entity that stands opposed in a dualistic way to other entities. Instead, it is the clearing in which entities (including thoughts, feelings, perceptions, objects, others) appear. The idea that humans are not entities but the clearing in which entities appear eventually helped Heidegger overcome not only dualism, but also anthropocentrism, the attitude that humankind is the source of all value and that all things must serve human interests. By maintaining that humans are authentic only when they let a thing manifest itself in ways consistent with its own possibilities, not merely in accordance with its instrumental value, Heidegger countered the anthropocentrism of much of Western thought. In examining his conception of nothingness, let us turn first to his early writings, particularly *Being and Time* (1927). Later, we shall consider the role of nothingness in his later (post-1935) writings.

The mystical notion of nothingness is at work in *Being and Time*, despite the fact that it is disguised in the complex vocabulary of philosophers like Kant. Following Kant, Heidegger asked the following sort of question: How is it possible for humans to understand entities *as* entities? To answer this question, he distinguished between the human understanding of things and the understanding we ascribe to animals. Birds are clearly able to apprehend entities; otherwise, they could not build nests or feed their young. But, so Heidegger argued, birds and other animals are not able to notice explicitly *that* things *are*.[5] Presumably, birds don't step back from their work to say, "Now that is a fine nest I'm building!" Moreover, we assume that birds don't have identity crises; they don't ask, "Why am I here and what will become of me? Who am I?" We humans understand ourselves and other things *as* entities, that is, as things that *are*. Early Heidegger concentrated on the human capacity for understanding the *being* of entities, a capacity revealed in our ability to use the verb "to be" in so many different ways.

Normally, philosophers conceive of understanding as a faculty of the "mind," the "thinking thing" that attempts to comprehend extramental "things." Heidegger, however, sharply criticized the Cartesian epistemological tradition, which conceived of humans as self-conscious substances, or as worldless subjects standing over against objects. Drawing on his study of Eckhart and other mystics, as well as on Kant, Heidegger maintained instead that the human being is not a thing but rather a peculiar kind of nothingness: the temporal-linguistic clearing, the opening, the absencing in which things can present themselves and thus "be." If humans are not things, then we have to define "knowing" in a different way than before. Knowing is not a relation between two things, mind and object. Rather, knowing occurs because the openness constituting human existence is configured in terms of the three temporal dimensions: past, present, future. These dimensions hold open the horizons on which entities may manifest themselves in determinate ways – for example, as instruments, objects, or persons. Heidegger's talk of the *a priori* character of the temporal horizons of human existence is analogous to Kant's talk of the *a priori* categories of the human understanding.

Human understanding, then, does not take place inside a mind locked in the skull. Instead, understanding occurs because human temporality is receptive to particular ways in which things can present or manifest themselves. Here it is important to emphasize that what we ordinarily take to be the ultimate constituents of "mind" – thoughts, beliefs, assertions, and so on – are for Heidegger phenomena that occur *within* the temporal clearing constitutive of human understanding. Hence, minds do not make thoughts possible; rather, *a priori* human understanding of being makes it possible for us to encounter and to conceive of ourselves as "minds" with "thoughts" separated from the "external world." For Heidegger, "thoughts" are not radically other than allegedly external entities, such as trees, cars, and books. Thoughts and cars are both entities manifesting themselves within and thus being understood as entities within the temporal clearing of human existence.

Just as in the case of "understanding," Heidegger defined "being" in a different way than most other philosophers. Traditionally, philosophers have defined the "being" of an entity as its ground or substance, that which provides the "foundation" for the thing. Plato called this foundation the eternal form of things; Aristotle, their substance; medieval theologians, their Creator. Refusing to conceive of being as a kind of superior entity, an eternal foundation, ground, cause, or origin for things, Heidegger argued that for something "to be" means for it to disclose or to present itself. For this presencing (*Anwesen*) or self-manifesting to occur, there must be a clearing, an opening, an emptiness, a nothingness, an absencing (*Abwesen*). Human existence constitutes the openness necessary for the presencing (being) of entities to take place. When such presencing occurs through the openness that I am, I encounter an entity *as* an entity; that is, I *understand* what it *is*. Heidegger used the term "Dasein" to name this peculiar receptivity of human existence for the being (self-manifesting) of entities. In German, *da* means "here" or "there," while *sein* is the German verb "to be." Hence, Dasein means the place in which being occurs, the openness in which presencing transpires. For Heidegger, neither temporality (absencing, nothingness) nor being (presencing, self-manifesting) is an "entity." Rather, they are the conditions necessary for entities to appear as such. We never "see" time or "touch" the presencing of things; rather, we see and touch the *things* that manifest or present themselves.

In the light of these remarks, the significance of the title of Heidegger's major work, *Being and Time*, becomes comprehensible. His aim here was to study the internal relationship between being and time. Because being and time, presencing and absencing, manifestness and nothingness lack any phenomenal or empirical properties, they seem to be "nothing" in the merely negative sense of an "empty vapor" (Nietzsche). For Heidegger, however, presencing and absencing "are" that which is most worthy of thinking.

What evidence, we might ask, is there for the claim that humans are really this temporal nothingness through which entities can manifest themselves and thus "be"? To answer this question, Heidegger appealed in part to an argument taken from Kant: the best way of accounting for the possibility of our understanding of entities is to postulate that we humans simply *are* the temporal openness or nothingness in which entities can appear *as* entities. In addition to such an argument, however, Heidegger maintained that the mood of anxiety reveals the nothingness lying at the heart of human existence. While contending that anxiety is perhaps the most basic human mood, he also observed that it is such a disquieting mood that we spend most of our lives trying to keep it from overtaking us. Our unreflective absorption in the practices of everyday life – family relations, schooling, job activities, entertainment – keep us distracted enough that we manage to conceal from ourselves the weirdness of being human. Anxiety tears us out of everyday absorption in things; it reveals them to be useless in the face of the radical mortality, finitude, and nothingness at the heart of human existence.

Why is human existence weird? Because humans are not things, but the clearing in which things appear. Although we are not fixed things, we define ourselves as if we were simply a more complex version of the things we encounter in the world: rational animals. Ordinarily, we identify ourselves with our thoughts, beliefs, feelings, attitudes, memories, bodies, material possessions, and so on. Such identification gives us a sense of stability and permanence, which covers up the essential groundlessness and emptiness of human existence. There is no ultimate "reason" for our doing what we do. We have to postulate our own reasons for doing what we do; we invent our own identities, although those identities to a great extent are determined in advance by social practices and norms that have evolved historically. Moreover, as groundless nothingness, humans are essentially dependent and receptive, finite and mortal. The mood of anxiety is so disturbing because it reveals that "at bottom" we are nothingness, that our existence is ultimately groundless, and that we are essentially finite and mortal. In the face of such disclosures, little wonder that most people flee from the mood of anxiety.

Early Heidegger claimed, however, that if we submit resolutely to what the mood of anxiety wants to reveal to us, we become authentic (*eigentlich*) in the sense of "owning" our mortal existence. As authentic, we assume responsibility for being the mortal openness that we already are. Assuming such responsibility is essential to human freedom. Instead of existing in a constricted manner – as egos with firm identities – we allow the temporal openness that we are to expand. This expansion allows things and other humans to manifest themselves in more complex, complete, and novel ways, rather than as mere objects or instruments for our ends.[6] Conversely, by fleeing from anxiety into everyday practices and distractions, we conceal the truth about our own mortal nothingness and are thus incapable of allowing things to manifest themselves primordially.

What early Heidegger says about authenticity may be compared to the famous Zen story about the "stages" of enlightenment. Before enlightenment occurs, mountains are mountains; at the moment of enlightenment, mountains cease being mountains; but then mountains become mountains once again. Zen enlightenment, *satori*, involves direct insight into one's radical groundlessness and nothingness. In the light of such a revelation, everyday practices (including working and eating) lose their meaning. Afterward, however, one reenters these practices, but in a way no longer burdened by ignorance about what it means to be human. Likewise for Heidegger, before becoming authentic one exists in accord with everyday practices; upon allowing anxiety to reveal one's utter groundlessness and nothingness, everyday practices slide away into meaninglessness; afterward, one takes up everyday practices once again, but not in a merely conformist manner.[7]

Instead, being authentic means being free to invigorate and to transform practices in light of the realization of their utter groundlessness. As groundless, things could be otherwise than they are at present. It is important to note, however, that for Heidegger freedom did not mean boundless license for the ego, but instead the capacity for human Dasein to "let things be" in ways other than as mere instruments for the ego. As the Zen tradition puts it, being enlightened means chopping wood and carrying water – but in a manner attuned to the presencing of things as it occurs beyond the dualism of "mind" and "body."

Heidegger's notion that humans are most free when they "let beings be" has been taken up as a slogan by some radical environmentalists, who object to treating nature merely as an instrument for human ends. Early Heidegger suggested that the instrumental disclosure of things played a primary role in human existence.[8] Later, however, he concluded that such instrumentalism was in fact a historical feature of Western history that began with the Greeks and culminated in the technological disclosure of things as nothing but raw material for human ends. Moreover, his early instrumentalism was intimately bound up with his twofold attempt to overcome the mind–body dualism that – especially in its scientific version – gave rise to the alienation at work in modern society.

One phase in this attempt involved conceiving of humans not as minds in skulls but rather as the temporal clearing or nothingness in which thoughts and trees, beliefs and cars can appear as entities. The other phase in overcoming dualism involved challenging those who privileged theoretical assertions and abstract knowledge over against pragmatic activity. Instead of conceiving of humans as worldless intellects making abstract assertions about external objects, Heidegger defined humans as being always already involved in myriad practices that utilize many different things. These things do not manifest themselves abstractly as "objects," but instead as tools involved in a complex set of relationships that constitute the "world" of human existence. Human existence, temporally oriented toward the future, is always pressing forward into possibilities opened up within the world. The practical involvements and practices of everyday life precede and make possible the theoretical knowledge so prized by philosophers. Heidegger emphasized the practical dimension of human existence by defining the very being of Dasein as "care." To be human means to be concerned about things and to be solicitous toward other people.

While early Heidegger sometimes spoke as if the "objectifying" tendencies of modernity were a result of humanity's intrinsic tendency to conceal deeper truths, he later concluded that the objectifying scientific view did not result from any human decision or weakness, but was instead a proper part of the technological disclosure of entities, a disclosure that was itself a dimension of the "destiny of being." The famous "turn" in Heidegger's thinking occurred when he concluded that he could no longer conceive of being in terms of human understanding, but instead had to conceive of human understanding as an aspect of being itself.

LATER HEIDEGGER'S CONCEPTION OF NOTHINGNESS

Following Kant, early Heidegger sometimes spoke of Dasein's temporal openness as if it were a faculty or capacity of humankind. And he often spoke as if the being of entities were somehow a function of human Dasein's understanding. Moreover, he depicted anxiety primarily as a personal phenomenon that called individuals to a less constricted way of understanding things. Later Heidegger altered these views. Ceasing to speak of temporality or nothingness as a dimension of human existence, he made clear that human temporality arises within a more encompassing "openness" or "region" that cannot be reduced to anything merely human. Later Heidegger emphasized that human existence is appropriated as the site for the self-disclosure or "being" of entities. Instead of conceiving of being from the perspective of human Dasein, then, Heidegger began "thinking" being in its own terms. This move was central to his attempt to abandon any remaining anthropocentrism discernible in his earlier work. In this connection, he concluded that "inauthenticity," that is, understanding things in a superficial and constricted way, was not a problem of individuals, but a widespread social phenomenon resulting from the self-concealment of being. The technological disclosure of entities, then, arose not because individuals were unable to endure anxiety, but instead because, since around Plato's time, being as such had increasingly withdrawn itself from human view. Correlatively, Western humanity was blinded to the fact that human existence is the clearing for the being of entities. Hence, Western humanity increasingly came to understand itself as a peculiar entity – the clever animal – driven to dominate all other entities for the sake of gaining power and security. Heidegger argued that the emergence of the technological age in the twentieth century was the inevitable result of the clever animals' craving for power.

From Heidegger's viewpoint in the thirties, Western humanity could be saved from technological nihilism only if Germany were granted another encounter with being and nothingness that was as powerful as the beginning granted to the ancient Greeks. Such an encounter, so he mistakenly believed, would be made possible by National Socialism, which revealed that the highest obligation and possibility of humanity were not to be the master of entities, but instead to be the historical clearing necessary for entities to manifest themselves in ways other than merely as flexible raw material.[9] Heidegger insisted that such a new beginning would require that humanity cease regarding itself as the lord and master, or the "ground," of entities. A transformed humanity would acknowledge its radically receptive, dependent, mortal, and finite status, thereby allowing itself to be appropriated (*ereignet*) as the site required for the presencing or being of entities to occur. Only in this way could humanity learn to "let beings be," that is, to allow things to manifest themselves in accordance with their own limits instead of in accordance with the limits imposed on them by scientific constructs and technological projects. Heidegger eventually concluded that the historical reality of National Socialism betrayed its "inner truth and greatness" by promoting a particularly virulent version of the technological disclosure of things, instead of opening up a new phase of Western history. Heidegger's lifelong refusal to renounce unambiguously his own "authentic" version of National Socialism is a source of concern for students of his thought.

The fact that modern humanity came to regard itself as the ground or foundation for entities resulted not from human decision, Heidegger maintained, but instead from the self-concealment of being itself. Plato conceived of being not as the dynamic presencing of entities, but rather as the eternally present, unchanging blueprint, form (*eidos*), or model for things in the realm of becoming. By conceiving of being as the permanently present grounding for entities, Plato initiated the 2,500-year history of metaphysics. Heidegger sought to transform this history by revealing that there is no eternal or final "ground" for things, that in fact what we mean by "being" is always shaped by historical factors.

The Romans gave a crucial twist to the metaphysical tradition by depicting the metaphysical ground as that which "causes" things to come into being. Henceforth, metaphysics became concerned primarily with telling the story of where things came from, how they were produced or created. Appropriating the metaphysical tradition, medieval theologians argued that for something "to be" meant for it to be created (produced) and preserved by the supreme entity, the Creator of biblical faith. In early modern times, human reason arrogated to itself the divine role as the ground of entities. Beginning with Descartes, Western humanity began to encounter entities as objects for the self-certain rational subject. For something to be meant for it to be capable of being represented – measured, quantified, known – by the subject. Modern science forced entities to reveal themselves only in accordance with theoretical presuppositions consistent with Western humanity's ever-increasing drive to gain control of everything. While during the industrial age the achievement of such control could be described as a means for the end of improving the human estate, during the technological era – which may be said to have commenced with the horrors of World War I – humanity itself has become a means to an end without purpose: the quest for power for its own sake, which Heidegger described as the sheer "Will to Will."

Later Heidegger differentiated his own meditations on being from theological and scientific accounts that search for the "causes" of things. He focused instead on the manifestness by virtue of which entities can first be encountered and only subsequently interpreted in terms of theoretical categories such as cause and effect, ground and consequent. He insisted that human reason cannot "ground" or "explain" the sheer presencing of things. Following the German mystic Angelius Silesius, he spoke of such acausal origination by saying, "The rose is without why; it blooms because it blooms" (SG 101–2). Moreover, later Heidegger also concluded that the "clearing" necessary for the self-manifesting of entities cannot be understood in terms of the Kantian model of the "temporal ecstases" of human existence. Rather, he argued that the clearing is constituted by a "thing" – whether natural or artifactual – that gathers mortals and gods, earth and sky into a kind of cosmic dance which frees up the inherent luminosity of things. The "world" constitutes itself by virtue of the spontaneous coordination or mutual appropriation of the appearances that arise – un-caused, from "no-thing" – moment by moment. Later Heidegger used the term *logos* to name this mutual coordination of appearances; hence, his claim that language (*logos*) lets things be. This account of the self-organization of uncaused appearances, which is close to Taoism, also provides the key to Heidegger's proximity to Mahayana Buddhism.

HEIDEGGER AND EASTERN THOUGHT: PRELIMINARY REMARKS

We know of Heidegger's debt to Meister Eckhart, whose writings reveal many congruences with Buddhism and other East Asian traditions.[10] And Heidegger himself was interested in Buddhism and Taoism. In one essay, for example, he noted the resonances between the Chinese term *tao* and his own notion of *Ereignis*, the "event of appropriation" that claims humanity as the site for the self-manifesting of entities. Such appropriation would change the course of Western history by freeing humanity from its compulsion to dominate things through technical means and by freeing humanity to adhering to the self-concealing "way" of things themselves (OWL 92; US 198). In fact, so intrigued was Heidegger by Taoism that he spent most of the summer in 1946 working with a Chinese student, Paul Shih-yi Hsiao, translating portions of the *Tao Te Ching*.[11] Otto Pöggeler, one of Heidegger's ablest commentators, reports that as early as 1930, to help settle a dispute on the nature of intersubjectivity, Heidegger cited a famous passage from Chuang-Tsu.[12] And William Barrett reports the possibly apocryphal story that upon reading one of D. T. Suzuki's books on Buddhism, Heidegger exclaimed that Suzuki voiced what Heidegger had been trying to say all along.[13] The fact that the Japanese have published seven translations of *Being and Time* gives credence to the idea that there is an important relation between Heidegger's thought and Buddhism.[14]

Those skeptical of the East Asian influence on Heidegger's thought point out his insistence that the "new beginning" that he envisioned for the West could arise only from the West itself, since it was in ancient Greece that there arose the "first beginning," which culminated in the technological disclosure of all things – including humans – as flexible raw material. In 1966 Heidegger said that the transformation of the technological impulse "cannot happen because of any takeover by Zen Buddhism or any other Eastern experience of the world.... Thinking itself can only be transformed by a thinking which has the same origin and calling" (OGSU 281; Sp 214–17).

In making such a distinction between East and West, Heidegger not only tended to downplay the impact of Eastern thinking on the German philosophical tradition (beginning with Leibniz and continuing through Nietzsche), but also seemed to be thinking metaphysically in accordance with a binary opposition between "East" and "West," an opposition that seems to privilege the West as the origin of the technological disclosure of things that now pervades the planet.[15] Nevertheless, in calling for another beginning that would displace the Western metaphysical quest for the ultimate ground of things, Heidegger questioned the validity of the West's claim to cultural superiority. Belief in such superiority hinges on the conviction that Western rationality, especially as manifested in science and technology, constitutes the ground for things: to be means to be a representation for the rational subject. In deconstructing metaphysical foundationalism, however, Heidegger revealed the groundlessness not only of rationality, but also of the historical project of mastery based on such rationality.

Heidegger maintained that, despite pretensions to the contrary, Western humanity never had control over its own destiny, including the rise of planetary technology. If such technology arises from trends in Western history, one might well make the case that it can best be "thought" in terms of Western discourse. While Heidegger himself believed that his own thinking could be enriched by his encounter with Eastern thinking, he also maintained that radically different kinds of languages forced Western and Eastern peoples to live in different "houses of being." His dialogue with the Japanese thinker and his incomplete translation of *Tao Te Ching* were efforts to bridge this linguistic gap. Before moving further into our examination of the Heidegger–Buddhism relation, we must pause to consider major features of Mahayana Buddhism, especially its idea of absolute nothingness.

THE BUDDHIST CONCEPTION OF NOTHINGNESS

Buddhism is a cosmological, psychological, and religious system which maintains that salvation arises from insight into the truth about reality. According to Mahayana Buddhism, the truth is that all things – including humans – arise moment by moment without causation, hence from absolute "nothingness" or emptiness, *sunyata.* Despite the apparent "solidity" of the phenomena we encounter, they are impermanent and "empty." So long as humans conceive of themselves as permanent things (such as egos), suffering ensues from the craving, aversion, and delusion associated with trying to make the impermanent permanent. Insight into the play of phenomena-arising-in-nothingness reveals that the ego, too, is impermanent and empty, merely a series of transient phenomena to which we assign the names "I" and "me." We suffer because we attempt to make the nothingness or emptiness that we "are" into a solid and enduring thing (an ego) that needs defending.

As opposed to the usual Western conception of nothingness as the absence of being or as mere chaotic negativity, Buddhists speak of absolute nothingness, *sunyata.* The Sanksrit word "*sunyata*" is derived from a term meaning "to swell." Something that looks swollen is hollow or empty on the inside. One commentator has noted that "this relationship is made still clearer by the fact that the mathematical symbol for zero was originally none other than the symbol for *sunyata.*"[16] Swelling also calls to mind pregnancy, a fact that suggests reading *sunyata* in some sense as a generative source that, because it transcends all categories that apply to ordinary phenomena, cannot be said either to cause or not to cause anything. Commentators sometimes speak of absolute nothingness – which transcends the polarities of being and nonbeing, cause and effect, subject and object, time and eternity, finitude and infinity – as the groundless ground, the unconditioned "origin" of all phenomena. This view of *sunyata* became important in Chinese Buddhism, influenced as it was by the notion of the Tao as the groundless ground of things.

However, a crucial Indian Buddhist thinker, Nagarjuna (c. 400

A.D.), warned that conceiving of absolute nothingness as such a transcendental origin would lead to a metaphysics of *sunyata* and, inevitably, to a new kind of dualism.[17] According to Mahayana Buddhism, overcoming all forms of dualism is a necessary condition for emancipation from the suffering brought about by experiencing the world as divided into ego-subject and objects. In combating such dualism, Nagarjuna emphasized *anatma,* the doctrine that there is no essence, core, or substance to things. According to this doctrine, all things arise together simultaneously and are radically codependent in the sense of mutually defining one another. This insight regarding internal relatedness or interdependent causation (*pratitya samutpada* in Sanskrit) not only undermines the notion of individual "substances" or "selves," but also rejects the dualistic idea that "sentience" is a capacity enabling some entities to "perceive" others. Entities are not perceived "by" the mind, but instead "perception" and "entity" are different ways of describing a unitary cosmic event of luminosity or self-manifesting, an event that cannot be understood as merely "mental." When we no longer experience the world dualistically as a collection of separate objects perceived by the mind, but instead as a moment-by-moment manifestation of interrelated phenomena, then we experience the whole universe as sentient, as inherently luminous.[18]

The most famous metaphorical expression of this insight, advanced by the Hua-yen school, is the jewel net of the god Indra. Into this infinite net, representing the universe, are set an infinite number of perfect gems, each of which reflects the light given off by all the other gems throughout the expanse of the net. The play of reflected light is codetermined simultaneously by all the gems, no one of which stands in a "superior" or "causal" relation to the others. Mahayana Buddhism holds that the phenomenal world is akin to such an interplay of reflected appearances, in which each thing is aware of its relation to all other things. These appearances have no ground; there is nothing "behind" what appears, no substantial "ground" or "essence" to cause them. All things arise together in an internally cosmic event of reflection, which is sentient though not usually self-conscious. Based on the insight that all appearances are ultimately empty, Mahayana Buddhists draw the conclusion that form *is* emptiness and emptiness *is* form, a paradoxical conclusion whose "proof" demands direct insight, which argument alone cannot provide.

The doctrine of the radical emptiness of all forms, derived from the doctrine of dependent coproduction, suggests that every form, every phenomenon, has equal worth. Since there are no essences, there is no hierarchy of phenomenal reality; hence, no one thing is subordinate to or lesser than any other. Each thing is uniquely itself, like a particular jewel reflecting the play of all other jewels in the cosmic phenomenal play arising as temporary-form-within-absolute-emptiness. Insight into the interdependency of all things reveals the falsehood of anthropocentrism: humans are not radically different from or better than other beings, but instead are moments in the play of phenomena.

If all things are internally related, there is no internal "substance" or "core" of entities, including humans. Human suffering (*dukha*) arises because people posit and identify with a substantial, unchanging ego at the core of the flux of experience. By identifying with this supposedly permanent self, we enter into the state of ignorance known as subject–object dualism. Such dualism is characterized by craving, aversion, and delusion, which combine to produce suffering. From one perspective, of course, there do seem to be individual things (including the ego) that are apparently connected by causal relationships. Hence, we speak of the laws of cause and effect at work among entities. From another perspective, however, as David Loy points out, "every moment and experience is momentary, uncaused because an end in itself, complete and lacking nothing."[19] Nothing "here" causes something else to happen "there." Attempts to explain how anything – including the self or the cosmos – "originates" fails to comprehend the radicality of dependent co-production. There is not even a "process" that "causes" one to enter into illusion and suffering, nor can one "do" anything to free oneself from illusion, for illusion already *is* enlightenment. There is no better "place" at which one should hope to arrive. Ultimately, there is no difference between *nirvana* and *samsara:* the nothingness of the phenomenal world of suffering is the same as the nothingness of *nirvana.* That is, form is emptiness, emptiness is form. Recognition of this fact is said to be the source of the extraordinary laughter that often accompanies *satori,* laughter that occurs when one apprehends that all attempts to "transcend" the phenomenal world in order to become "enlightened" are profoundly misguided. The longed-for *nirvana* is not other than the world of everyday life, although theoretical constructs prevent us from directly apprehending this liberating insight.

According to Mahayana Buddhism, Gautama Buddha opposed the traditional doctrine of the Upanishads and Vedas, according to which eternal Atman, the unchanging Divine Self, permeates and sustains things by constituting their ultimate essence, their true "self." For the Vedantic tradition, suffering ends only when one overcomes dualism by ceasing to cling to the illusory ego and identifying instead with the Absolute Self; for Mahayana Buddhism, suffering ends only when one overcomes dualism by ceasing to cling to the illusory ego and recognizing that there is no Absolute Self either. The conception of Buddhism as a life-denying tradition may be attributed to those adherents of Hinayana Buddhism who conceived of *nirvana,* the cessation of suffering, as being possible only for those few individuals who followed the arduous process of deconstructing the ego, encountering its emptiness, and thereby transcending the illusions of the world of appearance. Mahayana Buddhism affirms the possibility of and the need for saving *all* beings, since all "beings" are internally related – hence, the increasingly active role played by Mahayana Buddhists in the movement to protect nature from human abuse.[20]

THE RELATION BETWEEN HEIDEGGER'S THOUGHT AND MAHAYANA BUDDHISM

Heidegger's thought is close to that of Mahayana Buddhism, particularly Zen, in several respects. First, both maintain that inauthenticity or suffering arises from conceiving of oneself in a constricted manner: as an isolated ego craving security, avoiding pain, and seeking distraction. Both maintain that the "self" is not a thing, but rather the openness or nothingness in which the incessant play of phenomena can occur. Both criticize the dualistic view of the self as a cogitating ego standing apart from the "external" world. Both emphasize that the un-self-conscious nature of everyday practices reveals that people are not separate from things, but are rather directly involved with them. Human hands, diapers, the baby being cleaned up, the mixed feelings of aversion and affection – all these are moments of the same phenomenal event. No particular moment is privileged.

Second, both Heidegger and the Zen tradition maintain that once one is released from the constricted self-understanding associated with dualistic egocentrism, other people and things in the world no longer appear as radically separate and threatening, but instead as profoundly interrelated phenomena. Surrendering one's constricted ego-identity, and thus moving beyond dualism, enables one to become the compassion (Buddhism) or care (Heidegger) that one always already is. "Authenticity" (Heidegger) and "enlightenment" (Buddhism), then, result from the insight into nondualism, the fact that there are "not two," neither an "ego-mind" here nor "objects" there.

There is a difference between Heidegger's early and later idea of authenticity. Early Heidegger maintained that the moment of authenticity required resoluteness, a decision to allow human temporality to transform itself into a more radical openness for the self-manifesting of things. Later Heidegger, however, played down the voluntaristic dimension discernible in resoluteness and conceived of authenticity in terms of *Gelassenheit*, releasement from will. Interestingly, similarities between these two ways of conceiving of authenticity – as resoluteness and as releasement – are detectable in the Rinzai and the Soto Zen traditions, respectively.[21] Rinzai Zen emphasizes resoluteness in the face of the ego's resistance to transformation, while Soto Zen maintains that enlightenment can never be willed but can only be cultivated by learning to "let things be" in everyday life. The differences between the voluntarism of early Heidegger and Rinzai Zen, on the one hand, and the "letting be" of later Heidegger and Soto Zen, on the other, should not obscure their shared belief that "authenticity" or "salvation" involves becoming the nothingness that we already are, such that we are open for and responsive to the phenomena that show up moment by moment in everyday life.

While maintaining that one can never *resolve* to become authentic or enlightened, however, both later Heidegger and the Soto Zen master suggest that spiritual practices may help put one in the position of a paradoxical "willingness not to will," thereby preparing one for the releasement that brings one into the world appropriately for the first time.[22] While we may be familiar with the Zen emphasis on sitting meditation, proper breathing, and working with paradoxical koans, we may be somewhat less familiar with later Heidegger's claim that releasement may be cultivated by meditative practices, by proper breathing, and by contemplating paradoxical questions (Heideggerean "koans"). All of these practices are designed to bring one to the utter silence and stillness needed to become attuned to the openness or nothingness pervading all things.[23]

Third, later Heidegger and Buddhism both discount the primacy of causality in their account of "reality." For Heidegger, the self-manifesting or presencing of entities cannot be explained in causal terms. We can describe things in causal terms only *after* they have first manifested themselves as things. Likewise for Buddhism, causality is a conceptual scheme for relating phenomena, but these phenomena themselves are not "caused," for all phenomena arise simultaneously in mutual coproduction. Heidegger's account of the dance of earth and sky, gods and mortals, the dance in which things manifest themselves in the event of mutual appropriation, bears remarkable similarities to the Buddhist account of the moment-by-moment coproduction of self-luminous phenomena. To some extent, later Heidegger's thought and Buddhism alike are both versions of what we might call "phenomenalism." For them, there is "nothing" behind the appearances that constitute the furniture of our worlds.

Fourth, later Heidegger's cosmic dance is similar to Buddhism's cosmic coproduction. Mahayana Buddhism manifests cosmocentrism by noting that enlightened humanity exhibits compassion equally for all beings, not just for humans. Later Heidegger moved closer to the cosmocentrism of Mahayana Buddhism and away from his earlier anthropocentrism not only by calling for humanity to let all beings be, but also by no longer conceiving of the "clearing" as a human capacity or faculty. As I mentioned earlier, for later Heidegger, it is not human existence that gathers together a world; instead, the "thing" gathers together the "Fourfold" of earth and sky, gods and mortals. Dasein is a partner in a dance in which things impart to one another their appropriate place.

Fifth, both Heidegger and the Zen master suggest that, when authentic or enlightened, the "individual" exists beyond dualistic constraints, including those imposed by the distinction between "good" and "evil." In many different traditions, mystics have said – in effect – "Love God, and do what you will." The danger here, of course, is that a person may transgress moral boundaries when under the illusion that he or she has become "enlightened" or "authentic." Heidegger seems to have been gripped by such an illusion during his period of fascination with National Socialism.[24] Zeal for the mystical ideal of anarchy,[25] which allegedly brings forth boundless compassion, must be tempered by insight into humanity's enormous capacity for self-delusion.

Despite similarities, there are also important differences between Heidegger's thought and Mahayana Buddhism. Members of Japan's famous Kyoto school, such as Keiji Nishitani[26] and Masao Abe,[27] have offered the most extensive Buddhist discussions of the limits of Heidegger's thought. Nishitani and Abe are interested in Heidegger partly because his rigorous meditation upon nothingness may help to galvanize a Zen tradition that has become intellectually flabby. If Zen practitioners are willing to learn from Heidegger, however, Nishitana and Abe also suggest that Western proponents of his thought learn from Zen experience regarding the futility of metaphysical speculation.

Masao Abe argues that Heidegger, despite his interest in nothingness, never arrived at "absolute nothingness" because even his "meditative thinking" was still too connected with the metaphysical tradition.[28] Presumably, in the Zen Buddhist tradition someone truly "enlightened" would no longer "think," even in Heidegger's meditative manner, but would instead live a life without "goal" or "purpose," although a life of profound compassion as well. Heidegger's continued insistence on the importance of thinking also differentiates him from Meister Eckhart. As Reiner Schürmann points out, "For Meister Eckhart *gelâzenheit* as an attitude of man refers to thought only secondarily. Primarily it is a matter of a way of life – a life without representation of ends and purposes."[29]

According to Masao Abe, what follows the direct experience of absolute nothingness may be called Non-thinking to distinguish it from the usual opposition between thinking and nonthinking. Despite his critique of Heidegger's adherence to thinking, Masao Abe warns that

> because of its standpoint of Non-thinking, Zen has in fact not fully realized the positive and creative aspects of thinking and their significance which have been especially developed in the West. Logic and scientific cognition based on substantive objective thinking, and moral principles and ethical

realization based on Subjective practical thinking, have been very conspicuous in the West. In contrast to this, some of these things have been vague or lacking in the world of Zen. [Hence, Zen's] position in Not-thinking always harbours the danger of degenerating into mere not-thinking.[30]

Masao Abe charges that in spite of Heidegger's talk of nothingness, his emphasis on human existence "does not necessarily lead him to the completely dehomocentric, cosmological dimension alone in which the impermanence of all beings in the universe is fully realized."[31] Heidegger's own student, Karl Löwith, also argued that his mentor remained trapped within an anthropocentrism that blinded him to the cosmocentrism of ancient Greek thinkers such as Heraclitus.[32] Nevertheless, later Heidegger's notion of the "event of appropriation" (*Ereignis*), which gathers mortals together into the luminous cosmic dance with gods, earth, and sky, bears important similarities to Buddhism's mutual coproduction and Lao Tsu's *tao,* both of which are regarded as nonanthropocentric. *Ereignis, sunyata, tao:* these may be different names for the acausal, spontaneous arising and mutually appropriating play of phenomena. In suggesting that *Ereignis* "gives" time and being, Heidegger opens himself to the criticism that he is inventing a "metaphysics" of nothingness. Nevertheless, Dogen (1200–53 A.D.), founder of Zen's Soto sect, analyzed the temporality of absolute nothingness in a way that has significant affinities both with early Heidegger's notion of temporality as the "clearing" for presencing and with later Heidegger's notion of the mutually appropriative play of appearances.[33]

While both Heidegger and Mahayana Buddhists criticize anthropocentrism, both acknowledge that humanity is in some way special. If Buddhists regard human existence as *sunyata* brought to self-awareness, and if Heidegger conceives of human existence as the mortal clearing that allows things to manifest themselves, both also argue that this fact brings with it a distinctive responsibility: not to dominate or to constrict the appearing of entities, but rather to let things be.

Despite these similarities, we should not forget an important difference between *Ereignis* and *sunyata: Ereignis* supposedly "sends" the different modes of presencing that have shaped Western history in its Greek, Roman, medieval, modern, and technological eras.[34] Mahayana Buddhism might be suspicious of the way that, in Heidegger's "history of being," *Ereignis* seems to take on a generative, directive dimension that threatens to transform it into a metaphysical category, thereby undermining the nondualistic thrust of Heidegger's thought. Nevertheless, it is precisely because the relatively ahistorical Mahayana tradition lacks the conceptual resources necessary to confront the emergence of planetary civilization that Nishitani and other members of the Kyoto school have looked to Heidegger's thought for insight regarding how to relate *sunyata* to history.[35]

HEIDEGGER, BUDDHISM, AND DEEP ECOLOGY

Heidegger's notion of "letting things be" has made his thinking attractive for radical environmentalists interested in transforming humanity's currently destructive attitude toward nature. Both Heidegger's thought and Mahayana Buddhism have influenced a radical form of environmentalism called "deep ecology."[36] Unlike reform environmentalism, which fights pollution but remains anthropocentric, deep ecology argues that only a transformation of Western anthropocentrism and humanity–nature dualism can save the biosphere from destruction. Following Heidegger and Mahayana Buddhists, as well as other nonanthropocentric traditions, deep ecologists call on people to "let beings be."

Heidegger, Buddhism, and deep ecology each promotes its own version of ontological phenomenalism, the doctrine that "to be" means "to appear" or "to be manifest." Phenomenalism does not have to be subjectivistic; in other words, the event of appearing does not have to be restricted to or dependent on human awareness. In cosmic phenomenalism, human awareness is regarded as one mode through which appearing can occur. Mahayana Buddhism, with its claim that all things are empty of self or substance, but nevertheless intrinsically luminous and totally interrelated with the play of appearance, is an instance of such cosmic phenomenalism. Heidegger's thought is a more ambiguous case of such phenomenalism. A critic of Platonic essentialism, he was an equally strong opponent of subjective idealism. Yet if one combines his antiessentialism with his claims (1) that the ontological event of *appearing* is acausal and, hence, incapable of being explained by any narrative (mythical, religious, metaphysical, scientific) regarding how things may have been *produced,* (2) that being and appearing are in effect the same, and (3) that things manifest themselves in a mutually appropriative dance, then one discovers a position that is in many ways close to a kind of phenomenalism.

The deep ecologist Arne Naess, a noted Norwegian philosopher and naturalist, has been influenced both by Heideggerian and by Mahayana Buddhist phenomenalism. Naess argues that our everyday "experience" of what it means for things "to be" is shaped by gestalts that organize the concrete contents or phenomena. There are no "primary" qualities, substances, or "essences" of things; indeed, there are no "things" at all, if by "things" we mean solid, unchanging, isolated material objects. "Things" thus conceived are only useful constructs for dealing with the constantly changing and internally related phenomena constituting "experience." Naess says that "there is a similarity between this view and those expressed by the Buddhist formula *sarvam dharmam nihsvabhavam.* Every element is without 'self-existence.' "[37]

According to Naess, insofar as all things, including persons, lack substance or essence, there is no ultimate ontological divide between self and nature. Growing awareness of one's own insubstantiality brings with it, spontaneously, a growing *identification* with all phenomena. As Naess puts it, there is not "an environment," nor are there "people" who are placed "in" it.[38] "People" and "the environment" are abstract entities, functions of the discriminatory intellectual activity that projects interpretive schemata upon concrete contents, that is, upon the play of phenomena. For Naess and Heidegger, the scientific idea of nature as totality of matter–energy events has validity only so long as no absolute ontological claims are made for it. This idea of nature results from the projection of abstract categories such as "subject" and "object," "space" and "time," "matter" and "energy" onto phenomena for which no "explanation" can ever be given.

Reasoning vainly attempts to give ground to what is groundless: the flux of phenomena emerging moment by moment from the inexhaustible field of absolute nothingness. Insight into this nothingness undermines the constricted ego-pole "in here" defending itself against threatening others and objects "out there." Such insight reveals the ego and its objects to be gestalts whose contents are constituted by an infinite number of self-arising phenomenal events. Seeing into one's own original Buddha nature means being simultaneously

(1) those concrete contents, (2) the organizing gestalt, (3) the awareness of the contents/gestalt, *and* (4) the nothingness in which they all (including consciousness) manifest themselves. "Awakening" means shattering all dualisms, including the one between presencing and absencing, being and nothingness.

It may be objected that this kind of phenomenalism includes what seems to be two different notions of "appearing": (1) the event of a thing's appearing, its presencing, its self-manifesting; and (2) the emergence of a thing into presence by virtue of its own capacity for self-generation, as in the case of an animal being born or a plant sprouting. The first kind of appearing seems to require a site, human existence; the second kind of appearing does not.[39] For Heidegger, Naess, and Buddhism, however, such a distinction continues to presuppose that there "are" entities in a way that is distinguishable from what is meant above by the "appearing" of entities. Phenomenalist ontology holds that human existence is a specific modality of the luminosity characterizing all phenomena.[40] Human awareness brings this cosmic luminosity to self-awareness. Buddhism, Heidegger, and Naess all assign to human existence the special role of apprehending the groundless, empty play of phenomena. Humans exist most appropriately when their luminous openness is unconstricted by dualistic ego-consciousness. Freed from such dualism, people can enter into a new, nondomineering relationship with all things. Humans can encounter birds and trees, lakes and sky, humans and mountains not as independent, substantial, self-enclosed entities, but rather as temporary constellations of appearances: self-giving phenomena arising simultaneously.

To support their own view that nondualism discloses the truth about reality, deep ecologists often appeal to contemporary scientific trends that lead beyond atomism, mechanism, humanity–nature dualism, and reductionistic materialism and open the way for understanding natural processes as internally related, holistic events. Naess implies, however, that deep ecologists must keep in mind that what scientists mean by the "internal relatedness" of events is not necessarily the same as what Buddhism means by empty, self-arising phenomena.[41] Moreover, scientific findings regarding the interrelatedness of things cannot in and of themselves lead to the "compassion" (Buddhism, Naess) or "care" (Heidegger) required for "letting things be" in ways promoted by deep ecology. Required for such compassion or care is direct insight into the interrelatedness of things, insight that transforms the very structure of the one "person" gifted with the insight.

The issue of whether and how to resist the technological transformation of nature is made more complex by the following question: Does a phenomenalist ontology and its doctrine of *anatma* (no self-existence, no essence) provide a basis for criticizing or resisting the technological disclosure of entities? When Heidegger spoke of the self-limiting behavior of plants and animals, he meant that living things organize and produce themselves in accordance with limits that are not a function of the historical world in which trees and bees happen to be disclosed (EP 109; VA 98). Presumably, modern technology violates this self-limiting capacity, a capacity that would seem to be "essential" or at least "internal" to the organisms in question, by treating organisms like machines. Yet Heidegger, like Buddhists and Naess, also rejects the notion of essence. What, then, would be wrong with the technological disclosure of things?[42]

Heidegger would reply that there is a self-concealing dimension to things, a dimension he called "earth," which can never be brought to full appearance, especially not by the calculating disclosure at work in modern technology. Yet the "law of the earth" cannot be conceived as a "ground" for things analogous to eternal essences. Hence, the status of "earth" in Heidegger's thought needs further clarification.[43]

Regarding the technological disclosure of things, Buddhists would argue that even though all beings are merely temporary experiential gestalts, they are nevertheless sentient. It is wrong to inflict pain on sentient beings in the hopeless technological quest to make the ego immortal, all-powerful, and permanent. Because some beings are apparently more "sentient" than others, many Buddhists emphasize alleviating the suffering of humans and animals. Yet Buddhists also maintain that because all beings are interrelated, sentience cannot be restricted to a particular class of beings, especially if such restriction leads to a hierarchical scheme that justifies domination of some entities by others. Clearly, issues concerning what sorts of suffering people may inflict on nonhumans in order to feed, clothe, and house themselves are important and thorny, though they cannot be discussed here. Buddhism, Heidegger, and Naess argue that puncturing the illusion of permanent selfhood would alleviate the infliction of such suffering by freeing one from the illusory quest for total control. Being liberated from the illusion of egocentrism also frees one for spontaneous compassion toward other beings, human and nonhuman alike. One "lets things be" not for any external goal, but instead simply from a profound sense of identification with all things.

In the postmodern world envisioned by deep ecologists and other radical environmentalists, the thirst for knowledge would be tempered and guided by the wisdom associated with loving kindness for all things. Implementing the holistic view of life on earth fostered by Heidegger, Buddhism, and Naess, a view that decenters humankind and emphasizes care for all beings, however, would require an immense transformation. The rhetorical vehemence of some deep ecologists supporting this transformation has led critics to suspect them of being "ecofascists" who would sacrifice individuals for the good of the "organic whole."[44] The fact that Heidegger supported National Socialism and that many deep ecologists are attracted by his thought does nothing to reassure such critics. Social ecologists have argued that the environmental crisis has arisen not because of anthropocentrism, but rather from hierarchical and authoritarian attitudes that started in society and were consequently projected onto nature. Ecofeminists, in turn, charge that the real root of the environmental crisis is not anthropocentrism, but instead androcentrism: man-centeredness or patriarchy. Despite these important differences, however, all radical environmentalists would agree that humanity needs a new self-understanding that will eliminate humanity–nature dualism as well as the kind of anthropocentrism that justifies the heedless exploitation of nature. We must learn what it means to let beings – human and nonhuman – be. Changing human attitudes is fraught with political dangers, especially if utopian visions take the place of measured judgment. In seeking to change the humanity–nature relation, we must never forget that the twentieth century has been scarred by movements that promised salvation, but brought untold misery.[45]

NOTES

1 The best collection on Heidegger's relation to Eastern thinking is *Heidegger and Asian Thought*, ed. Graham Parkes (Honolulu: University of Hawaii Press, 1987). The following is a partial bibliography of

works on Heidegger and Eastern thought: Chang Chung-yuan, *Tao: A New Way of Thinking* (Heideggerian translation of *Tao Te Ching*) (New York: Harper & Row, 1975); Charles Wei-Hsun Fu, "Heidegger and Zen on Being and Nothingness: A Critical Essay in Transmetaphysical Dialectics," in *Buddhist and Western Philosophy: A Critical Study,* ed. Nathan Katz (New Delhi: Sterling, 1981); idem, "Creative Hermeneutics: Taoist Metaphysics and Heidegger," *Journal of Chinese Philosophy,* 3 (1976): 115–43; Peter Kreeft, "Zen in Heidegger's *Gelassenheit,*" *International Philosophical Quarterly,* 11 (December 1971): 521–45; Toshimitsu Hasumi, "Etude comparative de la philosophie de l'existence chez Heidegger et de la pensée philosophique du Zen," *Humanitas,* 19 (1978): 59–75; idem, *Elaboration philosophique de la pensée Zen* (Paris: La pensée universelle, 1973); Michael Heim, "A Philosophy of Comparison: Heidegger and Lao Tsu," *Journal of Chinese Philosophy,* 11 (1984): 307–35; Carl Olson, "The Leap of Thinking: A Comparison of Heidegger and the Zen Master Dogen," *Philosophy Today,* 25 (Spring 1981): 55–61; *Philosophy East and West,* 20 (July 1970), entire issue; John Steffney, "Transmetaphysical Thinking in Heidegger and Zen," *Philosophy East and West,* 27 (July 1977): 323–35; idem, "Man and Being in Heidegger and Zen Buddhism," *Philosophy Today,* 25 (Spring 1981): 46–54; idem, "Mind and Metaphysics in Heidegger and Zen Buddhism," *Eastern Buddhist,* new ser., 14 (Spring 1981): 61–74; Bernard Stevens, "Pratique du Zen et pensee de l'Etre," *Revue philosophique de Louvain,* 84 (1986): 45–76; Rolf von Eckartsberg and Ronald S. Valle, "Heideggerian Thinking and the Eastern Mind," in *The Metaphors of Consciousness,* ed. R. Valle and R. von Eckartsberg (New York: Plenum Press, 1981), pp. 287–311. The connection between Heidegger's thought and the Vedantic tradition has not been explored to any extent. But see J. L. Mehta's essay, "Heidegger and Vedanta: Reflections on a Questionable Theme," *International Philosophical Quarterly,* 51 (June 1978): 121–44, and Medard Boss, *A Psychiatrist Discovers India,* trans. H. Frey (London: Oswald Wolf, 1965).

2 Although a separate essay would be required to explore affinities between Heidegger's thought and Taoism, I shall on occasion mention such affinities because of Taoism's influence on both Chinese and Japanese Zen.

3 Concerning the deep ecological critique of anthropocentrism, see my essays "Toward a Heideggerean *Ethos* for Radical Environmentalism," *Environmental Ethics,* 5 (Summer 1983): 99–131; "Anthropocentric Humanism and the Arms Race," in *Nuclear War: Philosophical Perspectives,* ed. Michael Fox and Leo Groarke (New York: Lang, 1985), pp. 135–49; "The Crisis of Natural Rights and the Search for a Non-

Anthropocentric Basis for Moral Behavior," *Journal of Value Inquiry*, 19 (1985): 43–53; "Implications of Heidegger's Thought for Deep Ecology," *Modern Schoolman*, 64 (November 1986): 19–43.

4 On Eckhart and his importance for Heidegger, see John D. Caputo, *The Mystical Element in Heidegger's Thought* (Athens: Ohio University Press, 1977), and Reiner Schürmann, *Meister Eckhart: Mystic and Philosopher* (Bloomington: Indiana University Press, 1978). Both Caputo and Schürmann include comparisons of Heidegger and Zen as well. On St. Thomas Aquinas's mystical side, see Caputo, *Heidegger and Aquinas* (New York: Fordham University Press, 1982).

5 Heidegger discusses the question of animal understanding in great detail in *Die Grundbegriffe der Metaphysik: Welt-Endlichkeit-Einsamkeit, Gesamtausgabe* 29/30 (winter semester, 1929–30), ed. Friedrich-Wilhelm von Hermann (Frankfurt am Main: Vittorio Klostermann, 1983).

6 On the topic of authenticity, see Michael E. Zimmerman, *Eclipse of the Self: The Development of Heidegger's Concept of Authenticity*, 2d ed. (Athens: Ohio University Press, 1986). The final chapter includes a comparison of Heidegger and Buddhism.

7 On this topic, see Hubert L. Dreyfus and Jane Rubin, "You Can't Get Something for Nothing: Kierkegaard and Heidegger on How Not to Overcome Nihilism," *Inquiry*, 30 (1987): 33–76.

8 See Hubert L. Dreyfus, "Between *Techne* and Technology: The Ambiguous Place of Technology in *Being and Time*," in *The Thought of Martin Heidegger*, ed. Michael E. Zimmerman, Tulane Studies in Philosophy, 32 (New Orleans, La.: Tulane University Press, 1984), pp. 23–35. See also idem, *Heidegger's Confrontation with Modernity* (Bloomington: Indiana University Press, 1990), Chaps. 10 and 11.

9 See my essays "The Thorn in Heidegger's Side: The Question of National Socialism," *Philosophical Forum*, 20 (Summer 1989): 326–65; and "Philosophy and Politics: The Case of Heidegger," *Philosophy Today*, 33 (Summer 1989): 3–19. Concerning Heidegger's misguided view that National Socialism promised to offer an alternative to industrial nihilism, see my *Heidegger's Confrontation with Modernity*.

10 See, e.g., Rudolf Otto, *Mysticism East and West*, trans. Bertha L. Cracey and Richenda C. Payne (New York: Meridian Books, 1959); S. Radhakrishnan, *Eastern Religious and Western Thought* (Oxford: Oxford University Press, 1974); Daisetz T. Suzuki, *Zen and Japanese Culture* (Princeton, N.J.: Princeton University Press, 1970).

11 Paul Shih-yi Hsiao, "Heidegger and Our Translation of the *Tao Te Ching*," in *Heidegger and Asian Thought*, ed. Parkes, pp. 93–103.

12 Otto Pöggeler, "West–East Dialogue: Heidegger and Lao-Tzu," trans. Graham Parkes, in *Heidegger and Asian Thought*, p. 53.

13 William Barrett, Introduction to D. T. Suzuki, *Zen Buddhism* (Garden City, N.Y.: Doubleday, 1956), p. xi.

14 In an unpublished essay, "Die Übersetzbarkeit Heideggers' ins Japanische," Noriko Idada (Tokyo Metropolitan University) has commented on the difficulty of translating Heidegger into Japanese.

15 On this issue, see Evan Thompson, "Planetary Thinking/Planetary Building: An Essay on Martin Heidegger and Nishitani Keiji," *Philosophy East and West,* 36, No. 3 (1986): 235–52.

16 Hans Waldenfels, *Absolute Nothingness: Foundations for a Buddhist–Christian Dialogue,* trans. J. W. Heisig (New York: Paulist Press, 1980), p. 19.

17 The best available study on Eastern views of nondualism and how they compare with ideas of Western thinkers, including Heidegger, is David Loy's excellent *Nonduality: A Study in Comparative Philosophy* (New Haven, Conn.: Yale University Press, 1988).

18 For this point, I am indebted to David Loy.

19 David Loy, personal communication.

20 See Allan Hunt Badiner, *Dharma Gaia: A Harvest of Essays in Buddhism and Ecology* (Berkeley, Calif.: Parallax Press, 1990).

21 See Zimmerman, *Eclipse of the Self,* Chap. 8.

22 Western philosophers, including Nietzsche, have frequently interpreted Buddhism as preferring "nihilation" or "extinction" (*nirvana*) to life itself. In *Beiträge zur Philosophie* (GA 65 170–1), Heidegger spoke in a way which suggests that he shared Nietzsche's view, one that is inconsistent with Mahayana Buddhism. Heidegger's remark is somewhat cryptic: "The more un-entity [is] man, the less he anchors himself in the entity as which he finds himself, ever so nearer does he come to being. (No Buddhism! the opposite)."

23 On these issues, see my essay "Heidegger and Heraclitus on Spiritual Practice," *Philosophy Today,* 27, No. 2 (1983): 87–103.

24 It is worth noting that, in the Japanese middle ages, Samurai swordsmen sometimes trained at Zen monasteries, and that even today Japanese businessmen are at times sent to Zen monasteries to be "toughened up" for competition.

25 In his book *Heidegger on Being and Acting: From Principles to Anarchy,* trans. Christine-Marie Gros (Bloomington: Indiana University Press, 1987), Schürmann draws from Heidegger's writings the possibility of an anarchistic life, a life led "without why."

26 Keiji Nishitani, *Religion and Nothingness,* trans. Jan Van Bragt (Berkeley and Los Angeles: University of California Press, 1982).

27 Masao Abe, *Zen and Western Thought,* ed. William R. LaFleur (Honolulu: University of Hawaii Press, 1985).

28 Ibid., p. 119.

29 Schürmann, *Meister Eckhart*, p. 204.

30 Masao Abe, *Zen and Western Thought*, pp. 119–20.

31 Ibid., p. 67.

32 See, e.g., Karl Löwith, "Zu Heideggers Seinsfrage: Die Natur des Menschen und die Welt der Natur," *Aufsätze und Vorträge, 1930–1970* (Stuttgart: W. Kohlhammer, 1971), pp. 189–203.

33 On this topic, see Steven Heine, *Existential and Ontological Dimensions of Time in Heidegger and Dogen* (Albany: State University of New York Press, 1985). While his book is informative, Heine sometimes promotes Dogen's views at the expense of Heidegger's.

34 See Charles Wei-hsun Fu, "The Trans-onto-theo-logical Foundations of Language in Heidegger and Taoism," *Journal of Chinese Philosophy*, 1 (1975): 130–61.

35 See, e.g., Nishitani, *Religion and Nothingness*, Chap. 6.

36 See my essays "Toward a Heideggerean *Ethos* for Radical Environmentalism" and "Implications of Heidegger's Thought for Deep Ecology"; see also Dolores LaChapelle, *Earth Wisdom* (Los Angeles: Guild of Tutors Press, 1978), pp. 80–6. For analyses and bibliographies of deep ecology, see Bill Devall and George Sessions, *Deep Ecology: Living as if Nature Mattered* (Salt Lake City, Ut.: Peregrine Smith Books, 1985), and Warwick Fox, *Toward a Transpersonal Ecology* (Boston: Shambhala, 1990).

37 Arne Naess, "The World of Concrete Contents," *Inquiry*, 28 (December 1985): 417–28, p. 419. For a fuller exposition of Naess's views, see his *Ecology, Community, and Lifestyle: Outline of an Ecosophy*, trans. and revised by David Rothenberg (Cambridge: Cambridge University Press, 1989).

38 Ibid., p. 424.

39 See my essay "On Vallicella's Critique of Heidegger," *International Philosophical Quarterly*, 30 (March 1990): 75–100.

40 Note that in order to be true to the insight that being and nothingness, form and emptiness, are "the same," I should speak of the nothingness *as which* things come into presence, but such an expression defies good English.

41 For an exploration of whether modern science may contribute to the development of nondualistic awareness, see Ken Wilber, ed., *The Holographic Paradigm and Other Paradoxes* (Boulder: Shambhala, 1982).

42 For an insightful discussion of Heidegger's nonessentialist, pragmatic metaphysics and its relation to his interpretation of modern technology, see Mark B. Okrent, *Heidegger's Pragmatism* (Ithaca, N.Y.: Cornell University Press, 1988).

43 For a very helpful treatment of Heidegger's concept of earth, see Michel

Haar, *Le chant de la terre* (Paris: L'Herne, 1987). A translation is being prepared for Indiana University Press.

44 See, e.g., Murray Bookchin, "Social Ecology versus 'Deep Ecology,' " *Green Perspectives,* Nos. 4 and 5 (Summer 1987).

45 My thanks to David Loy and to Charles Guignon for their very helpful comments on earlier versions of this essay.

JOHN D. CAPUTO

10 Heidegger and theology

Heidegger's thought was from the start deeply interwoven with religious and theological concerns. We have recently learned from the searching historical investigations of Hugo Ott the details of Heidegger's early upbringing and education in the Catholic church. Heidegger was born in the conservative, Catholic farmlands of southern, central Germany, and his father was a sexton in St. Martin's Church, which stood across a quaint little courtyard not fifty yards from the Heidegger house. The Heidegger family was steadfastly loyal to the church in the controversy that followed the First Vatican Council when "liberal" Catholics rejected the proclamation of papal infallibility. The youthful Heidegger, brilliant and pious, was marked from the start for the Catholic priesthood. Through a series of scholarships funded by the church, one of which was intended for students seeking to do doctoral work on Thomas Aquinas, the poor but gifted young man was lifted out of these rural farmlands into the eminence of a German university career. Hugo Ott has discovered that Heidegger's earliest publications appeared in 1910–12 in *Der Akademiker,* an ultraconservative Catholic journal that toed the line of Pope Pius X. There in a series of book reviews the youthful Heidegger, still in his early twenties, spoke out against the danger of "Modernism" to the ageless wisdom of the Catholic tradition. Heidegger cites with approval the saying of "the great [Josef von] Görres": "Dig deeper and you will find yourself standing on Catholic ground."

Forced to break off his studies for the Catholic priesthood in 1911 for health reasons, Heidegger turned first to mathematics and the natural sciences and then to philosophy, where he was openly identified with the Catholic confession. His first teaching position was as a temporary substitute in the Chair of Catholic Philosophy at

Freiburg, and his first serious professional disappointment was his failure to secure permanent appointment to that chair in 1916.[1]

Heidegger's earliest philosophical and theological interests in those days centered on a new and promising appropriation of medieval scholastic philosophy in the light of his research into the foundations of modern logic and Husserl's refutation of psychologism. As a philosopher Heidegger rejected psychologism – the attempt to found logic and mathematics on the psychological makeup of the human mind – as a form of empiricism and relativism, even as he was opposed theologically to modernism as a form of historical relativism that threatened to undermine ageless theological truth. Heidegger saw a continuity between Husserl's "logical investigations," which put logic and mathematics on the foundation of pure phenomenology, and the Scotistic tradition of "speculative grammar" in the late Middle Ages. According to this tradition, which was profoundly antirelativist and antipsychologistic, the forms of grammar and of language (*modus significandi*) are a function of and reflect pure, universal forms of thought (*modus intelligendi*), which are themselves reflections of being itself (*modus essendi*).

But Heidegger also saw another side to the medieval tradition, let us say its "living" side as opposed to its logical and logocentric side, which is to be found in the religious life that animated what he called, following Dilthey, the medieval "experience of life" (*Lebenserfahrung*). We must understand, Heidegger insisted in the postscript to his habilitation dissertation, that the abstract and difficult theories of medieval philosophers and theologians proceed from a concrete experience of life, that such theories give conceptual expression to the "soul's relationship to God" as that is experienced in medieval life. To gain access to that dimension of medieval tradition Heidegger says that we must attend to medieval moral theology and medieval mysticism, in particular that of Meister Eckhart (GA 1 404, 410). For it is the mystical notion that the soul belongs wholly to God, that it is constituted by a kind of transcendence toward God, which we see writ large in the corresponding metaphysico-conceptual notion that the intellect has an inner harmony with and belongingness (*convenientia*) to being. This notion that thinking "belongs" (*gehört*) to being is one that Heidegger would always in some way or another maintain as a part of his own later views.[2]

By invoking the living significance of medieval mysticism Heidegger makes his first attempt at a "destruction" of the tradition – which does not mean to level or raze but rather to break through the conceptual surface of traditional metaphysics in order to "retrieve" or recover (*wieder-holen;* BT 437) its living roots and life-giving experiences. This is a gesture that Heidegger would repeat again and again throughout his life, so that the famous "de(con)struction" of metaphysics or of the "history of ontology" in *Being and Time* is always to be understood as a fundamentally "positive" operation, not a negative one (BT 44).

THE EARLY WRITINGS

In 1919, at the age of thirty, and on the occasion of the baptism of his first child, Heidegger broke with the Catholic faith. Writing to Engelbert Krebs, the young priest who had married Martin and Elfride in 1917 and who would have performed the baptism, Heidegger said:

> Epistemological insights, extending as far as the theory of historical knowledge, have made the *system* of Catholicism problematic and unacceptable to me – but not Christianity and metaphysics (the latter, to be sure, in a new sense).[3]

This is the first "turn" in Heidegger's thought, and its importance cannot be emphasized enough. For with the turn from Catholicism to Protestantism, the philosophical interests of the young thinker shifted from the questions of logic to those of history, from pure (Husserlian) phenomenology to what he called the "hermeneutics of facticity" (i.e., concrete life), and from dogmatic theology to the theology of the New Testament. He took his lead not from scholastic theologians like Aquinas, Scotus, and Suarez but from Pascal, Luther, and Kierkegaard, who in turn led him back to Augustine and Paul. Between 1919 and 1922 Heidegger – who identified himself in 1921 to Karl Löwith as a Christian theologian[4] – undertook an intensive study of the "factical experience of life" of the New Testament communities (in particular of their experience of time) in an effort to recover authentic Christian experience. Heidegger's model in this project was Luther's critique of Aristotle and medieval Aristotelian scholasticism. Luther, as has been pointed out by a recent historian of these affairs, even used the word "destruction" to describe his project of recovering an authentic scriptural Christianity beneath the conceptual scaffolding of medieval theology.[5] It is no exaggeration to say that Heidegger's attempt to formulate a "hermeneutics of facticity," or what came to be called in *Being and Time* an "existential analytic" (see BT 490, n. 1), which would mark out the distinctive traits of "factical life" – of Dasein – was inspired by Luther's critique of medieval metaphysical theology and Kierkegaard's critique of Hegelian speculative Christianity. The record of those investigations is now open as more and more of the early Freiburg lectures become available in the *Gesamtausgabe.* One of the most interesting of these lecture courses, the publication of which has been promised in the near future (GA 59/60), is Heidegger's lectures on St. Augustine, in which Heidegger attempts to retrieve the Christian experience of time that is concealed beneath the superstructure of Neoplatonic metaphysics in Augustine's writings.

The nearest prototype of the "destruction of the history of ontology" in *Being and Time,* and of what was later called "overcoming metaphysics," was this essentially theological project of 1919 in which Heidegger set out to recover the original categories of factical Christian life. At the same time, Heidegger was also undertaking a parallel project with regard to Aristotle. Unlike Luther, the young philosopher was not prepared to admit that God had sent Aristotle into the world "as a plague upon us on account of our sins."[6] On the contrary, Heidegger sought to break through Aristotle's system of metaphysical concepts, which was the side of Aristotle that medieval theology had seized upon, in order to discover its sources in "factical life." Aristotle had the greatest phenomenological sensitivities in the ancient world, Heidegger thought (BP 232; GA 24 328–9), and the task of the interpretation of Aristotle on which he had set out was to recover the living experiences – the factical structures of Greek and Aristotelian existence – that had taken conceptual form in Aristotelian philosophy. Heidegger's interpretations of Aristotle at this time were so rich and innovative that they inspired a generation of Aristotelian scholarship and were directly responsible for the appointment that Heidegger received from Marburg, where he began teaching in 1923 in close collaboration with the great Protestant New Testament theologian Rudolph Bultmann.

The work that eventually issued in the appearance of *Being and Time* – work thoroughly interwoven with theological questions –

consisted of a twofold retrieval, of Aristotle on the one hand and of New Testament life on the other. It appears to me that Heidegger thought that these two tasks were one, that the deconstructive retrieval of the categories of factical life would achieve the same results whether this was a matter of retrieving Greek or early Christian life, whether one were reading Aristotle's *Nicomachean Ethics* or the New Testament. For the categories of factical life – the categories of care and existence, of concern and instrumentality, of temporality and historicity – are what they are, wherever they are found. There is a peculiar kind of ahistoricism in Heidegger at this point, very likely one that was inspired by his attachment to phenomenology as a universal science and to the Husserlian ideal of the universal structures of the life-world that would be the same no matter where they would be realized. The goal of *Being and Time* – a very Husserlian and neo-Kantian goal indeed – was to "formalize" these factical structures, to give them a formal-ontological conceptualization that would be ontologically neutral to their concrete instantiation. That is what lay behind the famous distinction between the "existential" and the "existentiell," or the "ontological" and the "ontic," which is so central to the existential analytic. Heidegger's aim was to set forth universal *a priori* structures of existential life, of existing Dasein, without regard to whether such structures were in actual fact – that is, as an existentiell matter – Greek or Christian.

The goal of *Being and Time* was to keep the existential analytic free of any "existentiell ideal," any concrete, factical way to be – like Christian or Greek life. There is no suggestion at this point in Heidegger's writings that Greek existence was any more or less "primordial" than Christian existence. On the contrary they both represented "existentiell ideals" from which the existential analytic prescinded, of which the existential analytic represented the ontological formalization (BT 311; SZ 266).

Now it was precisely because *Being and Time* was in part the issue of an attempt to formalize the structures of factical Christian life that it was greeted with such enthusiasm by Protestant theologians like Bultmann (with whom it had in part been worked out). When Christian theologians looked into the pages of *Being and Time* they found themselves staring at their own image – formalized, ontologized, or as Bultmann said "demythologized." What *Being and Time* had discovered, Bultmann said, was the very structure of religious and Christian existence but without the ontico-mythical worldview that was an idiosyncratic feature of first-century cosmologies. The task of demythologizing Christianity for Bultmann came down to isolating the universal-existential structure of religious existence in general. Demythologizing sorts out existential structures like care, decision, temporality, and authenticity in the face of death from cosmological myths about heaven "above," hell "below," and the earth in between, myths about heavenly messengers who shuttle back and forth among these regions. Of the "historical" Jesus himself and what he actually taught we know nothing. Of the historical communities that were formed shortly after his death and that gave mythological formulation to their collective memories of Jesus we know a great deal, and they contain the essence of the Christian message, the saving truth. The task of theology, armed now with the Heideggerian analytic of existence, is to deconstruct and demythologize the canonical Gospels in order to retrieve their *kerygma,* the living-existential Christian message, one of existential conversion (*metanoia*), of becoming authentic in the face of our finitude and guilt, a task that faces every human being.[7]

When Bultmann "applied" *Being and Time* to Christian theology he was "de-formalizing" the existential analytic and articulating it in terms of a historically specific, existentiell ideal, namely, historical Christianity. The reason this deformalization worked so well was that the existential analytic was in the first place and in no small part itself the issue of a formalization of Christian factical life. Bultmann was largely reversing the process that had brought *Being and Time* about in the first place. I believe that much the same thing can be said of Paul Tillich – also a Marburg colleague of Heidegger – whose early existential theology draws on motifs in *Being and Time* that are themselves originally drawn from an analysis of the New Testament.[8]

Heidegger set forth his views on the relationship between universal phenomenological science and theology in one of his last lectures at Marburg, "Phenomenology and Theology."[9] Philosophy, as the science of being itself, differs "absolutely" from theology, which is an "ontic" science of a particular region of beings, not of universal being. Theology is a "positive" science because it deals with a positive, posited entity (a *positum*), which makes it more like chemistry than philosophy (PT 6–7; GA 9 48–9). The positum of Christian theology is "Christianness" (*Christlichkeit*), by which Heidegger means the factual mode of existing as a believing Christian, of existing in the history that is set into motion by the Cross, by the Crucified, by Christ on the cross (PT 10; GA 9 53–4). (These formulations reflect Heidegger's interest in the early twenties in Luther's theology of the cross.)[10] Theology is the work of bringing the existential rebirth that comes by faith to conceptual form. Theology is a science of faith, of existing faith-fully, of existing historically as a Christian. It does not make faith easier, but harder, because it does not give faith a rational grounding but shows rather that that is exactly what theology cannot do.

Theology is founded on faith and faith does not need philosophy; but theology, as a positive science, does (PT 17; GA 9 61). The "cross" and "sin" can be lived only in faith, but they can be conceptualized only with the help of philosophy. For faith is rebirth from sin, but sin is an onticoexistentiell determination of the ontological structure of guilt that is worked out in *Being and Time.* The Christian concept of sin depends on an adequate elucidation of the "pre-Christian" (universal ontological) concept of guilt. This dependence is not a matter of "deducing" it from guilt, but rather of receiving conceptual help and direction – or rather "codirection" and "correction" – from ontology. The theological concept of sin arises from the experience of faith, but it reaches conceptual *form* only with the help of philosophy. None of this denies, Heidegger thinks, the Pauline view of the mortal opposition between faith and philosophy. Indeed, it is this strife, this very foolishness that philosophy and faith seem to be to each other, which keeps each strong (PT 20–1; GA 9 66–7). Faith is philosophy's existentiell enemy, but it must consort with the enemy if it wants to assume conceptual theological form.

THE WAR YEARS

"Phenomenology and Theology" was Heidegger's farewell to Christian theology as a matter of explicit and personal concern. After he returned to Freiburg as Husserl's successor in 1928, his thought underwent another fundamental shift, a shift that once again was keyed to a changed theological attitude. This is the beginning of the darkest days of Heidegger's life and work. It culminated in his hellish endorsement of National Socialism and his ardent efforts to

Nazify the German university. He became an enthusiastic reader of Nietzsche, while Kierkegaard, Luther, and Aristotle faded into the background. Deeply influenced by the bizarre work of Ernst Jünger, his thought became excessively voluntaristic and heroic, far in excess of anything to be found in *Being and Time* itself. He told the tale of an encroaching nihilism, by which he meant the unwelcome effects of modernity and of modern liberal democratic institutions, all of which he saw as a bourgeois softness and love of comfort and which he simply identified with "value theory." In opposition to this "moribund semblance of a culture"[11] Heidegger argued for the love of danger, the need to expose oneself to the abyss of being, to venture to the outer limits of the groundlessness of being. That alone would give greatness and strength to the "German spirit" – the whole notion of "Dasein" and of universal *a priori* structures having now been contracted to a specifically German mode of being.[12] Such hardness of spirit would in turn keep the West safe from "the boundless et cetera" of American consumerism, on the one hand, and of Russian communism, on the other hand (IM 46; GA 40 49). All of this reached a philosophical crest, first in the famous "Rectoral Address" of 1933 and then in the 1935 lecture course *An Introduction to Metaphysics.*

This ominous development in Heidegger's thought is intimately related to a changing theological attitude. If he had begun as an ultraconservative Catholic, and if he had after 1917 become deeply involved in a dialogue with liberal Protestant historical theology, he was after 1928 deeply antagonistic to Christianity in general and to the Catholicism of Freiburg in particular, and he gives indications of having become personally atheistic. He became in his personal conduct at Freiburg a hostile opponent of Christianity. He would not accept the young Jesuits who came to Freiburg as his doctoral students, and he treated other Catholic students like Max Müller exceedingly badly. When their dissertations were submitted – under the direction of Martin Honecker, who held the Chair of Catholic Philosophy – Heidegger treated them with distance and even disdain. (After 1945 he claimed them as his students.) When Honecker died unexpectedly in 1941, Heidegger succeeded in having this chair abolished, the very one to which he himself had aspired a quarter of a century earlier.[13]

His philosophical work, always "methodologically" atheist, lost its ontological neutrality and became hostile to Christianity. If he thought, up to 1928, that both Greek and Christian existence, taken in their historical concreteness, exemplified the universal structures of factical existence, his position during the thirties was that Christianity was a decadent falling away from the primordiality of Greek experience. By "Greek" he meant the early Greeks, and he took Plato and Aristotle to represent the beginning of the metaphysical oblivion of being. The hostility that had invaded Heidegger's portrait of the relationship between philosophical questioning and Christian faith, between his methodological atheism and a more aggressive atheism, can be seen quite clearly in the following contrast. In 1922 he wrote:

> Questionability is not religious, but rather it may really lead into a situation of religious decision. I do not behave religiously in philosophizing, even if I as a philosopher can be a religious man. "But here is the art:" to philosophize and thereby to be genuinely religious, i.e., to take up factically its worldly, historical task in philosophizing, in action and a world of action, not in religious ideology and fantasy.
>
> Philosophy, in its radical self-positing questionability, must be in principle *a-theistic.* (GA 61 197)

The trick is to maintain oneself in radical "questionability," that is, the ability to raise radical questions, while responding to the claim of faith. Philosophical questioning is not and cannot become faith, without ceasing to be questioning, but the believer can hold his faith open and keep it free from dogmatic ideology only by sustaining the life of questioning. But in *An Introduction to Metaphysics* we read:

> Anyone for whom the Bible is divine revelation and truth has the answer to the question "Why are there beings rather than nothing" even before it is asked. . . . One who holds to such faith can in a way participate in the asking of our question but he cannot really question without ceasing to be a believer and taking all the consequence of such a step. He will only be able to act "as if." (IM 6–7; GA 40 5)

Later on in the text, Heidegger assails a work entitled *What Is Man?* by the Christian theologian Theodore Haecker, whose recent lecture at Freiburg had been angrily protested by the Nazi students:[14]

> If a man believes the propositions of Catholic dogma, that is his individual concern; we shall not discuss it here. But how can we be expected to take a

> man seriously who writes "What is Man?" on the cover of his book although he does *not* inquire, because he is *un*willing and *un*able to inquire? . . .
>
> Why do I speak of such irrelevancies in connection with the exegesis of Parmenides's dictum? In itself this sort of scribbling is unimportant and insignificant. What is not unimportant is the paralysis of all passion for questioning that has long been with us. (IM 142–3; GA 40 151)

Heidegger now clearly holds that there is an existential (if not a logical) contradiction between real philosophical questioning and religious faith. The believer does not have the passion – or the honesty – to enter the abyss of the questionability of being. In the view that he held at the time, that also makes the Christian faith a counterrevolutionary force from the standpoint of the National Socialist "renewal." The façade of questioning the believer puts up will always have a kind of fraudulent "as if" quality. The dishonest labors of Christian writers should not be mentioned in the same breath as the greatness of Greek thinkers like Parmenides.

Ironically, and in testimony to the power of Heidegger's thought as opposed to the smallness and perversity of the man, Heidegger was to exert enormous influence on Catholic theology precisely during this time. A series of Catholic luminaries heard these lectures during the thirties, including, in addition to Müller, Gustav Siewerth, Johannes Lotz, and above all Karl Rahner, all of whom were German Jesuits. Rahner unfolded the problematic of questioning in the direction of a "transcendental Thomism" first marked off by the Belgian Jesuit Maréchal. He held that questioning, as the radical opening of thinking to being, represented the dynamism or momentum of the mind toward God. He treated the fore-having of being by the understanding as a preunderstanding of God inasmuch as God is the being that is sought in all of our thought and action. In his second major work, *Hearers of the Word,* Rahner appropriated the thematics of speaking and hearing, claiming and being claimed, that Heidegger had begun to enunciate for the first time in the thirties in connection with his readings of the early Greeks. Rahner put Heidegger's reflections to a theological use, which argued that the believer is ontologically disposed to revelation, that there is a kind of ontological structure in Dasein in virtue of which its very being is to be addressed by being itself. That ontological structure, worked out in Heidegger's philosophical writings, articulates the condition of possibility of being claimed by the Word itself that the Father speaks to humankind. (Rahner also made significant use of Heidegger's conception of being-unto-death in a short treatise entitled *The Theology of Death.*)[15]

Once again, the question can be asked whether these young Catholic theologians found Heidegger's thought so amenable to theological application only because that thought had in the first place been significantly inspired by theological resources. Heidegger was giving a reading of the early Greeks that it is impossible to believe was not the result of a transference of the categories of Christianity to early Greek texts. He called in quasi-prophetic terms for an "other beginning" that resembled a kind of *metanoia* (conversion) and the coming of the kingdom, or even of the Second Coming. He viewed the relationship between being and thinking in Parmenides and Heraclitus in kerygmatic terms, arguing that these early Greeks took being to be "addressed" to man, that it laid claim to man, and that the Greeks conceived the being of man in terms of responsiveness and answerability to this claim. Heidegger went on to say that his deeply historical conception of being, which included even an "eschatological" conception of the "history of Being," was fundamentally Greek in inspiration. But it is clear to everyone but Heidegger's most fanatic disciples that he is clearly Hellenizing and secularizing a fundamentally bibilical conception of the history of salvation. He was in the most literal sense building a rival *Heilsgeschichte* to the biblical one that he had discovered in his New Testament studies.

One might object to this interpretation that Heidegger was simply demythologizing the history of salvation and giving it an ontological sense, which is no different from what he was doing in *Being and Time.* The difference, on my view, is that the later "history of Being" is every bit as mythological and just as much in need of demythologizing as the history of salvation it would purport to demythologize.[16]

As Kierkegaard had said a century earlier, the discovery of time and history was a Judeo-Christian one[17] – as was, we may add, the whole thematics of speaking and answering, claiming and being claimed. Heidegger had baldly appropriated the *kairological* – the *kairos,* the appointed time, the "moment" (*Augenblick*) of truth and decision in *Being and Time* (§67a) – and *kerygmatic* conceptions of human existence that he had learned from Christiantity in the first place and that were quite alien to the Greeks. It was these elements in his thought that the young Catholic theologians found so congenial to their own theological work. That is hardly surprising. Like Bultmann and the Protestant existential theologians before them, when they looked into Heidegger's texts, they beheld their own image.

THE LATER WRITINGS

After the war Heidegger largely succeeded in covering up his past involvement with National Socialism. A steady stream of new publications forged the image of the "later" Heidegger, previously known only to the small number of those who were able to follow his lectures during the war years. A whole new wave of Heideggerian thinking swept over Continental philosophy, encouraged especially by the enthusiastic reception Heidegger received from the French, which began with the French existentialist "misunderstanding" and continues today with French postmodernists. The 1947 "letter" to the French (to Jean Beaufret and to the philosophical world) set forth the "humanistic" limits of existentialism and the real demands of the "thought of Being" (BW 206–9). It was clear to everyone that Heidegger's thought had taken still another turn, one that we know today can be dated back to the 1936–8 manuscript entitled *Contributions to Philosophy,* which has only recently been published (GA 65).[18]

This later thinking had become radically antivoluntaristic, anti-Nietzschean. It construed classical Western "metaphysics" from Plato to the present age as the "oblivion" and "withdrawal" of being itself (and not a human error). It construed the metaphysics of the "will to power," whose most extreme expression is the contemporary technologizing of world and man, as the culmination of this history of oblivion. The task of "thinking" was now identified precisely as not willing, first by willing *not* to will and then by not willing at all (DT 59–60; GA 13 38–9). Here "willing" was taken in a general sense to mean not only choosing and willing in the determinate sense, but all conceptual or "representational" thinking, which goes to the very essence of the Western philosophical and scientific tradition. The heroic accents of the mighty "strife" between being and humanity – Heraclitus's *polemos,* which Heidegger liked to translate during the mid-thirties as *Kampf* (IM 61–2; GA 40 66) – disappeared. Instead of willing, Heidegger spoke of "letting be," using at this point the word *Gelassenheit,* one of the oldest and most revered parts of the vocabulary of the Rhineland mystics, in particular Meister Eckhart. Being is not something that human thinking can conceive or "grasp" (*be-greifen, con-capere*) but something that thinking can only be "granted." Thoughts come to us; we do not think them up (PLT 6; GA 13 78). Thinking is a gift or a grace, an event that overtakes us, an address visited upon us. The role of human beings is not, however, one of utter passivity but one of cooperation with and remaining "open" to being's advent. The work that man can do is not to will but to not-will, to prepare a clearing and opening in which being may come. This is not quietism but asceticism, the hard work of a kind of poverty of spirit. A debate began that continues to now about the place of "action" and ethics in Heidegger's thought, a debate that replays disputes in the classical literature on mysticism and ethical action, which itself goes all the way back to the biblical story of Mary and Martha and the medieval disputes about the relative merits of the *vita activa* and the *vita contemplativa.*[19]

Once again a fundamental shift in Heidegger's thinking took place and again with overt religious overtones. The strident antagonist of Christianity during the war years – himself a sometime Protestant and a sometime very ardent Catholic – had taken on a mystical air. With this latest turn Heidegger was, as he himself said, returning to his theological beginning (OWL 10; US 96). He was, we recall, quite interested in medieval mysticism as a youth and had intended to write a book on Meister Eckhart. He also had announced a lecture course on medieval mysticism for 1919, but the preparations for the course were apparently interrupted by the First World War and the course was never given.[20]

Heidegger's postwar relations with both Catholic and Protestant theologians were dramatically reversed. In the denazification trials held immediately after the war, a besieged Heidegger (he eventually had a minor breakdown) turned first for help from his old friend and counselor, the Archbishop of Freiburg Conrad Gröber, who had gained wide respect for holding his ground against the Nazis during the war (something of which Heidegger hardly approved in those years).

This is by no means to say that Heidegger's later thinking had returned to the faith of his youth. The mystical dimension of the later thinking is strictly a structural affair, a matter of a certain proportionality: the relationship of "thinking" to "being" is structurally like the relationship of the soul to God in religious mysticism. Thinking is directed toward being, not God. Being is not God but the event of manifestness, the happening of the truth of being, the coming to pass of the history of the epochal manifestations of being – from the early Greeks to the will to power. Being means very much what we might otherwise call history, but with two important differences: (1) history is understood as a history of truth or manifestness, of the various looks that being takes on over the ages (as *eidos* in Plato, as spirit in Hegel, as will to power in late modernity), as opposed to a political, military, social, or economic history;[21] (2) history is not human history but being's own, unfolding under the "initiative" of being's giving to and withdrawing from thought.

The status of God in Heidegger's later and more religiously, mystically keyed thinking is much debated. Heidegger does talk about God (and the gods) but it is a God who, from a Judeo-Christian point of view, has lost his sovereign lordship over history and become a function of being's history.[22] Thus, the epochal sending of the gods, the age of the Holy, has passed away and we now await a new god, a new and unpredictable sending of the Holy's graciousness, which appears to be a function of being's sending, not of God's will (BW 210). Heidegger at one point identified the lost age of the Holy as the time of the religion of the Greeks, of the Old Testament, and of the preaching of Jesus, indicating a kind of historicism about the various ways that the Holy can manifest itself or take on various historical forms, none of which is absolute (PLT 184; VA 183). Yet Heidegger shows a decided preference in these writings for the world of the early Greeks, for the Greek experience of being as *physis* and *aletheia,* and for an experience of the "gods" as a part of the "Fourfold." The Fourfold – earth and sky, mortals and gods – is a deeply Hölderlinian conception that Heidegger derived from his reading of Hölderlin's poetizing of the Greek world. So the god that emerges in Heidegger's late writing is a profoundly poetic god, a poetic experience of the world as something sacred and deserving of reverence. This god is a much more pagan-poetic god and much less Judeo-Christian, ethicoreligious God. It has virtually nothing to do with the God whom Jesus called *abba* or with the religion of the cross that Heidegger found in Luther. In fact, Heidegger's later writings are more suggestive of a kind of Buddhism, a kind of meditative, silent world reverencing, than of Judaism or Christianity.[23]

Understandably, Christian theologians have shown a remarkable interest in and been much nourished by Heidegger's later writings. These writings are marked by Heidegger's deeply – albeit generically – religious discourse of giving and receiving, grace and graciousness, saving and danger, address and response, poverty and openness, end time and new beginning, mystery and withdrawal and by a new thematics of the truly divine God. A new wave of post-Bultmannian Protestant theologians emerged that moved beyond Bultmann's "existential theology" and adopted a position that reflected Heidegger's own turn beyond the existential analytic. These theologians had a sharpened appreciation of the historicality and linguisticality of Heidegger's "thought of Being" and that is what they brought to bear on their theological work.

The key figure in this post-Bultmannian movement is Heinrich Ott. In his 1959 work entitled *Denken und Sein* (Thinking and being) Ott, a student of Karl Barth, who also has studied extensively with Bultmann, showed in effect that the later Heidegger's rejection of humanism opened up new possibilities for theology. It confirmed Karl Barth's long-standing objections to Bultmann (and to the Heidegger of *Being and Time*) and shows that Barth's theology of the primacy of God is in fact accommodated by the later Heidegger's turn toward being. Theology for Ott arises out of the experience of faith and is not a matter of scientific theological objectification, even as for Heidegger thinking speaks "out of the experience of thought" (PLT 1–14), out of thought's experience of being. Ott went on to construe the history of salvation as a history of disclosure comparable to Heidegger's history of the disclosure of being, and he put Heidegger's conception of language as "call" to use in interpreting biblical language. The sentences of the New Testament about the resurrection, for example, are not to be taken as propositional assertions of matters of fact but as a call to a new mode of being. Ott's work, and the whole impact of the later Heidegger on theological reflection, reached the United States in a volume entitled *The Later Heidegger and Theology*.[24]

In 1959, at a meeting with the old Marburgers, Heidegger led a day-long discussion on the relationship between his later "thinking" and Christian faith, in which he held that if his thought ruled out the God of metaphysics, it was by no means inconsistent with a nonmetaphysical relationship to God (PT 22–31; GA 9 68–79). The upshot of "thinking" for theology is to cease to think of God as *causa sui,* as the causal energy that creates and sustains the cosmos, and to turn instead to the God before whom one can dance or bend one's knee. This he calls the truly "divine God" (ID 72), and it reminds us of Pascal's injuncture to lay aside the God of the philosophers in favor of the God of Abraham and Isaac. This was a very open ended formulation of thinking in relation to religious faith, and it was precisely the path that Ott was pursuing.

This suggestion was also taken up in a forceful and interesting way on the Catholic side by the Freiburg theologian Bernard Welte. Welte argues that Heidegger's conception of the history of being tells the story of a technological darkening of the earth in which the illusion of human mastery overshadows the appearance of God. The "other beginning" of which Heidegger speaks signals a new age of the Holy, an epoch in which God can indeed be God. Welte also wrote sensitively about Meister Eckhart and the notion of *Gelassenheit,* and he produced an excellent essay comparing the later Heidegger, Meister Eckhart, and Thomas Aquinas (whose Dominican Chair at Paris Meister Eckhart had later occupied).[25]

Martin Heidegger died in 1976, in his eighty-sixth year. He was buried in the Catholic churchyard in Messkirch between his mother and his father. At Heidegger's request a Catholic mass was celebrated by Bernard Welte in the church of St. Martin's where Heidegger's father had been sexton, in whose shop in the basement of the church the young Martin had often played as a youngster. Welte, who was also a fellow townsman of Heidegger, delivered the eulogy. Welte said, quite rightly, that Heidegger's thought had shaken this century, that it was a thought that was always seeking, always under way. He related this being "on the way" to the Gospels' notion that he who seeks shall find:

> "He who seeks" – that could well be the title for all of Heidegger's life and thought. "He who finds" – that could be the secret message of his death.[26]

Had Heidegger come full circle, confirming what he said in *On the Way to Language* that his future lay in his theological beginning (OWL 10; US 96)? Was this Catholic end the repetition of his Catholic beginning? Was this the final turn on the path of thought?

NOTES

1 Hugo Ott, *Martin Heidegger: Unterwegs zu seiner Biographie* (Frankfurt: Campus, 1988), pp. 44–104; the Görres citation, p. 64; the grant to study Thomism, 79; passed over for chair, 91–2. For more on Heidegger's early Catholicism, see my *Heidegger and Aquinas: An Essay on Overcoming Metaphysics* (New York: Fordham University Press, 1982), Chap. 1.

2 The habilitation dissertation is found in GA 1. It has not been translated. I have discussed it in some detail in "Phenomenology, Mysticism, and the *Grammatica Speculativa,*" *Journal of the British Society for Phenomenology,* 5 (1974): 101–17. See also Roderick Stewart, "Signification and Radical Subjectivity in Heidegger's 'Habilitationsschrift,' " *Man and World,* 12 (1979): 360–86.

3 This letter can be found in *Heidegger and Aquinas,* p. 60; cf. 56.

4 Karl Löwith, "The Political Implications of Heidegger's Existentialism," *New German Critique,* 45 (1988): 117–34, at 121–2. For a commentary see Theodore Kisiel, "War der frühe Heidegger tatsächlich ein 'christlicher Theologe'? " *Philosophie und Poesie: Otto Pöggeler zum 60. Geburtstag,* ed. Annemarie Gethmann-Siefert (Berlin: Frommann-Holzboog, 1988), pp. 59–75. The letter itself can be found in D. Paperfuss and O. Pöggeler, eds., *Zur philosophischen Aktualität Heideggers,* vol. 2: *Im Gespräch der Zeit* (Frankfurt: Klostermann, 1990).

5 Edward John Van Buren, "The Young Heidegger," Ph.D. dissertation, McMaster University (1988), a revised version of which is forthcoming from Indiana University Press. See Van Buren's "The Young Heidegger: Rumor of a Hidden King (1919–1926)," *Philosophy Today,* 33 (Summer 1989): 99–108. See also Löwith, "Political Implications," as well as Otto Pöggeler, *Heidegger's Path of Thought,* trans. D. Magurshak and S. Barber (New York: Humanities Press, 1988), pp. 24–32, and idem, "Being as Appropriation," *Philosophy Today,* 19 (1975): 152–78, at 156–8.

6 *Selected Writings of Martin Luther (1517–1520),* ed. T. G. Tappert (Philadelphia: Fortress Press, 1967), p. 337.

7 See Rudolph Bultmann, *Kerygma and Myth* (New York: Harper & Row, 1961). On Heidegger and Bultmann, see John Macquarrie, *An Existentialist Theology: A Comparison of Heidegger and Bultmann* (New York: Harper Torchbooks, 1965); Hans-Georg Gadamer, "Martin Heidegger and Marburg Theology," in *Philosophical Hermeneutics,* trans. D. Linge (Berkeley and Los Angeles: University of California Press, 1976), pp 198–212.

8 See, e.g., Paul Tillich, *The Courage to Be* (New Haven, Conn.: Yale University Press, 1952).

9 "Phenomenology and Theology," in Martin Heidegger, *The Piety of Thinking*, trans. J. Hart and J. Maraldo (Bloomington: Indiana University Press, 1976), pp. 3–22.

10 See Alister E. McGrath, *Luther's Theology of the Cross: Martin Luther's Theological Breakthrough* (Oxford: Blackwell Publisher, 1985). See the work of Van Buren cited in note 5.

11 Martin Heidegger, "The Self-Assertion of the German University," trans. K. Harries, *Review of Metaphysics*, 38 (1985): 467–502, p. 480.

12 Jacques Derrida has discussed the nationalism of Heidegger's use of the word "spirit" in *Of Spirit: Heidegger and the Question*, trans. G. Bennington and R. Bowlby (Chicago: University of Chicago Press, 1989), Chap. 5.

13 Ott, *Martin Heidegger*, 259–67.

14 Ibid., pp. 255–9.

15 Rahner said that he had many good professors (*Schulmeister*) but only one teacher (*Lehrer*); see *Martin Heidegger in Gespräch*, ed. R. Wisser (Freiburg: Alber, 1970), pp. 48–9. See Rahner's *Spirit in the World*, trans. William Dych (New York: Herder & Herder, 1968); idem, *Hearers of the Word* (New York: Seabury Press, 1969); idem, *On the Theology of Death* (New York: Seabury Press, 1971). He also discussed *Being and Time* in "The Concept of Existential Philosophy in Heidegger," trans. A. Tallon, *Philosophy Today*, 13 (1969): 126–37. On Heidegger and Rahner, see Thomas Sheehan, *Rahner: The Philosophical Foundations* (Athens: Ohio University Press, 1985). For a discussion of Heidegger and Lotz, Siewerth, and Müller, see my *Heidegger and Aquinas*, Chap. 7.

16 See my "Demythologizing Heidegger: *Aletheia* and the History of Being," *Review of Metaphysics*, 41 (March 1988): 519–46.

17 Søren Kierkegaard, *The Concept of Anxiety*, trans. Reidar Thomte (Princeton, N.J.: Princeton University Press, 1980), pp. 89–90.

18 The only commentator who had access to *Contributions* was Otto Pöggeler. There are then three such turns: 1917–19, from Catholicism to Protestantism; ca. 1928, toward the extreme heroic, Nietzschean voluntarism; 1936–8: beyond voluntarism toward the "thought of Being."

19 John D. Caputo, *The Mystical Element in Heidegger's Thought* (Athens: Ohio University Press, 1978; rpt. New York: Fordham University Press, 1986), pp. 137–9.

20 Käte Oltmanns, a Heidegger student since 1925, published a book on Eckhart in 1935, which had been a dissertation done under Heidegger's direction; see Käte Oltmanns, *Meister Eckhart*, 2d ed. (Frankfurt: Klostermann, 1957). For a full account of these matters see my *Mystical Element*.

21 It is for just this reason that Charles Taylor in an unpublished essay,

quite rightly criticizes Heidegger for a "monomanic" conception of the history of the West.

22 John D. Caputo, "Heidegger's God and the Lord of History," *New Scholasticism,* 57 (1983): 439–64. For a famous exchange on this point, see Hans Jonas, "Heidegger and Theology," *The Phenomenon of Life* (New York: Harper & Row, 1966), pp. 244–9; and William Richardson, "Heidegger and God – and Professor Jonas," *Thought,* 40 (1965): 13–40.

23 There is a vast literature on Heidegger and Eastern religion. The best single volume is *Heidegger and Asian Thought,* ed. Graham Parkes (Honolulu: University of Hawaii Press, 1987). See also my *Mystical Element,* pp. 203–17.

24 Heinrich Ott, *Denken und Sein: Der Weg Martin Heideggers und der Weg der Theologie* (Zollikon: Evangelischer Verlag, 1959); idem, "The Hermeneutic and Personal Structure of Language," in *On Heidegger and Language,* ed. Joseph Kocklemans (Evanston, Ill.: Northwestern University Press, 1972), pp 169–93; idem, *Theology and Preaching,* trans. Harold Knight (Philadelphia: Westminster, 1965). See also J. Robinson and J. Cobb, eds., *The Later Heidegger and Theology* (New York: Harper & Row, 1963).

25 Bernard Welte, "The Question of God in the Thought of Heidegger," *Philosophy Today,* 26 (1982): 85–100; idem, "La Métaphysique de Saint Thomas d'Aquin et la pensée de l'histoire de l'être de Heidegger," *Revue des Sciences Philosophiques et Théologiques,* 50 (1966): 601–14. A good account of the later Heidegger and Catholic theology can be found in Richard Schaeffler, *Frömmigkeit des Denkens: Martin Heidegger und die Katholische Theologie* (Darmstadt: Wissenschaftliche Buchgesellschaft, 1978). See also *Heidegger et la question de dieu,* ed. R. Kearney and Joseph O'Leary (Paris: Grasset, 1980). The best recent work by a Catholic theologian with a distinctly Heideggerian inspiration is Joseph O'Leary, *Questioning Back: The Overcoming of Metaphysics in Christian Tradition* (Minneapolis, Minn.: Winston Press, 1985).

26 "Seeking and Finding: The Speech at Heidegger's Burial," in *Heidegger: The Man and the Thinker,* ed. Thomas Sheehan (Chicago: Precedent, 1981), pp. 73–5. See also Sheehan's useful biographical piece on Heidegger's early years (Chapter 2, this volume).

HUBERT L. DREYFUS

11 Heidegger on the connection between nihilism, art, technology, and politics

Martin Heidegger's major work, *Being and Time,* is usually considered the culminating work in a tradition called existential philosophy. The first person to call himself an existential thinker was Søren Kierkegaard, and his influence is clearly evident in Heidegger's thought. Existential thinking rejects the traditional philosophical view, which goes back to Plato at least, that philosophy must be done from a detached, disinterested point of view. Kierkegaard argues that our primary access to reality is through our involved action. The way things show up for a detached thinker is a partial and distorted version of the way things show up to a committed individual.

Kierkegaard defines the self as a relation that relates itself to itself. That means that who I am depends on the stand I take on being a self. Moreover, how I interpret myself is not a question of what I think but of what I do. I have to take up what is the given or factical part of my self and, by acting on it, define who I am. I understand myself as being a student, a teacher, the lover of a specific person, or the follower of a specific cause. Thus, the self defines itself by taking up its past by means of present actions that make sense in terms of its future. For Kierkegaard, then, the self can be understood as a temporal structure.

Given his emphasis on involvement, Kierkegaard was convinced that philosophical reflection has undermined commitment in the West. In his book *The Present Age,*[1] written in 1846, he gave a prophetic description of how all authority was disappearing, all concrete differences were being leveled, everything was becoming indifferent, giving rise to alternate fits of lethargy and excitement. Such was the victory of critical detachment over involved commitment. His whole work was devoted to the question: How can we get meaning and commitment back into our lives once we have gotten into the passionless, reflective attitude we are now in?

Heidegger calls the basic structure of human being – that each human being's way of being is an issue for it – *Dasein.* In his "existentialist" phase, during the twenties, Heidegger was interested in the ahistorical, cross-cultural structures of everyday involved experience. He worked out an interpretation of three basic ways of being (availableness, or "readiness-to-hand"; occurrence, or "presence-at-hand"; as well as Dasein) and their general structure (temporality) grounded in Dasein's ability to take a stand on its own being. These existential structures, Heidegger demonstrated, provided the conditions of the possibility of all modes of intelligibility. He also investigated the way the conformity to norms necessary for intelligibility opens up the possibility of flight into conformism, which levels down all meaningful distinctions.

But whereas Kierkegaard thought that leveling and lack of commitment had been accentuated to nihilistic proportions by the media, Heidegger in *Being and Time* writes as if leveling has been with humankind as long as tools have, and he sees nothing special in the present age. Around 1930, however, Heidegger began to investigate the understanding of being peculiar to modern Western culture. As he put it, in *Being and Time* "'phenomenology' and all hermeneutical-transcendental questions had not yet been thought in terms of the history of being" (EP 15). His early interest in the existential structure of the self had shifted to another Kierkegaardian concern – the lack of meaning and seriousness in the present age.

NIHILISM

In his lectures on Nietzsche in 1936 Heidegger quotes with approval Nietzsche's Kierkegaardian condemnation of the present age:

> Around the year 1882 [Nietzsche] says regarding his times, "Our age is an agitated one, and precisely for that reason, not an age of passion; it heats itself up continuously, because it feels that it is not warm – basically it is freezing. . . . In our time it is merely by means of an echo that events acquire their 'greatness' – the echo of the newspaper." (N I 47)

Heidegger agrees with Nietzsche that "there is no longer any goal in and through which all the forces of the historical existence of peoples can cohere and in the direction of which they can develop" (N I 157).

Nihilism is Nietzsche's name for this loss of meaning or direction. Both Kierkegaard and Nietzsche agree that if nihilism were complete, there would be no significant private or public issues. Nothing would have authority for us, would make a claim on us, would demand a commitment from us. In a non-nihilistic age there is something at stake; there are questions that all can agree are important, even if they violently disagree as to what the answers to these questions are. But in our age, everything is in the process of becoming equal. There is less and less difference among political parties, among religious communities, among social causes, among cultural practices – everything is on a par, all meaningful differences are being leveled.

Kierkegaard thought that the answer to nihilism was to make one's own individual absolute commitment. If you can commit yourself unconditionally – in love, for instance – then that becomes a focus for your whole sense of reality. Things stand out or recede into insignificance on the basis of that ultimate concern. You do not discover a significance that is already there. There is no basis for this commitment in the cosmos. Indeed, such a commitment is exactly the opposite of belief in an objective truth. You are called by some concrete concern – either a person or a cause – and when you define yourself by your dedication to that concern, your world acquires seriousness and significance.

The only way to have a meaningful life in the present age, then, is to let your involvement become definitive of reality for you, and what is definitive of reality for you is not something that is in any way provisional – although it certainly is vulnerable. That is why, once a society like ours becomes rational and reflective, such total commitments begin to look like a kind of dangerous dependency. The committed individual is identified as a workaholic or a woman who loves too much. This suggests that to be recognized and appreciated, individual commitment requires a shared understanding of what is worth pursuing. But as our culture comes more and more to celebrate critical detachment, self-sufficiency, and rational choice, there are fewer and fewer shared commitments. So commitment itself begins to look like craziness.

Heidegger comes to see the recent undermining of commitment as due not so much to a failure of the individual as to a lack of anything in the modern world that could solicit commitment from us and sustain us in it. The things that once evoked commitment – gods, heroes, the God-man, the acts of great statesmen, the words of great thinkers – have lost their authority. As a result, individuals feel isolated and alienated. They feel that their lives have no meaning because the public world contains no guidelines.

When everything that is material and social has become completely flat and drab, people retreat into their private experiences as the only remaining place to find significance. Heidegger sees this move to private experience as characteristic of the modern age. Art, religion, sex, education – all become varieties of experience. When all our concerns have been reduced to the common denominator of "experience," we will have reached the last stage of nihilism. One then sees "the plunge into frenzy and the disintegration into sheer feeling as redemptive. The 'lived experience' as such becomes decisive" (N I 86). That is, when there are no shared examples of greatness that focus public concerns and elicit social commitment, people become spectators of fads and public lives, just for the excitement. When there are no religious practices that call forth sacrifice, terror, and awe, people consume everything from drugs to meditation practices to give themselves some kind of peak experience. The peak experience takes the place of what was once a relation to something outside the self that defined the real and was therefore holy. As Heidegger puts it, "The loss of the gods is so far from excluding religiosity that rather only through that loss is the relation to the gods changed into mere 'religious experience' " (QCT 117; GA 5 76). Of course, private experience seems attractive only once the shared public world has lost its meaning and reality. Then one thinks (as if somehow it had always been the case and one had just discovered it) that, after all, it is the experience that matters. But sooner or later one finds that although private experience may have "energy" or "spontaneity" or "zing," it provides nothing in terms of which one can give consistency, meaning, and seriousness to one's life.[2] In Nietzsche's words "God is dead, and we have killed him."

Nietzsche, however, unlike Heidegger, finds the death of God liberating. He foresees a new stage of our culture that he calls "positive nihilism," in which each "free spirit" will posit, that is, create, his or her own values. Heidegger is not so sanguine. He sets out to investigate the history of the understanding of being in the West in order to understand how we did the terrible deed of killing God. One way he tells the story of the loss of meaning is by tracing the history of the very idea of values taken over uncritically by Nietzsche. Heidegger argues that to think of nihilism as a state in which we have forgotten or betrayed our values is part of the problem. Thinking that we once had values but that we do not have values now, and that we should regain our values or choose new ones, is just another symptom of the trouble. Heidegger claims that thinking about our deepest concerns as values *is* nihilism.

The essence of a value is that it is something that is completely independent of us. It is perceived, and then chosen or rejected. Values have an interesting history. Plato starts with the claim that they are what shows us what is good for us independent of our interests and desires. The idea of the good shines on us and draws us to it. Only with the Enlightenment do we arrive at the notion that values are objective – passive objects standing over against us – and we must *choose* our values. These values have no claim on us until we *decide* which ones we want to adopt. Once we get the idea that there is a plurality of values and that we choose which ones will have a claim on us, we are ripe for the modern idea, first found in the works of Nietzsche, especially in *Thus Spoke Zarathustra,* that we *posit* our values – that is, that valuing is something we do and value is the result of doing it. But once we see that we posit values, we also see that we can equally "unposit" them. They thus lose all authority for us. So, far from giving meaning to our lives, thinking of what is important to us in terms of values shows us that our lives have no intrinsic meaning. As long as we think in terms of value positing rather than being gripped by shared concerns, we will not find anything that elicits our commitment. As Heidegger says, "No one dies for mere values" (QCT 142; GA 5 102).

Once we see how thinking of the problem of nihilism in terms of lacking values perpetuates rather than combats the problem, we are ready to diagnose and seek a cure for our condition. According to Heidegger our trouble begins with Socrates' and Plato's claim that true moral knowledge, like scientific knowledge, must be explicit and disinterested. Heidegger questions both the possibility and the desirability of making our everyday understanding totally explicit. He introduces the idea that the shared everyday skills, concerns, and practices into which we are socialized provide the conditions necessary for people to make sense of the world and of their lives. All intelligibility presupposes something that cannot be fully articulated – a kind of knowing-how rather than a knowing-that. At the deepest level such knowing is embodied in our social skills rather than in our concepts, beliefs, and values. Heidegger argues that our cultural practices can direct our activities and make our lives meaningful only insofar as they are and stay unarticulated, that is, as long as they stay the soil out of which we live. If there is to be seriousness, it must draw on these unarticulated background practices. As Heidegger puts it in a later work, "The Origin of the Work of Art," "Every decision . . . bases itself on something not mastered, something concealed, confusing; else it would never be a decision" (PLT 55; GA 5 43). Critical reflection is necessary in some situations where our ordinary way of coping is insufficient, but such reflection cannot and should not play the central role it has played in the philosophical tradition. What is most important and meaningful in our lives is not and should not be accessible to critical reflection.

The cultural know-how that embodies our concerns is certainly not conscious, but neither does it appear to be unconscious. To get a sense of what this know-how is like, let us take a very simple case. People in various cultures stand different distances from an intimate, a friend, a stranger. Furthermore, the distances vary when these people are chatting, doing business, or engaging in courtship. Each culture, including our own, embodies an incredibly subtle shared pattern of social distancing. Yet no one explicitly taught this pattern to each of us. Our parents could not possibly have consciously instructed us in it since they do not know the pattern any more than we do. We do not even know we have such know-how until we go to another culture and find, for example, that in North Africa strangers seem to be oppressively close while in Scandinavia friends seem to stand too far away. This makes us uneasy, and we cannot help backing away or moving closer. It is through such responses that we got this know-how in the first place. As small children, when we began to interact with other people, we sometimes got the distances wrong. This made our parents and friends uneasy, and they either backed away or moved closer so that we gradually picked up the whole pattern. It was never made explicit. As a skill or *savoir faire* it is not something like a set of rules that could be made explicit.[3] Yet it embodies rudiments of an understanding of what it is to be a human being – hints of how important body contact is, and the relative importance of intimacy and independence.

Now practices like how far to stand from people are not all that are passed on by training and imitation. Our everyday know-how involves an understanding of what it is to be a person, a thing, a natural object, a plant, an animal, and so on. Our understanding of animals these days, for example, is in part embodied in our skill in buying pieces of them, taking off their plastic wrapping, and cooking them in microwave ovens. In general, we deal with things as resources to be used and then disposed of when no longer needed. A Styrofoam cup is a perfect example. When we want a hot or cold drink it does its job, and when we are through with it we throw it away. This understanding of an object is very different from what we can suppose to be the Japanese understanding of a delicate, painted teacup, which does not do as good a job of maintaining temperature and which has to be washed and protected, but which is preserved from generation to generation for its beauty and its social meaning. Or, to take another example, an old earthenware bowl, admired for its simplicity and its ability to evoke memories of ancient crafts, such as is used in a Japanese tea ceremony, embodies a unique understanding of things. It is hard to picture a tea ceremony around a Styrofoam cup.

Note that an aspect of the Japanese understanding of what it is to be human (passive, contented, gentle, social, etc.) fits with an understanding of what it is to be a thing (evocative of simpler times, pure, natural, simple, beautiful, traditional, etc.). It would make no sense for us, who are active, independent, and aggressive – constantly striving to cultivate and satisfy our desires – to relate to things the way the Japanese do; or for the Japanese (before their understanding of being was interfered with by ours) to invent and prefer Styrofoam teacups. In the same vein *we* tend to think of politics as the negotiation of individual desires, while the Japanese seek consensus. In sum, the practices containing an understanding of what it is to be a human being, those containing an interpretation of what it is to be a thing, and those defining society fit together. Social practices thus transmit not only an implicit understanding of what it is to be a human being, an animal, or an object, but, finally, an understanding of what it is for anything to be at all.

The shared practices into which we are socialized, moreover, provide a background understanding of what matters and what it makes sense to do, on the basis of which we can direct our actions. This understanding of being creates what Heidegger calls a *clearing* in which things and people can show up as mattering and meaningful for us. We do not produce the clearing. It produces us as the kind of human beings we are. Heidegger describes the clearing as follows:

> Beyond what is, not away from it but before it, there is still something else that happens. In the midst of beings as a whole an open place occurs. There is a clearing, a lighting. . . . This open center is . . . not surrounded by what is; rather, the lighting center itself encircles all that is. . . . Only this clearing grants and guarantees to human beings a passage to those entities that we ourselves are not, and access to the being that we ourselves are. (PLT 53; GA 5 39–40)

As we have noted, our cultural practices and the understanding of being they embody allow us to direct our activities and make sense of our lives only insofar as they are and stay unarticulated, that is, stay the atmosphere in which we live. These background practices are the concealed and unmastered that Heidegger tells us give seriousness to our decisions. Mattering lies not in what we choose, but in "that on the basis of which" we choose. The more our know-how is formulated and objectified as knowing-that, the more it is called up for critical questioning, the more it loses its grip on us. This is part of what Kierkegaard saw in his attack on modern critical reflection, and Heidegger in his attack on value thinking.

But this cannot be the whole story about nihilism. For there must always be a clearing – background practices containing an understanding of being – in order for things and people to be intelligible at all. And these will never be fully accessible to reflection. So there must be a deeper problem that Heidegger is pointing to. There must be something wrong with our current background practices that leads us to ignore them, causing us to seek meaning by choosing objective values and finally by positing personal values for ourselves. So Heidegger raises new questions: What is it to have a nihilistic clearing, how did we come to have one, and what can we do about it? Only when we have answered these, he holds, can we ask: Are there still left in our practices some remnants of shared meaningful concerns? If so, where are such remnants to be found? The strongest argument that some meaningful practices must have survived is that without some remnant of them we would not be distressed by nihilism. But before we can answer these questions, we must ask a prior one: How do practices give shared meaning to the lives of those who practice them?

THE WORK OF ART (WORLD AND EARTH)

For everyday practices to give meaning to our lives and to unite us in a community, they must be focused and held up to the practitioners. Clifford Geertz and Charles Taylor have discussed this important phenomenon. Geertz, for example, describes the role of the cockfight in Balinese society:

> It provides a metasocial commentary upon the whole matter of assorting human beings into fixed hierarchical ranks and then organizing the major part of collective existence around that assortment. Its function, if you want to call it that, is interpretive: it is a Balinese reading of Balinese experience, a story they tell themselves about themselves.[4]

Heidegger calls that interpretive function "truth setting itself to work," and anything that performs this function he calls a work of art. As his illustration of an artwork, Heidegger takes the Greek temple. The temple held up to the Greeks what was important, and so let there be meaningful differences such as victory and disgrace, disaster and blessing:

> It is the templework that first fits together and at the same time gathers around itself the unity of those paths and relations in which birth and death, disaster and blessing, victory and disgrace, endurance and decline acquire the shape of destiny for human beings. The all-governing expanse of this open relational context is the world of this historical people. (PLT 42; GA 5 29)

The Greeks whose practices were manifested and focused by the temple lived in a moral space of gods, heroes, and slaves, a moral space that gave direction and meaning to their lives. In the same way, the medieval cathedral made it possible to be a sinner or a saint and showed Christians the dimensions of salvation and damnation.[5] In either case, one knew where one stood and what one had to do. Heidegger would say that the understanding of what it is to be changes each time a culture gets a new artwork. Then different sorts of human beings and things show up. For the Greeks, what showed up were heroes and slaves and marvelous things; for the Christians, saints and sinners, rewards and temptations. There could not have been saints in ancient Greece. At best there could only have been weak people who let everybody walk all over them. Likewise, there could not have been Greek-style heroes in the Middle Ages. Such people would have been regarded as pagans – prideful sinners who disrupted society by denying their dependence on God.

Generalizing the idea of a work of art, Heidegger holds that "there must always be some being in the open [the clearing], something that is, in which the openness takes its stand and attains its constancy" (PLT 61; GA 5 48). Let us call such special things cultural paradigms. Talking of a paradigm focusing the practices seems almost inevitable. Compare Geertz: "It is this kind of bringing of assorted experiences of everyday life to focus that the cockfight . . . accomplishes, and so creates what, better than typical or universal, could be called a paradigmatic human event."[6]

A cultural paradigm collects the scattered practices of a group, unifies them into coherent possibilities for action, and holds them up to the people who can then act and relate to each other in terms of that exemplar. Works of art, when performing this function, are not merely representations or symbols, but actually produce a shared understanding. As Geertz put it: "Quartets, still lifes, and cockfights are not merely reflections of a pre-existing sensibility analogically represented; they are positive agents in the creation and maintenance of . . . sensibility."[7]

Charles Taylor makes the same point when he distinguishes *shared meanings,* which he calls intersubjective meanings, from *common meanings* "whose being shared is a collective act":

> It is part of the meaning of a common aspiration, belief, celebration, etc. that it be not just shared but part of the common reference world. Or to put it another way, its being shared is a collective act. . . .
>
> Common meanings are the basis of community. Inter-subjective meanings give a people a common language to talk about social reality and a common understanding of certain norms, but only with common meaning does this common reference world contain significant common actions, celebrations, and feelings. These are objects in the world that everybody shares. This is what makes community.[8]

In *The Structure of Scientific Revolutions,* Thomas Kuhn shows that scientists engaged in what he calls normal science operate in terms of such an exemplar or paradigm – an outstanding example of a good piece of work. The paradigm for modern science was Newton's *Principia.* All agreed that Newton had seen exemplary problems, given exemplary solutions, and produced exemplary justifications for his claims. Thus, for more than two centuries natural scientists knew that, insofar as their work resembled Newton's, they were doing good science.

The Newtonian paradigm was later replaced by the Einsteinian paradigm. Such a paradigm shift constitutes a scientific revolution. After such a revolution scientists see and do things differently. As Kuhn puts it, they work in a different world. They also believe and value different things, but this is less important. Kuhn is quite Heideggerian in holding that it is the paradigm that guides the scientists' practices and that the paradigm cannot be explained as a set of beliefs or values and so cannot be stated as a criterion or rule. As Kuhn notes: "That scientists do not usually ask or debate what makes a particular problem or solution legitimate tempts us to suppose that, at least intuitively, they know the answer. But it may only indicate that neither the question nor the answer is felt to be relevant to their research. Paradigms may be prior to, more binding, and more complete than any set of rules for research that could be unequivocally abstracted from them."[9] Kuhn further points out that "the concrete scientific achievement, as a locus of professional commitment, [is] prior to the various concepts, laws, theories, and points of view that may be abstracted from it." He adds that the paradigm cannot be rationalized: "The shared paradigm [is] a fundamental unit for the student of scientific development, a unit that cannot be fully reduced to logically atomic components which might function in its stead."[10] That the paradigm cannot be rationalized but only imitated is crucial to the paradigm's authority. It requires that the paradigm work by way of the background practices, in terms of which the scientists have a world. It also makes it possible for the scientists to agree without having to spell out their agreement.

At the time of a scientific revolution, however, Kuhn tells us that the paradigm itself becomes the focus of conflicting interpretations, each interpretation trying to rationalize and justify itself. Similarly,

Heidegger holds that a working artwork is so important to a community that people must try to make the work clear and coherent and to make everyone follow it in all aspects of their lives. But the artwork, like the scientific paradigm, exhibits a resistance to such rationalization. Any paradigm could be paraphrased and rationalized only if the concrete thing that serves as an exemplar symbolized or represented an underlying system of beliefs or values abstractable from the particular exemplar. But the whole point of needing an exemplar is that there is no such system, there are only shared practices. Heidegger calls the way the artwork solicits the culture to make the artwork explicit, coherent, and encompassing the *world* aspect of the work. He calls the way the artwork and its associated practices resist such totalization the *earth.*

Heidegger points out that world and earth are both necessary for an artwork to work. The temple must clarify and unify the practices – it must be "all-governing" – but being a concrete thing it resists rationalization. Such resistance is manifest in the very materiality of the artwork. Such materiality is not accidental. The temple requires the stone out of which it is made in order to do its job of showing man's place in the natural world, so that a temple made out of steel would not work. Likewise a tragedy requires the sound of poetry to create a shared mood and thus open up a shared world. Since it is made out of rock or sounds, the artwork shows that what is at stake cannot be captured in a system of beliefs and values. All those aspects of a cultural paradigm and the practices it organizes that resist being rationalized and totalized are included in Heidegger's notion of the earth. Earth is not passive matter, but comes into being precisely as what resists the attempt to abstract and generalize the point of the paradigm. And since no interpretation can ever completely capture what the work means, the work of art sets up a struggle between earth and world. This struggle is a necessary aspect of the way meaning inheres in human practices. It is a fruitful struggle in that the conflict of interpretations it sets up generates a culture's history.

Next Heidegger generalizes the notion of a cultural paradigm from a work of art to any being in the clearing that can refocus and so renew cultural practices:

> One essential way in which truth establishes itself in the beings it has opened up is truth setting itself into work. Another way in which truth

occurs is the act that founds a political state. Still another way in which truth comes to shine forth is the nearness of that which is not simply a being, but the being that is most of all. Still another way in which truth grounds itself is the essential sacrifice. Still another way in which truth becomes is the thinker's questioning, which, as the thinking of being, names being in its question-worthiness. (PLT 61–2; GA 5 49)

One can recognize an allusion to the covenant of God with the Jews and the Crucifixion. There is also a reference to the political act that founds a state. For example, the U.S. Constitution, like a work of art, has necessarily become the focus of attempts to make it explicit and consistent and to make it apply to all situations, and, of course, it is fecund just insofar as it can never be interpreted once and for all. The founding of a state could also refer to the act of a charismatic leader such as Hitler. This possibility will concern us later in this essay.

TECHNOLOGY

Cultural paradigms do not, however, always establish meaningful differences. There can be nihilistic paradigms. Such paradigms, instead of showing forth the earth on the basis of which our actions can matter to us, conceal the struggle between earth and world and celebrate our ability to get everything clear and under control. Thus, the current paradigms that hold up to us what our culture is dedicated to and is good at are examples of flexibility and efficiency, not for the sake of some further end, but just for the sake of flexibility and efficiency themselves. We admire the way computers are getting faster and faster and at the same time cheaper and cheaper, without knowing how we will use the incredibly flexible computing power they give us. Likewise, fast-food chains that give us cheap and instant service at any time of day or night stand out as technological triumphs of efficiency and adaptability. Heidegger's example is the power station of the Rhine:

The hydroelectic plant is set into the current of the Rhine. It sets the Rhine to supplying its hydraulic pressure, which then sets the turbines turning. This turning sets those machines in motion whose thrust sets going the electric current for which the long-distance power station and its network of cables are set up to dispatch electricity. . . . the energy concealed in nature is unlocked, what is unlocked is transformed, what is transformed is stored

> up, what is stored up is, in turn, distributed, and what is distributed is switched about ever anew. In the context of the interlocking processes pertaining to the orderly disposition of electrical energy, even the Rhine itself appears as something at our command. (QCT 16; VA 23)

All such paradigms deny that an understanding of being necessarily involves receptivity and mystery, and so they deny Heideggerian seriousness.

Again, a comparison with Kuhn can help us see Heidegger's point. According to Kuhn, a science becomes normal when the practitioners in a certain area all agree that a particular piece of work identifies the important problems in a field and demonstrates how certain of these problems can be successfully solved. Thus, a modern scientific paradigm sets up normal science as an activity of puzzle solving. It is the job of normal science to eliminate anomalies by showing how they fit into the total theory the paradigm sketches out in advance. In a similar way, the technological paradigm embodies and furthers our technological understanding of being according to which what does not fit in with our current paradigm – that is, that which is not yet at our disposal to use efficiently (e.g., the wilderness, friendship, and stars) – will finally be brought under our control, and turned into a resource. The contrast with the Greek temple is obvious. The temple is not a totalizing paradigm that makes everything clear and promises to bring it under control. The temple not only shows people what they stand for, but shows them that there is an earthy aspect of things that withdraws and that can never be articulated and dominated.

In the face of the totalizing tendency of the technological artwork, the earth's resistance to total ordering shows up as a source of what Kuhn calls anomalies. What cannot be ordered is treated as recalcitrant human beings who are deviant and must be reformed or as natural forces that have yet to be understood and mastered. All cultures inculcate norms of human behavior and find some order in nature, but ours is the only culture that tries to make the social and natural order total by transforming or destroying all exceptions. Kierkegaard already saw that the individual or exceptional was menaced by leveling. Heidegger sees that all our marginal practices are in danger of being taken over and normalized. It looks to us, of course, as if this is for our own good.

Heidegger, however, sees in these marginal practices the only possibility of resistance to technology. Greek practices such as friendship and the cultivation of the erotic are not efficient. When friendship becomes efficient networking, it is no longer the mutual trust and respect the Greeks admired. Likewise, the mystical merging power of the erotic is lost when we turn to private sexual experience. Similarly, Greek respect for the irrational in the form of music and Dionysian frenzy do not fit into an efficiently ordered technological world. Indeed, such "pagan" practices did not even fit into the Christian understanding of being and were marginalized in the name of disinterested agapē love and peace. These Christian practices in turn were seen as trivial or dangerous given the Enlightenment's emphasis on individual maturity, self-control, and autonomy.

In order to combat modern nihilism Heidegger attempts to point out to us the peculiar and dangerous aspects of our technological understanding of being. But Heidegger does not oppose technology. In "The Question Concerning Technology" he hopes to reveal the essence of technology in a way that "in no way confines us to a stultified compulsion to push on blindly with technology or, what comes to the same thing, to rebel helplessly against it." Indeed, he promises that "when we once open ourselves expressly to the *essence* of technology, we find ourselves unexpectedly taken into a freeing claim" (QCT 25–6; VA 33).

We will need to explain opening, essence, and freeing before we can understand Heidegger here. But already Heidegger's project should alert us to the fact that he is not announcing one more reactionary rebellion against technology, although many take him to be doing just that. Nor is he doing what progressive thinkers would like to do: proposing a way to get technology under control so that it can serve our rationally chosen ends. The difficulty in locating just where Heidegger stands on technology is no accident. Heidegger has not always been clear about what distinguishes his approach from a romantic reaction to the domination of nature, and when he does finally arrive at a clear formulation of his own original view, it is so strange that in order to understand it we are tempted to translate it into conventional platitudes. Thus, Heidegger's ontological concerns are mistakenly assimilated to ecologically minded worries about the devastation of nature.

Those who want to make Heidegger intelligible in terms of current antitechnological banalities can find support in his texts. During the war he attacked consumerism: "The circularity of consumption for the sake of consumption is the sole procedure which distinctively characterizes the history of a world which has become an unworld" (EP 107; VA 96). And as late as 1955, in an address to the Schwarzwald peasants, he points out: "The world now appears as an object open to the attacks of calculative thought. . . . Nature becomes a gigantic gasoline station, an energy source for modern technology and industry" (DT 50; G 19–20). In this address he also laments the appearance of television antennas on the peasants' dwellings and gives his own version of an attack on the leveling power of the media:

> Hourly and daily they are chained to radio and television. . . . All that with which modern techniques of communication stimulate, assail, and drive man – all that is already much closer to man today than his fields around his farmstead, closer than the sky over the earth, closer than the change from night to day, closer than the conventions and customs of his village, than the tradition of his native world. (DT 50; G 17)

Such quotes make it seem Heidegger is a Luddite who would like to return from consumerism, the exploitation of the earth, and mass media to the world of the pre-Socratic Greeks or the good old Schwarzwald peasants.

Nevertheless, although Heidegger does not deny that technology presents us with serious problems, as his thinking develops he comes to the surprising and provocative conclusion that focusing on loss and destruction is still technological: "All attempts to reckon existing reality . . . in terms of decline and loss, in terms of fate, catastrophe, and destruction, are merely technological behavior" (QCT 48; TK 45–46). Seeing our situation as posing a problem that must be solved by appropriate action is technological too: "The instrumental conception of technology conditions every attempt to bring man into the right relation to technology. . . . The will to mastery becomes all the more urgent the more technology threatens to slip from human control" (QCT 5; VA 14–15). Heidegger is clear this approach will not work. "No single man, no group of men," he tells us, "no commission of prominent statesmen, scientists, and technicians, no conference of leaders of commerce and industry, can brake or direct the progress of history in the atomic age" (DT 52; G 22).

Heidegger's view is both darker and more hopeful. He thinks there is a more dangerous situation facing modern man than the technological destruction of nature and civilization, yet this is a situation about which something *can* be done – at least indirectly. Heidegger's concern is the human *distress* caused by the *technological understanding of being,* rather than the *destruction* caused by *specific technologies.* Consequently, he distinguishes the current problems caused by technology – ecological destruction, nuclear danger, consumerism, and so on – from the devastation that would result should technology solve all our problems:

> What threatens man in his very nature is . . . that man, by the peaceful release, transformation, storage, and channeling of the energies of physical nature, could render the human condition . . . tolerable for everybody and happy in all respects. (PLT 116; GA 294)

The "greatest danger" is that

> the approaching tide of technological revolution in the atomic age could so captivate, bewitch, dazzle, and beguile man that calculative thinking may someday come to be accepted and practiced *as the only way* of thinking. (DT 56; G 27)

The danger, then, is not the destruction of nature or culture but certain totalizing kinds of practices – a leveling of our understanding of being. This threat is not a *problem* for which we must find a *solution,* but an *ontological condition* that requires a *transformation of our understanding of being.*

What, then, is the essence of technology – that is, the technological understanding of being, or the technological clearing – and how does opening ourselves to it give us a free relation to technological devices? To begin with, when he asks about the essence of technology we must understand that Heidegger is not seeking a definition. His question cannot be answered by defining our concept of technology. Technology is as old as civilization. Heidegger notes that it can be correctly defined as "a means and a human activity." But if we ask about the *essence* of technology (the technological understanding of being) we find that modern technology is "something completely different and . . . new" (QCT 5; VA 15). It even goes beyond using Styrofoam cups to satisfy our desires. The essence of modern technology, Heidegger tells us, is to seek to order everything so as to achieve more and more flexibility and efficiency: "Expediting is always itself directed from the beginning . . . towards driving on to the maximum yield at the minimum expense" (QCT 15, VA 23). That is, our only goal is optimal ordering, *for its own sake:* "Everywhere everything is ordered to stand by, to be immediately at hand, indeed to stand there just so that it may be on call for a further ordering. Whatever is ordered about in this way has its own standing. We call it standing-reserve" (QCT 17; VA 24). No more do we have subjects turning nature into an object of exploitation: "The subject–object relation thus reaches, for the first time, its pure 'relational,' i.e., ordering, character in which both the subject and the object are sucked up as standing-reserves" (QCT 173; VA 61). Heidegger concludes: "Whatever stands by in the sense of standing-reserve no longer stands over against us as object" (QCT 17; VA 24). He tells us that a modern airliner, understood in its technological essence, is not a tool we use; it is not an object at all, but rather a flexible and efficient cog in the transportation system. Likewise, we are not subjects who use the transportation system, but rather we are used by it to fill the planes.

In this technological perspective, ultimate goals like serving God, society, our fellows, or even ourselves no longer make sense to us. Human beings, on this view, become a resource to be used – but more important, to be enhanced – like any other: "Man, who no longer conceals his character of being the most important raw material, is also drawn into this process" (EP 104; VA 90). In the film *2001*, the robot HAL, when asked if he is happy on the mission, says: "I'm using all my capacities to the maximum. What more could a rational entity want?" This is a brilliant expression of what anyone would say who is in touch with our current understanding of being. We pursue the development of our potential simply for the sake of further growth. We have no specific goals. The human potential movement perfectly expresses this technological understanding of being, as does the attempt to better organize the future use of our natural resources. We thus become part of a system that no one directs but that moves toward the total mobilization and enhancement of all beings, even us. This is why Heidegger thinks the perfectly ordered society dedicated to the welfare of all is not the solution to our problems but the culmination of the technological understanding of being.

Heidegger, however, sees that "it would be foolish to attack technology blindly. It would be shortsighted to condemn it as the work of the devil. We depend on technical devices; they even challenge us to ever greater advances" (DT 53, G 24). Instead, Heidegger suggests that there is a way we can keep our technological devices and yet remain true to ourselves as receivers of clearings: "We can affirm the unavoidable use of technical devices, and also deny them the right to dominate us, and so to warp, confuse, and lay waste our nature" (DT 54; G 24–25). To understand how this might be possible, we need an illustration of Heidegger's important distinction between technology and the technological understanding of being. Again we can turn to Japan. In contemporary Japan traditional, nontechnological practices still exist alongside the most advanced high-tech production and consumption. The television set and the household gods share the same shelf – the Styrofoam cup coexists with the porcelain teacup. We thus see that the Japanese, at least, can enjoy technology without taking over the technological understanding of being.

For us to be able to make a similar dissociation, Heidegger holds, we must rethink the history of being in the West. Then we will see that although a technological understanding of being is our destiny, it is not our fate. That is, although our understanding of things and ourselves as resources to be ordered, enhanced, and used efficiently has been building up since Plato, we are not stuck with that understanding. Although the technological understanding of being governs the way things have to show up for us, we can be open to a transformation of our current cultural clearing.

Only those who think of Heidegger as opposing technology will be surprised at his next point. Once we see that technology is our latest understanding of being, we will be grateful for it. Our technological clearing is the cause of our distress, yet if it were not given to us to encounter things and ourselves as resources, nothing would show up *as* anything at all, and no possibilities for action would make sense. And once we realize – in our practices, of course, not just as a matter of reflection – that we *receive* our technological understanding of being, we have stepped out of the technological understanding of being, for we then see that what is most important in our lives is not subject to efficient enhancement – indeed, the drive to control everything is precisely what we do not control. This transformation in our sense of reality – this overcoming of thinking in terms of values and calculation – is precisely what Heideggerian thinking seeks to bring about. Heidegger seeks to make us see that our practices are needed as the place where an understanding of being can establish itself, so we can overcome our restricted modern clearing by acknowledging our essential receptivity to understandings of being:

> Modern man must first and above all find his way back into the full breadth of the space proper to his essence. That essential space of man's essential being receives the dimension that unites it to something beyond itself . . . that is the way in which the safekeeping of being itself is given to belong to the essence of man as the one who is needed and used by being. (QCT 39; TK 39)

This transformation in our understanding of being, unlike the slow process of cleaning up the environment, which is, of course, also necessary, would take place in a sudden gestalt switch: "The turning of the danger comes to pass suddenly. In this turning, the clearing belonging to the essence of being suddenly clears itself and lights up" (QCT 44; TK 43). The danger – namely that we have a leveled and concealed understanding of being – when grasped *as* the danger, becomes that which saves us. "The selfsame danger is, when it is *as* the danger, the saving power" (QCT 39; TK 39).

This remarkable claim gives rise to two opposed ways of understanding Heidegger's response to technology. Both interpretations agree that once one recognizes the technological understanding of being for what it is – a historical understanding – one gains a free relation to it. We neither push forward technological efficiency as our sole goal nor always resist it. If we are free of the technological imperative we can, in each case, discuss the pros and cons. As Heidegger puts it:

> We let technical devices enter our daily life, and at the same time leave them outside, . . . as things which are nothing absolute but remain dependent upon something higher. I would call this comportment toward technology which expresses "yes" and at the same time "no," by an old word, *releasement towards things.*[11] (DT 54; G 25)

One natural way of understanding this proposal holds that once we get in the right relation to technology, namely, recognize it as a clearing, it is revealed as just as good as any other clearing.[12] Efficiency – getting the most out of ourselves and everything else, "being all you can be" – is fine, as long as we see that efficiency for its own sake is not the *only* end for man, dictated by reality itself, but is just our current understanding. Heidegger seems to support this acceptance of the technological understanding of being as a way of living with technological nihilism when he says:

> That which shows itself and at the same time withdraws [i.e., our understanding of being] is the essential trait of what we call the mystery. I call the comportment which enables us to keep open to the meaning hidden in technology, *openness to the mystery.*
>
> Releasement toward things and openness to the mystery belong together. They grant us the possibility of dwelling in the world in a totally different way. They promise us a new ground and foundation upon which we can stand and endure in the world of technology without being imperiled by it. (DT 55; G 26)

Nevertheless, such acceptance of the mystery of the gift of an understanding of being cannot be Heidegger's whole story about how to overcome technological nihilism, for he immediately adds, "Releasement toward things and openness to the mystery give us a vision of a new rootedness which *someday* might even be fit to recapture the old and now rapidly disappearing rootedness in a changed form" (DT 55; G26). When we then look back at the preceding remark, we realize releasement gives only a "possibility" and a "promise" of "dwelling in the world in a totally different way"; it does not enable us to do so. Mere openness to technology leaves out much that Heidegger finds essential to overcoming nihilism: embeddedness in nature, or localness, and new shared meaningful differences. Releasement, while giving us a free relation to technology and protecting our nature from being distorted and distressed, cannot by itself give us any of these.

For Heidegger, then, there are two issues. One is clear: "The issue is the saving of man's essential nature. Therefore, the issue is keeping meditative thinking alive" (DT 56; G 27). This is a matter of preserving our sense of ourselves as *receivers* of understandings of being. But that is not enough: "If releasement toward things and openness to the mystery awaken within us, then we should arrive at a path that will lead to a new ground and foundation" (DT 56; G 28). Releasement, it turns out, is only a stage, a kind of holding pattern we can enter into while we are awaiting a new understanding of being that would give a shared content to our openness – what Heidegger calls a new rootedness. That is why each time Heidegger talks of releasement and the saving power of understanding technology as a gift, he then goes on to talk of the divine: "Only when man, in the disclosing coming-to-pass of the insight by which he himself is beheld . . . renounces human self-will . . . may [he], as the mortal, look out toward the divine" (QCT 47; TK 45). This is reflected in Heidegger's famous remark in his last interview: "Only a god can save us now."[13] But what does this mean?

To begin with, Heidegger holds that we must learn to appreciate marginal practices – what Heidegger calls the saving power of insignificant things – practices such as friendship, backpacking in the wilderness, and drinking the local wine with friends. All these practices remain marginal precisely because they resist efficiency. These practices can, of course, also be engaged in for the sake of health and greater efficiency. Indeed, the greatest danger is that even the marginal practices will be mobilized as resources. That is why we must protect these endangered practices. But just protecting nontechnical practices, even if we could succeed, would still not give us what we need, for these practices by themselves do not add up to a shared moral space of serious, meaningful options.

Of course, one cannot legislate a new understanding of being. But some of our practices could come together in a new cultural paradigm that held up to us a new way of doing things – a new paradigm that opened a world in which these practices and others were central, whereas efficient ordering was marginal. An object or event that would ground such a gestalt switch in our understanding of reality Heidegger calls a new god, and this is why he holds that only a god can save us.

What can we do to get what is still nontechnological in our practices in focus in a non-nihilistic paradigm? Once one sees the problem, one also sees that there is not much one can do about it. A new sense of reality is not something that can be made the goal of a crash program like the moon flight – another paradigm of modern technological power. A new paradigm would have to take up practices that are now on the margin of our culture and make them central, while deemphasizing practices now central to our cultural self-understanding. It would come as a surprise to the very people who participated in it, and if it worked it would become an exemplar of a new understanding of what matters and how to act. There would, of course, be powerful forces tending to take it over and mobilize it for our technological order, and if it failed it would necessarily be measured by our current understanding and so look ridiculous.

A hint of what such a new god might look like is offered by the music of the sixties. Bob Dylan, the Beatles, and other rock groups became for many the articulators of a new understanding of what really mattered. This new understanding almost coalesced into a cultural paradigm in the Woodstock music festival of 1969, where people actually lived for a few days in an understanding of being in which mainline contemporary concerns with order, sobriety, willful activity, and flexible, efficient control were made marginal and subservient to certain pagan practices, such as enjoyment of nature, dancing, and Dionysian ecstasy, along with neglected Christian concerns with peace, tolerance, and nonexclusive love of one's neighbor. Technology was not smashed or denigrated; rather, all the power of electronic communications was put at the service of the music, which focused the above concerns.

If enough people had recognized in Woodstock what they most cared about and recognized that many others shared this recognition, a new understanding of being might have been focused and stabilized. Of course, in retrospect it seems to us who are still in the grip of the technological understanding of being that the concerns of the Woodstock generation were not organized and total enough to sustain a culture. Still we are left with a hint of how a new cultural paradigm would work. This helps us understand that we must foster human receptivity and preserve the endangered species of pretechnological practices that remain in our culture, in the hope that one day they will be pulled together in a new paradigm, rich enough and resistant enough to give a new meaningful direction to our lives.

POLITICS

Heidegger's political engagement was predicated upon his interpretation of the situation in the West as technological nihilism, and of National Socialism as a new paradigm that could give our culture a new understanding of being. But the very same interpretation of the history of being that led Heidegger to support Hitler in 1933 provided the ground for his decisive break with National Socialism somewhere between 1935 and 1938. Between 1933 and 1935 Heidegger seems to have thought that following Hitler as a charismatic leader was the only way to save and focus local and traditional practices in the face of global technology as exemplified by the Soviet Union and the United States. In 1935 he says in a lecture course:

> From a metaphysical point of view, Russia and America are the same; the same dreary technological frenzy. . . . Situated in the center, our nation incurs the severest pressure. . . . If the great decision regarding Europe is not to bring annihilation, that decision must be made in terms of new spiritual energies unfolding historically from out of the center. (IM 31–2)

But by 1938, in "The Age of the World Picture," Heidegger sees technology as the problem of the *West,* and National Socialism, rather than the USSR and the United States, as the most dangerous form of what he calls, in Nazi terms, "total mobilization" (QCT 137; GA 5 97). Heidegger also criticized the belief in a *Führer* as the organizer of a total order as an example of faith in technological ordering.

> Beings have entered the way of erring in which the vacuum expands which requires a single order and guarantee of beings. Herein the necessity of "leadership," that is, the planning calculation . . . of the whole of beings, is required. (EP 105; VA 93)

After 1938, then, Heidegger thought of National Socialism not as the answer to technology and nihilism, but as its most extreme expression.

This gets us to one final question: To what extent was Heidegger's support of National Socialism a personal mistake compounded of conservative prejudices, personal ambition, and political naïveté, and to what extent was his engagement dictated by his philosophy? We have seen that Heidegger, like Charles Taylor and Robert Bellah more recently, holds that we can get over nihilism only by finding some set of shared meaningful concerns that can give our culture a new focus. Moreover, Heidegger sees no hope of overcoming nihilism if one accepts the faith in rational autonomy central to the Enlightenment. In fact, he sees the pursuit of autonomy as the cause of our dangerous contemporary condition. He counters the Enlightenment vision with a nontheological version of the Christian message that man cannot be saved by autonomy, maturity, equality, and dignity alone. Heidegger holds that only some shared meaningful concerns that grip us can give our culture a focus and enable us to resist acquiescence to a state that has no higher goal than to provide material welfare for all. This conviction underlies his dangerous claim that only a god – a charismatic figure, or some other culturally renewing event – can save us from nihilism.

To many, however, the idea of *a* god that will give us a unified but open community – one set of concerns that everyone shares if only as a focus of disagreement – sounds either unrealistic or dangerous. Heidegger would probably agree that its open democratic version looks increasingly unobtainable and that we have certainly seen that its closed totalitarian form can be very dangerous. But Heidegger holds that given our historical essence – the kind of beings we became in fifth century B.C. Greece when our culture gained its identity – such a community is necessary to us or else we will remain in nihilism. It is, he thinks, our only hope or, as he puts it, our destiny.

It follows for Heidegger that our deepest needs will be satisfied and our distress overcome only when our culture gets a new center. Our current condition is defined by the absence of a god:

> The era is defined by the god's failure to arrive, by the "default of god." But the default of god . . . does not deny that the Christian relationship with God lives on in individuals and in the churches; still less does it assess this relationship negatively. The default of god means that no god any longer gathers men and things unto himself, visibly and unequivocally, and by such gathering disposes of the world's history and man's sojourn in it. (PLT 91; GA 5 269)

Heidegger's *personal* mistake comes from having thought that Hitler or National Socialism was such a god. Yet Heidegger had already, in "The Origin of the Work of Art," developed criteria that could serve to determine whether a charismatic leader or movement deserved our allegiance. He stresses there that a true work of art must set up a struggle between earth and world. That is, a true work of art does not make everything explicit and systematic. It generates and supports resistance to total mobilization. Yet Heidegger chose to support a totalitarian leader who denied the truth of all conflicting views and was dedicated to bringing everything under control. Heidegger no doubt interpreted Hitler as setting up some sort of appropriate struggle. Unfortunately, there is no interpretation-free criterion for testing a new god, and such mistakes are always possible. Heidegger's *philosophy,* then, is dangerous because it seeks to convince us that only a god – a charismatic figure or some other culturally renewing event – can save us from falling into contented nihilism. It exposes us to the risk of committing ourselves to some demonic event or movement that promises renewal.

What sort of claim is Heidegger making when he tells us that Enlightenment welfare and dignity are not enough and that only a god can save us? How can one justify or criticize Heidegger when he reads our current condition as the absence of a god and our current distress as a sign of the greatest danger? – for only such a reading of the present age justifies risking commitment to some new cultural paradigm.

The first answer we might try to give is that Heidegger is offering a genealogical interpretation. He will focus on and augment our distress and show that it can be accounted for by telling a story of the progressive narrowing, leveling, and totalizing of the West's understanding of being. Such an interpretation has to make sense of more details of our history and present situation than any rival interpretation, and ultimately it must convince us by the illumination it casts on our current condition, especially on our sense of ontological distress or emptiness, if we have one.

But how could we know that our distress was due to the absence of a god rather than personal and social problems? One answer might be that we will just have to wait for the perfected welfare state and then see how we feel. If defenders of the Enlightenment are right, distress will be eliminated, whereas Heidegger, one might suppose, would expect that, as technology succeeds, the suffering will grow. But Heidegger does not make this claim. Heidegger admits and fears the possibility that everyone might simply become healthy and happy, and forget completely that they are receivers of understandings of being. All Heidegger can say is that such a forgetting of our forgetting of being would be the darkest night of nihilism. In such an "unworld," Heidegger could no longer expect to be understood. Only now, and only as long as he can awaken our distress and our sense of our receptivity to a mysterious source of meaning that creates and sustains us, can he hope that we will be able to see the force of his interpretation.

Such thinking is far from the "infallible knowledge"[14] many think

Heidegger claims. Indeed, Heidegger goes out of his way to point out that he can claim no infallibility for his interpretation. He writes to a student that "this thinking can never show credentials such as mathematical knowledge can. But it is just as little a matter of arbitrariness" (PLT 184; VA 183). He then goes on to repeat his reading of the West as having lost touch with the saving practices excluded by totalizing technology – practices that are nonetheless all around us:

The default of god and the divinities is absence. But absence is not nothing; rather it is precisely the presence, which must first be appropriated, of the hidden fullness and wealth of what has been and what, thus gathered, is presencing, of the divine in the world of the Greeks, in prophetic Judaism, in the preaching of Jesus. (PLT 184; VA 183)

And he immediately adds that he can claim no special authority: "I can provide no credentials for what I have said . . . that would permit a convenient check in each case whether what I say agrees with 'reality' " (PLT 186; VA 184). This is an appropriate warning since Heidegger's own political mistake reminds us that any guidelines must always be interpreted, and that if one opts for the charismatic one cannot avoid the risk. Thus, Heidegger's letter to the student fittingly concludes: "Any path always risks going astray. . . . Stay on the path, in genuine need, and learn the craft of thinking, unswerving, yet erring" (PLT 186; VA 185).

NOTES

1 Søren Kierkegaard, *The Present Age,* trans. Alexander Dru (New York: Harper & Row, 1962).

2 For evidence that Heidegger is right on this point, see Robert N. Bellah, Richard Madsen, William M. Sullivan, Ann Swidler, and Steven M. Tipton, *Habits of the Heart* (Berkeley and Los Angeles: University of California Press, 1985).

3 See H. L. Dreyfus and Stuart Dreyfus, *Mind over Machine* (New York: Free Press, 1982).

4 Clifford Geertz, *The Interpretation of Cultures* (New York: Harper Colophon Books, 1973), p. 448.

5 For a description of the dimensions and directions of moral space see Charles Taylor, *Sources of the Self* (Cambridge, Mass.: Harvard University Press, 1989).

6 Geertz, *Interpretation,* p. 450.

7 Ibid., p. 451.

8 Charles Taylor, "Interpretation and the Sciences of Man," *Philosophy and the Human Sciences* (Cambridge: Cambridge University Press, 1985), p. 39.

9 Thomas Kuhn, *The Structure of Scientific Revolutions,* 2d ed. (Chicago: University of Chicago Press, 1970), p. 46.

10 Ibid., p. 11.

11 Why Heidegger speaks of "things" here is a long and interesting story. In his essay "The Thing" in *Poetry, Language, Thought,* Heidegger spells out the way that certain things like a jug of wine can focus practices and collect people around them. Such things function like local, temporary works of art in giving meaning to human activities, but they do not focus a whole culture and so do not become the locus of a struggle between earth and world. Rather, they produce a moment of stillness and harmony. Albert Borgmann interprets and develops this idea in his account of "focal practices" (see A. Borgmann, *Technology and the Character of Contemporary Life* [Chicago: University of Chicago Press, 1984]). For an illuminating discussion of the importance for Heidegger of the thing, see also Charles Taylor's "Heidegger, Language and Ecology," in *Heidegger: A Critical Reader,* ed. H. Dreyfus and H. Hall (Oxford: Blackwell Publisher, 1992), pp. 247–69.

12 See Richard Rorty, "Heidegger, Contingency and Pragmatism," in *Heidegger: A Critical Reader,* ed. Dreyfus and Hall, pp. 209–30.

13 "Only a God Can Save Us," *Der Spiegel,* May 31, 1976.

14 Jürgen Habermas, "Work and Weltanschauung: The Heidegger Controversy from a German Perspective," *Critical Inquiry,* 15 (Winter 1989): 431–56, p. 456, rpt. in *Heidegger: A Critical Reader,* ed. Dreyfus and Hall, pp. 186–208.

CHARLES TAYLOR

12 Engaged agency and background in Heidegger

I

Heidegger's importance lies partly in the fact that he is perhaps the leading figure among that small list of twentieth-century philosophers who have helped us emerge, painfully and with difficulty, from the grip of modern rationalism. Others on the short list would include Wittgenstein and Merleau-Ponty. But one might claim some preeminence for Heidegger, in that he got there first. In the case of Merleau-Ponty, the breakthrough plainly built on Heidegger's work.

The emergence these philosophers helped us toward has, alas, been only partial and is still very contested; indeed, it is always menaced with being rolled back – hence the continuing relevance of their works, some of which appeared more than half a century ago.

In this essay, I shall discuss Heidegger, though with a side-glance at the others from time to time. I shall try to formulate the way in which his thinking takes us outside the traditional epistemology, using the notions of engaged agency and background.

My use of the term "rationalism" at the beginning of this essay could be contested, even by people basically sympathetic to the current of thought I am trying to articulate. There are a number of ways of formulating the outlook, more a set of semiarticulate assumptions, that Heidegger helped "deconstruct." It has a number of features, and we can argue which are most fundamental. In speaking of "rationalism" I am supposing that a certain conception of reason played a determining role. My view is, in short, that the dominant conception of the thinking agent that Heidegger had to overcome was shaped by a kind of ontologizing of rational procedure. That is, what were seen as the proper procedures of rational thought were read into the very constitution of the mind and made part of its very structure.

The result was a picture of the human thinking agent as disengaged, as occupying a sort of protovariant of the "view from nowhere," to use Nagel's suggestive phrase.[1] Heidegger had to struggle against this picture to recover an understanding of the agent as engaged, as embedded in a culture, a form of life, a "world" of involvements, ultimately to understand the agent as embodied.[2]

The issue of engaged agency merits some discussion because it is still difficult and controversial. What does "engagement" mean here? It is to say something like: the world of the agent is shaped by his or her form of life, or history, or bodily existence. But what does it mean to have one's "world shaped" by something? This is a relation subtly different from the ordinary causal link it is sometimes confused with.

Let us take a particular aspect of engagement, namely, being embodied; that is, let us focus on the way our world is shaped by our being bodily agents of the kind that we are. This is something different from the way some of our functions as agents are determined by physical causes. For instance, as a perceiving agent, I cannot now see the wall behind me. This can be explained by certain causal relations in physical terms: the light refracted off the surface of the wall behind me cannot reach my retina. The behavior of light and my physical constitution are so disposed as to make this impossible. In this sense, my embodiment undoubtedly shapes my perception, and hence in a sense my "world."

But this relation is rather different from the following example. As I sit here and take in the scene before me, this has a complex structure. It is oriented vertically, some things are "up," others are "down"; and in depth, some are "near," others "far." Some objects "lie to hand," others are "out of reach"; some constitute "unsurmountable obstacles" to movement, others are "easily displaced." My present position does not give me "good purchase" on the scene; for that I would have to shift farther to the left. And so on.

Here is a "world shaped" by embodiment in the sense that the way of experiencing or "living" the world is essentially that of an agent with this kind of body. It is an agent who acts to maintain equilibrium upright, who can deal with things close up immediately and has to move to get to things farther away, who can grasp certain kinds of things easily and others not, can remove certain obstacles and others not, can move to make a scene more perspicuous, and so on. To say that this world is essentially that of this agent is to say that the terms in which we describe this experience – for instance, those in quotes in the preceding paragraph – make sense only against the background of this kind of embodiment. To understand what it is to "lie to hand" one has to understand what it is to be an agent with the particular bodily capacities that humans have. Some creature from another planet might be unable to grasp this as a projectible term. Of course, the creature might work out some descriptions that were roughly extensionally equivalent. But to project this term the way we do, one has to understand what it is to be human.

Thus, there are two quite different kinds of relationship that might be expressed by saying that our experience is shaped by our bodily constitution. In the first – the case of the wall behind me – we note some consequences of this constitution for our experience, however characterized. In the second, we point out how the nature of this experience is formed by this constitution, and how the terms in which this experience is described are thus given their sense only in relation to this form of embodiment. The first kind of relation is asserted in an ordinary statement of contingent causality. The second concerns, by contrast, the conditions of intelligibility of certain terms. It is this second relation that I invoke in speaking of our "world being shaped" by body, culture, form of life. The ways in which our world is so shaped define the contours of what I am calling engaged agency – what Heidegger sometimes referred to as the "finitude" of the knowing agent.[3]

Now the other half of my claim is that the dominant rationalist view has screened out this engagement, has given us a model of ourselves as disengaged thinkers. In speaking of the "dominant" view I am thinking not only of the theories that have been preeminent in modern philosophy, but also of an outlook that has to some extent colonized the common sense of our civilization. This offers us the picture of an agent who in perceiving the world takes in "bits" of information from his or her surroundings and then "processes" them in some fashion, in order to emerge with the "picture" of the world he or she has; who then acts on the basis of this picture to fulfill his or her goals, through a "calculus" of means and ends.

The popularity of this view is part of what makes computer

models of the mind so plausible to lay people in our day. These models fit neatly into already established categories. The "information-processing" construal builds on a long-supported earlier conception, whereby atomic "ideas" were combined in the mind and made the basis of a calculation underlying action. Classical Cartesian and empiricist epistemologies provided earlier variants of this conception, which combine an atomism of input with a computational picture of mental function. These two together dictate a third feature: "factual" information is distinguished from its "value," that is, its relevance for our purposes. This separation is dictated by atomism, since the merely "factual" features can be distinguished from their having some role to play in our goals. But it is also encouraged by another underlying motivation, to be discussed later. In any case, the composite traditional conception has this third feature, which we might call "neutrality" whereby the original input of information is shorn of its evaluative relevance, is merely the registering of "fact."

Now in some respects this view has roots in the common sense of (in any case) our civilization, going back before the modern era. But in other important respects, this conception was shaped and entrenched in modern times. And one of the factors it was shaped by was modern reason – or so I want to suggest in my perhaps tendentious term "rationalism."

There are two facets of modern reason relevant here. The first is that the modern conception, starting with Descartes, focuses on procedure. Reason is not that faculty in us that connects us to an order of things in the universe, which itself can be called rational. Rather, reason is that faculty whereby we think properly. In its theoretical employment, reason serves to build a picture of the world. Rationality requires that we scrutinize this building closely and not let our view of things just form itself distractedly, or self-indulgently, or following the prejudices of our day. Rationality involves a careful scrutiny by thinking of its own processes. This determines the reflexive turn of modern rationalism. Careful construction of our picture of things requires that we identify and follow a trustworthy procedure. Modern thinkers differ on what this is, and there is a crucial and hotly contested difference in the seventeenth century between, for instance, that defined by the clear and distinct perception of Descartes and that organized around the rules of believable evidence of Locke.

But both views call for reflexive self-policing in the name of a canonical procedure.

More to the point, both procedures require that we break down our too hastily acquired beliefs into their components and scrutinize their composition to see if they are properly to be trusted. They both require that we treat candidate beliefs in this sense atomistically. Now a "method" of this sort is, in certain domains, an uncontestable advance over earlier ways of proceeding. The fateful step was not so much its formulation, but rather what I earlier called its ontologizing, that is, the reading of the ideal method into the very constitution of the mind. It was one thing to call on us to break down our beliefs into their possibly separable components, another to think that the primitive information that enters the mind must do so in atomic bits. The "simple ideas" of Locke are a classical example of such a reification of procedure, pouring it, as it were, in theoretical concrete and building it into the constitution of the mind itself.

But this reification has been immensely influential, conferring on the resulting model of the mind all the prestige and unchallengeable force that the procedures of reason have acquired in our civilization. The more we learn to treat things rationalistically, the more we are inclined to accept the corresponding view of how we "really" operate. The atomist-computational view owes part of its powerful hold on common sense to this.

"Simple ideas" result from reifying the procedure of challenging too hasty interpretations and inferences in order to get back to the basic data. But there was another important feature of correct, scientific thought as conceived in the seventeenth-century revolution that has also strongly influenced our ontology of the subject. This is the feature that Nagel calls "objectivity." Our thinking is objective when it escapes the distortions and parochial perspectives of our kind of subjectivity and grasps the world as it is. Seventeenth-century thinkers were impressed with the way our embodied experience and our ordinary way of being in the world (to use contemporary language) could mislead us. Descartes pointed out how the way we take our everyday experience leads us to attribute, say, the color to the object or to situate the pain in the tooth. These localizations were fine for Aristotelian theory, but the new mechanism showed that they were illusory. Only "primary" properties were really "in" the objects; "secondary" properties, like color, were effects produced in the mind by concatenations of primary properties in things. Seeing things as really colored was one of those distorting effects of our peculiar constitution as substantial union of soul and body. What comes to be called "objectivity" requires an escape from this.

Again, because of our situation in the world, we tend to "see" the sun "rising" and "setting," we "feel" directly that objects stop when they are no longer being pushed, and the like. One of the recurrent themes of seventeenth-century scientific discovery was the gap it showed between the real underlying constitution of things and the way things appeared to common sense. Sometimes the common appearance "regestalted" under the impact of the discovery: before Galileo, people "saw" that cannonballs shot straight forward and then dropped to the ground. Later, it was "obvious" that their trajectory was curved. But in very many cases, we still cannot help seeing things in the old way. The development of science since then has only entrenched this sense of strangeness, of the distance between underlying truth and our ordinary ways of seeing. An experience of everyday space that remains Euclidean coexists with our settled convictions about the curvature of space.

All this has nourished the aspiration to objectivity as Nagel defines it:

> The attempt is made to view the world not from a place within it, or from the vantage point of a special kind of life or awareness, but from nowhere in particular and no form of life in particular at all. The object is to discount for the features of our pre-reflective outlook that make things appear as they do, and thereby to reach an understanding of things as they really are.[4]

There is nothing wrong with this aspiration as it stands – except perhaps the hyperbolic form in which it is stated here. If we stated it slightly more modestly, as the goal of disengaging from those features of our prereflective outlook that we come to discover are distortive of reality, then it is not only unexceptionable but an indispensable condition of pursuing, say, modern physics. The fateful move was, once again, the ontologizing of this disengaged perspective, reading it into the depth constitution of the mind itself, and relegating the distortions to the periphery, either as a result of error, inattention, mere lapse or as a feature only of the brute preprocessed input, not touching the procedures of processing themselves.

Thus, the authors of the *Port Royal Logic* describe it as a culpable weakness in us that we tend to attribute color, heat, and the like to the things we experience.[5] They and the other foundational thinkers of seventeenth-century epistemology could agree that the input to our minds was extremely limited and lacunary, but the constitution of the mind as a thinking agency was unaffected by these limitations, which offered no real excuse for, even if they helped to explain the prevalence of, the distortions we typically fall prey to. The disengaged perspective, which might better have been conceived as a rare and regional achievement of a knowing agent whose normal stance was engaged, was read into the very nature of mind. This was the major motivation I alluded to earlier underpinning the third major feature in the modern "commonsense" view of the mind, the "neutrality" of the original input.

This ontologizing of the disengaged perspective took two major forms. One was dualism, as with Descartes. Disengagement can be seen as getting free of the perspective of embodied experience. It is this perspective that is responsible for our attributing the color to the object; it is this that makes us give disproportionate importance to the senses and imagination in our account of knowing. That the thinking activity of the mind is really in its essential character free from these distorting media shows that the mind is essentially nonbodily – so argues Descartes in the celebrated passage about the piece of wax that closes the second *Meditation.*

But what looks like a totally antithetical ontology could do just as well, that of monistic mechanism: thinking is an event realized in a body, mechanistically understood. This idea is given its modern form in Hobbes and thus has just as long a pedigree as the Cartesian alternative. Mechanism can do as well as dualism to underpin the disengaged perspective, because the underlying belief was that we need to attain this perspective in order to do justice to a mechanistic universe. This assumption is common ground to Descartes and his empiricist or mechanist critics. But to the extent that we understand our thinking mechanistically, we have to understand it outside of any context of engagement. The very relationship to something that defines a "world shaping," and hence identifies a form of agency as engaged, cannot be stated in a mechanistic perspective. The other relationship, that of the causal dependency of experience on some physical conditions, can of course figure in such an account. It is indeed of the essence of this kind of explanation. But nothing can be said about the conditions of intelligibility. That is why mechanists constantly misunderstand descriptions of experience as engaged as statements of causal dependency and are puzzled when they are described as denying such engagement. But, in fact, their denial is of the most effective sort, that of leaving a rival thesis no ontological room for coherent formulation.

To the extent that we explain thinking mechanistically, as with the present wave of computer-based theories of mind, what it means to say that the agent finds the input intelligible can be described only in terms of the operations it can put this input through. The unintelligible is what cannot be processed. But these operations are themselves mechanistically explained. So any statement of something like "conditions of intelligibility" for some input would have to take the form of some statement about how the mechanism is hard-wired or contingently programmed, that is, about the causal relations of the input to the series of steps it can trigger off. The "world-shaping" relation as defined earlier cannot be stated.[6]

Both dualism and mechanism are thus ontologies of disengagement. With the decline over the centuries in the credibility of the former, the latter has gained ground. But what has helped underpin the credibility of both, or rather of the view that sees these as the only two viable alternatives, is the power of the disengaged model of the mind, which draws on the prestige of the procedures of disengagement, channeling its authority, as it were, into a picture of the mind and its constitution that has the three features already mentioned. What I have called the ontologizing move brings about this (dubiously legitimate) transfer. The disengaged picture of mind then adds strength to mechanism; and since mechanistic explanations themselves have great prestige because of their association with the spectacular successes of natural science, support can also flow the other way as well. A picture of mind and an underlying theory of its explanation are thus locked into a posture of mutual support, and this complex has sunk deep into the common sense of our age. When one runs into trouble, the other comes to its support. If the picture can be made to seem implausible on the phenomenological level (and this is not hard to do), one can be reassured by the reflection that it all has to be explained mechanistically on a more basic level anyway and at that level that picture *must* be right. Reciprocally, the force of otherwise powerful arguments against mechanism is neutralized by the thought that in some sense we "know" that thinking is all information processing anyway, so surely some computer-based explanation must hold in the last analysis.

When I say that this rationalist model has entered common sense, I mean partly that the first reaction of most people when asked to theorize about thinking takes the form of this model, but also that it benefits from the onus of argument. That is, it stands as the default position. Powerful philosophical arguments have to be marshaled to convince people to think differently about these matters, to shake them out of what seems obvious. But in the absence of such a challenge the model itself seems to need no defense.

II

My claim here is that Heidegger is one of the principal sources of such powerful arguments that have helped to pry us loose from rationalism. In part, this was accomplished by our being made to appreciate the role of the background in one sense of this widely used term.

The sense I am pointing to here is that which arises inevitably in connection with any view of engaged agency. Engaged agency, as I described it earlier, is that agency whose experience is made intelligible only by being placed in the context of the kind of agency it is. Thus, our embodiment makes our experience of space as oriented up–down understandable. In this relation, the first term – the form of agency (e.g., embodiment) – stands to the second – our experience – as a context conferring intelligibility. When we find a certain experience intelligible, what we are attending to, explicitly and expressly, is this experience. The context stands as the unexplicited horizon within which – or to vary the image, as the vantage point from out of which – this experience can be understood. To use Michael Polanyi's language, it is subsidiary to the focal object of awareness; it is what we are "attending from" as we attend to the experience.[7]

Now this is the sense in which I use the term "background." It is that of which I am not simply unaware (as I am unaware of what is now happening on the other side of the moon), because it makes intelligible what I am uncontestably aware of; but at the same time I cannot be said to be explicitly or focally aware of it, because that status is already occupied by what it is making intelligible. Another way of stating the first condition – that I am not simply unaware of it – is to say that the background is what I am capable of articulating, that is, what I can bring out of the condition of merely implicit, unsaid contextual facilitator, and can make articulate in other words. In this activity of articulating, I trade on my familiarity with this background. What I bring out to articulacy is what I "always knew," as we might say, or what I had a "sense" of, even if I didn't "know" it. We are at a loss exactly what to say here, where we are trying to do justice to our not having been simply unaware.

But if the background is brought to articulacy, does it not then lose the second feature, that of not being the focal, explicit object? But this seemingly plausible inference is based on a misunderstanding.

Earlier I mentioned how the relation of "world shaping," which holds between a kind of agency and a certain form of experience, is easily confused with a psychophysical causal relation. But here we see that it can also be confused with another kind of relation, one between sentences, propositions, or thoughts. Someone's argument, for instance, can be "made more intelligible" by providing additional premises if it has initially been stated too elliptically. My enthymeme may not be fully plausible to you, but becomes so when I spell out the premises. There is a relationship of rendering intelligible that holds between speech acts – I explain to you what I was "on about" when I spoke earlier – which is based ultimately on logical relations between the sentences they put in play.

Now the "world-shaping" relation is neither of these. It is not a psychophysical link holding between states of affairs or events; nor is it a relationship of making intelligible holding between sentences. One of the great obstacles to winning recognition for this relation in our philosophical world is just that these two familiar forms of connection are thought to exhaust the space of possibilities. More specifically, it is often just taken for granted that if a relationship involves conferring intelligibility, it must hold between sentences or at least *representations* of some sort. The reasons behind my muddled and lacunary thoughts in the earlier example are further *thoughts*.

But the way in which my form of embodiment makes, for example, "lying to hand" or "too unwieldy" intelligible descriptions of some object is utterly different. The first term is not a representation or made up of representations. It is a really existent agent in the world. But, one might object, this is surely not the whole story. If my being humanly embodied makes "lying to hand" intelligible to me, this is because I have some "sense" of this embodied agency. This was the word I quite naturally had recourse to a few paragraphs back. That is perfectly true. Being this kind of agent means one has an implicit understanding, what Heidegger at one point calls a "pre-understanding" of what it is to act, to get around in the world, the way we do.

But this is not a matter of representations. The rationalist epistemology induces us to jump to this conclusion because it construes all our understanding as made up of representational bits in the way I described earlier. But this is not at all what preunderstanding is like. "Knowing our way about" is not a capacity that can be analyzed into a set of images on one side and a reality portrayed on the other. An analysis of this kind is certainly foreign to our lived experience, as Merleau-Ponty has shown.[8] To know one's way about is to be really moving around, handling things, dealing with things, with understanding. What is described in the last two words is not an extra layer of representations mirroring the effective actions; it conveys rather the way we inhabit these actions, differentiating them from certain autonomic processes in the body – digestion, for instance – or from what we may do in certain moments of blind distraction. An artificial-intelligence theory of bodily action may reconstruct an explanation in which inner representational states and computations on them play a role in enabling us to get about, but this has nothing to do with the way we live this capacity.

This background sense of reality is nonrepresentational, because it is something we possess in – that is inseparable from – our actual dealings with things. This is the point that is sometimes made by saying that it is a kind of "knowing how" rather than a "knowing that." The latter kind of knowledge is understood as consisting in having correct representations. We cannot do justice to our ordinary ability to get around if we construe it on the model of mind over against a world that it mirrors.

And it is also something that permits of what I called "articulation." I can become focally aware of where I am placing my feet; or I can say that I was taking your word in one way rather than another. This is neither a matter of fixing or saying expressly what was already formulated; nor is it one of totally fresh discovery. I am drawing on my sense of things to make these formulations or to rise to this explicit awareness. Articulation is a quite different process, for it calls on rather different skills and disciplines, even on quite different qualities of character, than describing independent realities. Think of the difference between articulating how you feel about someone and describing a scene involving that person. Of course, one may contaminate the other, but that is considered a vice. The tasks are distinct.

Our sense of things can be more or less articulate. But now we can see why the supposition that it could be totally articulate is misconceived in its very nature. I said that an engaged form of agency is one whose world is shaped by its mode of being. This mode of being provides that context in which the experience of this agent is intelligible, that is, has the sense it makes to the agent, as well as being understandable to an observer. World shaping is a matter of sense making. But the form can only determine the "sense" things make for the agent, because the agent has some "sense" of this form. The word in quotes in this sentence figures in two, closely related uses. "Up" and "down" have meaning for me because of my sense of what it is to be a creature embodied as I am. Engaged agents are creatures with a background sense of things.

But why can't it all be articulated? Because it isn't a matter of representations, but of a real context conferring sense. As a real context conferring sense, our form of life is also the essential background to any articulation being meaningful. The short answer to why complete articulacy is a chimera is that any articulation itself needs the background to succeed. Each fresh articulation draws its intelligibility in turn from a background sense, abstracted from which it would fail of meaning. Each new articulation helps to redefine us, and hence can open up new avenues of potential further articulation. The process is by its very nature uncompletable, since there is no limit on the facets or aspects of our form of life that one can try to describe or of standpoints from which one might attempt to describe it.

The supposition of complete articulacy arises out of the Procrustean outlook of modern rationalism. Our understanding is supposedly made up of a finite number of not yet expressly foregrounded representations that are in some sense already there. Beyond this it is all hard wiring. What this completely misses is the irreducible content–context structure of engaged agency.

One of the crucial distortions of the traditional rationalist epistemology was just that it had no place for this content–context structure. Ideas, the reified contents of the mind, were taken as bits of information. The background understanding in which they made sense either had to be ignored altogether or had to be treated like other bits of information. This leads to almost comical consequences at times, as in Hume's complaint that he can find no idea corresponding to the self. The same disability affects the contemporary heirs of this outlook who propound computer models of thinking.

The paradoxical status of the background can then be appreciated. It can be explicited, because we aren't completely unaware of it. But the expliciting itself supposes a background. The very fashion in which we operate as engaged agents within such a background makes the prospect of total explicitation incoherent. The background cannot in this sense be thought of quantitatively at all.

One of the features that distinguishes a view of human agency as engaged from the disengaged picture is that the former has some place for this kind of background. On the disengaged view, and in particular the mechanist theory that often underpins it, there is not, of course, an explicit rejection of this notion, but the entire issue to which it provides some answer does not arise. Intelligibility is assumed from the start and does not need a context to provide it. It is understood that the bits of input information are taken as such from the beginning and that the operations that follow amount to processing of that information. In the case of computer-based theories of the mind, this reading of input and process is built in to the very definition of what occurs as the realization of a program. Its being describable as such is a sufficient condition of its counting as such.[9]

Thus, it is not surprising that all the philosophies that have challenged the disengaged picture have had some place for a notion of the background. I already referred to Heidegger's notion of preunderstanding, or a prethematized understanding of our world. Wittgenstein makes use of a similar notion – for example, when he shows what has to be supposed as already understood when we try to define something ostensively or name something.

III

But the background does not just figure in these philosophies as a doctrine. It also plays a crucial role in their argumentative strategy. They overturn the disengaged picture through an articulation of the background that it too has to suppose. In doing this, they can be seen as answering a potential challenge that a defender of the disengaged view might throw back at his critic: if you're right, and we are always drawing on a background understanding that gives intelligibility to our experience, then even my account of the knowing agent in terms of the disengaged picture must draw on such a background to be intelligible to me. For according to you, what I am really describing is the disengaged stance, which you see as a special and regional achievement by an agent whose experience as a whole is made intelligible only by a background of the kind you invoke. As a special stance, one among the many possibilities of this agent, having a determinate place in his or her world, this must as well be made intelligible by some background understanding. So articulate for me the implicit understanding that I am allegedly drawing on; show me the preunderstanding I could not be doing without. Then I will have to believe you. Otherwise, stop prattling on about my being held captive by a picture, caught in a fly bottle, or suffering from *Seinsvergessenheit.*

The line of argument of the major "deconstructors" of the disengaged picture could serve as an answer to this challenge. It undermines the picture by bringing out the background we need for the operations described in the picture to make sense, whereby it becomes clear that this background cannot fit within the limits that the disengaged view prescribes. Once understood against its background, the account shows itself to be untenable.

The pioneer in this kind of argument, in whose steps all deconstructors find themselves treading, is Kant. Not that he intended to refute the disengaged view as such. But he did manage to upset one of its crucial features, at least in an earlier variant. The arguments of the transcendental deduction can be seen in a number of lights. But one way to take them is as a final laying to rest of a certain atomism of the input that had been espoused by empiricism. As this came to Kant through Hume, it seemed to be suggesting that the original level of knowledge of reality (whatever that turned out to be) came in particulate bits, individual "impressions." This level of information could be isolated from a later stage in which these bits were connected together – for example, in beliefs about cause–effect relations. We find ourselves forming such beliefs, but we can, by taking a stance of reflexive scrutiny (which, as we saw earlier, is fundamental to the modern epistemology), separate the basic level from our too hasty conclusions. This analysis allegedly reveals, for instance, that nothing in the phenomenal field corresponds to the necessary connection we too easily interpolate between "cause" and "effect."[10]

Kant undercuts this whole way of thinking by showing that it supposes, for each particulate impression, that it is being taken as a bit of potential information. It purports to be about something. The primitive distinction recognized by empiricists between impressions of sensation and those of reflection amount to an acknowledgment of this. The buzzing in my head is discriminated from the noise I hear from the neighboring woods, in that the first is a component in how I feel and the second seems to tell me something about what's happening out there. So even a particulate "sensation," really to be sensation (in the empiricist sense, i.e., as opposed to reflection), has to have this dimension of "aboutness." This will later be called "intentionality," but Kant speaks of the necessary relation to an object of knowledge. "Now we find that our thought of the relation of all knowledge to its object carries with it an element of necessity."[11]

With this point secured, Kant argues that this relationship to an object would be impossible if we really were to take the impression as an utterly isolated content, without any link to others. To see it as about something is to place it somewhere, at the minimum out in the world, as against in me, to give it a location in a world that, while it is in many respects indeterminate and unknown for me, cannot be wholly so. The unity of this world is presupposed by anything that could present itself as a particulate bit of *information*, and so whatever we mean by such a particulate bit, it could not be utterly without relation to all others. The background condition for this favorite supposition of empiricist philosophy, the simple impression, forbids us giving it the radical sense that Hume seemed to propose for it. To attempt to violate this background condition is to fall into incoherence. To succeed in breaking all links between individual impressions would be to lose all sense of awareness of anything. "These perceptions would not then belong to any experience, consequently would be without an object, merely a blind play of representations, less even than a dream."[12]

The transcendental deduction, and related arguments in the *Critique of Pure Reason,* can be seen as a turning point in modern philosophy. With hindsight, we can see them as the first attempt to articulate the background that the modern disengaged picture itself requires for the operations it describes to be intelligible and to use this articulation to undermine the picture. Once one goes through this transition, the whole philosophical landscape changes, because the issue of background understanding is out in the open. A crucial feature of the reified views that arise from ontologizing the canonical procedures of modern epistemology is that they make this issue invisible. The conditions of intelligibility are built into the elements and processes of the mind as internal properties. The isolated impression *is* intelligibly information on its own, just as the house is red or the table is square. It has all the particulate, separable existence of an external object. Locke treats simple ideas as analogous to the materials we use for building.[13] This outlook forgets that for something to be intelligibly *X* is for it to *count as* intelligibly *X,* and that there are always contextual conditions for anything to count as something.

In its original Kantian form, this revolution sweeps away the atomism of modern epistemology. In this respect, all those who have come after follow Kant closely. In a sense the very move that dereifies our account of the knowing agent has an inherently holistic bent. What was formerly built into the elements is now attributed to the background they all share.

Heidegger follows this pioneering Kantian form of argument. In *Being and Time,* he argues that things are disclosed first as part of a world, that is, as the correlates of concerned involvement, and within a totality of such involvements. This undercuts the first and third features of the disengaged picture, and hence makes the second feature inoperative. The first feature, the atomism of input, is denied by the notion of a totality of involvements. The third feature, neutrality, is undercut by the basic thesis that things are first disclosed in a world as ready-to-hand (*zuhanden*). To think of this character as something we project onto things that are first perceived neutrally is to make a fundamental mistake.[14]

Heidegger's discussion in *Being and Time* is sometimes taken by unsympathetic readers to be an interesting discussion of everyday existence that has no relevance to the philosophical issues of ontology he claims to be discussing. So we usually treat things as tools or obstacles in their relevance to our activities – what does this show about the priority of neutral information? Of course, we are not *aware* of things most of the time as neutral objects, but this does not show that the disengaged account is not right. Our ordinary everyday consciousness must itself be seen as a construct. We must not make the pre-Galilean mistake of thinking that things are as they appear, even in matters of the mind – so runs a common complaint by supporters of the disengaged view against "phenomenology."

But Heidegger's intention is plainly other than just reminding us of what it is like to live in the world at an everyday level. The purport of the argument is the same as Kant's and could be invoked like his as an answer to the challenge I voiced earlier. The aim is to show that grasping things as neutral objects is one of our possibilities only against the background of a way of being in the world in which things are disclosed as ready-to-hand. Grasping things neutrally requires modifying our stance to them that primitively has to be one of involvement. Heidegger, like Kant, is arguing that the comportment to things described in the disengaged view requires for its intelligibility to be situated within an enframing and continuing stance to the world that is antithetical to it, hence that this comportment could not be original and fundamental. The very condition of its possibility forbids us giving this neutralizing stance the paradigmatic and basic place in our lives that the disengaged picture supposes.

This argument about the conditions of possibility – the conditions of intelligibly realizing the stance – is carried in Heidegger's use of the term *ursprünglich* ("primordial"). This term does not just mean "prior in time," but something stronger. Our *ursprünglich* stance comes before, but also as a condition of, what follows and modifies it. The argument about conditions of possibility is also carried in his repreated use of the phrase *zunächst und zumeist* ("proximally and for the most part," according to the standard translation). Once again this sounds deceptively weak. But it is applied to a way of being that is not just there earlier and more frequently, but that also provides the background for what is not it.

In this essay, I have tried to show how Heidegger has helped to free us from the thrall of modern rationalist epistemology. I have formulated his line of thinking in terms of the notion of engaged agency. This in turn brings us to the notion of the background. But the idea of a background we can articulate figures not only as part of a new *picture* of the knowing agent. The series of philosophical arguments of Heidegger's existential analytic is itself such an articulation. The picture puts itself in motion. This pragmatic self-confirmation is what gives the existential analytic its peculiar force – a force that is very much needed to combat the hold of the disengaged understanding of agency in our culture.

NOTES

1 See T. Nagel, *The View from Nowhere* (New York: Oxford University Press, 1983).

2 Merleau-Ponty, whom I consider another of these great twentieth-century "deconstructors," focused more than anyone else on this issue of embodied agency. See especially *La phénoménologie de la perception* (Paris: Gallimard, 1945).

3 These two senses in which experience is shaped by embodiment help to explain the dialogue of the deaf between critics and exponents of artificial-intelligence-inspired theories of the mind. The former, e.g., Hubert Dreyfus and John Searle, have often insisted that the computer offers a model of "disembodied" consciousness. See Dreyfus's *What Computers Can't Do* (New York: Harper & Row, 1979); and Searle's "Minds, Brains and Programmes", in *Behavioural and Brain Sciences,* 3 (1980): 417–57. Proponents of the artificial intelligence model, insulted in the very heart of their materialist commitment, generally find this accusation unintelligible. But it is easy to see why the criticism is not understood. Proponents of strong artificial intelligence are thinking of the first kind of relation. The second kind has not yet swum into their conceptual ken, and hence they have great trouble understanding what they are being accused of.

4 Thomas Nagel, *Mortal Questions* (Cambridge: Cambridge University Press, 1979), p. 208.

5 The soul "ne s'est pas contentée de juger qu'il y avoit quelque chose hors d'elle qui étoit cause qu'elle avoit ses sentiments, en quoi elle ne se seroit pas trompée; mais elle a passé plus outre." "Et comme ces idées ne sont point naturelles, mais arbitraires, on y a agi avec une grande bizarrerie." A. Arnaud and P. Nicole, *La logique ou l'art de penser,* Pt. 1, Chap. 9 (Paris: Flammarion, 1970), p. 103.

6 This is, of course, what underlies the misunderstanding mentioned in

note 3 about the issue of "embodiment." Mechanists cannot formulate the issue without transcending their favorite explanatory language. It is odd that they have such trouble seeing that this language is so framed as to exclude engaged thinking, because with another part of their minds they are aware of this, and often say so. Thus, one of the original motivations for constructing computer realizations of reasoning was that realization on a program was thought to be a good criterion of formal rigor. A formally rigorous proof is one in which the transitions depend purely on the shape of the expressions, regardless of their semantic "meaning." But a proof can sometimes seem rigorous in this sense, and fail really to be so, because we can unawares be "supplying" some of the missing steps through the intuitive leaps we make as we check it. "Subjective" intelligibility is filling the gaps in formal argument. But if such a proof can be automated, that is, run on a machine, then we *know* that there can be no such surreptitious input from subjective intelligibility, and the proof must be valid. See John Haugeland's "automation principle: wherever the legal moves of a formal system are fully determined by algorithms, then that system can be automated" (in *Artificial Intelligence: The Very Idea* [Cambridge, Mass.: MIT Press, 1985], p. 83). Also Marvin Minsky: "If the procedure can be carried out by some very simple machine, so that there can be no question of or need for 'innovation' or 'intelligence,' then we can be sure that the specification is complete, and that we have an 'effective procedure' " (in *Computation: Finite and Infinite Machines* [Englewood Cliffs, N.J.: Prentice-Hall, 1967], p. 105).

7 See Michael Polanyi, *Personal Knowledge* (Chicago: University of Chicago Press, 1958), and *The Tacit Dimension* (Garden City, N.Y.: Doubleday, 1966).

8 See Merleau-Ponty, *La phénoménologie de la perception.*

9 See Daniel Dennett, *The Intentional Stance* (Cambridge, Mass.: MIT Press, 1988), Chaps. 2 and 7.

10 David Hume, *An Enquiry Concerning Human Understanding* (Oxford: Oxford University Press, 1966), Chap. 7.

11 "Wir finden aber, dass unser Gedanke von der Beziehung aller Erkenntniss auf ihren Gegenstand etwas von Notwendigkeit bei sich führe." Immanuel Kant, *Critique of Pure Reason,* trans. N. K. Smith (London: Macmillan Press, 1963), A 104.

12 "Diese [sc. Wahrnehmungen] würden aber alsdann auch zu keiner Erfahrung gehören, folglich ohne Objekt und nichts als ein blindes Spiel der Vorstellungen, d.i. weniger als ein Traum sein." Ibid., A 112.

13 John Locke, *An Essay Concerning Human Understanding* (Oxford: Oxford University Press, 1975), 2.2.2.

14 "The kind of Being which belongs to these entities is readiness-to-hand.

But this characteristic is not to be understood as merely a way of taking them, as if we were talking such 'aspects' into the 'entities' which we proximally encounter, or as if some world-stuff which is proximally present-at-hand were 'given subjective coloring' in this way" (BT 101). ("Die Seinsart dieses Seienden ist die Zuhandenheit. Sie darf jedoch nicht als blosser Auffassungscharakter verstanden werden, als würden dem zunächst begegnenden 'Seienden' solche 'Aspekte' aufgeredet, als würde ein zunächst an sich vorhandener Weltstoff in dieser Weise 'subjektiv gefärbt' " (SZ 71).

RICHARD RORTY

13 Wittgenstein, Heidegger, and the reification of language

What Gustav Bergmann christened "the linguistic turn" was a rather desperate attempt to keep philosophy an armchair discipline. The idea was to mark off a space for *a priori* knowledge into which neither sociology nor history nor art nor natural science could intrude. It was an attempt to find a substitute for Kant's "transcendental standpoint." The replacement of "mind" or "experience" by "meaning" was supposed to insure the purity and autonomy of philosophy by providing it with a nonempirical subject matter.

Linguistic philosophy was, however, too honest to survive. When, with the later Wittgenstein, this kind of philosophy turned its attention to the question of how such a "pure" study of language was possible, it realized that it was *not* possible – that semantics had to be naturalized if it were to be, in Donald Davidson's phrase, "preserved as a serious subject." The upshot of linguistic philosophy is, I would suggest, Davidson's remark that "there is no such thing as a language, not if a language is anything like what philosophers . . . have supposed. . . . We must give up the idea of a clearly defined shared structure which language users master and then apply to cases."[1] This remark epitomizes what Ian Hacking has called "the death of meaning" – the end of the attempt to make language a transcendental topic.

I take Frege and the early Wittgenstein to be the philosophers primarily responsible for imposing on us the idea that there *was* such a clear defined shared structure. In particular, we owe to Wittgenstein the idea that all philosophical problems can in principle be finally solved by exhibiting that structure. I take the later Wittgen-

Reprinted from *Essays on Heidegger and Others* (Cambridge University Press, 1990).

stein, Quine, and Davidson to be the philosophers who freed us from the idea that there is any such structure. The early Wittgenstein had defined the mystical as "the sense of the world as a limited whole." By contrast, the later Wittgenstein triumphed over his younger, more Schopenhauerian self by no longer feeling the need to be mystical, no longer needing to set himself over against the world as "the unsayable limit of the world."

The younger Heidegger, the author of *Being and Time,* was much more free of this Schopenhauerian urge than was the younger Wittgenstein. That book was filled with protests against the idea of philosophy as *theoria.* Heidegger saw that idea as an attempt to rise above the "guilt" and "thrownness" which he claimed were inseparable from Dasein's worldly and historical existence, an attempt to escape from the contingency of that existence. The younger Heidegger, had he read the *Tractatus,* would have dismissed that book in the same way as the older Wittgenstein dismissed it – as one more attempt to preserve the philosopher's autonomy and self-sufficiency by letting him picture himself as somehow above, or beyond, the world. The younger Heidegger would have seen the linguistic turn recommended by Frege and Wittgenstein as merely one more variation on the Platonic attempt to distance oneself from time and chance.

But although the younger Heidegger worked hard to free himself from the notion of the philosopher as spectator of time and eternity, from the wish to see the world from above "as a limited whole," the older Heidegger slipped back into a very similar idea. The limited whole which that Heidegger tried to distance himself from was called "metaphysics" or "the West." For him, "the mystical" became the sense of himself as "thinking after the end of metaphysics" – as looking back on metaphysics, seeing it as a limited, rounded-off whole – and thus as something we might hope to put behind us. The old Heidegger's final vision was of the West as a single gift of Being, a single *Ereignis,* a chalice with one handle labeled "Plato" and the other "Nietzsche," complete and perfect in itself – and therefore, perhaps, capable of being set to one side.

The young Wittgenstein had said, echoing Kant and Schopenhauer, that

> We feel that even when *all possible* scientific questions have been answered, the problems of life remain completely untouched. Of course there

are then no questions left, and this itself is the answer. . . . There are, indeed, things that cannot be put into words. They *make themselves manifest.* They are what is mystical.[2]

By contrast, the young Heidegger had no explicit doctrine of things that cannot be put into words, of *das Unaussprechliche.* Dasein was linguistic through and through, just as it was social through and through.[3] What the younger Heidegger tells us about the sociohistorical situation of Dasein is just what the older Wittgenstein tells us about our situation in regard to language – that when we try to transcend it by turning metaphysical we become self-deceptive, inauthentic.

But the older Heidegger retreated from sentences and discourse to single words – words which had to be abandoned as soon as they ceased to be hints (*Winke*) and became signs (*Zeichen*), as soon as they entered into relations with other words and thus became tools for accomplishing purposes. The younger – unpragmatical, mystical – Wittgenstein had wanted sentences to be pictures rather than merely tools. By contrast, the pragmatical young Heidegger, the philosopher of inescapable relationality (*Bezüglichkeit*), had been content to let them be tools. But the older, more pragmatical Wittgenstein became content to think of them as tools, about the same time that the older Heidegger decided his early pragmatism had been a premature surrender to "reason [which], glorified for centuries, is the most stiff-necked adversary of thought."[4]

On my reading of them, then, these two great philosophers passed each other in mid-career, going in opposite directions. Wittgenstein, in the *Tractatus,* started from a point which, to a pragmatist like myself, seems much less enlightened than that of *Being and Time.* But, as Wittgenstein advanced in the direction of pragmatism, he met Heidegger coming the other way – retreating from pragmatism into the same escapist mood in which the *Tractatus* had been written, attempting to regain in "Thought" the sort of sublimity which the young Wittgenstein had found in logic. The direction in which Wittgenstein was going led him to radical doubts about the very notion of philosophy as a provider of knowledge, and to a detranscendentalized, naturalized conception of philosophy as a form of therapy, as a *technē* rather than as the achievement of *theoria.* Heidegger had himself begun with just such doubts. But he was unable to sustain them, and so in the end he was driven to inventing "Thought" as a substitute for what he called "metaphysics." This led him to speak of language as a quasi-divinity in which we live and move and have our being, and of all previous Thought as a limited whole, a tale that had now been fully told.

So far I have been presenting a brief outline of a story which I shall tell in more detail. I shall begin my longer version with Wittgenstein's attempt to find a new way of doing philosophy.

Any attempt to preserve a method and a topic for armchair philosophy, one which will permit it to look down upon natural science and history, is likely to invoke the Kantian notion of "conditions of possibility." Whereas physics and history find conditions for the existence of actualities by discovering temporally prior actualities, philosophy can achieve autonomy only if it escapes from time by escaping from actuality to possibility. The Kantian strategy for achieving this escape was to replace an atemporal Deity with an atemporal subject of experience. Kant's "possible experience" – the domain whose bounds philosophy was to set – was purportedly smaller than the broader domain of logical possibility to which Wolff's ontotheology had claimed access. But it was enough for Kant's purposes that it overarched the domains of the scientists and the historians.

The linguistic turn was a second attempt to find a domain which would overarch those of the other professors. This second attempt became necessary because, in the course of the nineteenth century, evolutionary biology and empirical psychology had begun to naturalize the notions of "mind," "consciousness," and "experience."[5] "Language" was the twentieth-century philosopher's substitute for "experience" for two reasons. First, the two terms had an equally large scope – both delimited the entire domain of human inquiry, of topics available to human study. Second, the notions of "language" and "meaning" seemed, at the beginning of the century, immune to the naturalizing process.[6] Wittgenstein's *Tractatus* became the model around which the disciplinary matrix of analytic philosophy was molded. The preface to that book suggested (for the first time, as far as I know) the doctrine which Michael Dummett later put forward explicitly: that philosophy of language was first philosophy.

Philosophy of language, done in the manner of Frege, was supposed to produce conditions of describability, just as Kant had promised to produce conditions of experienceability. Describability, like experienceability, was supposed to be the mark of everything studied or exemplified by all areas of study other than philosophy. Language seemed able to avoid relativization to history, for description was thought to be a single indissoluble activity, whether done by Neanderthals, Greeks, or Germans. If one could give *a priori* conditions of the activity of description, then one would be in a position to offer apodeictic truths. To both Husserl and Frege, Brentano's thesis of the irreducibility of the intentional seemed to guarantee that the Kantian distinction between the *a priori* and apodeictic and the *a posteriori* and relative would remain secure. For even though the evolutionary transition from organisms which do not exhibit linguistic behavior to those which do could be explained naturalistically, linguistic behavior could not be adequately characterized in the terms used to characterize everything else in the universe. So the irreducibility of the intentional seemed to guarantee the autonomy of philosophy.[7]

The young Wittgenstein saw, however, what Frege and the young Russell had not seen: that the search for nonempirical truth about the conditions of the possibility of describability raises the self-referential problem of its own possibility. Just as Kant had faced the problem of rendering the possibility of transcendental philosophy consistent with the restrictions on inquiry which such philosophy purports to have discovered, so Frege and Russell had trouble explaining how knowledge of what they called "logic" was possible. The problem was that logic seemed to be an exception to the conditions which it itself laid down. The propositions of logic were not truth-functional combinations of elementary statements about the objects which make up the world. Yet "logic" seemed to tell us that only such combinations had meaning.

Russell had tried to solve this problem by reinventing the Platonic Forms. He had postulated a realm of otherworldly logical objects and a faculty of intellectual intuition with which to grasp them. But Wittgenstein saw that this led to a new version of the "third man problem" which Plato had raised in the *Parmenides* – the problem of how the entities designed to explain knowledge are known. Russell's logical objects, the Kantian categories, and the Platonic Forms were all supposed to make another set of objects – the empirical objects, the Kantian intuitions, or the Platonic material particulars – knowable, or describable. In each case, we are told, the latter objects need to be related by the former objects before they become available – before they may be experienced or described.

Call the lower-level entities, those which stand in need of being related in order to become available, entities of type B. These are entities which require relations but cannot themselves relate, require contextualization and explanation but cannot themselves contextualize nor explain. The Platonic Forms, the Kantian categories, and the Russellian logical objects are examples of what I shall call type A entities. These entities contextualize and explain but cannot, on pain of infinite regress, be contextualized or explained.

Those who postulate type A objects are always faced with the following self-referential problem: if we claim that no entity is available which remains unrelated by a form of relationship which cannot hold between unaided type B entities, then we have problems about the availability of the type A entities we postulate to lend the necessary aid. For if we are allowed to say that type A entities are their own *rationes cognoscendi,* or their own conditions of linguistic accessibility – that they make themselves available without being related to one another or to anything else – then we are faced with the question of why type B entities cannot themselves have this obviously desirable feature.

This dilemma is familiar from theology: if God can be *causa sui,* why should not the world be? Why not just identify God and nature, as Spinoza did? All type A entities, all unexplained explainers, are in the same situation as a transcendent Diety. If we are entitled to believe in them without relating them to something which conditions their existence or knowability or describability, then we have falsified our initial claim that availability requires being related by something other than the relata themselves. We have opened up the question of why we ever thought that there was a problem about availability in the first place. We have thereby questioned the need for philosophy, insofar as philosophy is thought of as the study of conditions of availability.

I shall define "naturalism" as the view that *anything* might have been otherwise, that there can be no conditionless conditions.[8] Naturalists believe that all explanation is causal explanation of the actual, and that there is no such thing as a noncausal condition of possibility. If we think of philosophy as a quest for apodicticity, for truths whose truth requires no explanation, then we make philosophy inherently antinaturalistic and we must agree with Kant and Husserl that Locke and Wundt operate at a subphilosophical level. Wittgenstein's *Tractatus* can be read as a heroic attempt to save philosophy from naturalism by claiming that type A objects must be ineffable, that they can be shown but not said, that they can never become available in the way that type B objects are.

As David Pears has pointed out in his admirable *The False Prison,* there is an analogy between Wittgenstein's discussion of the mysterious "objects" of the *Tractatus* and "the *via remotionis* in theology."[9] Of these objects, which form what he called "the substance of the World," Wittgenstein wrote as follows:

> If the world had no substance, then whether a proposition had sense would depend on whether another proposition was true.
> In that case we could not sketch out any picture of the world (true or false).[10]

No intrinsically simple objects, no pictures, and no language. For if analysis could not end with such objects, then whether a sentence had sense would depend, *horribile dictu,* upon whether another sentence were true – the sentence which specifies that two simpler objects making up a composite stand in the relevant compositional relationship. But when one asks what would be so horrible about *that,* Wittgenstein has no obvious answer.

On Pears's account, which seems to me right, what would be horrible about this situation would be that it would violate Wittgenstein's doctrine that "sense-conditions are ineffable." But, Pears sensibly continues, this just makes us wonder why they have to be ineffable.[11] His answer to this latter question is that if they were not ineffable we should have to give up the notion of "the limits of language," and therefore give up the doctrine that there is something which can be shown but not said.[12] Pears rightly takes this "doctrine of showing" to be the one closest to Wittgenstein's heart. He sums it up as follows:

> [Wittgenstein's] leading idea was that we can see further than we can say. We can see all the way to the edge of language, but the most distant things that we see cannot be expressed in sentences because they are the preconditions of saying anything.[13]

Another way in which Pears formulates this point is by saying that "if factual language could contain an analysis of its conditions of application, the language in which it analysed them would itself depend on further conditions. . . ."[14] This chimes with the following passage:

> Objects can only be *named.* Signs are their representatives. I can only speak *about* them: I cannot *put them into words.* Propositions can only say *how* things are, not *what* they are. The requirement that simple signs be possible is the requirement that sense be determinate.[15]

To sum up, if there were no objects, if the world had no substance, if there were no "unalterable form of the world,"[16] then sense would not be determinate, we would not be able to make ourselves pictures of the world, and description would be impossible. So the condition of the possibility of description must itself be indescribable. By way of parallel arguments, Plato concluded that the conditions of the possibility of the material world must be immaterial, and Kant that the conditions of the phenomenal world must be nonphenomenal.

The later Wittgenstein dropped the notion of "seeing to the edge of language." He also dropped the whole idea of "language" as a bounded whole which had conditions at its outer edges, as well as the project of transcendental semantics – of finding nonempirical conditions for the possibility of linguistic description. He became reconciled to the idea that whether a sentence had sense did indeed depend upon whether another sentence was true – a sentence about the social practices of the people who used the marks and noises which were the components of the sentence. He thereby became reconciled to the notion that there was nothing ineffable, and that philosophy, like language, was just a set of indefinitely expansible social practices, not a bounded whole whose periphery might be "shown." At the time of the *Tractatus* he had thought that the assemblage of philosophical problems formed such a whole, and that he had solved all these problems at once by drawing the consequences of the statement which, he claimed, "summed up the whole sense of [his] book": "what can be said at all can be said clearly, and what we cannot talk about we must pass over in silence."[17] He thought of philosophy as coextensive with an investigation of the possibility of meaning, and of that investigation as culminating in the discovery of the ineffable.

As Michael Dummett rightly says, if one adopts the point of view of Wittgenstein's *Philosophical Investigations,* there can be no such thing as a "systematic theory of meaning for a language." If one believes, with Dummett, that philosophy of language is first philosophy, then it follows that philosophy can never be more than therapeutic – can never set out positive conclusions.[18] As Thomas Nagel rightly says, Wittgenstein's later position "depends on a position so radical that it . . . undermines the weaker transcendent pretensions of even the least philosophical of thoughts." This position entails, as Nagel puts it, "that any thoughts we can form of a mind-independent reality must remain within the boundaries set by our human form of life."[19] Dummett and Nagel both see the later Wittgenstein as endangering philosophy by casting aside the picture which had held him captive when he wrote the *Tractatus* – the picture which Davidson has labeled the distinction of scheme and content. This is the distinction between what I have called type A entities and type B entities.

I would argue that this A-versus-B distinction is the least common denominator of the Greek distinction between universals and particulars, the Kantian distinction between concepts and intuitions, and the Tractarian distinction between the available and effable world and the unavailable and ineffable "substance of the world." The last version of this distinction is the most dramatic and the most revealing, since it sets out starkly the contrast between atomism and holism – between the assumption that there can be entities which are what they are totally independent of all relations between them, and the assumption that all entities are merely nodes in a net of relations.

Both Nagel and Dummett see a need to resist holism in order to preserve the possibility of philosophy. Both think of Davidson as endangering philosophy by embracing a thoroughgoing holism. They are right to do so, since Davidson's account of human linguistic behavior takes for granted, as the later Wittgenstein also did, that there are no linguistic entities which are intrinsically relationless – none which, like the "simple names" of the *Tractatus,* are by nature relata. But Davidson's holism is more explicit and thoroughgoing than Wittgenstein's, and so its antiphilosophical consequences are more apparent. Whereas in the *Philosophical Investigations* Wittgenstein still toys with the idea of a distinction between the empirical and the grammatical, between nonphilosophical and philosophical inquiry, Davidson generalizes and extends Quine's refusal to countenance either a distinction between necessary and contingent truth or a distinction between philosophy and science. Davidson insists that we not think either of language in general or a particular language (say, English or German) as something which has edges, something which forms a bounded whole and can thus become a distinct object of study or of philosophical theorizing. Bjorn Ramberg is right in saying that Davidson's principal motive is to avoid the reification of language.[20] So Davidson has no use for the idea that philosophical therapy is a matter of detecting "nonsense," of spotting "violations of language." Rather, it is a matter of spotting unproductive and self-defeating philosophical behavior – the sort of behavior which sends one, over and over again, down the same blind alleys (e.g., alleys labeled "realism," "idealism," and "antirealism").

Instead, Davidson asks us to think of human beings trading marks and noises to accomplish purposes. We are to see this linguistic behavior as continuous with nonlinguistic behavior, and to see both sorts of behavior as making sense just insofar as we can describe them as attempts to fulfill given desires in the light of given beliefs. But the realm of belief and desire – the so-called "realm of the intentional" – does not itself form an object of philosophical inquiry. Davidson agrees with Quine that neither the practical indispensability of the intentional idiom nor its Brentanian irreducibility to a behavioristic idiom gives us reason to think that there are type A entities called "intentions" or "meanings" which serve to relate type B entities.[21]

So much, for the moment, for Wittgenstein's and Davidson's attempts to escape from the idea that there is a discipline – philosophy – which can study conditions of possibility rather than merely conditions of actuality. I turn now to the early Heidegger's attempt to escape from this same idea – the idea of a discipline which lets us stand over and against the world of everyday practice by seeing it as God sees it, as a limited whole. I interpret the pragmatism of the first Division of *Being and Time* – the insistence on the priority of the ready-to-hand, the *Zuhanden,* over the present-at-hand, the *Vorhanden,* and on the inseparability of Dasein from its projects and its language – as a first attempt to find a nonlogocentric, nonontotheological way of thinking of things. It was a holistic attempt to eschew the scheme–content distinction, to replace a distinction between entities of type A and those of type B with a seamless, indefinitely extensible web of relations.

From the point of view of both *Philosophical Investigations* and *Being and Time,* the typical error of traditional philosophy is to imagine that there could be, indeed that there somehow *must* be, entities which are atomic in the sense of being what they are independent of their relation to any other entities (e.g., God, the transcendental subject, sense-data, simple names). For the later Wittgenstein, the best example of this mistake is his own earlier hope to discover the "unalterable form of the world," something which underlies the available or lies at the edges of the available, something which is a condition of the possibility of availability. When in the *Investigations* he is criticizing the Tractarian desire for "something like a final analysis of our forms of language," he says that it is as if we had in mind "a state of complete exactness" as opposed to whatever relative degree of exactness may be required for some particular purpose. This notion impels us, Wittgenstein continues, to ask "questions as to the *essence* of language, of propositions, of thought." He diagnoses the urge to ask such questions as due to the idea that "the essence is hidden from us." Obsession with this image of something deeply hidden makes one want to ask questions whose answers would be, as he says, "given once for all; and independently of any future experience."[22]

This last phrase sums up the idea that there is a nonempirical discipline which can tell us about the conditions of "all possible experience," or of all possible languages and forms of life. This is the idea which *Being and Time* rejected by insisting on the primordiality of the *Zuhanden,* on the fact that everything was always already related. The early Heidegger saw as clearly as the later Wittgenstein that the present-at-hand was only available in the context of pre-existent relations with the ready-to-hand, that social practice was the presupposition of the demand for exactness and for answers that could be given once and for all. Both saw that the only way in which the present-at-hand could explain the ready-to-hand was in the familiar unphilosophical way in which evolutionary biology, sociology, and history combine to give a causal explanation of the actuality of one particular social practice rather than another. Early Heidegger and late Wittgenstein set aside the assumption (common to their respective predecessors, Husserl and Frege) that social practice – and in particular the use of language – can receive a noncausal, specifically philosophical explanation in terms of conditions of possibility. More generally, both set aside the assumption that philosophy might explain the unhidden on the basis of the hidden, and might explain availability and relationality on the basis of something intrinsically unavailable and nonrelational.

One can imagine a possible Heidegger who, after formulating the Dewey-like social-practice pragmatism of the early sections of *Being and Time,* would have felt that his job was pretty well done.[23] But the early Heidegger was driven by the same urge to *purity* which drove the early Wittgenstein. The same drives which led Heidegger to develop the notions of "authenticity" and "being-toward-death" in the later portions of *Sein und Zeit* led Wittgenstein to write the final sections of the *Tractatus* – the sections in which the doctrine of showing is extended from logic to ethics. These are the so-called "Schopenhauerian" sections in which we are told such things as

> It is clear that ethics cannot be put into words. . . . It is impossible to speak about the will in so far as it is the subject of ethical attributes. . . . Death is not an event in life. . . . *How* things are in the world is a matter of complete indifference for what is higher. . . . It is not *how* things are in the world that is mystical, but *that* it exists. . . . Feeling the world as a limited whole – it is this that is the mystical.[24]

What is common to early Heidegger on authenticity and to the early Wittgenstein on the sense of the world as a limited whole is the urge to see social practice as *merely* social practice, thereby rising above it. This is the urge to *distance* the social practice to which one has been accustomed (though not necessarily to cease to participate in it) by seeing it as contingent – as something into which one has been thrown. So seen, it is something which one can only make authentic, only properly appropriate, by being able to say, with Nietzsche, "thus I willed it," thereby "becoming what one is."

To become authentic in this way is to see the requirement of mere accuracy (Heidegger's *Richtigkeit*) – the requirement to say what "one" (*das Man*) says, to give the right answers to "scientific" and "empirical" questions – as the requirement only of a "*limited* whole," of one possible ontic situation among others. This attempt to distance mere accuracy, to find something more important than giving the correct answers to intelligible questions, something more important than anything empirical science might offer, was encouraged by Kant's project of denying reason in order to make room for faith, and developed further by Schopenhauer, from whose hands both Nietzsche and the young Wittgenstein received it. It was also encouraged by Kierkegaard's and Nietzsche's sneers at Hegel's pretensions to scientificity and rigor.

But whereas the attempt to find what Habermas calls (following Adorno) "an Other to Reason" was common to the young Heidegger and the young Wittgenstein, Heidegger pressed it further as he grew older, whereas Wittgenstein gradually abandoned it. The crucial difference between their later selves is in their attitude toward the projects of their earlier selves. Whereas Heidegger came to feel that *Being and Time* was insufficiently radical, because "not yet thought through in terms of the history of Being" (EP 15; N2 415), Wittgenstein came to feel that the *Tractatus* was just a last outbreak of a disease from which he had been almost, but not quite, cured. Whereas Heidegger continued his own quest for authenticity by attempting to win himself a place in the history of Being as the first postmetaphysical Thinker, Wittgenstein's attitude toward philosophy became steadily more casual. Whereas the young Wittgenstein had had large quasi-Schopenhauerian things to say about such subjects as "the whole modern Weltanschauung,"[25] that sort of topic no longer surfaces in his later work. Heidegger becomes more and more interested in his own relation to history, and Wittgenstein less and less.

This is particularly clear in their respective attitudes toward metaphors of *depth* and *antiquity*. As Heidegger goes along, he worries more and more about whether he is being sufficiently *primordial*. Although Wittgenstein expressed sympathy with what he had heard of early Heidegger, one imagines that he would have mocked the later Heidegger's search for ever greater primordiality. That search would have seemed an instance of the process he described as "In order to find the true artichoke, we divested it of its leaves."[26]

The same opposition turns up if one looks at the way in which the two men change their attitudes toward language as a topic of study. The *Tractatus* starts out by telling us that the problems of philosophy are posed "because the logic of our language is misunderstood," but by the time we get to the *Philosophical Investigations* Wittgenstein is mocking the idea that there is any such logic to study. He mocks his younger self for believing that logic is "the incomparable essence of language," something "of purest crystal," something deeply hidden and graspable only after strenuous philosophizing. In the *Investigations* philosophy does not study a subject called "language," nor does it offer a theory of how meaning is possible – it offers only what Wittgenstein calls "reminders for a particular purpose."[27]

By contrast, the term "language" (*Sprache*) plays a very small role in *Being and Time,* and when it does occur, in section 34, it is subordinated to "talk" (*Rede*) and thus to Dasein. But by the time we get to the "Letter on Humanism," we find Heidegger saying "If the truth of Being has become thought-provoking for thinking, then reflection on the essence of language must also attain a different rank."[28] The stock of language rises as that of Dasein falls, as Heidegger worries more and more about the possibility that his earlier work has been infected with the "humanism" characteristic of the age of the world picture, about the possibility that Sartre had not misread him, and that Husserl had had a point when he said that *Being and Time* was merely anthropology.[29] More generally, Heidegger's turn from the earlier question "What are the roots of the traditional ontotheological problematic?" to the later question "Where do we stand in the history of Being?" is accompanied by a desperate anxiety that he be offering something *more* than, as he puts it, "simply a history of the alterations in human beings' self-conceptions."[30] So, at the same time as Wittgenstein was coming to see "language" as referring simply to the exchange of marks and noises among human beings for particular purposes, as no more denoting a real essence than does "game," Heidegger is trying desperately to think of the various houses of Being in which human beings have dwelt as "gifts of Being" rather than "human self-conceptions."

In order to justify my obvious preference for the later Wittgenstein over the later Heidegger, and my view that Heidegger's "turn" was a failure of nerve, I need to offer an account of the motives which dictated the trajectories of the two philosophers' careers. As I see it, they both started from a need to escape from what they both called "chatter" (*Geschwätz*),[31] a need for purity, a need to become authentic by ceasing to speak the language of the philosophical tribe within which they had been raised. The early Wittgenstein was convinced that this meant getting beyond language altogether. In his "Lecture on Ethics" Wittgenstein says that "the tendency of all men who ever tried to talk about Ethics or Religion was to run against the boundaries of language."[32] Elsewhere he said that "Man has the urge to thrust against the limits of language. . . . This thrust against the limits of language is *ethics*. . . ."[33] In a much-quoted letter he said that the point of the *Tractatus* was "an ethical one."[34] The *Tractatus* was supposed to help us get beyond chatter, help eliminate the temptation to try to say what could only be shown, to talk of type A entities in terms appropriate only to type B entities.

As Wittgenstein grew older, however, he became reconciled to the fact that the difference between chatter and nonchatter is one of degree. As he gradually became reconciled to the fact that he would never see the world as a limited whole, he gradually dropped the notion of the "limits of language." So he turned the *Tractatus* distinction between saying and showing into the distinction between assertions and the social practices which gave meaning to assertions. He thereby reinvented Heidegger's doctrine that assertion is a derivative mode of interpretation. The latter Wittgenstein would have heartily agreed with the claim in *Being and Time* that

> The pointing-out which assertion does is performed on the basis of what has already been disclosed in understanding or discovered circumspectively. Assertion is not a free-floating kind of behavior which, in its own right, might be capable of disclosing entities in general in a primary way: on the contrary it always maintains itself on the basis of Being-in-the-world. (BT 199; SZ 156)

This claim is the one developed in detail in Quine's and Davidson's holism – a holism deplored by Nagel and Dummett because, as Nagel put it, it shows a lack of humility, an "attempt to cut the universe down to size."

Anyone who, like Nagel and the later Heidegger, wants to retain a sense of humility, or a sense of gratitude, toward something which transcends humanity must insist that there are some uses of language which *are* cases of free-floating behavior. Such a philosopher must insist that the presentation of a succession of worlds revealed by social practices – world pictures – does not exhaust the function of language. So anyone who wants to escape from what Heidegger calls our "age of the world picture" must either resurrect the early Wittgenstein's doctrine of ineffability, as Nagel does, or else hypostatize language in the way in which the older Heidegger does in the following passage:

> Man acts as though he were the shaper and master of language, while in fact language remains the mistress of man. . . . For strictly, it is language that speaks. Man first speaks when, and only when, he responds to language by listening to its appeal.[35]

But the reification of language in the later Heidegger is simply a stage in the hypostatization of Heidegger himself – in the transfiguration of Martin Heidegger from one more creature of his time, one more self constituted by the social practices of his day, one more reactor to the work of others, into a world-historical figure, the first postmetaphysical thinker. The hope for such transfiguration is the hope that there is still the possibility of something called "thinking" after the end of philosophy. It is the hope that the thinker can avoid immersion in the "always already disclosed," avoid relationality, by following a single star, thinking a single thought. To break free of metaphysics, free of the world which metaphysics has made, would require that Heidegger himself be capable of rising above his time. It would mean that his work was not simply one more *Selbstauffassung,* one more human self-concept, for he would have escaped himself by escaping his time.

This hope is not to be mocked. It is the same hope which led Plato, Kant, and Russell to invent regress-stopping type A entities, and which led the young Wittgenstein to seek for the limits of language. But, from the point of view of the older Wittgenstein, it is a vain hope: the hope that one may, by coming to look down upon language, or the world, or the West, as a limited whole, become a type A entity oneself. Such an entity would be one which *imposes* limits. Without such an entity, the old Heidegger thought, language, or the world, or the West, is doomed to remain shapeless, a mere tohubohu. This attempt to avoid relatedness, to think a single thought which is not simply a node in a web of other thoughts, to speak a word which has meaning even though it has no place in a social practice, is the urge to find a place which, if not above the heavens, is at least beyond chatter, beyond *Geschwätz.*

But I think that the later Wittgenstein had concluded that there was no such place. He summed up the reason for the failure of the *Tractatus* when he said, in the *Investigations:*

So in the end when one is doing philosophy one gets to the point where one would like just to emit an inarticulate sound. – But such a sound is an expression only if it occurs in a particular language-game, which should now be described.[36]

The later Wittgenstein saw all philosophical attempts to grasp type A entities, all attempts to express the ineffability of such entities, as succeeding only in creating one more language-game.

From the later Wittgenstein's naturalistic and pragmatic point of view, we can be grateful to Heidegger for having given us a new language-game. But we should not see that language-game as Heidegger did – as a way of distancing and summing up the West. It was, instead, simply one more in a long series of self-conceptions. Heideggerese is only Heidegger's gift to us, not Being's gift to Heidegger.

NOTES

1 Donald Davidson, "A Nice Derangement of Epitaphs," in *Truth and Interpretation: Perspectives on the Philosophy of Donald Davidson,* ed. Ernest LePore (Oxford: Blackwell, 1986), p. 446.

2 *Tractatus Logico-Philosophicus,* trans. D. F. Pears and B. F. McGuiness (London: Routledge & Kegan Paul, 1961), 6.52–6.522.

3 I take the claim in *Being and Time* (BT 318; SZ 273) that "Conscience discourses solely and constantly in the mode of keeping silent" to be not a doctrine of inexpressibility but rather the doctrine that the realization that one must change one's life cannot be backed up with reasons – for such reasons could only be voices from one's past life. See Davidson on this point in his "Paradoxes of Irrationality" in Richard Wollheim and James Hopkins, eds., *Philosophical Essays on Freud* (Cambridge: Cambridge University Press, 1982), p. 305: "The agent has reasons for changing his own habits and character, but those reasons come from a domain of values necessarily extrinsic to the contents of the views or values to undergo change. The cause of the change, if it comes, can therefore not be a reason for what it causes."

4 Heidegger, "Nietzsche's Word: 'God is Dead' " (QCT 112; HW 247).

5 After Darwin, it became increasingly difficult to use the notion of "experience" in the sense Kant had tried to give it. For Darwin, by making Spirit continuous with Nature, completed the historicizing process which Hegel had begun. So those who wanted to preserve the notion of philosophy as a nonempirical science *relativized* the Kantian *a priori,* in

the manner common to Dilthey, Collingwood, Croce, and C. I. Lewis. They tried to keep intact the notion of a distinction between the formal and the material – the domain of philosophy and the domain of natural science. But this relativizing cast doubt on the notion of a "transcendental standpoint," and thus on the notion of "possible experience" as something the conditions of which could be specified. For a plurality of forms of experience or forms of consciousness looks much like a plurality of actualities, each of which may be presumed to have causal, naturalistically explicable conditions. Further, if the *a priori* could change, then it is no longer *a priori* enough, for philosophical arguments can no longer culminate in immutable, apodeictic truths.

In this situation, what was needed was to find something which looked as much like an indissoluble unity as Kant had thought "experience" to be, but which could not be subjected to relativization. For Husserl, this need was met by the realm which opened itself up to those highly trained professionals capable of performing transcendental-phenomenological reductions. For Frege and the young Wittgenstein, it was met by the notion of a language, construed in the sense condemned by Davidson, as referring to a "clearly defined shared structure."

6 What Hacking describes as the "death of meaning" brought about by Davidsonian holism I should prefer to describe as the naturalization of Fregean meaning. This description preserves the parallel with Darwin's naturalization of Kantian experience.

7 I have argued elsewhere, following leads provided by Quine and Davidson, that the irreducibility of one vocabulary to another is no guarantee of the existence of two distinct sets of objects of inquiry. On the current state of debate about the nature and importance of intentional ascriptions, see Daniel Dennett's suggestion that the great divide within contemporary philosophy of mind and philosophy of language comes between those who believe in "intrinsic intentionality" (Searle, Nagel, Fodor, Kripke, et al.) and those who do not (Dennett, Davidson, Putnam, Stich, et al.). Dennett develops this suggestion in chapters 8 and 10 of his *The Intentional Stance* (Cambridge, Mass.: MIT Press, 1987).

8 Historicism is a special case of naturalism, so defined.

9 See David Pears, *The False Prison* (Oxford: Oxford University Press, 1988), I:67.

10 *Tractatus*, 2.0211–2.0212.

11 Pears, *False Prison*, I:71–2.

12 More exactly, his answer is that ". . . we cannot give a complete account of the sense of any factual sentence. The reason . . . is that such an account would have to use language in order to identify the possibility presented by the sentence, and there is only one way for language to

latch on to this possibility and that is to exploit the same method of correlation. . . . There is only one way in which the ultimate grid of possibilities [the array of objects which form the substance of the world] imposes its structure on all factual languages, and in this case it has been pre-empted by the original sentence" (ibid., I:144).

13 Ibid., I:146–7.

14 Ibid., 1:7.

15 *Tractatus*, 3.221–3.23.

16 See ibid., 2.026–2.027: "There must be objects if the world is to have an unalterable form. Objects, the unalterable, and the subsistent are one and the same."

17 Ibid., "Foreword."

18 See Michael Dummett, *Truth and Other Enigmas* (Cambridge, Mass.: Harvard University Press, 1978), p. 453, and compare Dummett's "What Is a Theory of Meaning? (II)," in *Truth and Meaning*, ed. Gareth Evans and John McDowell (Oxford: Oxford University Press, 1976), p. 105. In the latter essay Dummett traces our philosophical problems back to "our propensity to assume a realistic interpretation of all sentences of our language, that is, to suppose that the notion of truth applicable to statements of this kind is determinately either true or false, independently of our knowledge or means of knowing" (p. 101). In contrast, Davidson is inclined to trace them back to the antiholistic implications of the assumption which Dummett (p. 89) calls "principle C," viz., "if a statement is true, there must be something in virtue of which it is true." Dummett mistakenly believed, at the time of writing this paper, that this principle was accepted by both himself and Davidson. Dummett's acceptance of this principle and his insistence on the need for an "atomic or molecular theory of meaning," as opposed to a thoroughgoing holistic one, stands to Davidson's view roughly as the *Tractatus* stands to the *Philosophical Investigations.*

19 Thomas Nagel, *The View from Nowhere* (Oxford: Oxford University Press, 1986), pp. 106–7.

20 See Bjorn Ramberg, *Donald Davidson's Philosophy of Language: An Introduction* (Oxford: Blackwell, 1989), p. 2 and chapter 8, *passim.*

21 See Quine's remark about Brentano at *Word and Object* (Cambridge, Mass.: MIT Press, 1960), p. 221, and Davidson's treatment of Brentanian irreducibility in "Mental Events," included in his *Essays on Actions and Events* (Oxford: Oxford University Press, 1980).

My picture of Quine and Davidson as taking the holism of the *Philosophical Investigations* to its limits helps bring out the frequently cited analogies between Wittgenstein and Derrida. See Henry Staten, *Wittgenstein and Derrida* (Lincoln: University of Nebraska Press, 1984). For analogies between Derridean and Davidsonian doctrines, see Samuel Wheeler, "Indeterminacy of French Interpretation: Derrida and Davidson," in *Truth and Interpretation: Perspectives on the Philosophy of Donald Davidson*, ed. Ernest LePore (Oxford: Blackwell, 1986), pp. 477–94.

In my picture, Davidson stands to Wittgenstein as Derrida stands to Heidegger: both of these more recent writers are trying to purify the doctrines of the earlier writer, trying to divest them of the last traces of the tradition which they had tried to overcome. Derrida's suspicion of what he calls "Heideggerian nostalgia" is the counterpart to Davidson's suspicion of the later Wittgenstein's distinction between "grammar" and "fact." Davidson and Derrida are both protesting against vestiges of what Derrida calls "logocentrism" – trying to free their respective predecessors from their last remaining attachments to the idea that philosophy can shield itself from natural science, art, and history by isolating what Derrida calls "a full presence which is beyond play." (Derrida, *Writing and Difference*, trans. Alan Bass [Chicago: University of Chicago Press, 1978], p. 279.) Texts for Derrida, and human behavior for Davidson, are both centerless networks of relations, networks which can always be redescribed and recontextualized by themselves being placed within some larger network. For both writers, there is no such thing as "the largest network" – no bounded whole which can be the object of specifically philosophical inquiry.

22 All the passages cited in this paragraph are from *Philosophical Investigations*, I, secs. 91–2. Norman Malcolm's admirable account of the relation of the *Tractatus* to Wittgenstein's later thought is entitled *Nothing is Hidden*, a reference to *Investigations*, I, sec. 126: "Philosophy simply puts everything before us, and neither explains nor deduces anything. Since everything lies open to view there is nothing to explain. For what is hidden, for example, is of no interest to us."

23 I am following Robert Brandom ("Heidegger's Categories in *Being and Time*," *The Monist* 66 [1983]) and Mark Okrent (*Heidegger's Pragmatism* [Ithaca, N.Y.: Cornell University Press, 1988]) in taking Heidegger's attack on Cartesianism as central to the achievement of *Being and Time*. See also Charles Guignon, *Heidegger and the Theory of Knowledge* (Indianapolis: Hackett, 1983), chapter 1, "Heidegger's Problem and the Cartesian Model." These writers agree in thinking that what Brandom describes as the recognition that social practice is determinative of what is and is not up to social practice is Heidegger's crucial insight in this work. See especially Brandom's interpretation of the claim that the analytic of Dasein is fundamental ontology as an expression of this recognition (Brandom, p. 389). I take the criticism of Husserl at *Prolegomena der Geschichte des Zeitbegriffs* (Heidegger, *Gesamtausgabe*, vol. 20 [Frank-

furt: Klostermann, 1979], p. 62), and Heidegger's claim on the following page that what is needed to get beyond Husserl is to clear up "the togetherness of *intentum* and *intentio*" as prefiguring the claim of *Being and Time* that, in Brandom's words, "Dasein-in-the-world-of-the-ready-to-hand is ontologically self-adjudicating."

24 These passages are extracted from *Tractatus* 6.421–6.52.

25 See *Tractatus* 6.371 – 6.372. Compare *Philosophical Remarks*, p. 7.

26 *Philosophical Investigations*, I, sec. 164.

27 Ibid., I, sec. 127.

28 BW 198; WM 149. Heidegger goes on to suggest that he already knew this when he wrote Section 34 of *Sein und Zeit*, but I think this claim to prescience should be taken with a grain of salt.

29 See N2 194, for a grudging admission on this point.

30 N4 138. The original is at *Nietzsche*, Vol. 2 (Pfulligen: Neske, 1961), p. 192: *eine Geschichte des Wandels der Selbstauffasung der Menschen.*

31 See McGuiness, ed., *Wittgenstein und der Wiener Kreis* (Frankfurt: Suhrkamp, 184), p. 69: "I think it obviously important that we put an end to all the chatter about ethics [*Geschwätz über Ethik*] – whether it is cognitive, whether values exist, whether "good" is definable, and so on." The context is his famous remark that he could understand what Heidegger meant by "Being" and "Angst." Compare Heidegger, *Was heisst Denken?* (Tübingen, 1954), p. 19: *Was einmal Schrei war: 'Die Wüste wächst . . .' droht zum Geschwätz zu werden* ([Nietzsche's words] 'The wasteland grows' were once a shout, but now threaten to become merely chatter).

32 Wittgenstein, "Lecture on Ethics," *Philosophical Review* 74 (1965), p. 13. For a detailed account of the connection between the *Tractatus's* doctrine of showing and Wittgenstein's ideas about spiritual perfection, see James Edwards, *Ethics Without Philosophy: Wittgenstein and the Moral Life* (Tampa: University Presses of Florida, 1982) – a book to which I am much indebted for my understanding of Wittgenstein. Unfortunately, I read Edwards's *The Authority of Language: Heidegger, Wittgenstein and the Threat of Philosophical Nihilism* (Tampa: University of South Florida Press, 1990) too late to use it when composing this paper. That book now seems to me the most illuminating of the many attempts to bring Heidegger and Wittgenstein together.

33 *Wittgenstein und der Wiener Kreis*, p. 68.

34 Englemann, *Letters from Wittgenstein*, ed. McGuiness, p. 143.

35 Heidegger, "Poetically man dwells . . ." (PLT 215–6; VA 190). (I have changed Hofstadter's "master" [for *Herrin*] to "mistress.")

36 *Philosophical Investigations* I, sec. 261.

BIBLIOGRAPHY

A complete, up-to-date bibliography of works by and about Heidegger would be a vast undertaking. Hans-Martin Sass's 1975 bibliography, which covered the period from 1917 to 1972, included entire chapters called "Heidegger in Japan" and "Literature on Heidegger in the Soviet Union" and already contained more than 3,700 entries! Fortunately, some excellent bibliographies are available listing writings on Heidegger up to 1980 or so. This bibliography is therefore quite selective, emphasizing recent works in English most likely to be helpful to students and nonspecialists. John Haugeland, who put together a complete bibliography of recent articles and books in English on Heidegger, has been most helpful in pinpointing some especially useful articles. In general, the bibliography that follows focuses on recent books and multiauthored collections, though a number of influential classics are also included. As a rule, when an essay has been reprinted in a collection, it is not listed again separately.

BIBLIOGRAPHIES

Franzen, Winfried. *Martin Heidegger.* Stuttgart: J. B. Metzler, 1976. (This volume provides a thorough overview of Heidegger's work in German, with carefully selected bibliographies arranged by topic.)

Lübbe, Hermann. *Bibliographie der Heidegger-Literatur, 1917–1955.* Meisenheim am Glan: A. Hain, 1957.

Nordquist, Joan, ed. *Martin Heidegger: A Bibliography.* Santa Cruz, Calif: Reference and Research Service, 1990.

Sass, Hans-Martin. *Martin Heidegger: Bibliography and Glossary.* Bowling Green, Ohio: Bowling Green State University, Philosophy Documentation Center, 1982.

Sheehan, Thomas, ed. *Heidegger: The Man and the Thinker.* Chicago: Precedent, 1981. (This valuable collection contains, in addition to important works by Heidegger and by scholars writing about him, a bibliography matching original writings to translations and a detailed bibliography of writings about Heidegger.)

SELECTED WORKS IN GERMAN

In 1974 the German publisher Vittorio Klostermann (Frankfurt am Main) began preparations for the publication of Heidegger's collected works (*Martin Heidegger: Gesamtausgabe*). Around 100 volumes are planned. The series will consist of four divisions: (I) published writings, 1910–70; (II) lectures from Marburg and Freiburg, 1923–44; (III) unpublished papers, 1919–67; and (IV) notes and fragments (including notes on previously published works, letters, summaries, notes on seminars, etc.). The publisher anticipates that twenty to thirty years will be needed to complete the project. Heidegger, who worked extensively with the editors of the *Collected Works* during the final years of his life, specified the form he wanted the volumes to have (e.g., no volume may contain an index). There is, however, some question whether these volumes will be the definitive edition for Heidegger scholarship. Those familiar with the project have suggested that Heidegger made revisions to the earlier manuscripts without this fact being explicitly noted in the texts. On this subject, see Thomas Sheehan, "Caveat Lector: The New Heidegger," *New York Review of Books*, December 4, 1980, pp. 39–41.

As of November 1991, the publication schedule for the *Collected Works* was as follows (volumes already published have publication dates in brackets; an asterisk denotes the anticipated date of publication):

Division I

1. *Frühe Schriften* (1912–16). Edited by Friedrich-Wilhelm von Herrmann [1978].
2. *Sein und Zeit* (1927). Edited by Friedrich-Wilhelm von Herrmann [1977].
3. *Kant und das Problem der Metaphysik* (1929). Edited by Friedrich-Wilhelm von Herrmann [1991].
4. *Erläuterungen zu Hölderlins Dichtung* (1936–68). Edited by Friedrich-Wilhelm von Herrman [1991].
5. *Holzwege* (1935–46). Edited by Friedrich-Wilhelm von Herrmann [1977].

6. Vol. 1, *Nietzsche I* (1936–39); Vol. 2, *Nietzsche II* (1939–46).
7. *Vorträge und Aufsätze* (1936–53). Edited by Friedrich-Wilhelm von Herrmann.
8. *Was heisst Denken?* (1951–2).
9. *Wegmarken* (1919–61). Edited by Friedrich-Wilhelm von Herrmann [1976].
10. *Der Satz vom Grund* (1955–6).
11. *Identität und Differenz* (1955–7).
12. *Unterwegs zur Sprache* (1950–9). Edited by Friedrich-Wilhelm von Herrmann [1985].
13. *Aus der Erfahrung des Denkens* (1910–76). Edited by Hermann Heidegger [1983].
14. *Zur Sache des Denkens* (1962–4).
15. *Seminare* (1951–73). Edited by Curd Ochwadt [1986].
16. *Reden* (1925–76). Edited by Hermann Heidegger.

Division II

17. *Der Beginn der neuzeitlichen Philosophie* (winter semester, 1923–4). Edited by Friedrich-Wilhelm von Herrmann [1993*].
18. *Aristoteles: Rhetorik* (summer semester, 1924).
19. *Platon: Sophistes* (winter semester, 1924–5). Edited by Ingeborg Schüssler [1992].
20. *Prolegomena zur Geschichte des Zeitbegriffs* (summer semester, 1925). Edited by Petra Jaeger. [2d ed., 1988].
21. *Logik. Die Frage nach der Wahrheit* (winter semester, 1925–6). Edited by Walter Biemel [1976].
22. *Grundbegriffe der antiken Philosophie* (summer semester, 1926). Edited by Franz-Karl Blust [1992].
23. *Geschichte der Philosophie von Thomas v. Aquin bis Kant* (winter semester, 1926–7). Edited by Helmuth Vetter [1993*].
24. *Die Grundprobleme der Phänomenologie* (summer semester, 1927). Edited by Friedrich-Wilhelm von Herrmann. [2d ed., 1989].
25. *Phänomenologische Interpretation von Kants Kritik der reinen Vernunft* (winter semester, 1927–8). Edited by Ingtraud Görland. [2d ed., 1987].
26. *Metaphysische Anfangsgründe der Logik im Ausgang von Leibniz* (summer semester, 1928). Edited by Klaus Held. [2d ed., 1990].
27. *Einleitung in die Philosophie* (winter semester, 1928–9). Edited by Otto Saame.

28. *Der Deutsche Idealismus (Fichte, Hegel, Schelling) und die philosophische Problemlage der Gegenwart* (summer semester, 1929). Edited by Ingtraud Görland [1993*].

29/30. *Die Grundbegriffe der Metaphysik. Welt-Endlichkeit-Einsamkeit* (winter semester 1929–30). Edited by Friedrich-Wilhelm von Herrmann [1983].

31. *Vom Wesen der menschlichen Freiheit. Einleitung in die Philosophie* (summer semester, 1930). Edited by Hartmut Tietjen [1982].

32. *Hegels Phänomenologie des Geistes* (winter semester, 1930–1). Edited by Ingtraud Görland. [2d ed., 1988].

33. *Aristoteles: Metaphysik IX* (summer semester, 1931). Edited by Heinrich Hüni. [2d ed. 1990].

34. *Vom Wesen der Wahrheit. Zu Platons Höhlengleichnis und Theätet* (winter semester, 1931–2). Edited by Hermann Mörchen [1988].

35. *Der Anfang der abendländischen Philosophie* (*Anaximander und Parmenides*) (summer semester, 1932). Edited by Heinrich Hüni.

36/37. *Sein und Wahrheit* (1933–4). Edited by Hartmut Tietjen [1992].

38. *Über Logik als Frage nach der Sprache* (summer semester, 1934).

39. *Hölderlins Hymnen «Germanien» und «Der Rhein»* (winter semester, 1934–5). Edited by Susanne Ziegler. [2d ed. 1989].

40. *Einführung in die Metaphysik* (summer semester, 1935). Edited by Petra Jaeger [1983].

41. *Die Frage nach dem Ding. Zu Kants Lehre von den transzendentalen Grundsätzen* (winter semester, 1935–6). Edited by Petra Jaeger [1984].

42. *Schelling: Vom Wesen der menschlichen Freiheit* (*1809*) (summer semester, 1936). Edited by Ingrid Schüssler [1988].

43. *Nietzsche: Der Wille zur Macht als Kunst* (winter semester, 1936–7). Edited by Bernd Heimbüchel [1985].

44. *Nietzsches metaphysische Grundstellung im abendländischen Denken: Die ewige Wiederkehr des Gleichen* (summer semester, 1937). Edited by Marion Heinz [1986].

45. *Grundfragen der Philosophie. Ausgewählte «Probleme» der «Logik»* (winter semester, 1937–8). Edited by Friedrich-Wilhelm von Herrmann [1984].

46. *Nietzsches II. Unzeitgemässe Betrachtung* (winter semester, 1938–9). Edited by Bernd Heimbüchel [1993*].

47. *Nietzsches Lehre vom Willen zur Macht als Erkenntnis* (summer semester, 1939). Edited by Eberhard Hanser [1989].
48. *Nietzsche: Der europäische Nihilismus* (second trimester, 1940). Edited by Petra Jaeger [1986].
49. *Schelling: Zur erneuten Auslegung seiner Untersuchungen über das Wesen der menschlichen Freiheit* (1st trimester, 1941). Edited by Günter Seubold [1991].
50. *Nietzsches Metaphysik* (1941–2). *Einleitung in die Philosophie – Denken und Dichten* (1944–5). Edited by Petra Jaeger [1990].
51. *Grundbegriffe* (summer semester, 1941). Edited by Petra Jaeger. [2d ed., 1991].
52. *Hölderlins Hymne «Andenken»* (winter semester, 1941–2). Edited by Curd Ochwadt [1982].
53. *Hölderlins Hymne «Der Ister»* (summer semester, 1942). Edited by Walter Biemel [1984].
54. *Parmenides* (winter semester, 1942–3). Edited by Manfred S. Frings [1982].
55. *Heraklit.* 1. *Der Anfang des abendländischen Denkens (Heraklit)* (summer semester, 1943); 2. *Logik. Heraklits Lehre vom Logos* (summer semester, 1944). Edited by Manfred S. Frings. [2d ed., 1987].
56/57. *Zur Bestimmung der Philosophie* (1919). Edited by Bernd Heimbüchel [1987].
58. *Grundprobleme der Phänomenologie* (winter semester, 1919–20). Edited by Hans-Helmuth Gander [1992].
59/60. *Vorlesungen Sommersemester, 1920 und 1921.* Edited by Claudius Strube and Bernd Heimbüchel.
61. *Phänomenologische Interpretationen zu Aristoteles. Einführung in die phänomenologische Forschung* (winter semester, 1921–2). Edited by Walter Bröcker and Käte Bröcker-Oltmanns [1985].
62. *Phänomenologische Interpretation ausgewählter Abhandlungen des Aristoteles zur Ontologie und Logik* (summer semester, 1922). Edited by Franco Volpi.
63. *Ontologie. Hermeneutik der Faktizität* (summer semester, 1923). Edited by Käte Bröcker-Oltmanns [1988].

Division III

64. *Der Begriff der Zeit* (1924).
65. *Beiträge zur Philosophie (Vom Ereignis)* (1936–8). Edited by Friedrich-Wilhelm von Herrmann [1989].

Besinnung (1938/39).
Die Überwindung der Metaphysik (1938/39).
Hegel (1938/39, 1942/43).
Die Geschichte des Seyns (1938/40).
Über den Anfang (1941).
Das Ereignis (1941–42).
Die Stege des Anfangs (1944).
Feldweggespräche (1945).
Das abendländische Gespräch (1946–1948).
Der Spruch des Anaximander (1946).
Das Wesen des Nihilismus (1946–1948).
Bremer und Freiburger Vorträge (1949, 1957).
Vorträge (18 lectures from 1915 to 1967 are listed)
Gedachtes.

Division IV

Comments on previously published writings (including *Being and Time*), notes for seminars, selected letters, summaries, etc.

The *Collected Works* editions of previously published volumes contain the pagination for the earlier editions in the margins. Some especially important works by Heidegger in German are the following:

Gelassenheit. 2d ed. Pfullingen: Günther Neske, 1960.
Holzwege. 5th ed. Frankfurt am Main: Vittorio Klostermann, 1972.
Kant und das Problem der Metaphysik. 2d edition. Frankfurt am Main: Vittorio Klostermann, 1951.
Nietzsche. 2 vols. 2d ed. Pfullingen: Günther Neske, 1961.
Der Satz vom Grund. 4th ed. Pfullingen: Günther Neske, 1971.
Sein und Zeit. 11th ed. Tübingen: Max Niemeyer, 1963.
Die Technik und die Kehre. Pfullingen: Günther Neske, 1962.
Unterwegs zur Sprache. 3d ed. Pfullingen: Günther Neske, 1965.
Vorträge und Aufsätze. 3d ed. Pfullingen: Günther Neske, 1967.
Was heisst Denken? Tübingen: Max Niemeyer, 1954.
Wegmarken. Frankfurt am Main: Vittorio Klostermann, 1967.

ENGLISH TRANSLATIONS

Basic Problems of Phenomenology. Translated by Albert Hofstadter. Bloomington: Indiana University Press, 1982.
Basic Writings. Edited by David F. Krell. New York: Harper & Row, 1977.
Being and Time. Translated by John Macquarrie and Edward Robinson. New York: Harper & Row, 1962.

The Concept of Time. Translated by William McNeill. Oxford: Blackwell, 1992.

Discourse on Thinking. Translated by John M. Anderson and E. Hans Freund. New York: Harper & Row, 1966.

"A Discussion between Ernst Cassirer and Martin Heidegger." Translated by Francis Slade. In *The Existentialist Tradition: Selected Writings.* Edited by Nino Langiulli. Garden City, N.Y.: Doubleday, 1971.

Early Greek Thinking. Translated by David Farrell Krell and Frank Capuzzi. New York: Harper & Row, 1975.

The End of Philosophy. Translated by Joan Stambaugh. New York: Harper & Row, 1973.

The Essence of Reasons. Translated by Terrence Malick. Evanston, Ill.: Northwestern University Press, 1969.

Existence and Being. Edited by Werner Brock. Chicago: Regnery, 1949.

Hegel's Concept of Experience. Translated by J. Glenn Gray. New York: Harper & Row, 1970.

History of the Concept of Time: Prolegomena. Translated by Theodore Kisiel. Bloomington: Indiana University Press, 1985.

Identity and Difference. Translated by Joan Stambaugh. New York: Harper & Row, 1969.

An Introduction to Metaphysics. Translated by Ralph Manheim. New Haven, Conn.: Yale University Press, 1959.

Kant and the Problem of Metaphysics. Translated by James S. Churchill. Bloomington: Indiana University Press, 1962. Retranslated by Richard Taft. Bloomington: Indiana University Press, 1990.

Martin Heidegger and National Socialism: Questions and Answers. Edited by Günther Neske and Emil Kettering. Translated by Lisa Harries. New York: Paragon House, 1990. (Contains "The Self-Assertion of the German University" [the rectoral address], "The Rectorate 1933/34: Facts and Thoughts," the *Spiegel* interview ["Only a God Can Save Us"], and "Martin Heidegger in Conversation" with Richard Wisser.)

The Metaphysical Foundations of Logic. Translated by Michael Heim. Bloomington: Indiana University Press, 1984.

Nietzsche I: The Will to Power as Art. Edited and translated by David F. Krell. New York: Harper & Row, 1979.

Nietzsche II: The Eternal Recurrence of the Same. Edited and translated by David F. Krell. New York: Harper & Row, 1984.

Nietzsche III: The Will to Power as Knowledge and Metaphysics. Edited by David F. Krell. Translated by Joan Stambaugh. New York: Harper & Row, 1987.

Nietzsche IV: Nihilism. Edited by David F. Krell. Translated by Frank A. Capuzzi. New York: Harper & Row, 1982.

On Time and Being. Translated by Joan Stambaugh. New York: Harper & Row, 1972.

On the Way to Language. Translated by Peter D. Hertz. New York: Harper & Row, 1971.

Parmenides. Translated by André Schuwer and Richard Rojcewicz. Bloomington: Indiana University Press, 1992.

The Piety of Thinking. Translated by James Hart and John Maraldo. Bloomington: Indiana University Press, 1976.

"Plato's Doctrine of Truth." Translated by John Barlow. In *Philosophy in the Twentieth Century*. Vol. 3. Edited by William Barrett and Henry D. Aiken. New York: Random House, 1962.

Poetry, Language, Thought. Translated by Albert Hofstadter. New York: Harper & Row, 1971.

The Principle of Reason. Translated by Reginald Lilly. Bloomington: Indiana University Press, 1991.

The Question of Being. Translated by William Kluback and Jean T. Wilde. New York: Twayne, 1958.

The Question Concerning Technology and Other Essays. Translated by William Lovitt. New York: Harper & Row, 1977.

Schelling's Treatise on Human Freedom. Translated by Joan Stambaugh. Athens: Ohio University Press, 1985.

"The Way Back into the Ground of Metaphysics" (Introduction to "What Is Metaphysics?"). Translated by Walter Kaufmann. In *Existentialism from Dostoyevsky to Sartre*. Edited by Walter Kaufmann. Cleveland: World, 1965.

What Is Called Thinking? Translated by Fred D. Wieck and J. Glenn Gray. New York: Harper & Row, 1968.

What Is Philosophy? Translated by William Kluback and Jean T. Wilde. New Haven: College and University Press, 1958.

What Is a Thing? Translated by W. B. Barton and Vera Deutsch. Chicago: Regnery, 1969.

"Why Do I Stay in the Provinces?" Translated by Thomas Sheehan. In *Heidegger: The Man and the Thinker*. Edited by Thomas Sheehan. Chicago: Precedent, 1981.

BACKGROUND AND BIOGRAPHICAL

Bubner, Rüdiger. *Modern German Philosophy*. Translated by Eric Matthews. Cambridge: Cambridge University Press, 1981.

Emad, Parvis. "The Place of Hegel in Heidegger's 'Being and Time.' " *Research in Phenomenology*, 13 (1983): 159–73.

Gadamer, Hans-Georg. *Philosophical Hermeneutics.* Edited and translated by David E. Linge. Berkeley and Los Angeles: University of California Press, 1976.

Philosophical Apprenticeships. Translated by Robert R. Sullivan. Cambridge, Mass.: MIT Press, 1985.

Habermas, Jürgen. *Philosophical-Political Profiles.* Translated by Frederick G. Lawrence. Cambridge, Mass.: MIT Press, 1983.

The Philosophical Discourse of Modernity: Twelve Lectures. Translated by Frederick G. Lawrence. Cambridge, Mass.: MIT Press, 1987.

Hollinger, Robert, ed. *Hermeneutics and Praxis.* Notre Dame, Ind.: University of Notre Dame Press, 1985.

Hoy, David Couzens. *The Critical Circle: Literature, History, and Philosophical Hermeneutics.* Berkeley and Los Angeles: University of California Press, 1978.

Kisiel, Theodore. "En Route to 'Sein und Zeit.' " *Research in Phenomenology,* 10 (1980): 307–27.

"On the Way to 'Being and Time': Introduction to the Translation of Heidegger's 'Prolegomena zur Geschichte des Zeitbegriffs.' " *Research in Phenomenology,* 15 (1985): 193–226.

"Why the First Draft of 'Being and Time' Was Never Published." *Journal of the British Society for Phenomenology,* 20 (January 1989): 3–22.

Makkreel, Rudolf A., and Scanlon, John, eds. *Dilthey and Phenomenology.* Lanham, Md.: University Press of America, 1987.

Megill, Allan. *Prophets of Extremity: Nietzsche, Heidegger, Foucault, Derrida.* Berkeley and Los Angeles: University of California Press, 1985.

Misch, Georg. *Lebensphilosophie und Phänomenologie. Eine Auseinandersetzung der Diltheyschen Richtung mit Heidegger und Husserl.* 3d ed. Darmstadt: Wissenschaftliche Buchgesellschaft, 1967.

Noreña, Carlos G. "Heidegger on Suárez: The 1927 Marburg Lectures." *International Philosophical Quarterly,* 23 (December 1983): 407–24.

Ott, Hugo. *Martin Heidegger: Unterwegs zur seiner Biographie.* Frankfurt am Main: Campus, 1988.

Palmer, Richard E. *Hermeneutics: Interpretation Theory in Schleiermacher, Dilthey, Heidegger, and Gadamer.* Evanston, Ill.: Northwestern University Press, 1969.

Petzet, Heinrich Wiegand. *Auf einen Stern zugehen: Begegnungen und Gespräche mit Martin Heidegger, 1929–1976.* Frankfurt am Main: Societäts-Verlag, 1983.

Pöggler, Otto. *Heidegger und die hermeneutische Philosophie.* Freiburg: Alber, 1983.

Ricoeur, Paul. "The Task of Hermeneutics." In *Heidegger and Modern Philosophy.* Edited by Michael Murray. New Haven, Conn.: Yale Univeristy Press, 1978.

Roberts, Julian. *German Philosophy: An Introduction.* Atlantic Highlands, N.J.: Humanities Press, 1988.

Schnädelbach, Herbert. *Philosophy in Germany, 1831–1933.* Cambridge: Cambridge University Press, 1984.

Seebohm, Thomas M. "The Problem of Hermeneutics in Recent Anglo-American Literature." *Philosophy and Rhetoric,* 10 (1977): 180–98, 263–75.

Seebohm, Thomas M., and Kockelmans, Joseph J., eds. *Kant and Phenomenology.* Washington, D.C.: University Press of America, 1984.

Sheehan, Thomas. "The 'Original Form' of 'Sein und Zeit': Heidegger's 'Der Begriff der Zeit' (1924)." *Journal of the British Society for Phenomenology,* 10 (May 1979): 78–83.

Sherover, Charles M. *Heidegger, Kant and Time.* Bloomington: Indiana University Press, 1971.

Solomon, Robert C. *From Rationalism to Existentialism: The Existentialists and Their Nineteenth-Century Background.* New York: Harper & Row, 1972.

Spiegelberg, Herbert. *The Phenomenological Movement: An Historical Introduction.* 2 vols. The Hague: Nijhoff, 1969.

Stapleton, Timothy J. *Husserl and Heidegger: The Question of a Phenomenological Beginning.* Albany: State University of New York Press, 1983.

Taminiaux, Jacques. "Poiesis and Praxis in Fundamental Ontology." *Research in Phenomenology,* 17 (1987): 137–69.

"The Interpretation of Greek Philosophy in Heidegger's Fundamental Ontology." *Journal of the British Society for Phenomenology,* 19 (January 1988): 3–14.

Wachterhauser, Brice R., ed. *Hermeneutics and Modern Philosophy.* Albany: State University of New York Press, 1986.

GENERAL

Barash, Jeffrey Andrew. *Martin Heidegger and the Problem of Historical Meaning.* Dordrecht: Nijhoff, 1985.

Bernasconi, Robert. *The Question of Language in Heidegger's History of Being.* Atlantic Highlands, N.J.: Humanities Press, 1985.

"Descartes in the History of Being: Another Bad Novel?" *Research in Phenomenology,* 17 (1987): 75–102.

Bernsen, Niels Ole. *Heidegger's Theory of Intentionality.* Odense: Odense University Press, 1986.

Bernstein, Richard J. "Heidegger on Humanism." *Praxis International,* 5 (July 1985): 95–114.

"The Rage Against Reason." *Philosophy and Literature,* 10 (October 1986): 186–210.

The New Constellation: The Ethical-Political Horizons of Modernity/Postmodernity. Cambridge, Mass.: MIT Press, 1992.

Bigelow, Patrick. "The Indeterminacy of Time in 'Sein und Zeit.' " *Philosophy and Phenomenological Research,* 46 (March 1986): 357–79.

Bourgeois, Patrick L., and Schalow, Frank. "The Integrity and Fallenness of Human Existence." *Southern Journal of Philosophy,* 25 (Spring 1987): 123–32.

Brandom, Robert. "Heidegger's Categories." *Monist,* 66 (July 1983): 387–409.

Bruzina, Ronald, and Wilshire, Bruce, eds. *Phenomenology, Dialogues and Bridges.* Albany: State University of New York Press, 1982.

Caputo, John D. "Three Transgressions: Nietzsche, Heidegger, Derrida." *Research in Phenomenology,* 15 (1985): 61–78.

Radical Hermeneutics: Repetition, Deconstruction, and the Hermeneutic Project. Bloomington: Indiana University Press, 1987.

"Demythologizing Heidegger: *Aletheia* and the History of Being." *Review of Metaphysics,* 41 (March 1988): 519–46.

"Incarnation and Essentialization: A Reading of Heidegger." *Philosophy Today,* 35 (Spring 1991): 32–42.

Carr, David. *Time, Narrative, and History.* Bloomington: Indiana University Press, 1986.

Ciaffa, Jay A. "Toward an Understanding of Heidegger's Conception of the Inter-Relation Between Authentic and Inauthentic Existence." *Journal of the British Society for Phenomenology,* 18 (January 1987): 49–59.

Dahlstrom, Daniel. "Heidegger's Last Word." *Review of Metaphysics,* 41 (March 1988): 589–606.

Dallmayr, Fred. *Between Freiburg and Frankfurt: Toward a Critical Ontology.* Amherst: University of Massachusetts Press, 1991.

Derrida, Jacques. *Margins of Philosophy.* Translated, with additional notes, by Alan Bass. Chicago: University of Chicago Press, 1982.

"On Reading Heidegger." *Research in Phenomenology,* 17 (1987): 171–85.

DiCenso, James. *Hermeneutics and the Disclosure of Truth: A Study in the Work of Heidegger, Gadamer, and Ricoeur.* Charlottesville: University of Virginia Press, 1990.

Dostal, Robert J. "The Problem of 'Indifferenz' in 'Sein und Zeit.' " *Philosophy and Phenomenological Research,* 43 (September 1982): 43–58.

"Beyond Being: Heidegger's Plato." *Journal of the History of Philosophy,* 23 (January 1985): 71–98.

Dreyfus, Hubert L. *Being-in-the-World: A Commentary on Heidegger's "Being and Time," Division I.* Cambridge, Mass.: MIT Press, 1991.

Dreyfus, Hubert L., and Hall, Harrison, eds. *Heidegger: A Critical Reader.* Oxford: Blackwell, 1992.

Edwards, James C. *The Authority of Language: Heidegger, Wittgenstein, and the Threat of Philosophical Nihilism.* Tampa: University of South Florida Press, 1990.

Emad, Parvis. *Heidegger and the Phenomenology of Values: His Critique of Intentionality.* Glen Ellyn, Ill.: Torey Press, 1981.

Farwell, Paul. "Can Heidegger's Craftsman Be Authentic?" *International Philosophical Quarterly,* 29 (March 1989): 77–90.

Fell, Joseph P. *Heidegger and Sartre: An Essay on Being and Place.* New York: Columbia University Press, 1979.

"The Crisis of Reason: A Reading of Heidegger's *'Zur Seinsfrage.'* " *Heidegger Studies,* 2 (1986): 41–65

Føllesdal, Dagfinn. "Husserl and Heidegger on the Role of Actions in the Constitution of the World." In *Essays in Honor of Jaakko Hintikka.* Edited by Esa Saarinen et al. Dordrecht: Reidel, 1979.

Frede, Dorothea. "Heidegger and the Scandal of Philosophy." In *Human Nature and Natural Knowledge.* Edited by A. Donagan, A. Perovich, and M. Wedin. Dordrecht: Reidel, 1986.

"Beyond Realism and Anti-Realism: Rorty on Heidegger and Davidson." *Review of Metaphysics,* 40 (June 1987): 733–57.

Fynsk, Christopher. *Heidegger, Thought and Historicity.* Ithaca, N.Y.: Cornell University Press, 1986.

Gelven, Michael. "Language as Saying and Showing." *Journal of Value Inquiry,* 17 (1983): 151–62.

Gillespie, Michael Allen. *Hegel, Heidegger, and the Ground of History.* University of Chicago Press, 1984.

Graybeal, Jean. *Language and the "Feminine" in Nietzsche and Heidegger.* Bloomington: Indiana University Press, 1990.

Grondin, Jean. *Le tournant dans la pensée de Martin Heidegger.* Paris: Presses universitaires de France, 1987.

Guignon, Charles B. *Heidegger and the Problem of Knowledge.* Indianapolis: Hackett, 1983.

"Heidegger's 'Authenticity' Revisited." *Review of Metaphysics,* 38 (December 1984): 321–39.

"On Saving Heidegger from Rorty." *Philosophy and Phenomenological Research,* 46 (March 1986): 401–17.

"Philosophy after Wittgenstein and Heidegger." *Philosophy and Phenomenological Research* 50 (June 1990): 649–72.

Haar, Michel "The End of Distress: The End of Technology?" *Research in Phenomenology,* 13 (1983): 43–63.

Martin Heidegger: Cahier a été dirige. Paris: L'Herne, 1983.

Le chant de la terre: Heidegger et les assises de l'histoire de l'être. Paris: L'Herne, 1987.

Heidegger et l'essénce de l'homme. Grenoble: Jerome Millon, 1990.

Hall, Harrison. "Love and Death: Kierkegaard and Heidegger on Authentic and Inauthentic Human Existence." *Inquiry,* 27 (July 1984): 179–97.

Haugeland, John. "Heidegger on Being a Person." *Noûs,* 16 (March 1982): 6–26.

Heim, Michael. "The Finite Framework of Language." *Philosophy Today,* 31 (Spring 1987): 3–20.

Herrmann, Friedrich Wilhelm von. *Subjekt und Dasein: Interpretationen zu "Sein und Zeit."* Frankfurt am Main: Klostermann, 1985.

Hoffman, Piotr. *The Human Self and the Life and Death Struggle.* Gainesville: University Press of Florida, 1983.

Doubt, Time, Violence. Chicago: University of Chicago Press, 1986.

Ihde, Don, and Silverman, Hugh J., eds. *Descriptions.* Albany: State University of New York Press, 1985.

Kockelmans, Joseph J. *On the Truth of Being: Reflections on Heidegger's Later Philosophy.* Bloomington: Indiana University Press, 1984.

A Companion to Martin Heidegger's "Being and Time." Washington, D.C.: University Press of America, 1986.

Kolb, David. *The Critique of Pure Modernity: Hegel, Heidegger, and After.* Chicago: University of Chicago Press, 1986.

Krell, David Farrell. *Intimations of Mortality: Time, Truth, and Finitude in Heidegger's Thinking of Being.* University Park: Pennsylvania State University Press, 1986.

Levin, David Michael. *The Opening of Vision: Nihilism and the Postmodern Situation.* New York: Routledge & Kegan Paul, 1988.

Löwith, Karl. *Heidegger: Denker in dürftiger Zeit: Zur Stellung der Philosophie im 20. Jahrhundert.* Stuttgart: J. B. Metzler, 1984.

Macomber, W. B. *The Anatomy of Disillusion: Martin Heidegger's Notion of Truth.* Evanston, Ill.: Northwestern University Press, 1967.

Magnus, Bernd. "Heidegger's Metahistory of Philosophy Revisited." *Monist,* 64 (October 1981): 445–66.

Maly, Kenneth and Emad, Parvis, eds. *Heidegger on Heraclitus: A New Reading.* Lewiston, N.Y.: Mellen Press, 1986.

Marx, Werner. *Heidegger and the Tradition.* Translated by Theodore Kisiel and Murray Greene. Evanston, Ill.: Northwestern University Press, 1971.

Marx, Werner, ed. *Heidegger Memorial Lectures.* Translated by Steven W. Davis. Pittsburgh: Duquesne University Press, 1982.

Mehta, Jarava Lal. *Martin Heidegger, the Way and the Vision.* Honolulu: University of Hawaii Press, 1976.

Mohanty, J. N. *The Possibility of Transcendental Philosophy.* Dordrecht: Nijhoff, 1985.

"Heidegger on Logic." *Journal of the History of Philosophy,* 26 (January 1988): 107–35.

Mugerauer, Robert. *Heidegger's Language and Thinking.* Atlantic Highlands, N.J.: Humanities Press International, 1988.

Mulhall, Stephen. *On Being in the World: Wittgenstein and Heidegger on Seeing Aspects.* London: Routledge & Kegan Paul, 1990.

Murray, Michael, ed. *Heidegger and Modern Philosophy: Critical Essays.* New Haven, Conn.: Yale University Press, 1978.

"Husserl and Heidegger: Constructing and Deconstructing Greek Philosophy." *Review of Metaphysics,* 41 (March 1988): 501–18.

Nenon, Thomas J., ed. *Spindel Conference 1989: Heidegger and Praxis.* Memphis, Tenn.: Memphis State University, 1990. *Southern Journal of Philosophy,* 28, suppl.

Okrent, Mark. "Hermeneutics, Transcendental Philosophy and Social Science." *Inquiry,* 27 (March 1984): 23–50.

"Relativism, Context, and Truth." *Monist,* 67 (July 1984): 341–58.

Heidegger's Pragmatism: Understanding, Being, and the Critique of Metaphysics. Ithaca, N.Y.: Cornell University Press, 1988.

Olafson, Frederick A. *Heidegger and the Philosophy of Mind.* New Haven, Conn.: Yale University Press, 1987.

Parkes, Graham, ed. *Heidegger and Asian Thought.* Honolulu: University of Hawaii Press, 1987.

Phenomenology: Descriptive or Hermeneutic. Pittsburgh: Duquesne University, Simon Silverman Phenomenology Center, 1987.

Phenomenology of Temporality: Time and Language. Pittsburgh: Duquesne University, Simon Silverman Phenomenology Center, 1987.

Pöggler, Otto, ed. *Heidegger: Perspektiven zur Deutung seines Werks.* Köln: Kiepenheuer & Witsch, 1969.

Martin Heidegger's Path of Thinking. Translated by Daniel Magurshak and Sigmund Barber. Atlantic Highlands, N. J.: Humanities Press International, 1987.

Rapaport, Herman. *Heidegger and Derrida: Reflections on Time and Language.* Lincoln: University of Nebraska Press, 1989.

Richardson, John. *Existential Epistemology: A Heideggerian Critique of the Cartesian Project.* Oxford: Clarendon Press, 1986.

Richardson, William J. *Heidegger: Through Phenomenology to Thought.* 3d ed. The Hague: Nijhoff, 1974.

Ricoeur, Paul. "The Human Experience of Time and Narrative." *Research in Phenomenology,* 9 (1979): 17–34.

"Narrative Time." In *On Narrative.* Edited by W. J. T. Mitchell. Chicago: University of Chicago Press, 1980.

"Phenomenology and Hermeneutics." In *Hermeneutics and the Human Sciences.* Edited by John Thompson. Cambridge: Cambridge University Press, 1981.

Time and Narrative. 3 vols. Translated by K. McLaughlin and D. Pellaner. Chicago: University of Chicago Press, 1984–6.

Rorty, Richard. *Philosophy and the Mirror of Nature.* Princeton, N.J.: Princeton University Press, 1979.

Consequences of Pragmatism. Minneapolis: University of Minnesota Press, 1982.

Contingency, Irony, and Solidarity. Cambridge: Cambridge University Press, 1989.

Essays on Heidegger and Others: Philosophical Papers. Vol. 2. Cambridge: Cambridge University Press, 1991.

Rorty, Richard, ed. *Heidegger and the History of Philosophy.* Special issue of *Monist,* 64 (October 1981).

Sallis, John. "End(s)." *Research in Phenomenology,* 13 (1983): 85–96.

"Heidegger/Derrida – Presence." *Journal of Philosophy,* 81 (October 1984): 594–601.

Echoes: After Heidegger. Bloomington: Indiana University Press, 1990.

Sallis, John, ed. *Deconstruction and Philosophy.* Chicago: University of Chicago Press, 1987.

Sallis, John, Moneta, Giuseppina, and Taminiaux, Jacques, eds. *The Collegium Phaenomenologicum: The First Ten Years.* Amsterdam: Kluwer, 1988.

Schmidt, Dennis J. "Between Hegel and Heidegger." *Man and World,* 15 (1982): 17–32.

"On the Obscurity of the Origin." *Philosophy Today,* 26 (Winter 1982): 322–31.

The Ubiquity of the Finite: Hegel, Heidegger, and the Entitlements of Philosophy. Cambridge, Mass.: MIT Press, 1988.

"In Heidegger's Wake: Belonging to the Discourse of the 'Turn.' " *Heidegger Studies* 5 (1989): 201–11.

Schrift, Alan D. "Reading Derrida Reading Heidegger Reading Nietzsche." *Research in Phenomenology,* 14 (1984): 87–119.

Schürmann, Reiner. *Heidegger on Being and Acting: From Principles to Anarchy.* Translated by Christine-Marie Gros and Reiner Schürmann. Bloomington: Indiana University Press, 1987.

Scott, Charles E. *The Language of Difference.* Atlantic Highlands, N.J.: Humanities Press, 1987.

"On the Unity of Heidegger's Thought." *Research in Phenomenology,* 17 (1987): 263–74.

Seifert, Josef. "Is the Existence of Truth Dependent on Man?" *Review of Metaphysics,* 35 (1982): 461–82.

Seigfried, Hans. "Against Naturalizing Preconceptual Experience." *Philosophy and Phenomenological Research,* 48 (March 1988): 505–18.

Shahan, Robert W., and Mohanty, J. N., eds. *Thinking about Being: Aspects of Heidegger's Thought.* Norman: University of Oklahoma Press, 1984.

Shapiro, Gary, and Sica, Alan, eds. *Hermeneutics: Questions and Prospects.* Amherst: University of Massachusetts Press, 1984.

Sheehan, Thomas. "Heidegger's Philosophy of Mind." In *Contemporary Philosophy: A New Survey.* Edited by Guttorm Floistad. The Hague: Nijhoff, 1983.

Silverman, Hugh J., ed. *Postmodernism and Continental Philosophy.* Albany: State University of New York Press, 1988.

Silverman, Hugh J., and Ihde, Don, eds. *Hermeneutics and Deconstruction.* Albany: State University of New York Press, 1985.

Silverman, Hugh J., Sallis, John, and Seebohm, Thomas M., eds.

Continental Philosophy in America. Pittsburgh: Duquesne University Press, 1983.

Silverman, Hugh J., et al., eds. *The Horizons of Continental Philosophy: Essays on Husserl, Heidegger, and Merleau-Ponty.* Dordrecht: Kluwer Academic, 1988.

Stambaugh, Joan. "Nihilism and the End of Philosophy." *Research in Phenomenology,* 15 (1985): 79–97.

Steiner, George. *Martin Heidegger.* Chicago: University of Chicago Press, 1987.

Stewart, Roderick M. "Heidegger and the Intentionality of Language." *American Philosophical Quarterly,* 25 (April 1988): 153–62.

Taminiaux, Jacques. *Dialectic and Difference: Finitude in Modern Thought.* Atlantic Highlands, N.J.: Humanities Press, 1985.

Heidegger and the Project of Fundamental Ontology. Translated by Michael Gendre. Albany: State University of New York Press, 1991.

Theunissen, Michael. *The Other: Studies in the Social Ontology of Husserl, Heidegger, Sartre, and Buber.* Translated by Christopher Macann. Cambridge, Mass.: MIT Press, 1984.

Tugendhat, Ernst. *Self-Consciousness and Self-Determination.* Translated by Paul Stern. Cambridge, Mass.: MIT Press, 1986.

Vallicella, William F. "Heidegger and the Problem of the Thing in Itself." *International Philosophical Quarterly,* 23 (March 1983): 35–44.

Watson, Stephen. "Heidegger, Rationality, and the Critique of Judgement." *Review of Metaphysics,* 41 (March 1988): 461–99.

White, Carol J. "Dasein, Existence, and Death." *Philosophy Today,* 28 (Spring 1984): 52–65.

"Heidegger and the Beginning of Metaphysics." *Journal of the British Society for Phenomenology,* 19 (January 1988): 34–50.

White, David A. *Logic and Ontology in Heidegger.* Columbus: Ohio State University Press, 1985.

Wood, David. "Heidegger after Derrida." *Research in Phenomenology,* 17 (1987): 103–16.

Zimmerman, Michael. "Heidegger's 'Existentialism' Revisited." *International Philosophical Quarterly,* 24 (September 1984): 219–36.

Eclipse of the Self: The Development of Heidegger's Concept of Authenticity. Rev. ed. Athens: Ohio University Press, 1986.

Heidegger's Confrontation with Modernity: Technology, Politics, and Art. Bloomington: Indiana University Press, 1990.

Zimmerman, Michael, ed. *The Thought of Martin Heidegger.* Tulane

Studies in Philosophy, Vol. 32. New Orleans, La.: Tulane University, 1984.

ETHICS AND POLITICS

Bernasconi, Robert L. " 'The Double Concept of Philosophy' and the Place of Ethics in *Being and Time.*" *Research in Phenomenology,* 18 (1988): 41–57.

Blitz, Mark. *Heidegger's "Being and Time" and the Possibility of Political Philosophy.* Ithaca, N.Y.: Cornell University Press, 1981.

Bourdieu, Pierre. *The Political Ontology of Martin Heidegger.* Translated by Peter Collier. Stanford, Calif.: Stanford University Press, 1991.

Brainard, Marcus, Jacobs, David, and Lee, Rick, eds. *Heidegger and the Political.* Special Issue of the *Graduate Faculty of Philosophy Journal,* 14–15 (1991). (Includes an extensive bibliography by Pierre Adler.)

Dallery, Arleen, Scott, Charles E., and Roberts, P. Holly, eds. *Ethics and Danger: Essays on Heidegger and Continental Thought.* Albany: State University of New York Press, 1992.

Dallmayr, Fred R. "Ontology of Freedom: Heidegger and Political Philosophy." *Political Theory,* 12 (May 1984): 204–34.

"Heidegger, Hölderlin and Politics." *Heidegger Studies,* 2 (1986): 81–95.

"Heidegger and Marxism." *Praxis International,* 7 (October 1987): 207–24.

Dauenhauer, Bernard P. "Heidegger's Contribution to Modern Political Thought." *Southern Journal of Philosophy,* 22 (Winter 1984): 481–86.

Derrida, Jacques. *Of Spirit: Heidegger and the Question.* Translated by Geoffrey Bennington and Rachel Bowlby. Chicago: University of Chicago Press, 1989.

Farías, Victor. *Heidegger and Nazism.* Edited by Joseph Margolis and Tom Rockmore. Translated by Paul Burrell, with the advice of Dominic Di Bernardi, and by Gabriel R. Ricci. Philadelphia: Temple University Press, 1989.

Ferry, Luc, and Renaut, Alain. *Heidegger and Modernity.* Translated by Franklin Philip. Chicago: University of Chicago Press, 1990.

Hans, James S. *The Question of Value: Thinking Through Nietzsche, Heidegger, and Freud.* Carbondale: Southern Illinois University Press, 1989.

Lacoue-Labarthe, Philippe. *Heidegger, Art, and Politics: The Fiction of the Political.* Translated by Chris Turner. Oxford: Blackwell, 1990.

Lyotard, Jean François. *Heidegger and "The Jews."* Translated by Andreas Michel and Mark S. Roberts. Foreword by David Carroll. Minneapolis: University of Minnesota Press, 1990.

Marcuse, Herbert, and Olafson, Frederick. "Heidegger's Politics." *Graduate Faculty Philosophy Journal,* 6 (Winter 1977): 28–40.

Marx, Werner. *Is There a Measure on Earth? Foundations for a Nonmetaphysical Ethics.* Translated by Thomas J. Nenon and Reginald Lilly. Chicago: University of Chicago Press, 1987.

McWhorter, La Delle. *Heidegger and the Earth: Issues in Environmental Philosophy.* Kirksland, Mo.: Thomas Jefferson University Press, 1990.

Nicholson, Graeme. "The Politics of Heidegger's Rectoral Address." *Man and World,* 20 (1987): 171–87.

Pöggler, Otto. *Philosophie und Nationalsozialismus: Am Beispiel Heideggers.* Opladen: Westdeutscher, 1990.

Rockmore, Tom, and Margolis, Joseph, eds. *The Heidegger Case: On Philosophy and Politics.* Philadelphia: Temple University Press, 1992.

Schalow, Frank. *Imagination and Existence: Heidegger's Retrieval of the Kantian Ethic.* Lanham, Md.: University Press of America, 1986.

"Toward a Concrete Ontology of Practical Reason in Light of Heidegger's Lectures on Human Freedom." *Journal of the British Society for Phenomenology,* 17 (May 1986): 155–65.

Schürmann, Reiner. "Adventures of the Double Negation: On Richard Bernstein's Call for Anti-anti-humanism." *Praxis International,* 5 (October 1985): 283–91.

Scott, Charles E. *The Question of Ethics: Nietzsche, Foucault, Heidegger.* Bloomington: Indiana University Press, 1990.

Sheehan, Thomas. "Heidegger and the Nazis." *New York Review of Books,* June 16, 1988, pp. 38–47.

Tymieniecka, Anna-Teresa, and Schrag, Calvin O., eds. *Foundations of Morality.* Boston: Reidel, 1983.

Wolin, Richard. *The Politics of Being: The Political Thought of Martin Heidegger.* New York: Columbia University Press, 1990.

Wyschogrod, Edith. *Spirit in Ashes: Hegel, Heidegger, and Man-Made Mass Death.* New Haven, Conn.: Yale University Press, 1985.

Zimmerman, Michael E. "Karel Kosik's Heideggerian Marxism." *Philosophical Forum,* 15 (Spring 1984): 209–33.

"Philosophy and Politics: The Case of Heidegger." *Philosophy Today*, 33 (Spring 1989): 3–20.
"The Thorn in Heidegger's Side: The Question of National Socialism." *Philosophical Forum*, 20 (Summer 1989): 326–65.

AESTHETICS AND LITERARY THEORY

Bove, Paul A. *Destructive Poetics: Heidegger and Modern American Poetry*. New York: Columbia University Press, 1980.
Brogan, Walter. "The Battle Between Art and Truth." *Philosophy Today*, 28 (Winter 1984): 349–57.
Bruns, Gerald L. *Heidegger's Estrangements: Language, Truth, and Poetry in the Later Writings*. New Haven Conn.: Yale University Press, 1989.
Eiland, Howard. "The Way to Nearness: Heidegger's Interpretation of Presence." *Philosophy and Literature*, 8 (April 1984): 43–54.
Foti, Veronique M. *Poiesis-Sophia-Techne: Between Heidegger and Poets*. Atlantic Highlands, N.J.: Humanities Press, 1991.
Halliburton, David. *Poetic Thinking: An Approach to Heidegger*. University of Chicago Press, 1981.
Harries, Karsten. "Meta-Criticism and Meta-Poetry." *Research in Phenomenology*, 9 (1979): 54–73.
Kockelmans, Joseph J. *Heidegger on Art and Art Works*. Dordrecht: Nijhoff, 1985.
Murray, Michael. "The Conflict between Poetry and Literature." *Philosophy and Literature*, 19 (April 1985): 59–79.
Schrift, Alan D. *Nietzsche and the Question of Interpretation: Between Hermeneutics and Deconstruction*. New York: Routledge & Kegan Paul, 1990.
Spanos, William V., ed. *Martin Heidegger and the Question of Literature: Toward a Postmodern Literary Hermeneutics*. Bloomington: Indiana University Press, 1979.
Tymieniecka, Anna-Teresa, ed. *The Philosophical Reflection of Man in Literature*. Boston: Reidel, 1982.
Vattimo, Gianni. "Aesthetics and the End of Epistemology." In *The Reasons of Art*. Edited by Peter McCormick. Ottawa: University of Ottawa Press, 1985.
Warminski, Andrzej. *Readings in Interpretation: Hölderlin, Hegel, Heidegger*. Minneapolis: University of Minnesota Press, 1987.
White, David A. *Heidegger and the Language of Poetry*. Lincoln: University of Nebraska Press, 1979.

Wright, Kathleen. "The Place of the Work of Art in the Age of Technology." *Southern Journal of Philosophy,* 22 (Winter 1984): 565–82.

SCIENCE AND TECHNOLOGY

Borgmann, Albert. *Technology and the Character of Everyday Life: A Philosophical Inquiry.* Chicago: University of Chicago Press, 1984.

Borgmann, Albert, and Mitcham, Carl. "The Question of Heidegger and Technology: A Critical Review of the Literature." *Philosophy Today,* 31 (Summer 1987): 99–194.

Bourgeois, Patrick L. "Fundamental Ontology, Scientific Methods, and Epistemic Foundations." *New Scholasticism,* 56 (Fall 1982): 471–9.

Caputo, John D. "Heidegger's Philosophy of Science." In *Rationality, Relativism and the Human Sciences.* Edited by Joseph Margolis. Nijhoff, 1986.

Durbin, Paul T., ed. *Research in Philosophy and Technology.* Vol. 2. Greenwich, Conn.: JAI Press, 1979.

Durbin, Paul T., and Rapp, Friedrich, eds. *Philosophy and Technology.* Dordrecht: Reidel, 1983.

Emad, Parvis. "Technology as Presence: Heidegger's View." *Listening,* 16 (Spring 1981): 131–44.

Fandozzi, Phillip R. *Nihilism and Technology: A Heideggerian Investigation.* Washington, D.C.: University Press of America, 1982.

Kelly, Michael. "On Hermeneutics and Science: Why Hermeneutics is not Anti-Science." *Southern Journal of Philosophy,* 25 (Winter 1987): 481–500.

Kockelmans, Joseph J. *Heidegger and Science.* Washington D.C.: University Press of America, 1985.

Kolb, David A. "Heidegger on the Limits of Science." *Journal of the British Society for Phenomenology,* 14 (January 1983): 50–64.

Leder, Drew. "Modes of Totalization: Heidegger on Modern Technology and Science." *Philosophy Today,* 29 (Fall 1985): 245–56.

Loscerbo, John. *Being and Technology: A Study in the Philosophy of Martin Heidegger.* The Hague: Nijhoff, 1981.

Rouse, Joseph. "Kuhn, Heidegger, and Scientific Realism." *Man and World,* 14 (1981): 269–90.

"Heidegger's Later Philosophy of Science." *Southern Journal of Philosophy,* 23 (Spring 1985): 75–92.

Sawicki, Jana. "Heidegger and Foucault: Escaping Technological Nihilism." *Philosophy and Social Criticism*, 13 (Winter 1987): 155–76.

THEOLOGY AND RELIGIOUS STUDIES

Ballard, Bruce W. *The Role of Mood in Heidegger's Ontology.* Lanham, Md.: University Press of America, 1991.

Bonsor, Jack Arthur. *Rahner, Heidegger, and Truth.* Lanham, Md.: University Press of America, 1987.

Caputo, John D. *Heidegger and Aquinas: An Essay on Overcoming Metaphysics.* New York: Fordham University Press, 1982.

The Mystical Element in Heidegger's Thought. New York: Fordham University Press, 1986.

Gall, Robert S. *Beyond Theism and Atheism: Heidegger's Significance for Religious Thinking.* Dordrecht: Nijhoff, 1987.

Kovacs, George. *The Question of God in Heidegger's Phenomenology.* Evanston, Ill.: Northwestern University Press, 1990.

Macquarrie, John. *An Existentialist Theology: A Comparison of Heidegger and Bultmann.* New York: Macmillan, 1955.

Mehta, Jarava Lal. *Philosophy and Religion: Essays in Interpretation.* New Delhi: Indian Council of Philosophical Research in association with Munshiram Manoharlal Publishers, 1990.

Robinson, James McConkey, and Cobb, John B., Jr., eds. *The Later Heidegger and Theology.* Westport, Conn.: Greenwood Press, 1979.

Sheehan, Thomas. "Metaphysics and Bivalence: On Karl Rahner's 'Geist in Welt.' " *Modern Schoolman*, 63 (November 1985): 21–43.

Staten, John C. *Conscience and the Reality of God: An Essay on the Experiential Foundations of Religious Knowledge.* Berlin: de Gruyter, 1988.

Thiselton, Anthony C. *The Two Horizons: New Testament Hermeneutics and Philosophical Description with Special Reference to Heidegger, Bultmann, Gadamer, and Wittgenstein.* Grand Rapids, Mich.: Eerdmans, 1980.

Tropea, Gregory. *Religion, Ideology, and Heidegger's Concept of Falling.* Atlanta: Scholars Press, 1987.

Welte, Bernhard. "God in Heidegger's Thought." *Philosophy Today,* 26 (Spring 1982): 85–100.

Williams, John R. *Martin Heidegger's Philosophy of Religion.* Waterloo, Ontario: Wilfrid Laurier University Press, 1977.

Zimmerman, Michael E. "Heidegger and Bultmann: Egoism, Sinfulness, and Inauthenticity." *Modern Schoolman*, 57 (November 1980): 1–20.

PSYCHOLOGY AND PSYCHOTHERAPY

Faulconer, James E., ed. *Reconsidering Psychology: Perspectives from Continental Philosophy.* Pittsburgh: Duquesne University Press, 1990.

Hoeller, Keith, ed. *Heidegger & Psychology.* Special Issue of the *Review of Existential Psychology & Psychiatry.* Seattle, 1988.

McCall, Raymond J. *Phenomenological Psychology: An Introduction, with a Glossary of Some Key Heideggerian Terms.* Madison: University of Wisconsin Press, 1983.

Medina, Angel. "Heidegger, Lacan and the Boundaries of Existence: Whole and Partial Subjects in Psychoanalysis." *Man and World*, 18 (1985): 389–403.

Messer, Stanley B., Sass, Louis A., and Woolfolk, Robert L. *Hermeneutics and Psychological Theory: Interpretive Perspectives on Personality, Psychotherapy, and Psychopathology.* New Brunswick, N.J.: Rutgers University Press, 1988.

INDEX